Reframing Todd Haynes

a Camera Obscura book

Reframing Todd Haynes
Feminism's Indelible Mark

Theresa L. Geller and Julia Leyda,
EDITORS

DUKE UNIVERSITY PRESS
Durham and London 2022

Printed in the United States of America on acid-free paper ∞
Designed by A. Mattson Gallagher
Typeset in Chaparral Pro and Cronos Pro by Westchester Publishing Services

Library of Congress Cataloging-in-Publication Data
Names: Geller, Theresa L., editor. | Leyda, Julia, editor.
Title: Reframing Todd Haynes : feminism's indelible mark / Theresa L. Geller and Julia Leyda, editors.
Other titles: Camera obscura book (Duke University Press)
Description: Durham : Duke University Press, 2022. | Series: A camera obscura book | Includes bibliographical references and index.
Identifiers: LCCN 2021029092 (print)
LCCN 2021029093 (ebook)
ISBN 9781478015390 (hardcover)
ISBN 9781478018001 (paperback)
ISBN 9781478022626 (ebook)
Subjects: LCSH: Haynes, Todd—Criticism and interpretation. | Motion picture producers and directors—United States. | Queer theory—In motion pictures. | Feminism and motion pictures—United States. | BISAC: PERFORMING ARTS / Film / History & Criticism | SOCIAL SCIENCE / Gender Studies
Classification: LCC PN1998.3.H385 R4473 2022 (print) | LCC PN1998.3.H385 (ebook) | DDC 791.4302/33092—dc23/eng/20211104
LC record available at https://lccn.loc.gov/2021029092
LC ebook record available at https://lccn.loc.gov/2021029093

Cover art: Production still from *Carol*, 2015. Courtesy of *Carol* / Number 9 Films Limited.

For Chantal Akerman (1950–2015)

CONTENTS

PART II. **Intersections and Interventions**

PART III. **Intermediality and Intertextuality**

ACKNOWLEDGMENTS

First and foremost, we express our deepest gratitude to our contributors for their patience and commitment during the lengthy preparation of this volume. We are indebted to them for their contributions to this project and their steadfast support over the years. Sincerest thanks are also due to Patricia White and the editorial collective of *Camera Obscura* for adopting this book for their series. Nick Davis and Maria San Filippo generously offered advice along the way. Grinnell College, Sophia University, and the Norwegian University of Science and Technology provided funding assistance at various stages of the book's development.

Theresa L. Geller acknowledges the Beatrice Bain Research Group at the University of California, Berkeley, and the Whitney Center for the Humanities at Yale University, as both helped support the completion of this project. She also thanks Patrick Flanery, Andrew van der Vlies, Steve Choe, Michelle Risacher, Youngbin Song, and especially Jess Issacharoff, who played the Eve Arden role of steadfast buddy through all the melodrama.

Julia Leyda owes innumerable debts of thanks spanning this book's long gestational process; it is impossible to even remember, much less list, them all. This project took shape during major relocations, from Japan to Germany to Norway, becoming part of the luggage even as it transformed along the way. She has leaned heavily on Diane Negra, Christopher Shore, and Nina Lager Vestberg, availing herself of their seemingly endless supply of kindness, advice, and cheerleading.

Elizabeth Ault assiduously shepherded the volume at Duke University Press, where the copyediting team performed superlative and sensitive work to clarify and correct every part of the manuscript. This book may not have come into being at all without the aid of David E. Maynard, who provided unflagging support and patience through all the trials, tears, and tribulations.

INTRODUCTION

Feminism's Indelible Mark

Theresa L. Geller

> Feminist theory has left an indelible mark on my own critical—and creative—thinking. . . . For me, everything I questioned about what it meant to be a man—and how much my sexuality would perpetually challenge those meanings—could be found in arguments posed by feminists. What can I say? I identified.
>
> —TODD HAYNES, *Far from Heaven, Safe, and Superstar: The Karen Carpenter Story: Three Screenplays* (2003)

"Something Quite Different"

For three decades, Todd Haynes has been making film and media attuned to the almost imperceptible shifts in our culture as they happen. From the AIDS epidemic and an increasingly toxic celebrity culture to the financial crisis and the devastating effects of environmental deregulation, his projects are uniquely calibrated to these subtle changes, registering in their formal experimentation and rarified thematics an ever-evolving affective history of the present. Yet Haynes's films do this by returning us to a different historical moment, inviting us to rethink our own from another place and time. Although his body of work has been concatenated in terms of a loosely defined "queer" style or generic categories such as melodrama,[1] the incontrovertible distinction of each of his projects is that their narratives are situated in a different era, or in multiple eras, as in the case of

Wonderstruck (2017), *Velvet Goldmine* (1998), and *I'm Not There* (2007). He is the only living filmmaker whose entire body of work consists of period dramas, and yet this very work is lauded as postmodern, experimental, and, in many ways, cutting-edge filmmaking. As he explains, "I see things about the present more clearly when I'm looking through the frame of the past: I think it's very hard to assess the present moment that we are in" (quoted in Aftab 2017). Haynes's exceptional acumen for assessing the present as it unfolds has earned his work well-deserved critical accolades. Among a pool of films representing eighty-four years of cinema from twelve countries, the British Film Institute named *Carol* (2015) the best LGBTQ film of all time, and the *Village Voice* declared *Safe* (1995) the best film of the 1990s. Because of its philosophical themes concerning illness, *Safe* has remained "ahead of its moment," as Haynes puts it, as fitting an allegory of the AIDS crisis at the time of its release as it is of a global pandemic decades later, evident in the renewed attention it received when COVID-19 struck (Haynes, quoted in Tobias 2014).[2]

The iconoclastic independent filmmaker has recently garnered significant attention for quietly building a body of meaningful media work aimed at "thinking about identity and representation ... [in which] ideas and issues and progressive politics ... coexist," in the filmmaker's words (quoted in Lim 2010). *Todd Haynes: The Other Side of Dreams* at the Lincoln Center in New York (2015) and *Sparks on Celluloid: Haynes + Vachon* at the San Francisco Museum of Modern Art (2017), both retrospectives the director helped curate, and a lengthy in-depth profile in the *New Yorker* (Lahr 2019), brought Haynes's oeuvre and its contexts to new viewers and dedicated fans alike.[3] Haynes has steadily garnered wider critical recognition for his "outsider's perspective," because, as Cate Blanchett attests, "the authenticity of that perspective" has produced quietly revolutionary media- and genre-spanning work for the past three decades (quoted in Jagernauth 2016). While other independent filmmakers moved into the mainstream, Haynes has held fast to the outsider status cultivated by artists and activists who characterized the movement known as New Queer Cinema (NQC), with which he is most often identified by film critics and scholars to this day. And yet, most of his work has now been released since the turn of the millennium, the point at which NQC had been declared to have run its course (Pick 2004, 103).[4]

Politically and aesthetically nonconformist, Haynes has built a career essentially outside the industry, averaging about four years between features until the mid-2010s. Not only did the frequency of Haynes's releases increase—with *Carol* (2015), *Wonderstruck* (2017), and *Dark Waters* (2019) coming at two-year intervals—but these literary adaptations also represented a departure from his consistent practice of writing the material he directs. Whereas *Carol* recalls Haynes's earlier melodramas, the others move in new directions: *Wonderstruck* is a young-adult film bearing the imprint of his art-house sensibility nonetheless, and *Dark Waters* is a docudrama thriller in the vein of *Erin Brockovich* (Steven Soderbergh, 2000). And yet all of these are also period dramas, proving once again Haynes's claim that "even though I mostly make period movies, they are all contemporary at the same time" (quoted in Jenkins 2015). Significantly, despite nearly one hundred award nominations, with at least half resulting in wins, only with his first official studio movie, *Dark Waters*, and ads for Revlon (2017) and Givenchy (2018) did critics begin to wonder whether Haynes might be flirting with the mainstream. Yet Haynes's new (and first) documentary film, *The Velvet Underground* (2021), is a clear retort to such suspicions, demonstrating a return to form (and content) in a film that epitomizes the experimentalism and avant-garde aesthetics for which the "outsider" band was known, and that greatly impacted Haynes as a filmmaker.

Trained as a painter but making films since he was in high school, Haynes established himself with the controversial *Poison* (1991), an experimental tripartite feature that exemplified the traits of the group of independent, low-budget films that B. Ruby Rich (1992) dubbed "New Queer Cinema." These films shunned positive gay images and subverted both narrative structure and film style, inspired by the AIDS crisis and the assimilation of poststructuralist thought into the academy. Winner of the Grand Jury Prize at the Sundance Film Festival, *Poison* quickly became the subject of political scrutiny for its National Endowment for the Arts funding, and led to invitations for Haynes to appear on television talk shows to debate Republicans about arts financing, making him the movement's default (and exceptionally articulate) spokesperson. Despite, or possibly because of, his notoriety in the media, Haynes balked at the prospect of being pigeonholed as a filmmaker of NQC, claiming that he "was eager to move on from it and do something quite different in my second film" (quoted in Winslet 2011). Yet that film—*Safe* (1995)—secured his position in NQC by providing film critics and scholars formal terms with which to further define the movement. The film's idiosyncratic style and opaque narrative resonated with the anti-assimilationist, anti-identity politics that defined the emergent subfield of queer theory. Although some critics chose to ignore the fact that *Safe* "doesn't have gay themes in it at all," Haynes hoped the film's thoroughgoing critique of identity and representation would allow his work to be seen in a different light: "As opposed to feeling part of a current cinematic movement among gay filmmakers ... [my work] shares a criticism of mainstream culture that goes beyond content and that does affect forms" (quoted in Saunders 2014, 41).

Despite his ambivalence about his NQC branding, Haynes, more than others of his cohort (such as Gus Van Sant and Gregg Araki), has been designated the keeper of the flame for the movement for obvious reasons. Certainly the fact that Haynes returned to "gay themes" in his next films, *Velvet Goldmine* (1998) and *Far from Heaven* (2002), cemented this association; both joined *Poison* and *Dottie Gets Spanked* (1993) as crucial pillars in the canon of NQC.[5] More significantly, these very different films established the two main strands of Haynes's work, which, as he describes, "fall into categories: the melodramas, which are typically women's stories, and the more exuberant, eccentrically structured films about musical artists" (quoted in N. Davis 2015a). Both categories rationalize setting his stories in other historical periods; yet these strands are not as distinct as they might first seem for other reasons too, as this volume demonstrates by foregrounding the "women's stories" that traverse both. It is this attention to women's stories that distinguished Haynes's work from the start, making him "an exception among male queer directors ... not least because he enables queer to function inclusive of women" (Pick 2004, 106). His exceptional focus on women may be why Haynes was eager to shed his label as a director of NQC, especially because, from his perspective, NQC was never about what motivated or shaped his work but rather, "the movement, as it was branded, basically identified a market" (quoted in Lim 2010).[6] Although the movement "was extinguished almost as soon as it was named" because queer themes became mainstream almost overnight, film critics and scholars have continued to frame Haynes's career in terms of NQC (Lim 2010). Yet, when asked directly which association best governs how the industry and audiences perceive him now—that is, "with New Queer Cinema, with the 'woman's film,' with activist work, [or] with academic approaches to semiotics"—Haynes avers: "For the most part, people notice my career's obvious attentiveness to female subjects and the very great actresses I've worked with" (N. Davis 2015b).

Haynes is notably not resistant to this sort of market identification. He has no qualms about being branded a director of women's films: "These days ... anybody who is making women's stories a priority is distinct from the ongoing, tiresome turn to the male spectator as our sole value. It's a distinction I completely appreciate and feel I've earned and am proud to hold" (quoted in N. Davis 2015b). Haynes has shown exceptional consistency in his choice of creative collaborators (Christine Vachon, Julianne Moore, Cate Blanchett, Maryse Alberti, Sandy Powell, et al.), and in "subjects" that confront cinema's and society's continuing "problem with women" (Haynes, quoted in MacKenzie 2016). For all these reasons, Haynes is widely recognized as a woman's film director, with *Carol* and *Far from Heaven* his largest box office draws to date. This collection of essays, therefore, undertakes a unique project in Haynes criticism: to integrate the multiple perceptions of the director, creating a more complete understanding of Haynes as an artist-activist mobilized by academic theorizations of gender and cinema. Synthesizing these perspectives, the volume privileges those things for which Haynes is most noted today, specifically his persistent interest in the political and formal possibilities afforded by the genre of the woman's film and his collaboration with women in front of and behind the camera.

As fans recognize, and as reviewers and interviewers consistently note, "Haynes has always focused on stories about women," and he is eager to explain why: "[Stories about women] always—maybe more than films about men—contain the limits of social burden ... and the choices they make in carrying on the institutions of the family, satisfying men, raising children—there's less freedom of movement in women's lives'" (quoted in Thompson 2016). It is this political perspective that makes his film and media work pointedly *feminist* rather than simply "about" women. Indeed, Haynes's persistent feminist commitments as a queer filmmaker provided the grounds for producers Vachon and Elizabeth Karlson to defend their choice of a man to tell Patricia Highsmith's story, affirming "he couldn't have been a better choice for the undeniably feminist film"; screenwriter Phyllis Nagy agrees, noting that "this material was *absolutely* for Todd ... whether or not he's a female" (Simon 2015, emphasis in original). Haynes's cross-gender identifications—a theme throughout this volume—is allegorized in the film itself. During a key scene, the eponymous Carol Aird (Cate Blanchett) places a new camera firmly in the hands of Therese Belivet (Rooney Mara), an expensive and thoughtful gift from a wealthier, older woman meant to encourage the young ingénue's interest in photography. Taking photos of the enigmatic, alluring Carol, Therese bears a metonymic relationship to Haynes, who, as a child, had to be bribed to stop drawing only women in his sketch pads (figure I.1) (R. White 2013, 133). Of course he never really stopped, as he explains to Kate Winslet, remaining "drawn

I.1 Therese behind the camera stands in for Haynes himself—one of many cross-gender identifications to be found in his work.

to female characters ... because they don't have as easy or as obvious a relationship to power in society, and so they suffer under social constraints" (2011). In this way, Therese also figures Haynes as a student of art and semiotics at Brown University, guided by mentors who introduced him to the "arguments posed by feminists" that shape his films.

Reframing Todd Haynes: Feminism's Indelible Mark contends that no thorough consideration of Haynes's work can afford to ignore the crucial place of feminism within it, evident not only in his recurring focus on female characters and his continuing commitment to collaborations with women behind the camera, but also, and most significantly, in the influence of feminist theory on his aesthetic vision, discernible in the visual and narrative design of his oeuvre. Therefore, this volume reframes Haynes's long and continuing career in the emergent critical rubric of "new feminist cinema" to shed new light on the expanding arc of the director's work. "Any narrative of twenty-first-century cinema could be, and perhaps should be, written through feminist films," So Mayer (2016a) suggests, and "one such narrative would reflect the emergence of openly feminist cismale filmmakers," identifying "*Camera Obscura*'s special issue on Todd Haynes" for its study of Haynes's "intersectional filmmaking and its importance for feminism" (6). Whereas Mayer speculates that the narrative of feminist male filmmakers is crucial to the development of "new feminist cinema," this particular lineage within feminist cinema remains essentially unexplored. Nearly two decades after the publication of "Todd Haynes: A Magnificent Obsession" (2004), *Reframing Todd Haynes* contributes to the narrative of new feminist cinema by exploring Haynes's "women's stories," including films rarely identified as such, even as it questions the essentialist notion of "woman" throughout.

In the films that make up new feminist cinema, as loosely characterized as NQC before it, "a politicized point of view can be sensed in an ethical approach to narrative choices, but also through film form" (Mayer 2016a, 9–10). Haynes's films exemplify this commitment to form, insisting that his "experiments in form" are inseparable from "the invigorating notion of gender as a product of ideology," inspired by "the complexity—and diversity—of feminist thought, from its incorporation of Marx and Freud to its reexamination of film and society" (Haynes 2003, viii). It is this focus on the ideology of gender that de-essentializes his film practice. Although his films stand out for their attention to women characters and women's concerns, the performance of femininity across bodies and genders is crucial to all of his media work. Haynes may well be recognized for his films' social and cinematic construction of femininity, memorably conveyed by the "great actresses" with whom he collaborates, but he is equally indebted to feminist theory for challenging "what it mean[s] to be a man"—and how nonnormative sexualities undercut those meanings. A focus on nonnormative sexualities—reading Haynes's films as primarily queer—has dominated academic and popular criticism of his work, often eclipsing the feminist arguments he repeatedly references as the early inspiration for his filmmaking: "It was 1981 when I started [at Brown University]," Haynes recalls, "only just a few years after some of the seminal writing, particularly cutting-edge feminist film theory, had first come on the scene. . . . I found myself identifying and relating quite closely" (quoted in R. White 2013, 134). And as recently as 2015, he reaffirmed that "New French theory and feminist film criticism . . . paved the way for my asking theoretical questions about representation and narrative form and feminism" (quoted in Cooke 2015). Without disputing his place in the queer film canon, which has been thoroughly documented in extant scholarship,[7] this volume turns its attention to the questions that Haynes has long posed in his film work—questions that reflect the indelible mark of five decades of feminist theory on the filmmaker's "creative thinking."

Although, as Haynes claims, "the world has just continued to move far away from the kinds of radical questions that I felt free to ask during the *feminist* schooling that I enjoyed and grew from" (quoted in R. White 2013, 162, emphasis added), his work has persistently pursued such questions for several decades now. Indeed, this book contends that Haynes is the most significant male director in the canon of new feminist cinema, which is defined as expressly activist and often noted for politicized revisions of "women's genres." In *Film Feminisms: A Global Introduction*, Kristin Lené Hole and Dijana Jelača assert that "feminist films can, and have frequently been made by male directors" (2019, 27), pointing to Haynes's *Far from Heaven* (2002) as a key example, and elaborating on how *Carol* appropriates "the male gaze and desire . . . [as] the audience is invited to identify with Therese's gaze and align with her lesbian desire towards Carol—an act of looking that actively undermines the patriarchal and heteronormative sexualizing of women onscreen" (54). Notably, this analysis of *Carol* is remarkably consistent with Haynes's own claims about the origins of his filmmaking, explaining to Gus Van Sant (2015) that it emerged "out of feminist film theory in the '70s. Laura Mulvey. That whole movement. And the notion of the male spectator, the male gaze. All of these terms now feel extremely integrated if not outmoded or defunct, yet they still have residence and are formative." If college-era Haynes is aligned with the budding artist Therese, feminist theory—notably, as far from singular today as it was from the start—is more akin to Carol, the experienced older woman, privileged in many ways, yet also embattled and world-weary. Any engagement with feminist thought at the current moment must reflect on its institutional privileges and its long-fought struggles—and the stories told about them. Such reflection informs the organization of this volume, which maps the shifting terms of feminist film inquiry as it has developed over the past half century.

Although the terms of '70s feminist film theory, as Haynes acknowledges, have been declared "defunct" if not dismissed outright,[8] recent feminist film criticism has proven they nonetheless "still have residence" in the critical formulations of new feminist cinema. Directed toward woman-made cinema, this scholarship develops a nonlinear approach to film feminisms to reveal new feminist cinema's often obscure(d) connections to film history and theory—the project driving *Reframing Todd Haynes* as well, but one turned to the cinema of a gay male independent filmmaker (see Bolton 2015; Margulies and Szaniawski 2019; Mulvey and Rogers 2015; and P. White 2015c). "What's 'new' about the twenty-first century 'new feminist cinema,'" as Mayer explains, "is its negotiation of a transgenerational feminist film history of four decades within a reflexive awareness of the interruption and re-vision of feminisms, and interconnectedly of film cultures, in the new millennium" (2016a, 6). The story of twenty-first-century cinema that this volume narrates through Haynes's work takes as its starting point the director's training in feminist film theory and his proclivity for telling "women's stories," making his work a model for the interconnectedness of feminist and queer film cultures.

In the example of Haynes's films, NQC's celebrated experimental aesthetics can be traced back to feminist film theory and women's film culture. As Mary Ann Doane explains, "much of the film practice of the 1970s and 1980s allied itself with the avant-garde through a project of negation, a systematic interrogation and undermining of classical [Hollywood] codes of sexual looking and imaging" (2004a, 1231). A student of Doane, Leslie Thornton, and Michael Silverman at Brown in the early 1980s, Haynes interrogated the classical codes of sexual looking in painting and filmmaking, beginning with *Superstar*—a film he asserts "collects all the themes and instincts of every film I have made since in one little movie. It's about pop culture, women, domestic life; it experiments with formal traditions; it sets up boundaries that the viewer has to overcome" (quoted in Cooke 2015). Although it was a collaborative project with Cynthia Schneider, *Superstar*'s themes reappear throughout his work, but they are most often recognized as (and reduced to) "a content idea," as Haynes puts it, overlooking the "structural idea[s]" behind his experimentation with preexisting forms (Laskawy 2014, 21). Thus, his work "about" women and domestic life have earned him popular recognition as a "woman's director," a label he is happy to embrace: "If these kinds of stories [that raise questions about choices we do or do not have] find greater expression in domestic tales that are driven by female characters, then I'm thoroughly proud to be part of that tradition. And it is a tradition!" (N. Davis 2015b).[9] In this assignation, however, the feminist idea(l)s motivating his experimental filmmaking remain obscured.

By reframing Haynes as director of new feminist cinema, this collection affords a clearer understanding of the formal innovations of his film work. The "tradition" of the woman's film activates most of Haynes's key feminist thematics and experiments with "form," which to him "is everything. It's the first question about how to approach a story and why you are telling it and what kind of traditions you are evoking" (quoted in Hopewell 2017). Directly influenced by Doane's (1987) critical contribution to the "invention" of the genre and its subgenres, Haynes studied such films (with her) not to replicate them but rather to identify in them "stress points and perturbations [that] can ... be activated as a kind of lever to facilitate ... another cinematic practice"—one not possible within "the traditional forms and conventions of Hollywood narrative," because these, by (feminist) definition, cannot sustain the exploration "of female subjectivity and desire" (13). Haynes's postmodern women's films pull this lever, posing crucial questions about femininity, "narrative form and feminism"—and thus are constitutive of "another cinematic practice" grounded in formal experimentation. "The cultural work feminist critics performed in 'inventing' the genre of the woman's film," as E. Ann Kaplan argues, has directly impacted "feminist cinema practices in the current postmodern moment ... inspiring feminist directors to imagine aspects of their social and political worlds through a genre lens" (2012, 71, 72). Although Kaplan is likely thinking only of women directors here ("their"), Haynes is arguably the most well known and prolific of the "independent directors outside Hollywood" doing just such work in "the postmodern, feminist era" (73). The woman's film functions as a key generic framework through which Haynes's cinematic experimentation is mapped throughout this collection precisely because it undercuts auteurist claims to the uniqueness of the (male) director's vision.

Haynes's women's films fly in the face of auteur theory's claims for the originality of the auteur, as they evoke not only the original tradition but also the feminist counter-cinema that first recited and reworked the subgenre in their formal experiments. Indeed, not just Haynes's women's films bear the "indelible mark" of second-wave feminist filmmaking; its formal experimentalism is evident even in his student thesis, *Assassins: A Film concerning Rimbaud* (1985), in which, he admits, "people will see the influence of Fassbinder, for sure ... [but I was also] translating different influences" in shots that were "very Laura Mulvey," referring to her film with Peter Wollen, *Riddles of the Sphinx* (1977) (N. Davis 2015a). Women's cinema of the '70s and '80s drew heavily on the classical woman's film despite its avant-garde aesthetics, and Haynes's work reflects this feminist "interruption and re-vision" of the tradition, revising it for the same reasons. Noted for its "pleasurable reworking" and "ironic undercutting" of that genre "both attractive to and manipulative of women—the melodrama," women's cinema established a nonpatriarchal film language by "draw[ing] on, criticiz[ing] and transform[ing] the conventions of cultural expressions traditionally associated with women: the melodramatic story of doomed love,... the 'family romance,' and ... the family melodrama" (Kuhn [1982] 1994, 171). Haynes has noted that films like Sally

Potter's *Thriller* (1979) and Chantal Akerman's *Jeanne Dielman, 23, quai du Commerce, 1080 Bruxelles* (1975), which "were beginning to work with commercial genres ... using the experimental vernacular," impacted him and Vachon "tremendously" (quoted in MacDonald 2014, 154). Such critical transformations of the melodrama clearly shaped *Superstar*, *Safe*, *Far from Heaven*, *Mildred Pierce*, and *Carol*, but they also inflected his other works, as several contributors demonstrate. Feminist counter-cinema's reworking of the tropes of the woman's film provided Haynes the experimental film language for "another cinematic practice"—one that negotiates transgenerational feminist history and film culture to interrogate the affective conditions of the present.

"Cultural Tremblings"

That Haynes frequently turns to the woman's film, like the feminist filmmakers before him, is of little surprise as the gestalt of his filmmaking is one of affective belatedness. Feminist film theory has long argued that the fantasy of the woman-centered melodrama is time-based, premised on the affective register of "the pathos of the 'too late,'" as Linda Williams (1991, 10–11) formulates it. Yet this narrative dilatoriness is equally present in his musical biographies; as Haynes asserts, "pop music ... provides those true Proustian moments, unlocking sensations, unlocking our imagination" (quoted in Murray 2014, 143). This Proustian sensibility permeates Haynes's work because all of his films are set in previous eras.[10] About Haynes's arguably most exuberant musical, *Velvet Goldmine*, Nick Davis observes: "On the one hand, it is a gender-bending, pleasure-baiting, hormone-firing, freely adapting, time-warping, glitter-bombing, assumption-testing spectacle and soundscape.... On the other hand, *Velvet Goldmine* emits a palpable melancholy ... pin[ing] ... for relatively recent pasts" (2013, 246). This melancholy is a result of how and *why* Haynes persistently engages "relatively recent pasts." Acknowledging his consistent tendency to draw on earlier forms of popular culture to frame the past while also differentiating his work from the larger trend of "retro" cinema, Haynes explains: "We're learning how to refer to and play with other genres; I just think sometimes the style precedes the purpose and the content. We need to know why we're looking at the past and what we're trying to learn from it and ultimately how it's informing the present" (quoted in Farber 1989, 22). Haynes's films thus strive for historical dialectics, limning the conditions of the present by returning to older genres

I.2 Another stand-in for Haynes, Jarvis Cocker recites women's stories and experiences through the temporal drag of Sondheim's lyrics.

and themes to re-enliven their particular affective register at a different historical juncture.

The short film *I'm Still Here*, which appears in the documentary *Six by Sondheim* (2013), exemplifies these dialectics, encapsulating his cinematic projects writ small by emphasizing the pathos behind the camp surface of the famous ballad. In it, Haynes provides a unique interpretation of one of Sondheim's more famous—and potentially more campy—songs, one usually performed by elder stateswomen of musical theater such as Elaine Stritch or Debbie Reynolds, but here performed by the lanky singer Jarvis Cocker of the band Pulp, who interprets the song lyrics for and through the many women sitting in the diegetic audience of a smoky bar (figure I.2).[11] Less crooning to his female listeners than identifying with them, Cocker seems a perfect stand-in for the director who is best known for telling women's stories. Offering a striking synecdoche for his body of work, *I'm Still Here*, like *Superstar*, weds the musical form to the woman's "weepies" by intercutting the song's performance with stoic close-ups of the women in the audience, implying their personal experiences of suffering in the lyrics. This metonymic relation to Haynes's oeuvre only deepens when the framing documentary informs the viewer that Sondheim, a gay artist, wrote the song thinking about Joan Crawford's long career—a career revivified by her role in Michael Curtiz's *Mildred Pierce* (1945). As he does with his return to that text and the woman's film generally, Haynes creates a layered portrait of women's struggles and survival, allowing Sondheim's lyrics to imply the melodramas behind the unknown women's faces in the diegetic audience.

In many ways, this short underscores Haynes's response to the question of his identifying as a "woman's director": "I'm pleased if I'm doing anything to reinvigorate a discussion in movies about women's stories, women's status, and women's experiences—and also, stories that aren't by definition affirmative or heroic" (N. Davis 2015a). His choice of verbs—to *re*invigorate—acknowledges the existence of previous vigorous discussions about women's stories and social status in feminist theory that Haynes has long sought to rekindle. Sondheim's lyrics, of course, are anything but heroic or affirmative: "Reefers and vino, rest cures, religion and pills, and I'm here; Been called a 'Pinko,' commie tool, got through it stinko by my pool..." (Sondheim 1971). Such lines recall Carol White's "rest cure" and Mildred's final line, "Let's get stinko," and like all his films, the lyrics return to specific moments in history ("In the Depression, was I depressed?... I got through Herbert and J. Edgar Hoover") through the frame of women's less-than-affirmative experiences of them. More to the point, the personal experiences of history denoted in Sondheim's lyrics are presented in the juxtaposition of events set in the past with the present tense declarative, "and I'm here." At each "I'm here," Haynes employs lighting and close-ups to carve out the space and consideration that these complex and compelling women are due. In an analogous way, *Reframing Todd Haynes* carves out space for the long overdue critical consideration of Haynes's feminist film practice, which draws on the relatively recent pasts of feminist theory and film culture to provide a much-needed window on the present.

Haynes's avant-garde aesthetics and politicized narratives find their origins in feminist critiques of representation (or "semiotics") and in the activism of the AIDS crisis. And yet, despite his repeated proclamations, in every book-length study of the director (excluding *Camera Obscura*'s special issue), and in most published articles, the words *feminism* and *feminist* barely make an appearance outside of quotations from Haynes himself.[12] The fact that most Haynes criticism tends to omit or ignore the feminist arguments with which he expressly identifies to stress the newness of queer theory (and NQC) is consistent with how Clare Hemmings (2011) describes the stories told about each. A teleological story has taken hold, as Hemmings explains, in which "feminist and queer theory are counterposed usually with the emphasis on the former's untrendy focus on oppression and the latter's seductive emphasis on 'individual' performance" (119). Fortunately, scholars of "queer feminist criticism" challenge these stories by unpacking the political implications of such specious claims. Queer feminist criticism, a "strange" neologism invented by Robyn Wiegman, describes not so much "a collaboration between queer *and* feminist criticism but ... a distinct body of work in its own right ... [defined by] a set of shared political and theoretical genealogies [that have] in some cases revis[ed] the very inheritances of queer theory along the way, such that the famous distinction between sexuality and gender ... is repealed as a theoretical universalism" (2014, 19–20n1). Indeed, it is precisely this distinction that has made it too easy to disavow Haynes's feminism and efface the specific theoretical origins of his filmmaking.

Envisioned as a contribution to this "distinct body of work," this volume approaches Haynes's period work, which to date includes every feature and his television projects, as a creative archive of queer feminist historiography. Haynes's filmmaking, like queer feminist scholarship, "attends to the condition of the present through the analytics of affect and time" (Wiegman 2014, 5). Haynes's projects are catalyzed by the same epistemological aims as queer feminist scholarship, drawing on past eras and their forms to provide an affective aesthetics—if not an analytics—fitting our own historical moment(s). He admits: "I try to be motivated by what's around me, the cultural tremblings that surround us.... [But] I always seem to go to another time to draw some sort of frame around the time we are in" (quoted in Hopewell 2017). Included here is new research on Haynes's film and media that expressly draws on queer feminism's political and theoretical genealogies, including its revisions of established narratives. Like the queer feminist criticism with which Haynes's work has long been synergistically aligned, his film work is centrally concerned with queer negativity, engaging the affects of shame, melancholia, pathos, and failure. Haynes's more recent projects, however, have begun to reflect the "different set of terms" needed to analyze the conditions of the present: "debt, crisis, precarity, bare life, biopolitics, neoliberalism, and empire" (Wiegman 2014, 5). Several chapters directly engage queer feminism's critical concepts, situating the volume's project within its purview as opposed to traditional auteur criticism, which is interrogated from the outset.

Haynes is uniquely skilled in translating contemporary affect in film and media set in other eras, as several contributors specifically detail. The contributors who engage queer feminism's conceptual archive come at it from differing terms and perspectives, reflective of the distinctive, and sometimes contradictory, approaches within the field itself. For example, the "bi-polar" interpretations of affect in queer feminist criticism, evident in the distinctions between J. Halberstam's "converting loss into heroic loserdom" and Lauren Berlant's (2011) much more skeptical anatomization of "optimism's cruelty," are "important not as competing interpretive strategies or opposite world views, but as evidence and evocation of the collective *affect* of 'The times we're in'" (Wiegman 2014, 6). *Carol* may be seen to integrate these perspectives, which Patricia White's analysis sketches out, accessing melancholic queer histories before Stonewall through Highsmith's writing while heralding asynchronous lesbian erotics to buffer against progressive assimilationist narratives. Other conceptual frameworks such as "empire" or "bare life," however, delimit the political traction of queer feminism's negative affect, redemptive (Halberstam) or not (Berlant), as Danielle Bouchard and Jigna Desai assert in their critical reassessment of *Safe, Wonderstruck*, and *Carol*.

Whereas part I, "Influences and Interlocutors," stresses the compensatory work of negative affect and its heroic losers—twilight lovers, glam rockers, and various social outcasts—part II moves toward the pole of optimism's cruelty. Patrick Flanery zeroes in on this in his examination of the HBO miniseries *Mildred Pierce* (2011), in which he details how Haynes, like Berlant, confers "meticulous attention on the psychic and social environments in which [his] objects of study struggle to live . . . offering them (and us) an interpretive sensorium of the intimate detail" (Wiegman 2014, 6). Indeed, the chapters collected in part II, "Intersections and Interventions," take as their object of study "the psychic and social environments" of Haynes's women's stories, paying special attention to the ways these environments come into conflict. Haynes's women-centered melodramas reject redemption in favor of simply detailing the suffering of his protagonists, even at the risk of "disappointing" the work's political aims, as Sharon Willis anatomizes in her canonical essay on *Far from Heaven*. Such detailing describes the visual and narrative work of Haynes's "women's films," but not only his women's films, as Jess Issacharoff demonstrates by turning our attention to *Poison*'s women.

Although Haynes's cinematic contemplation of suffering is foreshadowed in his high school short *The Suicide* (1978), it becomes explicitly political during his college years, as he avows in his introduction to the screenplays for *Superstar*, *Safe*, and *Far from Heaven*: "If there exists between them a sisterhood of sorts, aligning them as stories about women or even experiments in form, the imprint of feminism would clearly be at its core" (Haynes 2003, viii). It is this relationship between feminism and Haynes's experiments with form that tethers part III's focus on Haynes's stories about women. In "Intermediality and Intertextuality," it is evident that even though films like *Dottie Gets Spanked* and *I'm Not There* may feel more assuring in their queer premise that "being undone is a way of overcoming, even when life still feels bad" (Wiegman 2014, 6), their feminist imprint is no less clear. Because Haynes's women's stories, major or minor, circumscribe their objects of study to white women's struggles, however, this imprint is potentially attenuated, as both Willis and Bouchard and Desai detail in their interventions.

Although only some contributors directly engage queer feminism's critical terms, all share its impulse "to reconfigure feminism and queer theory as co-operative rather than discrete theoretical traditions" (Hemmings 2011, 189). Using a wide range of critical frameworks, from star and fan studies to media archeology, each chapter attends to the affective asynchronies discernible in Haynes's film work. Haynes admits, "I feel that going back to the past deepens and makes more exciting the journey or the transport that a film offers us.... I also feel that in some ways, when period films have issues that reflect back—or forward—to contemporary issues, they're almost stronger" (quoted in Jenkins 2015). While much Haynes criticism acknowledges such transports, most often as pastiche, citation, or homage, this volume theorizes three decades of media practice in terms of the "outmoded or defunct" that names a particularly queer feminist relation to time and affect. Purposefully out of sync, Haynes opts "for a kind of overt aesthetic and temporal disjunction," Elena Gorfinkel argues, as his "films are *about* anachronism as much as they *use* anachronism as an aesthetic resource ... employ[ing] 'outmoded' or obsolete elements within their *mise-en-scène* and narrative" (2005, 155). More than simply using obsolete "elements," Haynes's works rely in toto on the affective structures of anachronistic forms and thematics to reorient our perspective on the present.

To this extent the volume is shaped by the notion of "temporal drag," following Elizabeth Freeman's redefinition of "drag ... as the act of plastering the body [and texts] with outdated rather than just cross-gendered accessories, [and] whose resurrection seems to exceed the axis of gender and begins to talk about, indeed talk back to, history" (2010, xxi). Translating the pull of the past on the present in affective and affecting scenarios, temporal drag in Haynes's work takes the form of deep intertextuality, or what many identify as his richly allusive cinephilia and fascination with popular media and celebrity culture—the central organizing through-line of part III, "Intermediality and Intertextuality." *Reframing Todd Haynes* illuminates the feminist origins (and ends) of Haynes's cinematic temporal drag to explore the ways his film and media model "a kind of *temporal* transitivity that does not leave feminism, femininity, or other so-called anachronisms behind" (Freeman 2010, 63). Yet critics who have situated Haynes's films in the archive of temporal drag (e.g., Dana Luciano, Cüneyt Çakırlar) frequently elide the specific context of feminist historiography in which the term arises for Freeman. Experiencing the "pull backward" of feminism's waves, "its forward movement [that] is also a drag back," Haynes's work resonates with Freeman's theoretical project, which seeks to replace feminism's generational logic with "a notion of 'temporal drag' [as] the movement time of collective political fantasy" (65). And yet the director is only footnoted in Freeman's *Time Binds* as an exceptional filmmaker of NQC, acknowledging his importance in the spurious "lacuna" of research on cinema's reworking of history as social construction that "is currently being filled in cinema studies, particularly in essays on the work of Todd Haynes" (2010, 182n11).[13]

Haynes is surprisingly absent from Freeman's archive, which is mostly experimental film and media, because her project is to explore affective registers other than suffering. He shares the same history as all of her other visual artists, nonetheless: "Born between 1960–70 . . . coming of age in the afterlife of sixties, [a] successor to mass movements whose most radical elements were often tamed, crushed or detoured. . . . [His] political experience unfolded in and moved outward from the 1980s, when the feminist, lesbian/gay, and AIDS movements met continental theory" (Freeman 2010, xiv). Haynes is one of the most self-aware artists of his historical positioning and inheritance in just these terms in interview after interview.[14] With his training in semiotics and feminist theory, Haynes wasn't just a "witness" but actually led the charge in "the semiotic warfare eventually known as 'queering'"; he cofounded the art activist group Gran Fury, which "brought deconstructive reading practices and grassroots activism together, laying the groundwork for . . . queer theory" (Freeman xiv–xv). One important contribution of recent queer feminist criticism is the genealogical work of excavating these foundations, tracing them back to the "arguments posed by feminists," as Hemmings, Sara Ahmed (2017), Jennifer Nash (2019), and Freeman, among others, have all undertaken in their respective contributions to the field. Haynes, of course, has long asserted that these arguments form the bedrock of his "creative thinking," claiming "that it wasn't until gay theory was ushered in . . . that I realized how significant and important feminism is" (quoted in Wyatt 1993, 7). It is this recursive allegiance to feminism that is reflected in the temporal drag of much of his work. Haynes's period work, "in its chronotopic disjunctiveness," to borrow Freeman's phrasing, epitomizes "a temporal economy crucial to queer performance [but] harnesse[d] to . . . movements that go beyond the shimmyings of individual bodies and into the problematic relationship between feminist history and queer theory" (2010, 68). This relationship is expressly addressed in the chapters by White, Julia Leyda, Issacharoff, Davis, Noah Tsika, and Willis, and it is implicit in the feminist reframings throughout the volume in their meticulous attention to various transgenerational feminist histories.

The impetus for this volume is the desire to rethink Haynes's cultural production in terms of the antiteleological engagement with social history paradigmatic of queer feminist criticism. In Haynes's cinema, the varied frames of history, figured against the conceptual ground of feminist politics, are his attempt to "intercede in the current direction of the world . . . to interrupt the contemporary moment with a [filmic] practice of the untimely," and as Jane Elliott insists, "such interruptions need not appear historically new" (2006, 1701). And yet they cannot just be a repetition of the past either. In the organization of the volume, the aim is to tease out this contradiction: diverse contributions are placed in dialogue through a specific set of feminist frameworks. Temporal drag, albeit implicit, specifies the queer feminist logic behind the book, because, as Freeman posits, it names "a counter-genealogical practice of archiving culture's throwaway objects, including the outmoded masculinities and femininities from which useable pasts may be extracted" (2010, xvii). *Reframing Todd Haynes* is organized around these very counter-genealogical practices, from restoring outmoded lesbian or young girls' fantasies and the creative work to which these fantasies give rise, as explored in part I, to the regressive femininities of defunct film genres that tethers part II, and the archiving of culture's throwaway objects that mobilizes part III. Haynes's recollection of supposedly "outmoded" feminist film theories is redoubled in his citation of older genres and intertexts. As such, his work embodies the aims of temporal drag, which creates "a *productive* obstacle to progress, a usefully distorting pull backward, and a necessary pressure on the present tense" (Freeman 2010, 64, emphasis in original). Haynes's film and media, the book argues, exert just such a necessary feminist pressure on the present.

"Experiments in Shape and Feeling"

As the quotations in the preceding paragraphs have shown, Haynes persistently draws attention to the legacies of feminist film criticism and women's art practice in his work, making his own authorship visible as a constituent part of a larger body of artistic and theoretical work—work developed in large part to counter auteur theory's and genre criticism's gendered foreclosures. Haynes's career thus paradoxically affords a unique opportunity to disrupt the auteurist edifice, smuggling in the very terms of that edifice's undoing in its most privileged figure—the white male director. The established response to auteur theory's endemic sexism, which has been much noted of late (Marghitu 2018; Mayer 2016b; and Shambu 2018), is the proliferation of scholarly research on women filmmakers, rekindled in exciting new directions with Mayer's *Political Animals: The New Feminist Cinema* (2016a) and Patricia White's *Women's Cinema, World Cinema* (2015c), which "models ... an expanded, critical, interrogatory post-auteurism" (Shambu 2018). Several contributors extend this model to Haynes's film and media, beginning with White's chapter on *Carol*. Accordingly, this book departs from the chronological structure typical of auteurist companion studies, opting instead for a post-auteurist framework developed in conjunction with the concept of new feminist cinema. With the aim of democratizing authorship, many contributors here trouble Haynes's status as auteur by foregrounding women's contributions to works that are expressly polyvocal and heteroglossic.

Part I of *Reframing Todd Haynes*, "Influences and Interlocutors," deconstructs the founding conceit of auteur theory by approaching his work through the feminist concept of authorship. "The concept of auteurship," as Hole and Jelača explain, "is imbued with a sense of creative authority historically denied to women ... [and] inherently invites hagiographic celebrations of a filmmaker's artistic achievement, while the concept of authorship is more democratic and less burdened by such demands for high artistic recognition" (2019, 9). Focusing on Haynes's collaborations with smart, creative women—artists in their own right—the contributors challenge reductive notions of the (male) auteur in analyses that tease out the dialogical implications of film production and reception. By recuperating the contributions of women to his work, these chapters develop a feminist dialogics that challenges "the myth of the solo auteur" by "reinforcing the concept that it takes many people to create art ... [which] doesn't devalue the work, it just acknowledges what actually goes into making it"

(Derschowitz 2019, 60).[15] In this way, part I amplifies the multiple voices that speak through, with, and back to works organized under the name "Todd Haynes." White, for one, examines the ways in which Haynes's *Carol* can be read as a complex palimpsest that bears the imprint of its lesbian authors, Highsmith and Nagy. White's chapter highlights the democratic potentials of film authorship (as opposed to auteurism) by drawing out the multiple authors of its images (postwar women photographers such as Helen Levitt and Vivian Maier, costume designer Sandy Powell, producers Vachon and Karlson) and narrative (Highsmith, Nagy). She goes on to show that Haynes's commitment to such polyvocality opens the text to new interlocutors throughout its afterlife.

Julia Leyda, too, examines the ways Haynes's films invite viewers to collaborate in a film's meanings well after production. In her close reading of the doll scene in *Velvet Goldmine* (1998), Leyda suggests the film authorizes fan appropriation, evinced in the slash fiction produced, mostly by women, in the years since its release. The schoolgirls in the doll scene allegorize the repurposing of gay male desire echoed in the fan fiction that arose as part of the film's reception. Akin to the lesbian subculture surrounding *Carol*, women appropriate the narrative and characters for their own purposes and fantasies—an appropriation Haynes models in his own fandom, repurposing popular culture for his own use. To this extent, Leyda and White both foreground intermediality to amplify the heteroglossia of Haynes's film work, intimating how the self-authorizing technologies of social media may well provide the grounds for auteurism's eventual undoing.

Whereas White's chapter introduces the breadth of interlocutors shaping Haynes's works, Rebecca Gordon and David Maynard and I examine the implications of taking such influences seriously, focusing on Julianne Moore and Christine Vachon, respectively. By rack-focusing on Haynes's collaborators, these chapters undermine some of the most cherished precepts of auteur theory. Because these interlocutors are women, granting them an authorial presence throws the male canon into question, as Maynard and I make clear in our discussion of Vachon. For Gordon, on the other hand, the meanings generated by Moore's body and the suffering it registers may well be a form of embodied resistance beyond the director's ken. Abjection is central to Gordon's quite literal anatomization of Julianne Moore's body in Haynes's women's films, from her only partially hidden pregnant body in *Far from Heaven* to her actually anorexic body in *Safe*. Indeed, Moore's characters are typical of Vachon's films, inclusive of

Haynes's work but extending far beyond it. Maynard and I argue Vachon's work is inhabited by characters who seem to revel in "self-destruction, passivity, sacrifice, and masochism"; we identify in these themes, however, an antisocial feminism that, following the work of Halberstam (2011), "renarrat[es] abjection as resistance" (Wiegman 2014, 6).

By widening the temporal frame to include the production histories of Haynes's films and their transmedia afterlife, part I solidifies a narrative about Haynes that firmly places his work in the tradition of new feminist cinema. Returning to the feminist theorists and filmmakers that influenced Haynes's *Safe*, my own essay takes to task the "manspreading machinery" of auteurism that Girish Shambu defines as "an ingenious mechanism for ceaselessly multiplying discourse on a limited number of directors . . . usually, men" (2018). Situating the film in a transgenerational genealogy of feminist counter-cinema, the chapter provides an altogether different context from the male genius-auteur tradition in which his work is commonly placed. Rather than "admit that female filmmakers . . . influence individual male filmmakers—or even culture more broadly," interviewers and critics have ignored the substantial influence of Chantal Akerman on *Safe*, emblematizing a deep misogyny endemic to auteur theory (Mayer 2016b). My discussion of *Safe*'s indebtedness to women's experimental cinema and the feminist culture that shaped it provides a pivot to part II, which approaches Haynes's work in terms of the interruption and re-vision of feminisms that further challenge the auteurist paradigm.

Whereas part I's contributors attend to the conceptual and contextual frames mobilized by Haynes's media work, part II, "Intersections and Interventions," reframes Haynes's film work from the standpoint of intersectional feminist politics, foregrounding issues of class, race, nation, sexuality, and whiteness that have intervened into feminism's foundational claims about gender as a (singular) category of analysis. The first chapter in part II reminds us that, as early as 1991, Haynes was forthright about the "reductive" tendency to label him as a gay filmmaker: "I don't consider myself a gay filmmaker, and I don't consider *Poison* an exclusively gay film" (Laskawy 2014, 20)—a claim Issacharoff illustrates by returning to the film's other sections, "Hero" and "Horror," which literally frame the critically privileged section, "Homo." Returning to *Poison*'s forgotten women enables Issacharoff to recuperate the feminist scholarship that made queer social theory (and NQC) imaginable. Her chapter demonstrates how cross-gender identification in Haynes's work figures the intersectional and, at times, familial relationship between queer and feminist theory evident throughout this volume. Part II, in this way, explores Haynes's "intersectional filmmaking and its importance for feminism," assessing his work less in terms of collaborative authorship, as part I does, than the arguments posed by feminist theory that have developed over the last several decades (Mayer 2016a, 6).

Poison was made at the height of the AIDS crisis, responding to a critical moment in history; two decades later, Haynes would react to a different crisis, the financial crisis, with yet another intersectional work—one attuned to the particular affective experiences produced by late capitalism in the new millennium. As both *Dark Waters* and *Mildred Pierce* adumbrate, neoliberalism has captured Haynes's attention in recent years: "Where is the outside now? Who stands beyond capitalism? Who is questioning corporate culture? The market has won. It accepts gay and lesbian lives because those people can spend money like anyone else. It is issues of poverty and race that need attention now" (quoted in Cooke 2015). Haynes, true to form, locates this "outside" inside the family and its cinematic genres, as Flanery suggests in his reading of *Mildred Pierce*. He traces an emergent aesthetic form in the temporal drag of Haynes's adaptation of James M. Cain's novel—an aesthetic originating in the changed affective atmosphere following the financial crisis of 2008. Reading it as an exemplum of Berlant's "situation tragedy," Flanery tracks the recurrent disappointments of failed fantasies of the good life in *Mildred Pierce* to the logics of neoliberalism. Sounding the depths of these resonances, Flanery's chapter links the intersectional politics of gender and class experienced as perpetual crisis to the temporality of televisual serialization.

The dialectics of Haynes's *Mildred* relies on its anachronistic return to a set of thematics that found the maternal melodrama in its heyday when the problems of motherhood were intimately tied to issues of social class. Willis argues the discursive limits of the form for transcoding critical race and intersectional feminist politics. Overlooked in responses to Willis's critique—those who have sought to defend *Far from Heaven* against the "disappointments" and inconsistencies she maps out in its political ambit—is the trope of "maternal plenitude" and its topos of suffering that shapes her intervention.[16] Addressed to women, the maternal melodrama figures centrally in woman's culture, as Berlant (2008) details, yet the form "has mobilized fantasies of what black and working-class suffering must feel like in order to find a language for [the white woman's] own more privileged suffering at the hands of other women, men, and callus institutions" (6). Such fantasies, as Willis shows through her extensive media archeology, form the political undertow of *Far from Heaven*, and Haynes's own words bear this out: "It's the gay man, Frank Whitaker, who has the most freedom.... He's not as intensely visible as Raymond the gardener, who has to move. But Cathy is at the bottom of the hierarchy; she gives up the love object, loses the husband, and is left with the responsibility of the children" (quoted in MacDonald 2014, 163). Sybil—who, as the family's black maid, actually takes care of the children in the Whitaker home—doesn't even appear on this scale of ranked oppressions, intimating the perspectival blind spots that accompany Haynes's women's films, even when critically queer.

The last two chapters of part II, in this way, bring into view the more troubling residue of cinematic fantasies that are reactivated in Haynes's filmic allusions—fantasies that operate as the historical ground against which Haynes's white protagonists figure. Both Willis's and Bouchard and Desai's interventions trouble what sort of narratives and which kinds of bodies are read as feminist, queer, or both, intimating that Haynes's citation of classic films, from D. W. Griffith to Douglas Sirk, raises concerns feminist film critics cannot ignore. In posing such questions, these chapters reject the hagiographic tendencies of auteur theory in favor of an intersectional feminist perspective that demands film criticism be more attentive and amenable to other kinds of histories and other sorts of subjects. Drawing attention to his construction of white femininity and the racialized politics of looking in several of his films, Bouchard and Desai revisit their earlier claims (2005) about *Safe*—a film that came on the scene at a critical moment in the institutionalization of feminism, and one that thematizes a similar sense of entitlement in its representation of whiteness within the broader context of US imperialism. In identifying certain troubling motifs in *Carol* and *Wonderstruck* (2017), they trace out increasingly problematic relations of looking in his films that Haynes once challenged in *Safe*. As a filmmaker who has come to see class and race as priorities for cinematic representation, Haynes's image repertoire of white femininity (and marginalized women and children of color) certainly begs scrutiny, as Bouchard and Desai prove in the closing chapter of part II.

The final part of the volume, "Intermediality and Intertextuality," offers a critical model that moves precisely in this direction by reading Haynes's work through a series of feminist companion texts in media history. Temporal drag manifests in his films through a self-conscious creative practice of media archeology in which Haynes scaffolds his meditations on the present to the affective work of a range of media forms and material objects. Bouchard and Desai, to this extent, afford a transition to part III in their discussion of *Wonderstruck*, a film that figures media archeology's privileged objects—particularly early cinema and the "captured exotica" of museums—along with the subfield's more troubling aims, as Elsaesser identifies: "to fetishize 'memory' and 'materiality' in the form of trauma and loss" (2016, 206). The film's obsessive attention to the materiality of cultural objects set in their specific sociohistorical contexts (or not, in the case of the Natural History Museum, as Bouchard and Desai address) reminds us that such fetishizing has long typified Haynes's work. His film and media curate an array of "defunct" objects and cultural forms, mostly involving outmoded genres of music (e.g., the easy listening, folk, and glam rock of the '60s and '70s) and film, especially the subgenres of the woman's film as Doane (1987) identifies them: the films of medical discourse, the maternal melodrama, the love story, and the paranoid gothic film. Yet, as the final chapters demonstrate, Haynes's intertextuality is coeval with his interest in intermedia, turning his "textual drag" of older cinematic, televisual, and musical genres into opportunities to lovingly contemplate past movements in architecture, photography, painting, design, fashion, and much more.

Although media archeology remains loosely defined, the general consensus of its traits is remarkably descriptive of Haynes's media practice: "discontent with linear narratives . . . , the need to 'read [media history] against the grain,' . . . to 'dig out' forgotten, suppressed and neglected histories . . . reconfigur[ing] the temporalities of past and future" (Elsaesser 2016, 183). Haynes's films certainly undertake such work in their anachronistic pull backward, but it is their attention to "reading" popular media texts against the grain on which the latter chapters focus. Moreover, what makes his own "readings" of popular culture pointedly feminist is his choice of intertexts. Most are recognizable feminist "companion texts [that] spark a moment of revelation in the midst of an overwhelming proximity" (Ahmed 2017, 16), and, as the contributors elaborate, in Haynes's imaginative worlds, such companion texts provide a wealth of feelings and resources "to make sense of something . . . beyond [our] grasp" (16), like our own present moment in history. Lynne Joyrich's chapter, for example, maps *Far from Heaven*'s numerous cinematic intertexts, particularly Sirk's domestic melodramas, that are well-established feminist companion texts. Indeed, Haynes, as J. Hoberman (2002) observes, "first encountered Sirk in college in the 1980s at a moment when academic interest in his movies was stimulated by a feminist reappraisal and radical rereading of so-called women's pictures." For Joyrich, *Far from Heaven*'s intertextuality invites a deeper media archeology through these companion texts' "outmoded ... accessories," including the television console and the wired telephone, along with other material objects that make up their particular affective sensorium. Attending to the semiotics of objects of mediation, she makes the case for Haynes as a dialectician of new technologies, as these objects intercede into and redirect characters' communications and desires.

Bridget Kies's essay builds on Joyrich's materialist reassessment of melodrama, but rather than do so through the objects within the diegetic frame, she looks to the technology of its transmission: the television. Reflecting the recent historical turn in feminist media studies, Kies situates *Mildred Pierce* in the context and history of HBO programming. Kies tunes in to the gendered divisions that shape televisual discourse and define cable branding through the framing of *Mildred Pierce* as an HBO miniseries, situating it within the larger context of the history of media industries. In this context, the miniseries signals a double feminization, both as maternal melodrama and as television itself, which has long been theorized as a feminized medium. This feminization of forms is also central to Mary R. Desjardins's chapter, which explores the meanings of the female body and female agency evoked by the anorexic body in *Superstar*—or its avatar in the form of a Barbie doll, adding yet another layer of intermediality to a film about the pop singer and television icon Karen Carpenter. Desjardins situates the experimental video in the broader context of feminist cultural criticism, reading Haynes's work with feminist classics such as Lynn Spigel's research on Barbie and Susan Bordo's work on eating disorders to vet the film's claims about the female body, stardom, and, especially, biography, as Desjardins notes in her added coda.[17] Forerunners in feminist intermedia studies, Desjardins's and Joyrich's essays first appeared in *Camera Obscura*. They thus bridge the book to its own companion text, that journal's special issue.

Barbie dolls in *Superstar* evoke a recognizable object from childhood with its own "*haptic* historiography ... negotiating with the past and producing historical knowledge through visceral sensations" (Freeman 2010, 123, emphasis in original). In *Dottie Gets Spanked* (1993), such haptics are bound to the act of spanking. The deep intertextuality generated by Haynes's fictionalized Lucille Ball, "Dottie," and the queer child who worships her affords Noah Tsika the opportunity to undertake an extensive media archeology of female stardom in the age of television, implicitly responding to the question Desjardins poses in her coda about how to theorize biography from a feminist perspective and anticipating Nick Davis's chapter on *I'm Not There*. In his study of Cate Blanchett's Dylan and Charlotte Gainsbourg's Claire, Davis finds both performances to be equally mimetic and denaturalized, akin to Ball's complexly queer mimicry anatomized in Tsika's analysis. In her performance of Claire, Gainsbourg evokes the feminist companion texts of the era, Davis argues, particularly the writing of rock critic and radical feminist Ellen Willis. Together, the last two chapters develop an intermedial archeology that explicates Haynes's unique "*dialectics* of feeling," mapping out in his work how "we feel through and with representational, technological, and social forms whose histories are uneven and overlapping" (Freeman 2010, 127, emphasis in original).

Taking its cue from Haynes's cinematic dialectics, *Reframing Todd Haynes* offers a critical practice appropriate to new feminist cinema narrated through the frame of authorship in order to disrupt the tropes of auteur criticism. In his experiments in shape and form catalyzed by the insights of feminist film theory of the '70s and '80s, Haynes refuses to fetishize the "new" in work that is nonetheless uncannily contemporary. Haynes's film and media, in this way, afford a rich archive of companion texts that suggest "perhaps when we think about the question of feminist futures, we need to attend to the legacies of feminist pasts" (Ahmed 2003, 236). By returning to feminist film theory's privileged forms, especially the woman's film, Haynes has created an oeuvre of "social political critique," bringing the genre's "latent radicality and embedded critical perspectives of modern life" to the surface of the screen in creatively anachronistic experimental narratives (Haynes, in Kohn, 2011). Such work incarnates queer feminist criticism's temporal drag in its interrogations of time and affect. Evoking the "specters of feminism," his film and media may "look politically anachronistic," but as Freeman insists—and Haynes proves time and again—"there are those of us for whom queer politics and theory necessarily involve not disavowing . . . feminism and its histories" (2010, 59, 62). From his collaborative work with (and inspiration from) women throughout his career to the "radical questions" his work has consistently posed across several decades, Haynes's unwavering feminist commitments have left their own indelible mark on culture and on our understanding of film and media.

NOTES

I thank Patricia White and Lynne Joyrich for their thoughtful contributions and feedback to this introduction.

1 Recent examples include Jonathan Goldberg's 2016 book *Melodrama: An Aesthetics of Impossibility* and Wim Staat's "Todd Haynes' Melodramas of the Unknown Woman: *Far from Heaven*, *Mildred Pierce*, and *Carol*, and Stanley Cavell's Film Ethics" (2019). Both Staat and Goldberg explicitly distance themselves from all feminist readings of Haynes's films and ignore—or, worse, denigrate—feminist writing on melodrama generally.

2 The *New Yorker*, for one, framed it as "A Tale of Two Plagues" (Roth 2020). Reconsiderations of *Safe* since COVID-19 have appeared in popular magazines such as *Vanity Fair*, *Vogue*, *W Magazine*, and *Jezebel*. See Cills (2020), Collins (2020), Hahn (2020), Munzenrieder (2020).

3 Haynes retrospectives in the US followed the one held during the 2012 Munich Film Festival. The director was later awarded the Pardo d'onore Manor lifetime achievement award at the Locarno Film Festival and feted with a tribute to his career at the Mill Valley Film Festival.

4 Rich, who coined NQC, now sees it as less of a "movement" than a "moment" (2001, 114–18).

5 Both *Safe* and *Superstar* are not so easily integrated into the NQC canon; the latter obviously predates the movement by four years. Those who make the case for *Safe* do so by reading the film as an AIDS allegory. Others, like Michael DeAngelis, gloss over *Safe* when using Haynes's work to define "the characteristics of new queer filmmaking" (2004, 41).

6 Haynes remains adamant in defining NQC in specifically formal terms: "The thing I dug about New Queer Cinema was being associated with films that were challenging narrative form and style as much as content.... Queerness was, by definition, a critique of mainstream culture. It wasn't just a plea for a place at the table. It called into question the table itself" (quoted in Lahr 2019).

7 Haynes's role in NQC is the organizing principle of James Morrison's volume, but it also anchors Haynes's inclusion in nearly every study of NQC, including Benshoff and Griffin (2006) and Michele Aaron (2004). Nick Davis (2013) stands apart for his nuanced reading of *Velvet Goldmine* "as a film to which New Queer Cinema had been leading ... to force it along different paths" (244–45).

8 See Geller (2018) for a discussion of the backlash against feminism within film studies.

9 If Haynes sounds defensive of the tradition of the woman's film, he has good reason, as critics often dismiss it out of hand. Goldberg (2016), for one, refuses to take seriously Haynes's own claim that his films are part of this tradition, insisting that he must be joking (33). Hoberman (2002) also dismisses the tradition as "so-called."

10 Haynes often refers to Marcel Proust in interviews; see Lahr (2019) and Polito (2008).

11 Frank Rich notes Haynes's "decidedly unorthodox" approach to Sondheim in Pogrebin (2013).

12 In Morrison's 2007 anthology, the term *feminism* (applied to Haynes) only appears in Pick's discussion of *Safe*. Rob White (2013) acknowledges that *Safe* alludes to Akerman's "feminist anti-epic" but never uses the term to describe *Safe*. White's few references

to feminism are symptomatic of the discomfort many critics have with it; White never once ascribes it to Haynes or his work (6, 42, 44), despite its being used in the synopsis on the back cover: "Todd Haynes films are … underpinned by a serious commitment to feminism." Only Haynes, in the concluding interview, repeatedly raises the topic of feminism and feminist film theory.

13 The discussion of history as social construction is an established subfield of film studies, one led, in fact, by Haynes's mentor at Brown, Phil Rosen. Such ill-informed claims are common in queer theory outside of film studies—a problem in queer feminism I discuss elsewhere (Geller 2013).

14 For example, see the interview with Keith Phipps (2014, 94).

15 Derschowitz cites Thomas Kail, director of *Fosse/Verdon* (2019), a Time's Up–era miniseries conceived to correct the erasure of Gwen Verdon's contributions from Fosse's body of work.

16 It may be because Willis breaks with auteurist hagiography in criticizing Haynes that Goldberg, who is fully within it, condemns her for the ideas he (inaccurately) ascribes to her: "She wants the satisfaction of the happy ending" (2016, 42).

17 For Ahmed, "By feminist classics, I mean … the texts that reach us, that make a connection … [often] ones assumed to be dated, to belong to a time that we are in no longer" (2017, 17).

PART I

Influences and Interlocutors

1 Lesbian Reverie
Carol in History and Fantasy

Patricia White

The plot of Todd Haynes's rapturously received lesbian romance *Carol* (2015) is framed as a reverie: in early 1950s New York, an unformed young store clerk and aspiring photographer, Therese Belivet (Rooney Mara), recalls in flashback her affair and painful breakup with the title character, Carol Aird, a dissatisfied society matron played by Cate Blanchett. Therese's reverie resolves with her decision to be a lesbian, to return to Carol. As a pre-Stonewall tale made in the era of marriage equality by a queer auteur skilled in cinematic pastiche, the film itself is a kind of lesbian reverie.[1] Set amid lonely city streets, Midwest diners, and roadside motels, where lesbianism is associated with paranoia and unfit motherhood, *Carol* occupies the affective terrain of what Heather Love (2007) calls "feeling backwards." The characters and the plot remain remarkably sketchy; the film's quality of reverie is conveyed in its exquisite design, cinematography, and score.[2] *Carol* is a story of love between women that pleasurably suspends time and action in its period mise-en-scène, dilatory diegesis, and spectatorial address. But as an adaptation of a novel written "back then" that sustains, rather than (only) punishes, the heroines' and the audience's desire, the film takes subsequent histories (of feminist and queer culture) into account, without resolving as an identitarian or utopian fable. What does Haynes's approach permit in the present moment of queer representation? How does the film activate the force of the queer and movie past, and for whom?

My reading of *Carol* explores the temporality, aesthetics, and affective structure of reverie to uncover how a contemporary viewer may be engaged as the subject of the film's fantasy. That a viewer can be so engaged is illustrated by the extravagant mainstream critical praise that heralded *Carol*'s release—it garnered six Academy Award nominations—and by the subterranean but no less extravagant fan dedication that keeps it alive on Tumblr. That other viewers don't feel so addressed is illustrated in the comments of dissenters who find the film "easy to admire but hard to hold close" (Zacharek 2015), a criticism of "coldness" often leveled at Haynes's period reconstructions. My own captivation with *Carol* is overdetermined by an enduring friendship with the director and a critical engagement that takes me back to the terrain of my first book, *Uninvited: Classical Hollywood Cinema and Lesbian Representability*, which used Haynes's work to reflect on the queer psychic imprint of the Hollywood past in the process I call "retrospectatorship" (1999, 197). Haynes has acknowledged that "making a film about the love between two women was really a tribute to the lesbians in my life"—my writing on the film, folding together inter-, extra-, and close textual analysis, is a tribute in turn. Framing questions of authorship in terms of fantasy, I argue that Haynes and his collaborators create formal structures through cinematography, mise-en-scène, and score that open critical access to the historical stakes and emotional force of the film's source text, Patricia Highsmith's fiercely beloved 1952 novel *The Price of Salt,* while remaining rooted in the queer and feminist present. Demonstrating the film's embeddedness in a rich legacy of cinematic signifiers of lesbianism, I conclude with a discussion of fan practices that find in *Carol*'s revision of lesbian/film history a still-potent vocabulary of desire.

Carol's screenplay by acclaimed lesbian playwright Phyllis Nagy, who became friends with Highsmith in the decade before the author's death in 1995, is faithful to the novel's wish-fulfilling staging of an intergenerational, class-aspirational, head-over-(high) heels seduction fantasy. It also captures the novel's strong strain of compulsion, threat, and anxiety. But it is Haynes's direction, with its precise calculation of the effect of every decision, from casting to color palette to undergarment to film stock, that is responsible for *Carol*'s emotional sweep, the exact inflection of the "lover's discourse" it speaks (Barthes 1978). A film theorist's dream director, Haynes schooled his actors in the attitude of the "amorous subject" by giving them copies of Roland Barthes's poetic text *A Lover's Discourse* to prepare for their roles. Ultimately, the encounter he stages between Hollywood and Highsmith exerts a queer gravitational pull toward history. As filmmaker John Waters (2015) mused: "Maybe the only way to be transgressive these days is to be shockingly tasteful. This Lana Turner–meets–Audrey Hepburn lipstick-lesbian melodrama is so old-fashioned I felt like I was one year old after watching it. That's almost reborn." Waters aptly assesses Haynes's near simulacrum of a movie past dominated by white female stardom and fueled not so much by camp as by affect of infantile intensity. Waters also suggests that the turn toward the past can open up new futures for queer representation, an insight crucial to assessing the importance of Haynes's work at the intersection of queer and feminist, gay male and lesbian, indie and mainstream representational practice.

Carol certainly resonates with Haynes's ongoing reworking of the terms of the classical Hollywood women's picture. In the maternal melodramas *Far from Heaven* (2002) and *Mildred Pierce* (2011), for example, Haynes uses the heroines' struggles with subjectivity and desire to construct an affective vision of the past that challenges patriarchal authority in the present. *Carol* differs from *Far from Heaven*, Haynes points out in interviews, in its grayer and grittier photojournalism-inspired aesthetic and in its setting, far from Hollywood as it were, during the uncertain years before Eisenhower-era affluence. But it differs most momentously in its direct exploration of that *other* kind of love—lesbian desire—that, as I argued in *Uninvited*, so often traverses the sacrificial scenarios of the Hollywood women's picture without breaking into the diegesis. As an undergraduate at Brown University, Haynes studied with Mary Ann Doane, whose influential 1987 study named the disposition of these 1940 melodrama heroines in the resonant, ambiguous phrase "the desire to desire." Haynes's affinity with his heroines, and his mobilization of Hollywood women's films as intertexts, acknowledges a cultural trope of amorous, glamorous femininity that resonates with (some) gay men (see Farmer 2000). *Carol* returns that identification between gayness and femininity to lesbians on the level of both spectatorship and content. Therese and Carol, unlike Haynes's other heroines, get what they want.

Lesbian Adaptation

Women profoundly shape Haynes's work both internally, through the psychic investments I've indicated, and externally, through his collaborations—most notably with college friend and Killer Films founder Christine Vachon, who has produced all his films since *Poison* (1991). In the case of *Carol*, the formidable status of Patricia Highsmith and the participation of Vachon and Nagy—the latter known for her successful stage adaptation of Highsmith's *The Talented Mr. Ripley*—queer a reading in terms of singular (male) creative genius. Indeed, Haynes came on board more than a decade into this female-driven project.[3]

Arguably, the production delay and even the film's slowly staged release added to its sense of belatedness. It is a quiet, period romance with, as the British censor's certificate has it, "infrequent" (if "strong") sex, released alongside righteous lesbian civil rights films like *Freeheld* (2015). Belatedness functions as what Elizabeth Freeman calls "temporal drag"—a queer mode of "feeling the historical" that pulls us toward Highsmith's darker times and disposition (2010, 62). The film's attitude toward that past is neither indulgent nor triumphalist.[4] *Carol* doesn't gratify our wishful projections onto the past with a portrait of Greenwich Village bars frequented by interracial butch-femme couples styled after pulp novel covers. Nor does it endorse a progressive, coming out–into–rights and visibility narrative. Rather, it invites us to dwell in the half-light of a Cold War–era segregated closet whose door is beginning to crack, rewarding our patience with what Dana Luciano, in her reading of *Far from Heaven*, evocatively calls "an opening to the affective forces of another time—a feminine dilation on the past" (2007, 266).

Highsmith published the cryptically titled *The Price of Salt* in 1952 under the pseudonym Claire Morgan. Indirection and subterfuge have long been part of the novel's appeal to its lesbian readers, who found wrapped in its paperback cover a modernist-inspired work whose ending—"Therese walked toward her"—diverged notably from the payback required in lesbian pulp fiction of the time. By the time Bloomsbury reissued the novel in 1990 under the title *Carol* and Highsmith's real name, the lesbian clandestine life it recorded belonged to a bygone era. Highsmith's afterword recounts the genesis of the novel in an autobiographical incident, at the same time giving it an almost hallucinatory pitch. Highsmith had taken a seasonal sales job at Bloomingdale's to supplement her income as she awaited publication of her first novel, *Strangers on a Train* (1950), when "into this chaos of noise and commerce, there walked a blondish woman in a fur coat. She drifted towards the doll counter with a look of uncertainty—should she buy a doll or something else?—and I think she was slapping a pair of gloves absently into one hand" (1990, 308).[5] As Highsmith describes the catalyzing effect of this moment: "It was a routine transaction, the woman paid and departed. But I felt odd and swimmy in the head, near to fainting, yet at the same time uplifted, as if I had seen a vision" (309).

The film adaptation revives the frisson of living in the shadows with twilight images of midcentury lust and anxiety, coded gestures, longing glances, and double-edged words. *Carol*, with its pre-Stonewall somberness, exhibits "the backward turn" in queer culture—not a condescending look back from the enlightened present, but rather an attention to and affective investment in negativity that honors queer history's losses (Love 2007, 5). It doesn't so much turn away from a present political moment as attend to the power of an occluded history. Haynes's customary attention to detail serves not verisimilitude but rather the image of a historical moment—in this case, 1952 before postwar posterity painted Americans' aspirations in full, garish Technicolor. Haynes constructs from Nagy's script and Highsmith's anxious seduction fantasy a picture of the lesbian past animated by the feminized structures of feeling and queer authorial stylings of the Hollywood woman's picture, as well as by an intervening feminist and queer history of art and activism. This collaboration puts a particular spin—call it a swoon—on the queer feeling for the past.

Flung out of Time

Carol shows the price that the eponymous heroine, a wealthy, discontented suburban wife and mother, willingly pays for her taste of salt—a headlong affair with a shop girl she meets in a department store during the Christmas rush. But *Carol* also does something trickier. It successfully transports the viewer into the place of the sales clerk, a young woman as blank in experience, background, and character as the "I" of Daphne du Maurier's *Rebecca* (1938)—if equally watchful and ardent. Nagy notes of the challenges of adapting *The Price of Salt*: "Because Therese is Pat's stand-in, she is virtually character-free. Which is fine for a book, but doesn't really work in a movie."[6] The problem as Nagy poses it is that filmic narration is both subjective and objective—we see Therese seeing Carol. The film responds to this challenge by subtly opening onto Carol's perspective and her vulnerability. It also responds to it formally. We frequently look in on scenes through windows and doorways, strain to see around objects or figures blocking our view, move with the camera instead of the characters, or dwell on an echoing sound. The device of a cinematic narrator who is both "virtually character-free" and a proxy for lesbian authorial desire is key to *Carol*'s success as an adaptation that is also unmistakably a film signed by Todd Haynes. The film's drifting mood, spare frames, and sketchy plot, its

1.1 Carol's fraught touch on Therese's shoulder is a quotation from *Brief Encounter.*

precise gestures and camera setups, invite the viewer to share in a story suspended in time while remaining located in history.

The film begins with a flourish as a crane moves up from a subway grate—the underground rumble anticipates the motif of trains and cars carrying us into subjective space and time. The floating camera soon enters a posh New York hotel restaurant where the smartly dressed Carol and Therese are taking tea. Thrust into the point of view of an intruding male acquaintance, we interrupt a conversation choked with emotions that we can't begin to decipher. The two women quickly take leave of each other, their parting platitudes belied by the branding touch of Carol's hand on Therese's shoulder (figure 1.1). The scene pays homage to the framing structure of David Lean's *Brief Encounter* (1945), whose lovers will forever remain relegated to opposite train platforms. *Carol*'s exquisite lovelorn sensibility owes as much to that romantic classic as it does to Highsmith's masterful inscription of the obsessive mind; from the conjunction of the two emerges a different romantic outcome.

Most of the rest of the film is told in flashback. Therese's reverie reveals how the women met by chance, grew closer, and shared a bittersweet road trip before being forced to part under threat of the loss of Carol's daughter, Rindy. Through the framing device the end is implied at the beginning: we know the lovers will be separated; we are invited to luxuriate in the sheer impossibility of their romance. By the time the film's plot finally catches up to a reprise of its first scene, the full extent of the encounter's pathos is clear. This time, we hear the women's conversation and learn that Carol has relinquished custody of Rindy and moved out on her own. Nervously, she invites Therese to come and live with her. But, once burned, twice shy: the now-poised young woman declines. This time her exit is excruciatingly emotional. Now we hear Carol's "I love you" before Therese's acquaintance Jack interrupts their tête-à-tête. Carol's admission attempts and fails to take back the "I release you" with which she closed her earlier letter to Therese. Slight changes in the cutting of the scene the second time we see it double down on its invocation of the sacrificial ethos of the woman's picture.

But let's return to the staging of Therese's flashback, which encompasses this replay of the scene, for it is what happens within that reverie that determines Therese's own change of heart.[7] In *Brief Encounter*, the protagonist Laura narrates her would-be affair with Alec in an internal monologue addressed to her husband; *Carol* makes its temporal shift visually instead, with Therese's reflection in the rain-streaked window of the car. Looking through glass becomes a central visual motif in the film, one that materializes the cinematographic process of looking through a lens. Therese's blurred features resemble the cover art of a midcentury paperback novel. The indistinct image represents Therese's subjectivity both as a blank space at the film's center that the spectator must fill and as the point from which all the story's characters, emotions, and events are projected. An image of her first glimpse of Carol floats up and recedes as Therese travels downtown, until a shot from inside a glass case displaying a toy train set transitions us decisively to the flashback that will bring the women to this evening, to this end. Crossing this threshold marks the audience's entry into a fictional world, just as, for the two hours required to watch the movie, the audience shares the temporality of reverie. Steve Macfarlane's 2015 review in *Slant* cannily describes the film's timing: "*Carol* isn't even a love story; it's a tenuous chronology of two characters striving to get a love story started." In its almost arduous passage, the film has time to work on the viewer's body as the thought of Carol works on Therese's.

Mise-en-Scène of/and Desire

Feminist theorists have brought the psychoanalytic concept of fantasy to bear on similar scenarios of reverie in classical woman's pictures as a way of complicating accounts of spectatorial identification.[8] Jean Laplanche and

J. B. Pontalis ([1967] 2006) define fantasy in a suggestively cinematic way as a script or "*mise-en-scène* of desire." "It is not the object that is desired but its setting," they note, glossing Freud's account of his patients' various elaborations of the simple script: "a child is being beaten" (318–19). The sketchy details repression leaves in its wake (Who is the child: self or sibling? Who is punishing it: mother or father? What is its misdeed? What is its aim: pleasure or pain?) are filled in by films and fictions that invite the onlooker to find and respond to a version of her most deeply conflicted, desiring self in their constructed worlds. But as Teresa de Lauretis emphasizes in her work on lesbian spectatorship, the textual place from which to regard a particular fantasy's unfolding is not equally hospitable to all spectators. In a manner often correlated with gendered genre preferences, the viewer may refuse the invitation or expend equal psychic intensity repudiating it. Haynes's oeuvre plays quite knowingly with these ideas, explicitly quoting Freud's text in *Dottie Gets Spanked* (1993) and, more significantly, formally activating these processes. In an uncanny doubling of such authorial preoccupations, *Carol*'s lesbian fantasy of maternal seduction is imbedded in a memorable account Highsmith gives of writing the novel on which it is based.[9]

The evening after her encounter with "the blondish woman," Highsmith recounts, she drafted the "entire story" that became *The Price of Salt*: "It flowed from the end of my pen as if from nowhere—beginning, middle, end. It took about two hours, perhaps less" (1991, 309). The book's thin plot and careful scene-setting befit its origin in an erotic reverie that lasted precisely the duration of a feature film. The form of the fantasy—the lovers' postponement of gratification, their flight from the law, their separation—betrays the fact, as Laplanche and Pontalis note, that "the prohibition is invariably present in the actual formation of the wish" (1967, 318). The beating fantasy is a seduction fantasy that has undergone repression. When Freud's daydreamers were asked whether they were doing the spanking or being spanked in their erotic reveries, they could answer only vaguely: "I am probably looking on" ([1919] 1953, 186). Highsmith goes on to tell us that the creative fever turned out to be the onset of chicken pox, and she describes the symptoms with a striking level of detail given the brevity of her account of the novel and its writing: "The face, torso, upper arms, even ears and nostrils are covered or lined with pustules that itch and burst. One must not scratch them in one's sleep, otherwise scars and pits result" (1990, 309). The description of convulsive embodiment itself functions as a symptom of the productivity of the erotic fantasy that would become the novel, the hesitation to scratch its anticipatory pleasures.

In another key text on fantasy, "Creative Writers and Day-Dreaming," Freud argues that "the purely formal—that is, aesthetic—yield of pleasure which [the artist] offers us in the presentation of his [or her] phantasies" functions like a bribe, lowering our resistance, shielding us from shame over the naked erotic and ambitious wishes behind the stories we enjoy ([1907] 1953, 153). A swirl of artistic inspiration and childhood infectious disease informs the gripping portrait of lesbian desire in *The Price of Salt*, whose status as "creative writing" rather than authorial daydream is secured by the pseudonym Claire Morgan. It is this original fantasy of seduction, I argue, that is strong enough to bubble up sixty years later in the filmic rendition of Highsmith's swimmy "vision"—like the "little blister on the skin" that appeared on the writer's abdomen (1990, 309).

For theories of fantasy offer a way to look at Haynes's and Highsmith's distinct authorial contributions. The formal qualities that have so dazzled some viewers—the fluid camera, hypnotic pace, cool color temperature, spare musical cues and compositions—are "bribes" that others refuse. With its proliferation of thresholds and reflections, *Carol* seems deliberately to figure this provisional entrée to the film's mise-en-scène of lesbian desire. Even the grainy Super-16 filmstock of Edward Lachman's cinematography brings our eye to the surface of the image.

Haynes collected dozens of images of midcentury street photography in preparation for the film. The visual vocabulary of city streets and shop windows blurred by rain and reflected traffic is inspired by the work of Saul Leiter. Carol and Therese drift in and out of focus in these frames, their vivid red accents signaling danger and desire. Postwar women photographers including Esther Bubley, Ruth Orkin, Helen Levitt, and Vivian Maier provided models for interiors, New York street scenes, and Therese's very avocation—in the novel she's a set designer rather than a photographer. The film has the perfect period styling one has come to expect in a Haynes film, and this styling is given a distinctive weightlessness by the frequent shooting through glass. Mise-en-scène itself comes to signify desire. Carol's bourgeois accoutrements—scarves, wraps, purses, and especially gloves—beckon the onlooker with their sensuous silks, leathers, and furs. (Haynes acknowledges that he took on the project in part because of costume designer Sandy Powell's enthusiasm for doing another "frock film" together.) Therese responds to such tactile erotics when, shown into their room at Chicago's Drake Hotel, she exclaims, "This furniture, this fabric!"

Ultimately, I argue, the formal features of Haynes's film provide entrée for historical as well as erotic fantasy—they bribe the viewer into experiencing a desired vision of the past at the same time they signal the limits of the fantasy. Behind the barriers figured on and as the surface of the image lies a segregated postwar America on the brink of momentous social change. In the transitional shot of the toy train set inside the display case, a black lawn jockey functions literally as a sign of obdurate racial hierarchies invisible to the film's characters. In this sense, the film's attention to detail directs us to read Therese's fantasy in historically specific terms as invested in the white, class, and normative gender privilege that Carol embodies. For Carol and Therese, deviance is cloaked in the consumer privileges of white femininity. In the first of the nondescript hotel rooms the couple shares on the road, Carol flirts by putting makeup and perfume on Therese. The erotic play at the game of "cosmetics counter" points back to the film's primal scene: the female paradise of the department store, with Therese serving as both vendeuse and goods.

Lesbian Scripts

When Therese arrives at her post at Frankenberg's one chilly morning, she pauses by the train set display before turning on the lights of the toy department. Goods and Christmas cheer beckon from the screen, like an uncanny shop window to the past. Within moments strikes the *coup de foudre* upon which the entire romance turns, the kernel of reality upon which Highsmith built her tale. Therese looks up from the doll counter to find a blonde woman in a fur coat across the room. Larger than life, the woman fondles her long gloves in one hand before meeting Therese's gaze briefly and getting lost in the crowd (figure 1.2). A slap of the gloves (the gauntlet) on the counter, and Carol is beside Therese, inquiring about a doll for her young daughter. Therese suggests the train set instead. "Done," says Carol, having picked up the gift she came for and, for all intents and purposes, the shop girl with it. But the norms of 1950s femininity, and the pleasures of anticipation, require the viewer to wait another hour for this mutual and obviously sexual desire to be fulfilled. Carol (deliberately, we suspect) leaves her gloves behind.

As I've suggested, the story plays out as a maternal seduction fantasy, a clichéd scenario that nevertheless has purchase in a text influenced by midcentury Freudianism and Highsmith's own troubled relationships to women, starting with her mother. Therese is positioned as the pre-oedipal

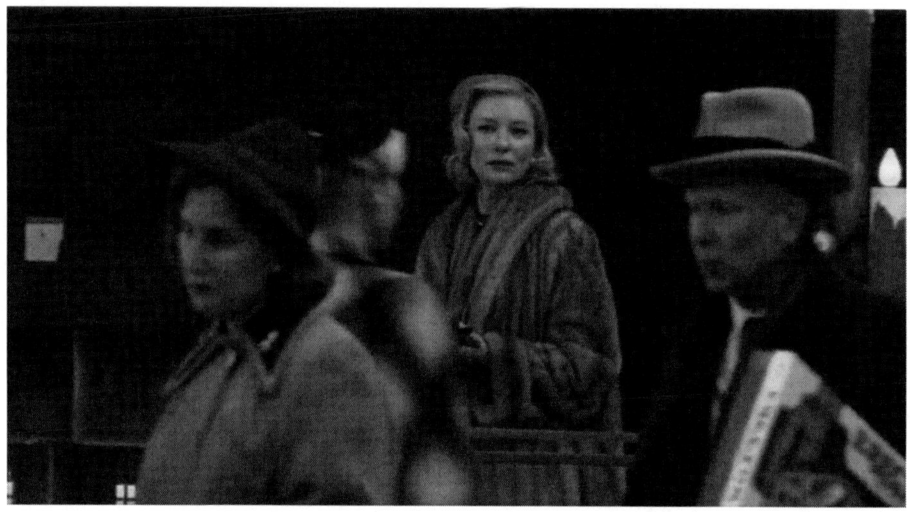

1.2 The *coupe de foudre* between the lovers recalls Highsmith's memory of working as a salesgirl.

bisexual child who desires the mother sexually. Carol invokes the younger woman's nonnormative gender by calling her "strange"—"an angel, flung out of space"—a characterization enhanced in the film by Mara's flat, guileless delivery. And initially, at least, Therese's femininity is less distinct than her youthfulness. Designer Sandy Powell emphasizes this with childlike costumes: a coat with a trimmed hood, a beret, a tam o'shanter. In fact, Therese's wardrobe could serve as well for Carol's daughter, Rindy, whose pageboy hairstyle she shares. Soon Therese will take Rindy's place, living out the female fantasy of being and/or having "something else besides a mother," a famous line from *Stella Dallas* (1937) that distills for me the erotics of the maternal melodrama (P. White 1999, 97–99).

These psychic positions are taken up in what Elaine Marks (1979) recognizes as the primary topos of lesbian literature since Sappho, the girls' boarding school. Lunching with Carol, Therese wears a white blouse and pinafore in which she looks strikingly like a different Therese, the heroine of softcore auteur Radley Metzer's adaptation of Violette Leduc's sexy Sapphic schoolgirl memoir, *Therese and Isabelle* (1968). The pedagogical dimensions of lesbian seduction also are aligned with class mobility. When Therese arrives at Carol's suburban manse for the first time, she is greeted at the door by both the housekeeper and Rindy. The former presents a different possible role for Therese to play in Carol's life of bourgeois anomie. Indeed,

Therese is promptly pressed into serving tea. When Carol's husband Harge (Kyle Chandler) blusters in, he looks right past the mousy young woman, eyes blinded by class privilege. When he later turns in fury to demand, "How do you know my wife again?" it is as if he suddenly registered her lesbian challenge to the domestic mise-en-scène. Yet the film pointedly contrasts Therese with a visible, working-class-coded butch-femme couple spotted lurking in a record store. When, after her breakup with Carol, the younger woman gets a job in the photo department of the *New York Times*, her femme styling becomes more confident and her class mobility more plausible, both developing with her "eye."

The confident career lesbian that Therese will become can be previewed in lesbian actress Sarah Paulson's role as Carol's best friend and ex-lover, Abby, who evokes one of classical Hollywood's reliable methods for encoding the lesbian as a tough, wisecracking supporting character—she's Eve Arden to Blanchett's Joan Crawford. But here, the sidekick's lesbianism is acknowledged; Abby voices the erotic and historical truths that queer-coded supporting characters like Thelma Ritter's Birdie in *All about Eve* (1950) only hint at (see P. White 1999, chap. 5).[10] Yet, if Paulson almost steals the show with lesbian verisimilitude in her supporting role, it is decisively as leading lady that Blanchett plays Carol. The older woman appears to Therese, and the spectator, as glamorous, sexy, and mysterious as Grace Kelly bending in for a kiss in the famous slow-motion point-of-view shot in Alfred Hitchcock's *Rear Window* (1954). It is Kelly, in fact, after whom Nagy patterned her vision of Carol. Less a convincing characterization of a lusty lesbian than a foregrounding of the fact that it is Blanchett playing one, the just-this-side-of-campy performance is a key element of the film's historical imaginary, a realization of how the larger-than-life female stars of postwar cinema could be experienced as one's own personal seductresses. More specifically, the "Hitchcock blonde" as a type hints at Highsmith's erotic investment in snobbery, wealth, and whiteness. With her dignified bearing and ability to pass as straight, Carol is an avatar of the cinematic figure Robert J. Corber (2011) calls the Cold War femme, a Kinsey-era housewife or other feminine woman whose imagined sexual duplicity channels anxiety about masculine identity, racial hierarchies, and national security.

Sisters to this Production Code–era type in European art films are the elegant predatory lesbians and silky vampires whom Carol is styled and played to evoke. Richard Dyer inventories the type: "She is commonly shown positioned ... behind the more sexually indeterminate (i.e., she might go

1.3 *Carol* stages an iconic lesbian seduction.

'either way') woman ... drawing the other woman into her thrall, not by direct assault or honest seduction but by stealth" (1993, 37). There is no mistaking Carol's kinship with Giovanna Galletti's fascist in *Rome, Open City* (1945) or Delphine Seyrig's blood countess in *Daughters of Darkness* (1971), for she approaches Therese precisely the way these figures do, first as the younger woman sits at the piano and finally in the long-withheld seduction, which occurs in front of a mirror (P. White 2015a) (figure 1.3).

Viewers feel these sinister dimensions of queer love as they follow the lovers across lonely stretches of highway, from hotel room to hotel room, waiting like the detective on their tail for them to "be" lesbians. On the run before their "crime" has been committed, the lovers play out Highsmith's exquisitely attuned paranoid imagination, nurtured in McCarthy-era America. In the movie, the couple's punishment comes with dream-logic swiftness, the morning after they've consummated their love, in the form of an ominous telegram informing Carol that her husband has hired a private detective who has captured recordings of their dalliance and plans to use them against her in court. If, as Laplanche and Pontalis assert, "defensive operations ... are themselves inseparably bound up with the primary function of phantasy" ([1967] 2006, 318), the pathos of the couple's thwarted love—which reaches its peak in Carol's letter that follows hard on the telegram—may even exceed the passion of its expression. "Dearest ... I release you," Blanchett's voiceover memorably emotes.

Carol in Heaven and in Hell

"It would be Carol in a thousand cities, a thousand houses, in foreign lands where they would go together, in heaven and in hell . . . ," Therese tells herself at the end of *The Price of Salt*. Although the film, too, brings Carol and Therese back together with extravagant emotion, simply to call the ending happy is to sell its complexity short. Therese resolves to go back to Carol after the film has replayed the scene of their parting. It is as if she is moved, as we are, by the reverie that comprises most of the film's running time, and changes her mind. The final scene begins with a low-angle shot of Therese under a street lamp against the twilight, a Cindy Sherman–esque reprise of the cover of a lesbian pulp novel like Ann Bannon's *Odd Girl Out* (1957) (figure 1.4). As she turns to catch a cab uptown, she passes the only black people to reach the film's foreground, as if Therese's sudden self-awareness is an opening to a social awareness that threatens to burst the bubble of the film's historical fantasy. When Therese arrives at the posh hotel restaurant where Carol is dining with friends, she sweeps the room with her gaze, eventually finding Carol in profile, a visual reference to Scottie's first vision of Madeline in Ernie's restaurant in *Vertigo* (1958). As Therese stands perfectly still in the next shot, the camera tracks in to highlight her gaze, as the musical cue comes in over the diegetic restaurant sounds and swells over a point-of-view sequence of Therese making her way across the crowded room toward her lover. When Carol finally turns slightly away from her conversation partner, as if magnetized by Therese's gaze, she meets it not with the tear-stained face that *Brief Encounter*'s heroine would have shown had things turned out differently, but with cocked head and bright red lips curling into a slightly carnal smile. In the next shot of Therese, from Carol's point of view, the camera tracks back slightly, reversing its earlier motion as if pulling Therese back into Carol's ambit; the smallest smile appears on Therese's face. The final shot continues to move toward Carol before the film cuts to black and the music ends just as abruptly.

In a homonormative world of "happily ever after," Therese would cross the room and join the sparkling dinner crowd, perhaps discussing her and Carol's plans to move in together. Instead the lovers remain separated, the hard sound and image cut leaving them in their exclusivity, in an eternally present tense, struck into stillness by a second electric return of the gaze. The viewer is pleasurably suspended in the cyclical temporality of fantasy

1.4 Therese's moment of self-recognition resembles the cover of a lesbian pulp novel.

even as she is definitively shut out. Savoring the film's tantalizing taste of the past, she gets an inkling of a queer future. The film ends with neither renunciation nor lesbian visibility, but on the brink of makeup sex. *Carol* hits melodrama's beat of "just in time" rather than "too late," an important revision of the scenarios of loss and exclusion that characterize Haynes's body of work (Neale 1986), exemplified in the craft and care of Highsmith, Haynes, and his collaborators, and extended, I think, to the viewer.

Harold, They're Lesbians

Insisting on the film's lesbian address is important in the face of its universalizing reception, which often took a retrograde approach to the film's interest in a mediated queer past. Not since *Blue Is the Warmest Colour* (Abdellatif Kechiche, 2013), and for different reasons, has a lesbian film so beguiled cinephile circuits. The word *swoon* appears with dizzying frequency in reviews that herald Haynes as an expressive auteur, Cukor-esque in his sensitive direction of powerhouse actresses. *Carol*, we are told in *Salon*, "isn't just a lesbian movie, it is a classic American romance" (O'Hehir 2015). *Entertainment Weekly*'s Joe McGovern (2015) regrets "the usage of simplistic language such as 'lesbian romance'" when describing the film, because the fact that "*Carol* is about a love story between two women," he assures readers, "hardly limits the film's thematic power to a same-sex point of view." The film's well-heeled projection of midcentury sapphism slides into a signifier of universal love and cinematic art, the rare and the ineffable, thus obscuring the sleazier side of Highsmith's own sexual compulsion, which, I have argued, survives in the very structure of the story's seduction fantasy. But even if "You don't have to be a woman who falls in love with women to get swept off your feet by *Carol*" (Berman 2015), plenty of its intended audience, and several of its key creative personnel, *are* such women. Though it's "not for lesbians only" (Cole 2015), the film captures that "same-sex" point of view in ways film history has long denied.

Lesbian comedian and *Saturday Night Live* (NBC, 1975–) regular Kate McKinnon blew the lid off the decorousness of *Carol*'s reception and ushered the film into the canon of camp with her impersonation of Carol in a video directed by Joel Gallen for the 2016 Independent Spirit Awards broadcast. Taking on Blanchett's mannerisms with drag-queen precision, McKinnon speaks the hidden sexual agenda of the movie's "glove lunch," intercut with Mara's reaction shots from the scene in which she first meets Carol ostensibly to return her customer's gloves.[11] In the skit, McKinnon-as-Carol tires of the younger woman's tentativeness and the clueless interjections of comedian Kumail Nanjiani playing the waiter, and joins, at the next table, a pair of seasoned dykes played by lesbian celebrities Jane Lynch and Wanda Sykes. The parody conjures a quotidian gay world of lust and racial diversity. Blanchett plays her role as award presenter just as broadly when the show cuts back to the ceremony and she grabs co-presenter Mara's breast.

Some fan genres display a "gloves off" willingness to speak the lustiness of the film—fan fiction imagines in detail what happens after the lovers' restaurant reunion and the final cut to black. Other lesbian viewers responded reverentially to *Carol*'s discretion. Fans on social media testify to feelings that recall the onset of Highsmith's own crush: "I felt odd and swimmy in the head, near to fainting, yet at the same time uplifted, as if I had seen a vision" (1990, 309). Even before the film's release, the professional-looking Tumblr "Miss Belivet" offered insider updates, tracking release dates, nominations, awards, and in-person appearances, and presenting each newly released production still or clip with fetishistic care, anticipating the film's own pleasures of holding back. Fan sites proliferated: some creators felt as though they had been personally addressed by the film, and their Tumblrs attest to this feeling by playing on Carol's letter to Therese—"Dearest, there are no accidents, and everything comes full circle." In such fugitive images, fans cherish the film's moments of loss and longing. Allison Tate's short film *Carol Support Group* (2017) explores the film's activation of that classic malady of the female fan: overidentification. One member of the film's support group for fans addicted to the film, a dead ringer for Carol Aird, refuses the therapeutic discourse, defiantly walking out of the session with everyone else following—and leaving her gloves behind to tempt others.

Speaking the fan vernacular most eloquently are the many *Carol*-inspired GIFs, portable, low-resolution images whose format supports simple animation. There are GIFs online for every lustful glance, averted gaze, and sharp intake of breath in the film. The GIF in its very format works as an analog for the subtle, almost undetectable turn in spectatorship from the objective to the subjective, the social to the psychic, the representation to the moment of address. The GIF is suspended in time, a badge of seduction, the aesthetic bribe that puts "secret" lesbian codes into circulation. *Carol* is prized by young lesbian viewers who may never have seen the classic melodramas to which it pays homage; my hope is that it provides a queer portal to this past.

The *Carol* meme that had the greatest viral success provides a particularly apt play on the open secret of Hollywood history. Overheard at a matinee screening of *Carol*, an older woman said to her husband: "Harold, they're lesbians." The hashtag #haroldtheyrelesbians calls up witty mash-ups using the title treatment of the film's box office rival, *Star Wars: The Force Awakens* (2015); candid shots of the film's stars together; fan art in manga style; and, significantly, images and GIFs of other popular cultural phenomena loaded with lesbian so-called subtext (figure 1.5).[12] Here, viral media practices send us back to, rather than drive us away from, the theatrical cinema experience, in a dialectic between the exclusive (and exclusionary) repertoire of celluloid sapphism and the infinite ways of making it one's own. I like to think the older woman's comment is less one of shock (Harold, they're lesbians!) than impatience (*Harold*, they're *lesbians*)—evidence of female spectators who knew what was going on with those midcentury women's pictures all along. Such proliferating fan practices challenge those who find Haynes's films distant and cold, as they spin erotic reveries out of precisely the details whose surface perfection distracts the naysayers.

1.5 A *Carol* meme became the subject of inventive fan art (Kylie O'Neil).

Carol offers a retrospective vision of a film of the 1950s, a lesbian "classic" not made in the image of the present. The romantic nostalgia it no doubt inspires is ghosted by a critique of the exclusions that bound Highsmith's world. Even the online fandom that desires Therese and Carol's reunion stutters in its staging of happily ever after. By layering my reading of the film with its intertexts, I inscribe authorial politics and the viewer's subjective desire within a potent film-historical seduction fantasy, one that engages viewers across a queer temporality of both belatedness and anticipation.

NOTES

My sincere thanks go to B. Ruby Rich, editor of *Film Quarterly*, where I first published on *Carol*, and to Teresa de Lauretis, whose visit to Philadelphia inspired me to return to theories of fantasy and spectatorship. I am grateful to those who invited me to present this as work in progress, including Shawn Shimpach and Lisa Henderson at the University of Massachusetts, Amherst; Anna Shechtman at Yale; and Jackie Stacey, Clara Bradbury-Rance, and the participants in the Sexuality Summer School at the University of Manchester, where I had the immense good fortune of having Richard Dyer as interlocutor. Thanks also to Terry Castle, Lara Cohen, Theresa Geller, Amelie Hastie, Liz Karlsen, Heather Love, Bakirathi Mani, Bryan O'Keefe, Cynthia Schneider, Jennifer Stott, Allison Tate, Christine Vachon, Kat, and the many anonymous *Carol* fans on Tumblr. For Todd Haynes: everything comes full circle.

1 On politics, emotion, and pastiche in Haynes's *Far from Heaven*, see Dyer (2007, 147–49).
2 The film was shot by Edward Lachman, and cut by Affonso Gonçalves. Judy Becker was the production designer, with costumes by Sandy Powell and score by Carter Burwell. All have worked with Haynes on other projects.
3 At the behest of producer Dorothy Berwyn, Phyllis Nagy produced her first screen adaption of *Carol* in the late 1990s and offered the script to Rose Troche, director of the breakthrough lesbian drama of the New Queer Cinema, *Go Fish* (1993), produced by Vachon and Tom Kalin, but Troche passed. After the rights to *The Price of Salt* lapsed, English producer Liz Karlsen fought hard to get them, seeing the film as an important feminist project. Financing remained elusive even with Blanchett attached and the backing of Film Four executive Tessa Ross. Finally, Karlsen approached Vachon, her collaborator on an earlier project with Nagy and a Highsmith fan. Only then did Haynes come on board, and the project moved forward with Harvey Weinstein's backing.
4 See N. Davis (2007), Dyer (2007), Luciano (2007), and O'Neill (2004) on history in Haynes.
5 The lesbian publisher Naiad Press was the first to issue a new edition of *The Price of Salt* in 1983 with an afterword by the author. Still using the pseudonym Claire Morgan, Highsmith talks briefly about 1940s gay life but does not include the story of the blondish woman that appears in the afterword to the Bloomsbury edition. This discrepancy was pointed out to me by Terry Castle, editor of the Norton critical edition of Highsmith's novel.
6 Phyllis Nagy, interview with the author, August 17, 2015.
7 Attending the film's New York premiere, Edie Windsor, successful plaintiff in the Supreme Court case that overturned the Defense of Marriage Act, who met her lover Thea Spyer in a Greenwich Village restaurant in the early 1960s, recalled the thrill of that ending.
8 In "Time and Desire in the Women's Film," Tania Modleski explores the flashbacks in *Letter from an Unknown Woman* in light of Freud's comment that hysterics "suffer from reminiscences" (1984, 29).
9 In *Dottie Gets Spanked* (1993), Haynes explores the influence of popular culture—specifically the powerful image of a female star—on a queer child, with explicit reference to Freud's texts and these theories. See *Uninvited* (1999) for my reading of the film in relation to lesbian spectatorship.

10 Surveillance is part of the imagination from which the character springs: Highsmith kept the address of the "blondish woman" and stalked her at her New Jersey home. In her fictional portrait of Carol, Highsmith also draws on her lover, Virginia Catherwood, whose husband used secret recordings against her in a child-custody battle.

11 The skit resurrects the style of Jane Cottis and Kaucyila Brooke's hilarious videotape about lesbian subtexts in Hollywood film, *Dry Kisses Only* (1990), which cuts shots of Brooke into a scene from *All about Eve*. She wears Eve's (Ann Baxter) rumpled raincoat and tells a wartime dyke sob story to Bette Davis/Margo Channing, who nods her head sympathetically, her face smeared with cold cream.

12 "Harold, they're lesbians" was overheard and reported by Tumblr user @thcully on December 11, 2015, according to the Tumblr Memedocumentation, memedocumentation.tumblr.com/post/136322720365/explained-harold-theyre-lesbians-meme. Kylie O'Neil, posting on social media as MuffinPines, created the original fan artwork shown in figure 1.5.

2 Playing with Dolls

Girls, Fans, and the Queer Feminism of *Velvet Goldmine*

Julia Leyda

A gentle love scene is being played out by the hands and off-screen voices of two young English Girls. The scene is shot romantically, with soft lighting and heavy diffusion.

CURT DOLL My career was on the skids, mate. And you fished me out o' the muck. You got me back on my feet, you did.

BRIAN DOLL It was nothing, chum. I wanted to help you make more of that far-out sound. I love your music, my son, and I love—

The Brian doll turns away. The Curt doll walks up to him from behind.

CURT DOLL (*softly*) You don't have to say it, mate.

The dolls turn toward each other and embrace. They slowly, tenderly go down to the floor.

—TODD HAYNES, *Velvet Goldmine: A Screenplay* (1998)

This scene in which two unnamed schoolgirls use Barbie-style dolls to act out a seduction between two of the film's central characters, British glam star Brian Slade (Jonathan Rhys Meyers) and American rock icon Curt Wild (Ewan McGregor), occurs, with no explanation, about seventy minutes into

Todd Haynes's 1998 film *Velvet Goldmine*. The film never shows the girls' faces, nor attempts to explain the abrupt insertion of this scene into an already challenging narrative structure. Critics point to the scene as a nod to Haynes's *Superstar: The Karen Carpenter Story* (1987), yet Haynes himself has repeatedly asserted that this scene is more than a knowing self-reference: it is a *mise-en-abyme* for the entire movie (figure 2.1). He tells Amy Taubin (1998) that "the little girls holding up their Barbies and speaking through them is exactly what I'm doing in the entire film." Designating the schoolgirls as avatars of the gay male filmmaker, Haynes lays claim to his hallmark queer feminist practice. Studies of his creative oeuvre tend to draw hermeneutic distinctions between his works that explicitly engage with what feminist film studies has demarcated the "woman's film" (such as *Superstar*, *Safe*, *Far from Heaven*, *Mildred Pierce*, and *Carol*) and his other works whose categorization poses more challenges, among them those with "queer" content centered mainly on male characters, such as *Poison* and *Velvet Goldmine* itself. This chapter, however, in supporting the wider argument animating this book, insists on a strategic re-vision of this divide.[1] Although not itself a melodrama along the conventions that feminist film scholars have outlined (Doane 1987; Modleski 1984; Williams [1984] 2000), *Velvet* deploys affective strategies drawn from Haynes's lifelong immersion in the melodramatic form and his affinities for feminist film studies of it.

Most of Haynes's films, including *Velvet Goldmine*, evoke powerful emotion in conjunction with a reassertion of the artifice of aesthetic forms; this combination operates in his woman's films, but also here, in a quite different kind of movie. In a conversation with Oren Moverman (1998), Haynes elaborates: "The doll scene . . . does represent the film as a whole, and maybe in the most complete way. A lot of it has to do with the game of laughing and feeling aware of the construct—in a fun way, not in a Brechtian, didactic way. There's humor in glam rock, there's irony and wit; it's often about the . . . inherent artificiality of our so-called natural world. And yet it ends up being very moving" (xx). Taking up Haynes's oft-repeated claim that the disruptive doll scene represents *Velvet Goldmine*, this chapter critically reassesses the film, arguing that its central concern is with the fluidity of gender appropriation, which permeates the rest of the film and is performed with aesthetic pleasure and intense emotion by female fans and queer male stars alike. In this way, *Velvet Goldmine* exemplifies Haynes's queer feminism, a neologism invented in order to mend the specious division of queer theory from its feminist origins. The co-constitutive nature of queer theory and feminism, as Lynne Huffer demonstrates in her call for a "queer femi-

2.1 *Velvet Goldmine*'s dolls scene nods to *Superstar* and serves as mise en abyme for the entire film.

nist ethics," demands "concerted attention to the specifically ethical stakes of queer versus feminist conceptions of sexual practices, laws, norms, and artistic production" (2013, 9). In terms of artistic production, there may be no better model of the ethical commitments of queer feminism than Haynes, whose work refuses and refutes such spurious divisions. Haynes's films provide a pedagogy of reciprocity between queer theory and feminism, exemplifying an ethics that refuses the "versus" to insist on the political stakes shared by queers and feminists alike. Here I show that even those films heretofore considered significant primarily for their interventions into queer representation and historiography, like *Velvet Goldmine*, can serve as fruitful case studies for his queer feminism.

By ironizing the presumed realism of heteronormativity, the doll scene represents an interruption, an interlude within the male-centered film that calls into question the taken-for-granted categories of not only male and female, but also straight, gay, and bisexual. In this way, portraying schoolgirls enacting a gay romance scene, it offers a playful answer to Judith Butler's question, "What happens to the subject and to the stability of gender categories when the epistemic regime of presumptive heterosexuality is unmasked as that which produces and reifies these ostensible categories of ontology?" (1990, xxx). Moreover, the film continues to echo this instance of "gender trouble" in its representations of women, troubling boundaries between normative gendered and sexual identities and between reality and fantasy. Highlighting the giddy pleasure of gender play while also scripting a scene of their own exclusion, the girl figures in the doll scene in *Velvet Goldmine* enact a feminist allegory that invites us to see the girls and women in the film as stand-ins for not only the filmmaker, but ourselves as viewers. *Velvet Goldmine* articulates the female fan and her place in the queer male world of glam rock through the doll scene on several levels, portraying girls as active and engaged fans and storytellers interested in adult romance, and as emblems of possibilities for a female–gay male alliance.

The doll scene highlights the girl fans' interest in their idols' romantic relationship, yet the fan in *Velvet Goldmine* is primarily represented by Arthur (Christian Bale), the protagonist and audience surrogate, whereas female characters occupy more marginal roles in which they are shunted aside or remain unnamed. The doll scene encapsulates a sexual and gendered dynamic that finds sharper articulation and resonance in the adult character of Mandy Slade (Toni Collette), Brian's wife, modeled on Angie Bowie, and in the many unnamed girl fans who people the film, all of whom affiliate themselves with the glam performers through costuming and makeup, and through their erotic interest. Interestingly, Haynes reports that the film is his most popular among young female viewers (Leyda 2012). Like young female fans of Haynes's film, these characters derive pleasure from the work of the queer male artist, drawing a liberatory power from the potentialities it offers them. Yet Mandy's character also embodies the circumscribed role of women under patriarchy, during the sexual revolution of the 1970s and its aftermath in the conservative 1980s. *Velvet Goldmine* juxtaposes the two historical moments through visual style and affective signifiers: opposites mark out the blithe, colorful glam 1970s and the bleak, anemic 1980s, where ultimately only nostalgia remains for the disillusioned.

Velvet Goldmine portrays the 1970s phenomenon of glam rock, propelled into the media spotlight by the outrageous self-presentation of its practitioners, idols and fans alike. Indeed, part of the shock value of glam rock lay in its overt rejection of essentialized gender and sexual categories—the boy and girl fans wore long hair, makeup, and platform shoes, and the (mostly) male stars flaunted their bisexuality on stage and in the press. Until now, *Velvet* has been studied primarily in terms of its interventions in the queer archive, yielding convincing and eloquent interpretations of how the film figures the oblique operations of shame, cultural memory, and trauma (Bennett 2010; N. Davis 2007; J. Dean 2007; O'Neill 2004). Chad Bennett's article, for example, features an illuminating close reading of the doll scene and contextualizes the shame that often accompanies fandom by introducing quotations from case studies of real-life female Bowie fans Julie and Sheila, who are identified as queer only in their intense desire for and identification with the queer star image of Bowie (2010, 31–33). Despite the fact that Bennett's two examples of fan narratives and the two children in the doll scene are girls titillated by queer male glam performance, his analysis doesn't push beyond his focus on the three central male characters, neglecting to investigate the positioning of girls in the affective ecologies of fandom in *Velvet Goldmine*. Whereas previous studies of this film situate it (quite rightly) within the purview of queer theory, this chapter seeks to tilt-shift and refocus attention by placing the secondary female characters at the center, attending to how their identifications with and desires for male glam idols are portrayed and problematized.

Positioned as onlookers and fans, female characters take active roles in encouraging and mentoring the queer male glam stars, even while the fan position is primarily occupied by Arthur, the fan around whom the story is focalized as he researches his 1970s idols ten years later. His 1984 investigation as a journalist leads him to remember his youth in 1970s England through extensive flashbacks, which make up most of the film; the exuberance of those times strikes a stark contrast with the Orwellian present day of the film, when many of the achievements of the sexual revolution seem lost or irrelevant in the face of the corporate, quasi-totalitarian conservative backlash of the Thatcher-Reagan years. The main characters in the film, along with Arthur, are Brian Slade, the glam star and subject of Arthur's research, and Curt Wild, Brian's proto-punk American lover from that time. Outside this triad are the female characters: Mandy Slade, Brian's bisexual, bicultural American wife; Shannon, Brian's loyal assistant; and numerous unnamed girls and women.

The dynamic interplay among female fans, glam rock, and queer artists comprise the narrative and visual excitement in much of *Velvet Goldmine*, and this chapter teases out some of the complex tangle of sexual and gendered affinities and tensions between fans and artists, both within the film itself and in its reception. Girls and women occupy an unstable ground, both in the film and as fans of the film, in their relations to the queer male characters and filmmaker. Though Haynes positions Arthur the fan at the center of the story, he also provides provocative female fan figures in more tangential roles. Indeed, although Haynes has spoken in interviews of his own identification with the girl fans in the doll scene, he is also aligned with the queer male characters in the film who inspire the admiration of the young women in his film audience. This constantly evolving dialectic between artist and audience, male and female, becomes clearer through an analysis of the doll scene, the character of Mandy, and the glam images of female fans scattered throughout the film.

Playing with Dolls: Girl Fans and Queer Male Idols

Velvet Goldmine's doll scene presents a fan-produced interlude embedded within the movie's other narratives. The two girls in school uniforms are playing with Curt and Brian dolls while lying on a pink carpet among stuffed animals, Barbies, toys, Brian Slade records, crayons, jacks, and jars of sequins strewn around on the floor (figure 2.2). Amid all these signifiers of girlish femininity, the doll play is also a twist on the romance plots common in fairy tales and Hollywood movies, centered on a love scene and a kiss. Using modified and lovingly costumed dolls, two girls perform their romantic fantasy of Brian and Curt as stars and lovers, turning the objects of their admiration and desire into objects of play and fantasy. The stars have become children's toys, acting at the whim of the girls' imagination.

To theorize the complex interactions of gender and sexuality at play in the doll scene, I turn to fan fiction generated by *Velvet Goldmine* fans and to academic studies of the fan phenomenon of slash fiction (see also R. White 2013, 69). Slash fiction is a variety of underground fan fiction that invents same-sex intimacies among fictional characters (from books, films, or television) who were not originally portrayed as explicitly gay, usually written by women about queer male sexual experiences; the most widely discussed early slash fiction, K/S, paired Captain Kirk and Mr. Spock from the television series *Star Trek* (H. Jenkins 1992; Penley 1992). And although the characters of Brian, Curt, and Arthur in *Velvet Goldmine* are already portrayed as queer, the fan fiction available online embellishes on the pairings in the movie by developing relationships beyond where they go on-screen, such as Arthur and Curt as a cohabiting couple and new pairings and threesomes among minor characters.[2]

If we read the doll scene in the context of the slash fiction phenomenon, it is clear that *Velvet Goldmine* portrays the girls' "slashing" of Brian and Curt's pop star images as what Richard Berger (2010) calls "a subversive form of appropriation" that "allows for a critical reception of mainstream ... texts, in the queering of such texts" (173). Berger refers to online communities of slash fiction readers and writers, but I think his point applies to the fans in the film as well—their fantasies and scripts constitute a "new dialog

2.2 The doll scene is enacted in a pink-suffused child's room, with two girls sprawled on the floor amid the trappings of their inventive play.

between an established media text, its transgressive slash fic potential, and the dynamics of community members" (173). Irony is implicit in the doll scene in that the already queer characters are being slashed within the film itself, and in what is usually assumed to be a heteronormative context of girls playing with dolls. This scene suggests that the girls in the film, and the fans generally, not only consume popular culture but also appropriate, produce, and repurpose it.

As Lawrence Grossberg (1992) argues, "Fans' investment in certain practices and texts provides them with strategies which enable them to gain a certain amount of control over their affective life" (65). The girls create a romantic scene between two pop stars to entertain themselves and exert control over their sexual and gendered identities, at least in their imaginations. Their affective investment in the male lovers is simultaneously radical and touching. Similarly, the largely female writers of slash fiction during the same period produced "a transgressive commentary on the mainstream portrayals of heterosexuality and the later crude stereotyping of homosexuality" (Berger 2010, 177). The complex identifications and affiliations inherent in the female-authored male love story are a crucial element in *Velvet Goldmine*, one that the filmmaker himself acknowledges.

In an interview with Taubin (1998), Haynes explains that the film is all about fans, including the mobile sexual identities of girls and boys, fans and stars. I quoted a snippet from this interview earlier, but it bears reproducing in full here: "I wanted to show that it wasn't a problem for girl fans to enter that world and play out their desires with two boys instead of a boy and a girl. But ultimately, the little girls holding up their Barbies and speaking through them is exactly *what I'm doing in the entire film*. It's not the story of Bowie and Iggy. It's *what we do* with what they put out there. That's the work of the fans" (104, my emphasis). Here Haynes positions himself in the place of the schoolgirls, who perform a romance narrative peopled by their idols in a scene in his movie about fictionalized characters inspired by his real-life glam rock idols. As a creator of slash fiction himself, in this sense, Haynes the storyteller emphasizes the agency and power of the fan rather than the star. The schoolgirls in the doll scene are, as I proposed in my conversation with Haynes, "storytellers ... controlling the narrative" (Leyda 2012; 2014, 205). He characterized the narrative impulses in their cross-gender play and repurposing of "feminine" toys: "I think that's how we all begin to externalize our desires: through storytelling. Dolls are a tool that lends itself to that; they are supposedly made for little girls, and I loved dolls when I was a kid" (Leyda 2014, 205). Haynes's doll scene points to what he calls "the core of the intense affect that is felt by these kinds of characters in popular culture," even (or especially) when they are crossing erotic or gendered boundaries (205).

Stephen doCarmo (2005) refers to the entire movie as slash fiction, which he defines as "a type of storytelling that rewrites and reworks mass-market fictions to suit the interests and desires of the people (traditionally women) doing the rewriting" (397). Haynes heartily agrees that the film is itself a work of slash fiction: "I wasn't really interested in getting inside the closed doors of these famous subjects and that's why a fictionalization of this unique period made sense. We all already fictionalize and fill in and fantasize. And we see it too in the whole slash fiction phenomenon, which I didn't even know about until *Velvet Goldmine*, and in which *Velvet Goldmine* has itself become a category" (Leyda 2012; 2014, 206). His point about the power of the fans and our interest in them, as well as or perhaps more so than in the famous pop star characters, foregrounds the role of gender as well: the male director compares himself to the girls playing with their idols, even as he has made a film—widely admired by girls and women—focalized around a male fan and his relationships, imagined and real, with his idols.

Haynes's queer feminism emerges through these schoolgirls and their appropriation of the queer male romance narrative, although the relation of women to gay men has rarely been theorized in relation to his films. In *Fags, Hags, and Queer Sisters: Gender Dissent and Heterosocial Bonds in Gay Culture*, Stephen Maddison (2000) probes the fraught coalitions and conflicts between heterosexual women and gay men through his theory of heterosociality, which he defines as an alternative set of relations to the homosocial, male-only gay society. He points to close bonding and friendships between women and gay men, describing "fag hags" and "queer sisters" as figures important to queer theory: "Rather than suppress bonds with women,... gay male-female identification opens the possibility of a denaturalization of gender difference, an attempt therefore to re-imagine gender power" (93–94). Maddison's argument takes slash fiction as an example of heterosocial potential, which could provide "women with an opportunity to appropriate homoeroticism as the means to enact an empowering identification with a subject position through which they may exhibit power ... , while being able to avoid such an identification slipping into a ventriloquism of patriarchal dominance" (100). Implicit in female-authored slash fiction, then, is not only a transgression of the original text and its characters, but also a movement toward identifying with an "other" gendered and sexual subject position that does not entail the objectification of women. As Haynes points out, he "wanted to show that it wasn't a problem for girl fans to enter that world and play out their desires with two boys instead of a boy and a girl" (Taubin 1998, 104). That movement into the world of male-male romance offers the girls a sense of agency and freedom, demonstrating the co-constructedness of Haynes's queer aesthetics with his feminism.

As the girls script and perform the doll romance between male lovers, they are able simultaneously to express "female heterosexual specular pleasure in male physicality" and to enact "queer sistership through an identification with male homosexuality" (Maddison 2000, 100); Maddison does critique female-authored slash stories for the ways in which they reveal their own limitations as still relatively heteronormative and as implicit disavowals of lesbianism, for example. Yet for the purposes of this analysis of *Velvet Goldmine*, these limitations are beside the point. Although this love scene may have very little to do with a realistic male-male seduction scene, it does give the girls a chance, through private play, to imagine an eroticism outside their own subject positions, beyond the confines of the feminine object in a heteronormative script. Whether the schoolgirls are straight or not, the scene validates their interest in causing gender trouble through their play.

Set amid the '70s sexual revolution, as the women's liberation movement converged with the popular and newly acceptable curiosity about alternative forms of sexual expression, *Velvet Goldmine* portrays the spirit of experimentation and erotic freedom in the doll scene. At a time when more people were experimenting with pornography and nonmonogamous relationships, and when open discussion of sexual practices and identities, including queer sexualities, was becoming more widespread, the fan girls in *Velvet Goldmine* are coming of age and creating their own stories. At the same time, the scene reveals the transitional nature of that time and place, in that the girls are still enacting a conventional romantic script, albeit with two men instead of a man and a woman: the script explicitly emphasizes this conventionality in its call for romantic lighting and diffusion (Haynes 1998, 79). In the doll scene, same-sex romance is verbally repressed—"you don't have to say it"—ironically echoing the famous taboo on homosexuality as the love that dare not speak its name.[3] In this case, the Brian doll doesn't need to say it because the girls can see it and imagine it and make the dolls act it out. The girls author the scene as they like, including both conventional and revolutionary elements, exercising their freedom to improvise in any direction they choose.

The dolls are also an explicit self-reference to Haynes's notorious 1987 movie *Superstar: The Karen Carpenter Story*, a Karen Carpenter biopic "acted" entirely by Barbie-type dolls and voiced by offscreen actors. Common to both movies is the doll as a metaphor for the objectification and commodification of the star—including the damage to the star's body and spirit and the voracious appetite of the fans (see Desjardins, this volume; Landy 2003). Unlike the dolls in *Superstar*, however, the Curt and Brian dolls don't really "impersonate" the people—or act the roles—they represent; the girls visibly orchestrate and improvise the men's roles in their own high, girlish voices—for example, the doll representing the American Curt speaks in an English accent and uses the word *mate*. The glam stars themselves are commodified and objectified in a manner analogous to molded plastic dolls, but in a more utopian way, to show the creativity and power of the fan to appropriate and manipulate images; at the same time, the scene underscores the movie's political point about the power of popular culture to have an impact on the daily lives of ordinary people. As Henry Jenkins argues, "there is something empowering about what fans do with those texts in the process of assimilating them to the particulars of their lives" (1992, 284). The girls playing with dolls in *Velvet Goldmine* do certainly constitute a portrayal of fans performing what Jenkins calls an "exceptional reading" (284). The use of dolls in this scene in *Velvet Goldmine* can be seen ironically: both as a portrayal of the commodification of the stars as mass-produced toys *and* as the tools with which the young girls subvert the heteronormative scripts that are assumed to accompany such gender-specific child's play.

Reminding his own fans of the aesthetic provocation of *Superstar*, Haynes pushes *Velvet Goldmine*'s formal experimentation and celebration of artificiality to their limits while also simultaneously provoking a powerful affective response from his audiences—just as glam rock did. In an interview with *Rolling Stone* magazine, he explains this notion of glam as film form:

> I was trying to replicate how glam rock worked as a form, as a style.... The challenge was to accomplish what I think is so amazing about Bowie and particularly Roxy Music ... pushing it to the limit of camp, but also emotionally resonant.... Most rock & roll is defined by its authenticity, its ability to shed the surface and the makeup. These artists could foreground the artificiality, make it powerful. That is a trick I tried hard to get into the film—to be full of wit and irony and literary shit but to be moving and enveloping, an emotional trip. (Fricke 1998, 64)

Acknowledging that although his techniques in *Velvet Goldmine* may be defamiliarizing, they are not meant to produce a distance but quite the opposite, particularly in the doll scene, Haynes describes his film as a pastiche of both the artificiality and the affect of glam rock. *Velvet Goldmine*'s eye-popping excesses of makeup and costumes, especially in its glam rock performance set pieces, bring a theatrical flair that the film always contextualizes within the adoring eyes and emotional investments of its fans, besotted "with its rhythm, its meter, its color. And that's something I was trying to do with this film" (Moverman 1998, xx).

At the height of the sexual revolution, the out queer sexuality of Brian Slade makes it possible for young girls to act out a romantic love scene between two male pop stars they admire. *Velvet Goldmine* portrays this potentially liberatory power that fans can claim as a result of the popularity of glam rock stars, yet at the same time the film problematizes the role of girls and women in this largely male script. The girls' choice of two male figures tacitly acknowledges that women, even at the height of the sexual revolution and women's movement, still are not as free to act as men are. The character of Mandy Slade echoes the actions of the girls in the doll scene, dressing characters and shaping narratives as she invests herself in the creation of Brian's star image and orchestrates their public personae as an out bisexual glam rock couple. If Mandy represents the real-world possibilities for girl fans to grow up and live their glam dreams in creative self-exploration along with queer male allies in the 1970s, she also serves as a figure of warning in the 1980s, when she has been cast aside by Brian and largely forgotten as a pop culture icon in her own right. The utopian promises of the sexual revolution as benefiting women and gay men fail to deliver equal rewards, and Mandy narrates her abandonment.

Mandy Slade and the Ambivalent Position of Women in *Velvet Goldmine*

While researching the movie, Haynes read Angela Bowie's memoir *Backstage Passes* (1993), in which she describes the importance of costuming and appearance in the early glam years. She recounts swapping outfits with her husband and describes one of David Bowie's first business decisions after becoming moderately successful: hiring a full-time costumer. As one of the primary sources behind the fictional characters of Mandy and Brian Slade, Angela Bowie's account of those years details her active role in shaping David Bowie's career and his public image. Likewise, the character of Mandy is a key informant in Arthur's investigation, and her role in fostering the rise of the glam star becomes clear as she and others tell the story. The personal and professional relationship between Mandy and Brian is manifest in their costumes, which provide a visual articulation of their individual development and that of their partnership. Yet her bleak black outfit in 1984 also expresses Mandy's devastation in the wake of her relationship with Brian and, by extension, the film's refusal to gloss over the abandonment of its lead female character in a clear commentary on the quite different outcomes for men and women in the backlash years (figure 2.3).

Mandy is a knowing and worldly party girl in a sheer silver sequin dress when she and Brian first meet in 1969, when he is still a hippie with long frizzy hair, relatively new to the scene. At that party she is making out with Jack Fairy, a character based on queer icon Jack Smith (MacDonald 2014), whose influence Mandy emphasizes to Arthur in her voiceover: "Jack was truly the first of his kind. A true original, everyone stole from Jack" (Haynes 1998, 57). Her character is portrayed as cosmopolitan, sophisticated, and dancing on the cutting edge of fashion and pop culture on the eve of the glam era. Although both characters bear traces of the transition from '60s into '70s style, her metallic dress foreshadows the glitter era particularly well. This scene is part of a montage, set to Roxy Music's "Ladytron," in which Mandy and Brian meet and become lovers—as in the doll scene, it combines the trappings of conventional boy-meets-girl romance and love at first sight with a daring approach to sexuality.

Their relationship, portrayed mostly via flashbacks narrated with Mandy's voiceover during her interview with Arthur, involves the experimentation in sexuality and polyamory typical of the sexual revolution. Although they are an opposite-sex married couple, they are both out as nonmonogamous and bisexual. The sexual liberation of women with the arrival of easy and accessible forms of birth control certainly paved the way for Mandy's free lifestyle, but she is also ensconced in the heart of London's gay club scene. Haynes describes Mandy, like Sally Bowles in *Cabaret*, as a "type of camp female character [that] has basically vanished from our cultural landscape, [who] owes a great deal to the gay male sensibility of the time" (Moverman 1998, xix). She performs her embodied female sexuality on the stage, introducing Brian's act, making reference to her *guiche*, or perineum (the tissue between the vagina and anus), and eliciting scandalized laughter from the mostly gay male audience (see also Frueh 1999; O'Neill 2004). This interaction between the female character and the gay audience draws on their similarities (of anatomy, of raunchy humor) and their differences (her reference to the vagina), while structurally echoing in reverse the performer/fan gender dynamic that mostly dominates the film (male stars, female fans). Indeed, Mandy feeds on the energy of the gay nightclub where she first meets Brian, and she revels in her "fag hag" or queer sister role as emcee, but I would argue that the relationship between Mandy and the gay male sensibility goes both ways.

Brian and Mandy's relationship can be seen as that of a performer and his fan, but it is also frequently portrayed as an equal partnership. Their coupled status is often expressed visually, in ways that broadcast their commitment and challenge notions of gender differences and similarities: first, through late '60s-style androgyny and the visual suggestion of facial resemblance, and later as they become more "glam" and artificial-looking, with their twinned costuming, hair, and makeup, as in the press conference in which Brian openly announces his sexuality. In that scene, Mandy's public persona, like Brian's, seems designed to shock and challenge—both wear chartreuse and black animal-print outfits with platform shoes, makeup, and red hair with blunt-cut bangs, although Mandy's rainbow glitter eye makeup is more elaborate. The camera also draws attention to their androgynous resemblance to one another in the stylized love scene that took place during what Mandy's voiceover tells us was "the most stimulating and reflective period in our marriage" (Haynes 1998, 61) (figure 2.4).

2.3 Mandy Slade's chunky black sweater, plain hairstyle, and unadorned face tell us much of her state of mind in 1984, though she is still partial to shiny jewelry, as the heavy silver rings attest.

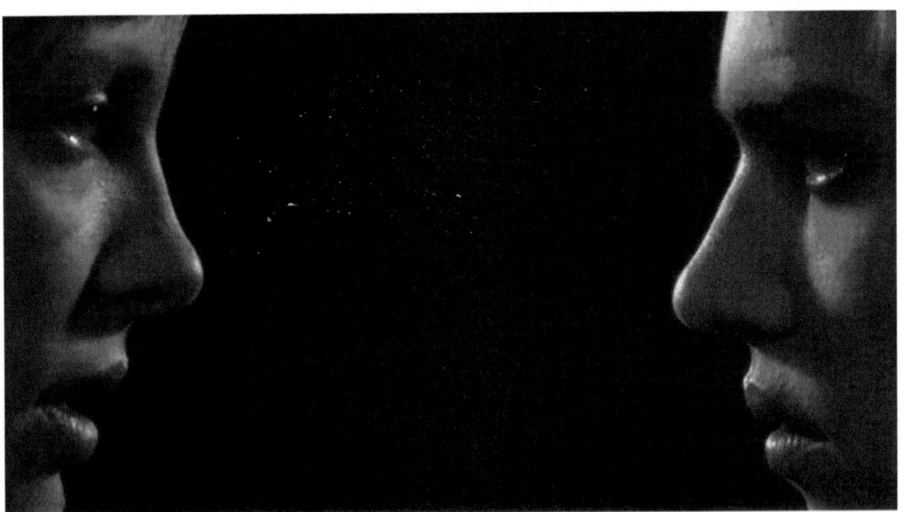

2.4 Mandy and Brian, a beautiful androgynous couple, face one another and pledge their love.

Mandy's character develops several different striking looks throughout the movie, which contribute to the development of her character: first as a bohemian party girl, then as Brian's glam twin. Her self-styled, fashion-forward image in the 1970s inspires and complements those of the pop idols with whom she lives and works. In this sense, she represents a grown-up fan girl who now, instead of styling her dolls to act out her fantasies, dresses herself and her partner in a real-life performance of queer nonmonogamous romance. Yet although Mandy exerts a strong influence over Brian's career and image in the early days of their relationship, she is ultimately excluded from his life. In her scenes set in the movie's present time (1984), Mandy sports a stripped-down, minimalist, post-punk look—in short, the opposite of glam. She wears no visible makeup, a heavy black sweater with black leggings and tall leather boots, chunky silver rings, and plain bleached hair with dark roots; her manner has none of the smug, playful naughtiness that she and Brian reveled in at the press conference. During her meeting with Arthur in an almost empty bar, she also seems to have lost her part-time English accent, saving it only for moments of extreme sarcasm. The stark overhead lighting and near monochrome color palette exemplify the way the film's visual style for the 1980s scenes produces an aesthetic and a political break with the '70s segments, which were frantic with color, movement, and visual effects such as filters and zooms. The embittered '80s Mandy Slade is reduced to playing pub gigs, still trading on her glam ex-husband's name.

Mandy's persona has evolved over the years, and it shows in her costuming: her all-black '80s outfit is consistent with the stark, colorless images of 1984 throughout the film, in contrast to the vibrant color explosions of the glam-era flashbacks. Yet her latest incarnation is also a figure for the marginal role of the woman in the glam slash story: she was an active participant, an erotic fellow traveler, gallivanting with her queer male and female lovers throughout those heady days, but in the end she is left behind, forgotten, divorced, in post-punk widow's weeds. Brian has transformed himself into a plastic pop commodity, erasing his previous transgressive stage identity and taking a new name; he has a successful career, selling out stadiums and endorsing right-wing politicians. Although Arthur and Curt appear depressed and demoralized in their '80s scenes, they still have access to the treasured green gemstone pendant that symbolizes queer artistic endeavor, which has changed hands from Oscar Wilde to Jack Fairy to Brian to Curt to Arthur (see Fontenot 2008, 169). Alas, there is nothing for Mandy but stale cigarettes and straight Scotch in a dive bar.

Mandy constitutes a counterpoint to the utopian giddiness of the glam scenes: even as she serves as a role model for liberated female sexuality in the '70s, in her last scenes it appears as if her character has been punished, as in conventional Hollywood films, for her transgressions. None of the main characters can sustain the exuberance of the glam era, but Mandy's character pays a steep price for the freedom and experimentation she enjoyed in the heyday of glam, resembling the leads of the "fallen woman" films of classical Hollywood before the Hays Code (L. Jacobs 1991). Haynes generates a kind of double exposure in *Velvet Goldmine*, simultaneously portraying the freedom that briefly allowed boys and girls, men and women to construct themselves, borrowing one another's tools and props at will, and that freedom's sad eclipse as patriarchy and conservative politics vigorously reasserted themselves in the next decade. His queer feminism ensures that although the film's male couple and narrator dominate the narrative, its women articulate their own gender-specific experiences of that heady period and its aftermath.

Makeup, Femininity, and Glam Girls

The film represents cosmetics, traditionally a woman's domain, as an important marker of glam rock for male stars and their male fans. The makeup becomes a visual metaphor for the gender-bending, artificial aesthetic of glam rock, originating in the borrowing of makeup between male and female fans, and between fans and stars, suggesting a porous boundary between gender norms that are traditionally seen as essentialized and fixed. Transgression of such boundaries was one of the sources of social and sexual anxieties during the 1970s glam rock phenomenon and the wider context of that decade's sexual revolution: not only did popular culture portray young people identifying as both gay and straight, it also portrayed bisexuality as a sexual orientation that disregarded that binary and insisted on a third option. Haynes alludes to that rejection of fixities and binaries implicit in bisexuality with a Norman O. Brown quotation, inserted as an intertitle on a hot-pink background: "Meaning is not in things but in between them." The association of male bisexuality with women characters throughout the film complicates any emphasis on *Velvet Goldmine* solely for its gay thematics—the co-presence of same-sex male relationships alongside male-female relationships resists that categorization even as the movie contains breathtakingly powerful representations of male-male pairings. The most obvious interpretation of the quotation is in terms of bisexuality and the characters within the film, but it also applies to the web of relationships implicitly surrounding *Velvet Goldmine*—among the film, its audience, and its director.

The movie frequently shows us anonymous female fans, at concerts, on TV, and in the background shots, dressed and made up in glam style, with an aggressively artificial aesthetic sense. These female fans are younger and less polished than the older, more professional glam rockers—a distinction the film also makes poignantly in its flashbacks to Arthur's awkward teen years and his often less than successful attempts to re-create their looks. The movie places the glam star Brian constantly in front of dressing-room mirrors getting professionally made up and coiffed, contrasted with scenes of Arthur and his glam friends cavorting with hair dye, cosmetics, and cheap jewelry in front of their mirrors. Brian's neurotic isolation in his persona of Maxwell Demon, sitting surrounded by his reflections like a descendent of Dorian Gray in a queer glam Douglas Sirk video, is very different from the endearing camaraderie of the young fans. We see Arthur and his glam roommates in their underwear, wrestling over a contested piece of lipstick, reflected in a dressing-table mirror. Throughout the film, Arthur's heartbreaking, earnest failed imitations mark him as the focal character for fans in the audience. A similar youth and vulnerability comes through in the shots of young women fans, analyzed in more detail below.

But the movie also illustrates how that appropriation of femininity changes the female fans' attitudes toward makeup and such supposedly "feminine" things.[4] Instead of signaling conformity to traditional femininity, wearing makeup in the brash glam style provides girls a way to assert a more aggressive sexual agency, eschewing the natural hippie look for a self-consciously made-up style. Haynes describes his own teen fascination with glam as "forbidden, dangerous; something I associated with the tougher girls in school—the 'smoker girls' who were very in the know. They started dressing differently and making themselves up differently" (Moverman 1998, x). Linking his attraction to glam rock with his memory of these intimidating older girls and their new approaches to style, Haynes grants to the girl fans an ambivalent place in his own personal history and in the history of glam rock.

The teenage girls from Haynes's past seem to appear in the film in the fan scenes, sporting—like younger, less elaborate versions of Mandy and the women in Brian's entourage—what he calls a "very dressed-up, shiny, cosmeticized look" (Moverman 1998, x). Instead of sitting before multiple mirrors in elaborate dressing rooms, the young fans do their makeup together in the street. Their collective ownership of their makeup, applied in the mirrorlike reflection of a shop window, links these fans with Arthur and his friends described earlier: they refine and exhibit their glam style out in public, further defamiliarizing and denaturalizing the femininity and mystification that traditionally adheres to beauty rituals (figure 2.5). Through their imitation of male glam rock stars—in their makeup and fashion in particular—the female fans create for themselves a tough, flashy image that runs interestingly parallel to that of the male glam stars and fans. Indeed, it can be considered transgressive for women to wear makeup and sequins *only because* the men are now also wearing makeup; the crossing over of makeup from women's domain to men's and back again has a liberating result for female glam fans as well. Joanna Frueh's meditation on the film describes the influence the queer male star personas exert on her: "Promiscuous beauties Wild and Slade dispel my fear of inhabiting tartish style" and "dare us into luxuriant self-invention" (1999, 88). Frueh's personal and poetic essay emphasizes the influence of the glam stars and the movie itself on audiences and fans, including the way that queer male stars affect female fans who may see them as offering permission to embrace more glam looks for themselves. Akin to Maddison's notion of "queer sisters," Frueh's identification with the queer glam stars and what she aptly names the glam tartish style on the screen can be seen "as a means of enacting gender dissent" and "resisting alignment as feminized objects of heterosexuality" (Maddison 2000, 100).

The opening credits sequence features a high-energy series of shots of glam fans running through the streets of London and then lined up outside a concert hall. The colorful clothes, long hair, and glitter makeup appear on boys and girls in these shots. The kinetic excitement expressed in the shots of the running fans is tempered with the more controlled tracking shots of fans standing in line: putting on makeup, smoking, talking, and even looking directly at the camera. These images show how girls embrace the queer glam look that runs counter to the previous hippie generation's premise of femininity's naturalness and authenticity, often marked by a rejection of, or less visible use of, cosmetics. On the contrary, the glam girls have a different relation to their identities and sexualities—sharing makeup with boys, painting glitter on their faces, they acknowledge that they are constructing themselves, creating their own images as they like, and challenging essentialized notions of gender. As Frueh puts it, they exercise a "luxuriant self-invention" (1999, 88).

The girls' challenge is embodied in their tough, tarty images and is amplified by the feminist aesthetics inherent in the way Haynes and his cinematographer, Maryse Alberti, film them. One pair of glitter girls confront

2.5 Girl and boy glam fans share their makeup as they apply it in the street using shop windows as mirrored surfaces.

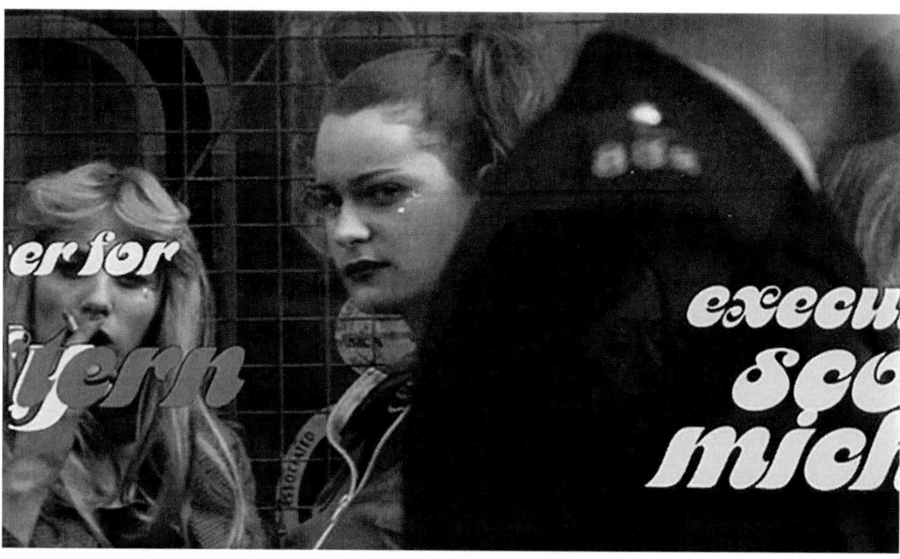

2.6 The bold gaze of a glitter-faced glam girl challenges the camera as a policeman walks past and her friend pensively smokes a cigarette.

the viewer through their sustained direct gaze into the camera (figure 2.6), claiming the gaze for themselves and disrupting their status as objects to be looked at, as Laura Mulvey (1975) famously formulated the woman's position in Hollywood film, by behaving as we in the audience do, as viewing subjects. These girls, with their cigarettes and glitter makeup, are not smiling or posing for the camera; they are looking at it levelly, through narrowed eyes, without comment or reaction. Rather than Mulvey's theory of the woman as object, these shots call to mind some of the later theories of cinematic spectatorship: Teresa de Lauretis's notion of double identification, for instance, in which she argues that the female spectator simultaneously identifies with both the (allegedly male) gaze and the (typically female) image (1984, 144). In their active looking, returning the camera's gaze and confronting the audience through sustained eye contact, these glam girls sassily inhabit their doubled position as objects of the camera, which they seem to see as they break the fourth wall, and as agents of looking themselves, as they gaze into the camera, back at us. As Haynes tells Taubin (1998), "The whole act of looking was foregrounded in the glam era in ways it hadn't been before in pop music. The lyrics, the melodrama of the music, the staging, are all about the act of looking. So that the roles we all play in life are highlighted by the roles they play on the stage. It offers you the invitation to become the thing you're looking at, to dress up, to experiment." The fan girls' knowing, assertive interaction with the camera in the credits sequence echoes the schoolgirls' engagement with their pop idol dolls—as fans, as storytellers, and as active audience members.

In a circular pattern of influence, the glam girls take inspiration from the glittery male pop stars they see on television and in popular music—who wear makeup as part of their sexually ambiguous star image—and reappropriate from the stars "feminine" tools like makeup that those stars have themselves appropriated from a conventionally feminine realm. In this context, makeup is no longer a tool to enhance femininity, in "natural," heteronormative opposition to a traditional masculinity—a binary in which the woman is the object, seeking to attract the attention of the dominant male. Rather, both boys and girls use makeup to emulate the bisexual glam stars they admire. In the motif of glam makeup, *Velvet Goldmine* again portrays the repurposing of allegedly "feminine" commodities for more transgressive ends; like the schoolgirls using dolls to act out a same-sex seduction scene, these images of girls and boys in glam makeup comment on and complicate the lipstick and eyeliner that earlier generations of women took as traditional markers of their gender identity.

Glam rock in *Velvet Goldmine* is a brief, utopian moment of self-invention that fleetingly enables new and exciting forms of gendered and sexual expression and identification. The film, however, also conscientiously points out the hollowness of nostalgia in the final shot of an old radio playing an old Roxy Music song, "2HB," itself a nostalgic paean to classical Hollywood star Humphrey Bogart with the refrain "fade away never." In its portrayal of a sparkling instant of women's and queer liberation, and in its honest evocation of that temporary escape route slamming shut, *Velvet Goldmine* remains true to the historical contexts of its very fabricated fairy story. This complex movie opens itself to a range of interpretive tools, but in this chapter I have endeavored to demonstrate the usefulness of restoring to the scholarly toolbox an awareness of Haynes's deep-seated queer feminism and his fascination with the affective dynamics of the woman's film.

NOTES

For feedback on the endless versions of this chapter I must thank Joshua Paul Dale, Alexandra Ganser, Theresa L. Geller, Rebecca Gordon, Therese Grisham, Sheila Hones, Leopold Lippert, Hogara Matsumoto, David Maynard, Kimiyo Ogawa, Karen Shimakawa, Christopher Shore, Chris Tedjasukmana, and Marie Thorsten.

1 See also Jess Issacharoff's chapter on *Poison* in this volume for an excellent articulation of this argument.

2 The archive of *Velvet* fan fiction online is called *Satellite of Love*, and was last updated in 2005 but remains online; meanwhile, fans continue to publish *Velvet Goldmine* stories in other online communities such as FanFiction.net. The *Velvet* fanfics are written in English, French, Spanish, and Portuguese, and some have many online comments. For example, as of this writing, a total of 218 fan fiction entries related to *Velvet Goldmine* are available on FanFiction.net, three of them from 2017, ranging in length from about nine hundred words to more than fourteen thousand; recent numbers have hovered between three and nine per year, declining from their high point of thirty in 2002.

3 The epigraph at the beginning of Taubin's 1998 piece on *Velvet Goldmine* in the *Village Voice*, entitled "Fanning the Flames," is a line not from a glam rock hit, but from blues standard "Back Door Man" by Willie Dixon and Chester Burnett, released by Howlin' Wolf (1960) and the Doors (1967): "The men don't know, but the little girls understand." Clearly Taubin also understands; the review closes with this nugget: "When Miramax, *Velvet Goldmine*'s North American distributor, test-screened the film, it found that it scored highest with female audiences under 25. 'I always knew,' says Haynes, 'that the perfect boy is a girl.'"

4 I'm grateful to Tara Nicole Brown for making this point during one of our many discussions of the movie.

3 Todd Haynes and Julianne Moore
Collaboration and the Uncontainable Body

Rebecca M. Gordon

> In order to tell a story, the [artist] has only an instant at his disposal . . . and he must thus choose it well, assuring it in advance of the greatest possible yield of meaning and pleasure. . . . This crucial instant, totally concrete and totally abstract, is . . . the *pregnant moment*. . . . The pregnant moment is just this presence of all the absences (memories, lessons, promises) to whose rhythm History becomes both intelligible and desirable.
>
> —ROLAND BARTHES, *Image-Music-Text* (1977)

Todd Haynes's interest in grappling with ways to convey ideas about heteronormative patriarchy, female agency, and the visibility/invisibility of the female body has been evident since his first feature film, *Superstar: The Karen Carpenter Story* (1987), in which he used Barbie dolls to portray the physical and psychic decline of Karen Carpenter. In his subsequent films, Haynes has continued these explorations of ideology and style, but with real actors. Doing so makes Haynes's films more cinematically complex, but to work with live actors inevitably positions some meanings outside his power to manage. Haynes's collaborations with Julianne Moore, arguably his best female partner as an actor, brings these tensions between theoretical intent and corporeality to the fore, for in the course of working with Haynes on *Safe* (1995) and *Far from Heaven* (2002), Moore's body underwent significant physical changes that influenced her expressive capacities in ways neither Moore nor Haynes could always predict.

Safe was Moore and Haynes's first collaborative effort. During the making of this film about a California housewife who develops an unspecified "environmental illness," Moore deliberately lost several pounds to physically express the process of deterioration. Although her decision caused unanticipated and unintentional damage to her health, Moore's transformation made visible her character Carol White's meek acceptance of her fate, and made tangible Haynes's critique of the moral certainties central to the "disease movie" genre. While finishing postproduction on *Safe* and envisioning further collaboration with Moore, Haynes conceived a project based on the films of Douglas Sirk. Haynes imagined a woman of the 1950s forced to navigate two social crises of her day that would not have been explicitly addressed in melodramas of the period: homosexuality and interracial desire. After ruminating for years, Haynes wrote the script for *Far from Heaven*. He conceptualized Moore's character, Cathy Whitaker, as "someone in a social setting that was restricted, that would have to encounter a discrepancy with her own feelings and needs, but [who] ultimately ... would [have] no real escape.... She would just have to learn about those contradictions" (Kugler 2002). Because Cathy can neither understand nor help her husband Frank "beat" his homosexuality, she must keep her confusion and sense of inadequacy to herself; because Cathy cannot single-handedly overcome the racism in her town, she resigns herself to losing her new love, Raymond, tamping down desire because showing her attraction to a black man is as taboo as feeling it. Moore loved the script, and a year later the film was in production; what she did not tell Haynes until shooting began, however, was that she was pregnant.

Both Moore and Haynes made light of Moore's pregnancy at publicity junkets for *Far from Heaven*. Moore claimed that doing the film with an ever-growing belly was a good distraction, "because being pregnant was so tedious" (P. Fischer 2002). To questions about how her condition altered the film's production, as costume design and production schedules had to be tweaked in order to minimize chances of showing Moore's girth, Haynes insisted that it really didn't matter for the finished film. He did, though, ask journalists not to dwell on the fact, because "if you look for it, you'll see it, but it's just not important" (Kugler 2002). Yet even as Haynes asked journalists not to focus too much on Moore's body, he also admitted that being pregnant "gave her great 1950s breasts" (Kugler 2002).

This downplaying of Moore's pregnancy is in keeping with Moore and Haynes's greater concern for the ideas *Far from Heaven* conveys, but it is also ironic. Moore's body underwent significant changes as her pregnancy advanced during the film's production. Because *Far from Heaven* was not shot chronologically, Moore's body fluctuates in size throughout the edited film. Insofar as her character, Cathy, must absorb private hurts while maintaining social decorum, Moore's physical changes register the film's theme of repression and convey Cathy's metaphorical "swallowing" of the homophobia, racism, and hypocrisy that buffet her throughout the film.

In both *Safe* and *Far from Heaven*, Moore's characters powerfully express women's experiences that remain invisible to or disallowed by society; through working with Moore, Haynes's theoretical and stylistic explorations, feminist in impulse and intent, find themselves having to cope with the reality of the female body—and with what he himself identifies as women's suffering. Nonetheless, Moore's sometimes-visible pregnancy in *Far from Heaven* suggests—figuratively, not narratively—the historical fact of the generational delay Haynes wished to thematize in his film. An educated heterosexual woman in the mid-twentieth century fails to escape the status quo and must stifle her generation's ills in the fiber of her body, leaving it to another generation to face those ills. Moore's pregnancy during the making of *Far from Heaven* was an aleatory event, not a theatrical or scripted one, and her body's shifting size throughout the course of the film is due to the nonlinearity of shooting and editing processes rather than the needs of the story; nevertheless, Moore embodies the arguments at play in *Far from Heaven*, even beyond deliberate narrative design. Her work lends Haynes's films what Bertolt Brecht (1992) referred to as a "gestic" quality for, once framed by Haynes's ideological intent, her performances exceed what "naturalistic" acting calls for.

Pregnant Moments and the Pregnant Actor

For Brecht, according to Roland Barthes, the *gest* is "a gesture or set of gestures (but never a gesticulation) in which a whole social situation can be read" (1977, 74). As George Kouvaros (2006, 60) explains it, the gest is distinguishable from other gestures used in performance, in that whereas most gestures are concerned with subjective inner states, the gest shifts the focus of action away from a character's personalized inner drama toward the explication of a social meaning. For its social meaning to be recognized as such, however, the gest must be properly "framed." Barthes argues that the tableau-like nature of Brecht's epic theater, or Sergei Eisenstein's cinema, provides the ideal conditions for the legibility of the gest, for the tableau marks the selection of *the* significant narrative moment in which an entire composition can be read in an instant.

This crucial instant, when socially meaningful gest and narrative idea are perfectly aligned in visual representation, creates what Barthes calls the "pregnant moment" (1977, 73).[1] The "pregnant moment" marks the artistic communication of a vital point, when performance and frame, or action and context, coincide to "guide meaning toward its ideality" (75). Barthes argues that such moments can act as "hieroglyph[s] in which we can read at a glance ... the present, the past, and the future, i.e., the historical meaning of the represented gesture" (73). Because the tableau—the ideologically framed moment, scene, or shot—works to present an ideal meaning, the actor's responsibility is less to "act" than "to present the very knowledge of the meaning" called for in the tableau (74). One implication of this responsibility is that unintended or accidental gestures on the part of the actor, when performed within that framed moment, can still communicate a vital point, take on the weighted social import of the gest, and create a "pregnant moment."[2]

Of course, pregnant actresses are not what Barthes meant. Nonetheless, pregnant moments emerge in *Far from Heaven*, I contend, as a result of Moore's literal pregnancy. That is, moments that show the painful contradictions Cathy must negotiate, and that then exceed the narrative's confines to comment on the state of interracial relations and homosexuality as understood in society *now*, are moments when Moore's pregnancy shows. It is not visible as a "bump," which costume designer Sandy Powell was careful to conceal, but is discernible through Moore's stance, the placement of her arms, the rhythm of her gait, the suggestion of weightiness. Through such gestures—which I read as accidental, unintentional, or extranarratorial, as Haynes and Moore asked viewers not to look for them—Moore provocatively presents "a hieroglyph" in which we can read the present, the past, and possibly the future of our own time, in which race and sexuality remain volatile topics of conversation and social policing. In effect, Moore's pregnant body literalizes the historical dilemma thematized in *Far from Heaven*, signifying beyond Moore's careful character construction and Haynes's self-conscious intent. Moore's performances in *Safe* and *Far from Heaven* demonstrate her skill as an actor and her and Haynes's combined skill as collaborators, but in *Far from Heaven*, her body conveys meanings in addition to those she or her director deliberately devised.

Moore's pregnancy during the making of *Far from Heaven*, however, also allowed gestures and movements unnecessary to the narrative and her character to be captured in performance, where they communicate unanticipated meaning. If during much of the film Moore is not visibly pregnant, at other points in the film Moore's pregnancy shows—as Haynes and Moore both knew but asked viewers to ignore. Several of the points when Moore's pregnancy is most visible, I argue, coincide narratively with Cathy's most difficult negotiations of her social setting and her desires. Whereas Haynes and Moore collaborated on the creation and performance style of Cathy, neither director nor actor could entirely control Moore's physical changes, including changes that give rise to gestures and motions typical of pregnant women. Nonetheless, those movements, arising within the narrative context of Haynes's film, help telegraph the film's chief intention: to provoke its audience not only to recognize the genre reimagined before them but to realize what 1950s melodrama could *not* have represented. Thus, Moore's pregnant body made possible certain "pregnant moments."

Conceiving and Embodying Collaboration: *Safe*

From their first meeting at auditions for *Safe* (1995), Moore revealed a capacity for making her body physically index the concepts driving Haynes's work. In that film, Carol White, a bourgeois housewife living in Southern California, develops an "environmental illness"—an unpredictable and sometimes violent reaction to fumes, smells, and, it seems, her own house. Although she seeks treatment, her malady worsens, leading to Carol's slow deterioration. In the screenplay, Haynes describes Carol as "pretty in a remote, quiet way. She is most comfortable when the world goes about its business, accepting (by ignoring) her as one of its own. The thin weakness of her speaking voice combined with a kind of emotional laxity make her seem removed at times, distant from herself" (2003, 104). For Haynes, hearing Moore's audition for *Safe* was definitive, because until then Carol had been too weird a character to picture. As he explained to Sarah Hebron (2003) of the *Guardian*, "There was a conceptual sense of her in my mind, but she wasn't a living, breathing thing yet. And with Julianne, suddenly I felt like, 'Oh my God, this could work!'" What worked was Moore's method of embodying the character. Moore clarifies: "I kept thinking, I don't want her to have a voice; I want her to talk on top of her vocal cords, as if her voice was not connected to her body. I wanted her to be invisible.... And that was what was so gratifying about that collaboration for me—. . . I felt that [Todd] and I were in sync about an idea" (Hebron 2003).

Moore's command of technique made Carol White possible in other ways, as well. Throughout the film, Moore uses rounded pronunciation and a singsong voice with a nasal quality that vividly conveys Carol's minimal self-possession. Moore further developed Carol's marginal subjectivity through Haynes's visual design. When shooting on *Safe* began, Moore and Haynes did not know each other well, so to help Moore understand his aesthetic, Haynes let her look through the camera to see how he composed shots. Haynes also shared his storyboards to show Moore how he imagined Carol in each scene. Moore describes an especially enlightening sketch of the baby shower scene, a description that provides insight into her process as an actor:

> [Todd] had one group of women standing on one side [of a double living room] and on the other he had drawn me on the side of frame. . . . The figure had her head bent so without having any discussion about the acting, he'd already told the whole story in that frame. . . . As an actor, I just look at that, I can see the emotion in that scene and know how to fill it that way. And I'm completely satisfied because I've had the dual experience of leaning on his structure and his preparation while at the same time having the freedom to let the acting happen at the moment in that frame. (Hebron 2003)

Moore's process points to techniques such as "imagination work," developed by actor and director Michael Chekhov and derived from Konstantin Stanislavski's "emotion-memory" method. This technique allows the actor to suffuse her acting with emotions of her own that are analogous to the emotions experienced by the character. Moore's desire to "let things happen in the frame" speaks to improvisation, suggesting varieties of movement training; that Moore renders Carol so believably remote hints at Brechtian training as well. I point out these techniques primarily to signal that Moore's eclectic approach is of a piece with the plasticity Haynes admires in her work.

As Carol's illness worsens, Moore's gestures and facial expressions convey Carol's growing fear, as well as an increasingly severe detachment between body and self. One morning soon after Carol has begun to notice symptoms such as nosebleeds, her husband hugs her to comfort her. Carol seems to be crying so hard she is heaving; however, Carol is, in fact, ill, and she vomits on her husband's feet. Not long after, Carol experiences

3.1 Carol sits up in bed, disoriented.

a severe asthma attack for no clear reason. She stays in bed the next day and seems confused when her husband checks on her. In a close-up shot in profile, she stares ahead briefly then asks, "Oh God, what is this? . . . Where am I? . . . Right now?" "We're in our house," her husband answers, uneasily. "In Greg and Carol's house." The answer doesn't soothe the disoriented Carol, whose lips quiver and eyes tear up; she tries to smile but her chin trembles, her brow furrows, and she begins to cry (figure 3.1).

Finally, after being hospitalized for mysterious seizures, Carol seeks help at the New Agey Wrenwood Center for the treatment of environmental illnesses. There she tries to internalize the retreat's therapy culture of affirmation and positive thinking but has trouble doing so. The retreat's leader tells her, "Your feelings are entirely normal. We're just about trying to absorb as many tensions as we can so you can get on with healing." Carol responds, haltingly and defensively, "Oh I know . . . I know . . . I'm just still learning, um, you know . . . um . . . the words." At the end of the film, Carol moves into a sterilized, porcelain-lined igloo, the ultimate safe house. She tries out the language of the treatment center, tentatively reciting, "I love you . . . I . . . I really love you" into a mirror. The shot is framed in close-up such that Carol looks out at the audience, but by this time Carol has weakened so much that it is doubtful whether she knows who "I" is. Commenting on this moment, Mary Ann Doane notes that, although the close-up is the conventional visual marker of interiority, Carol's profession of love is "unconvincing, and the mirror scene is anything but subjectivity regained" (2004b, 9–10). That Carol is so unconvincing in this moment is a measure of how well Moore and Haynes managed to invest a conventional "movie of the week" tableau with a gestic quality that critiques that genre's pieties.

In *Safe*, Moore embodies Haynes's concept of a woman who can't articulate herself or her place in the world. In addition to using acting techniques to suggest Carol is slowly vanishing, however, Moore deliberately lost ten pounds. This decision was Moore's, not a request from Haynes. It unintentionally led her to develop anorexia and amenorrhea: "I wanted to look as thin as possible; I wanted to look like someone who is disappearing, which would create a sense of a person's body betraying them. So then I started to lose weight.... God, it was horrible! When I wrapped up the movie, my blood pressure was 80/60 or something. I wasn't menstruating and I developed that swollen-belly thing.... I went below where I should have gone" (Boorman and Donahue 1996, 220–21). Male actors receive the lion's share of attention for undergoing strenuous weight gain or loss, especially to play well-known figures; Moore lost weight, however, to better convey *an idea*. Moore's skill in conveying that idea renders Carol's deterioration so credible that Moore's work as a performer may escape notice. Anat Pick, for example, credits "Carol's diminishing physique" as an element of the film's logic of disembodiment (2007, 147). But such a logic depends on the efforts of a very embodied actor. Scholars and critics do not interpret Moore's body, at various points in *Safe*, and certainly in its final moments, as *her* body, but rather as a hieroglyph, having been represented repeatedly within Haynes's visual design (or, we might say, within the film's tableaux).

The effects of Moore's weight loss during the making of *Safe* were not always predictable, yet those physical changes aligned with and extended Haynes's concept: in collaboration, Haynes and Moore produced a correspondence of idea and performance. Haynes and Moore's collaborative efforts in *Far from Heaven* likewise embody the ideas they wish to convey, though in this instance, the nature of physical change during pregnancy, of indie film funding, and consequently of indie film editing meant that the expressive effects of Moore's body sometimes eluded both collaborators' control.

Performance Style and Styles of Containment in *Far from Heaven*

Haynes's reasons for making *Far from Heaven* were multiple, but they sprang primarily from a desire to revisit the woman's film and a desire to work with Moore again (Michael 2003). In the introduction to a collection of his screenplays, Haynes explains that the melodramas of Sirk and Max Ophüls "always astounded [him]," for "beneath the lush, teeming surfaces" of films like *All That Heaven Allows*, *Written on the Wind*, and *The Reckless Moment* "are claustrophobic stories of disillusionment and resignation, of women locked up in houses who emerge, in the end, as lesser human beings for all they surrender to the ways of the world" (2003, xiii–xiv). Understanding that on-screen suffering is most likely to "provoke deep recognition and social critique" when the sufferer is a woman, to Haynes it seemed that the woman-centered 1950s melodrama, as a form, could be the ideal vehicle for a contemporary exploration of race and sexuality, "reveal[ing] how volatile those subjects remain today—and how much our current climate of complacent stability has in common with that bygone era" (xiv).

Haynes's vision for the film required lights, filters, props, and exteriors that would evoke the appropriate Sirkian Technicolor look. His vision also necessitated directing actors in the mannered performance techniques of the period. Haynes identified Moore's performance as critical, for "ultimately the woman's role is the one we were trying to focus on.... You know, it's really on her shoulders to keep it going and to maintain decorum and a sort of tradition" (Kugler 2002). As in *Safe*, Moore's challenge in collaborating with Haynes on *Far from Heaven* was to physically convey an abstract concept.

Moore understood from the outset that Haynes's intention was to revisit the 1950s Hollywood melodrama not as realist drama but as style, including performance style. As she explained to *Film Monthly*, "We're not making a movie about the Fifties but a movie that uses the style of films of the Fifties. So, in a sense, the Fifties could not have existed for us to make this film, only the films of the Fifties could" (P. Fischer 2002). As she did for Carol in *Safe*, Moore modulated her voice to a timbre and speed reflective of Cathy's desire to keep her conventional life running smoothly. The breathy musicality of Cathy's voice signals restraint; this explodes, however, in rare moments of anger, such as when Cathy defends her friendship with Raymond Deagan (Dennis Haysbert), her African American gardener, to her husband. Re-creating the look and feel of a 1950s melodrama also required specific ways of moving. Moore's tightly cinched, wide-skirted dresses pressed her body into an attitude of constriction, and her look—different from the sheath dresses worn by Moore's fellow female actors—suggests a conservative sensibility at odds with what we learn of Cathy's "liberalism" (in college, Cathy used to play summer stock theater with "all those steamy Jewish boys," which earned her the moniker "Red").

A further challenge Moore faced during the making of *Far from Heaven* was, of course, her pregnancy. Because *Safe* was filmed chronologically, Moore's weight loss coincided narratively with Carol's slow deterioration. Funding and scheduling issues, however, required that many of *Far from Heaven*'s later scenes be shot earlier—and far out of narrative sequence. Thus, as the film's producer Christine Vachon and Bunn (2006) relate, Moore was at her most pregnant in scenes that appear *earlier* in the film. And although Moore's body is not overtly referred to as pregnant in critical pieces on the film, such extrafilmic knowledge seems to circulate unofficially in the praise Moore and Haynes received for their work.

Both popular and scholarly pieces on *Far from Heaven* have expressed Moore's talent at conveying Haynes's ideological aims through the notion of Moore as a vessel or container. For example, in a review for Salon.com, Andrew O'Hehir (2002) writes, "With Julianne Moore blazing at its center in red and gold, like a bouquet of autumnal foliage in a fine china vase, Todd Haynes's 'Far from Heaven' is an explosion of synthetic delights." He continues: "In obsessively emulating the style, tone and posh suburban settings of legendary 1950s director Douglas Sirk, Haynes has paradoxically set himself free.... Haynes hasn't left queer theory behind with 'Far from Heaven'; instead ... he's found exactly the right *container* for it" (emphasis mine). By moving swiftly from an introduction that situates Moore at the "blazing center" of *Far from Heaven* to discovering that the film is "exactly the right container" through which to revisit the Sirkian melodrama, O'Hehir seems to suggests that Moore both shapes and is contained by Haynes's work. Scholars have also suggested that Moore's character, Cathy, functions as a sort of vessel, holding together both the narrative strands of the film and its historical connection to the women's film. Doane remarks that "in Haynes's cinema, it is always women who try to hold the world and its contradictions at bay with a perfection, a seamlessness, and an embrace of a faultless naïveté.... However, they always fail; something goes awry, and the world comes crashing in" (2004b, 5–6). In this case, the world crashes in on two fronts: first, Cathy discovers that her husband is homosexual and beginning to act on his desires; then, feeling lonely and discarded, she finds comfort in her friendship with a black man, a deviation her town will not abide.

The idea of Moore as a vessel or container for Haynes's 1950s-inspired narrative can suggest that Moore functions primarily as "muse" to Haynes's directorial genius, a gendered stereotype of actor-director relationships that Moore and Haynes actively oppose, or, further, it can convey the impression that Moore played Cathy "straight," not differentiating between the acting styles typical of classical Hollywood and the more distanced, self-referential techniques Moore employs. On the other hand, throughout the making of *Far from Heaven*, Moore's body was literally, if somewhat crudely, a *container*: she was carrying her second child at the time. Yet this physical fact upends the metaphor of woman as vessel-like muse for the artist's imagination, for a vessel or container is generally designed to maintain its shape. In this case, what Moore's body was doing during the making of the film (growing, shifting) and what Cathy was designed to do (maintain the status quo, conceal secrets) uncannily contradict one another.

Like a good Cold War wife, Cathy subscribes to a policy of containment, fending off external threats—including her husband's homosexuality—through the smooth running of her household. By the end of the film, Cathy's husband has divorced her to be with a new lover, while Cathy's new love, Raymond, and his daughter have left Hartford for Baltimore and, they hope, safety. Diegetically speaking, in the film's final scenes Cathy need no longer absorb, conceal, or contain so much, but these scenes were shot early in the film's production, and Moore is visibly less pregnant. Moore's body telegraphs Cathy's aloneness in a manner both motivated by and extrinsic to the narrative as writ. Earlier in the film, however, Cathy—like a container—must keep things in their place. Through voice and gesture, Moore conveys the shocks and injuries of Cathy's predicament; careful not to pass on those shocks, Cathy absorbs them in exchange for the private experience of pain.

Cathy's capacity to absorb secret hurts falters when she discovers Frank (Dennis Quaid) in the arms of another man while delivering dinner to his office one night. She flees, and then waits for Frank at home in the dark. When he returns, Cathy, dazed, attempts to chat about the roofer's estimate. Finally, she says, "I can't . . . ," and Frank begins to explain that a long time ago, he had "problems." Their conversation proceeds in a halting series of unfinished statements:

CATHY What if? . . . I mean, there must be people . . .

FRANK I . . . I don't know.

CATHY Because, otherwise, I don't know what I . . .

After a long pause, Frank responds, "Alright." His resigned tone indicates that Cathy's need to contain his confession—indeed, his homosexuality—has "won," but in the process Cathy endures a massive blow to her sense of normalcy.

Richard Dyer describes the performances in *Far from Heaven* as both "held in" and "held off" (2007, 175–76). The characters address one another formally, holding each other at a distance, and imitate the unironic emotional intensity of 1950s melodrama so well as to "present the very knowledge of the meaning" of the genre (Barthes 1977, 74). This held-in style, and the thematics of containment that intersect it, shatter violently when Frank confronts Cathy over being seen in public with Raymond Deagan, giving way to more overt gestures. Moore's movements trace the difficult moral terrain Cathy inhabits as a supportive yet betrayed wife and a loyal yet naive friend.

The sequence begins after Cathy and Raymond spend an afternoon together, walking in the woods and then dancing at Raymond's neighborhood diner. Unfortunately, they are spotted by the town gossip. Cathy returns home to a ringing phone: her friend Eleanor reports that Cathy has been seen with a black man, and the whole town is talking. Shocked, Cathy denies it, turning her back to the camera. Her voice remains mellifluous and innocent but her left hand moves toward her mouth, connoting guilt. At that moment, Frank comes home from work, drunk. Cathy hangs up the receiver and steps forward to join him, but Frank demands, "Just tell me one goddamn thing: is it true?" Pressed to defend herself and Raymond, Cathy's voice escalates in pitch; when she sticks up for "the idea of a white woman even *speaking* to a colored man," she is screaming. This scene is the only time she raises her voice during the film. She faces Frank, but her body turns slightly in an attitude of self-protection; she is still but her body shakes, furious. She gesticulates toward him with her right hand, almost in a fist, while her left hand wavers at her side. As the scene proceeds, Cathy lowers her voice and her right hand; she tells Frank, "We won't be seeing the man again," her body indicating prostration.

Throughout the course of developing her character, Moore sought to make Cathy sympathetic; Haynes, however, saw Cathy as the "oppressor"—a kind of police officer patrolling, though artlessly and not deliberately cruelly, the rigid limits of her social group and time (Michael 2003). Moore's command of melodrama's presentational, self-contradictory style, among other techniques, nonetheless allows her to straddle this complicated ground. Her gestures in this scene recall not only 1950s Hollywood melodrama performances but also the nineteenth-century stage.[3] These echoes of earlier performance styles thus have a gestic quality, for they produce an intellectually visible critique of the historical situation Moore performs.

To reiterate, Barthes defines the pregnant moment, through reference to Brecht, as the instant when the gest (a socially weighty and socially legible gesture) and the primary idea in a work of representational art are perfectly aligned and "framed" for the spectator and both social meaning and narrative meaning can be "read" in a single instant. Brecht trained his actors through methods that would, he theorized, lead to performances with the intended political force; but for Barthes, how the pregnant moment emerges may be a matter of serendipity as much as careful selection of aesthetic elements.[4] Barthes writes that in the tableau the actor "must present the very knowledge of [its] meaning"; this knowledge, which the actor must demonstrate "by an unwonted supplement," is "neither his human knowledge nor his knowledge as actor," yet still he must "guide meaning toward its ideality" (1977, 74–75). The actor's deliberate "actorly" choices may or may not be what causes the spectator to grasp meaning from the attitude of the body before him or her. Barthes further explains how the body and vocal music create something new as a result of the commingling of their particular rhythms and affects. He traces how the personhood of the performer insinuates its way into performance: "The grain is the body in the voice as it sings, the hand as it writes, the limb as it performs" (188). And if a body changes throughout the course of a performance, it, too, could create meaning anew, and in unanticipated ways.[5]

Despite Haynes's and Moore's insistence that her pregnancy did not seriously affect the production of *Far from Heaven*, and the film crew's active work to conceal her growing girth, Moore's body can be identified—or, perhaps more accurately, sensed—as pregnant in the film, telegraphing meanings that exceed Haynes's and Moore's conscious, deliberate decisions. As such, Moore's acting opens upon what Merleau-Ponty called the flesh of the world, the great interwoven texture of co-implication that makes everyone both patient and agent at once, subject and object of processes that ultimately mock any pretense that humans are self-starting "agents" in the world. To the extent that Haynes's and Moore's aim in *Far from Heaven* is to suggest how the social taboos of the 1950s are still with us, and that we should not pride ourselves on being able to address homosexuality and interracial desire more articulately now than what this film imagines possible in the 1950s, Moore's pregnant moments illustrate "[the] presence of *all* the absences (memories, lessons, promises) to whose rhythm History becomes

3.2 Cathy waits in lavender.

intelligible and desirable" (Barthes 1977, 73). As I argue below, Moore's body signifies this goal of the film beyond the character of Cathy as scripted.

Pregnant Moments

The least encouraging of the film's pregnant moments, for it suggests how deeply institutionalized our social attitudes remain, finds Cathy in the office of Dr. Bowman, a psychiatrist. Frank agrees to see Dr. Bowman early in the film, after admitting his "problems" to Cathy; the hope is that Frank will be "cured." Cathy is asked to wait outside. On this occasion her entire outfit is lavender, including her gloves and handbag; the waiting room is lavender as well (figure 3.2).

Lavender is Cathy's signature color, which conveys, according to Sharon Willis, her sympathy for homosexuals in the film's color economy (2003, 149). It also signifies her connection to Raymond (he rescues a scarf of this color for her, and Cathy wears it when she waves goodbye to him at the end). But to be enveloped in lavender is visually overwhelming, and Cathy's body suggests something other than sympathy. She squeezes her waist with her inner forearms, gripping her purse squarely in front of her. Moore's torso, if one looks for it, is somewhat thick in this scene, and her movements suggest a physical mass in proportion with her hopes but out of proportion with her understanding. In this moment Cathy tries to absorb a great deal: her husband's "illness," her lack of access to his emotional life, and what these mean for her future. The volume of uncertainty that Cathy must contain is telegraphed through the hints of awkwardness in Moore's body. Extradiegetically, this scene is a pregnant moment insofar as it critiques a medical field whose mode of "treating" homosexuality (through electroshock aversion therapy, in particular) is hardly distant memory.

The Whitakers' annual society house party is the most ideologically loaded scene in the film. Cathy, a perfect hostess, sails through the night absorbing her guests' racist remarks ("What happened in Little Rock couldn't happen here.... For one thing, there are no Negroes in Hartford!") and containing fiery situations as they arise, including her drunk husband's insults of Cathy's looks ("It's all smoke and mirrors, fellas; you should see her without her face on!"). Eleanor even speaks to Cathy in a quiet moment ("I've never seen Frank so soused!"), but Cathy, in her voice of fluid containment, excuses Frank's behavior as a symptom of overwork. Indeed, Cathy remains remarkably calm all evening, even while her guests recognize tension in the room (about Frank's behavior, at least, not their own racism). Cathy even laughs with her guests' jokes about her "kindness to Negroes"—her conversation with Raymond at an art gallery the previous day has become the talk of her social circle. Cathy barely indicates her awareness of the genteel hostility in the room.

At the same time, Moore's body says more than Cathy's story allows. The scene had to be reshot late in the production schedule, when Moore was at her biggest (her waist grew from twenty-six to thirty-six inches during the course of shooting). Costume designer Sandy Powell called in experts who used Magic Markers to shade Moore's party gown because not enough money was left in the $14 million budget to make another. Only rarely is Moore's entire body visible on screen; she is expertly hidden behind other guests and the furniture. But when she moves, her hips sway and her torso undulates in ways that indicate a different sense of balance than Cathy's other female guests have. When Frank pulls Cathy down to sit on the sofa arm next to him, Moore's movement suggests that her body carries more weight than her dress shows. Moore's body weight is more evident just after the party, when Cathy steps up into the darkened living room to rehash the night's events with Frank, and to regret the night's "ugliness." In that step up, there is a hint of physical effort.

A hostess with impeccable manners, Cathy willingly tamps down unpleasantness for the sake of smooth social functioning; at the same time, Moore's literally weighty body gives figural heft to the social issues Cathy cooperates in repressing—specifically, in this scene, racism. The pregnant moment in Barthes's terms is literalized in the party scene: Cathy's readiness to conform to social expectations in 1958, the film's "now," makes it clear to the audience watching in the early twenty-first century that some other event—either one in the future of the film's characters or, more likely, an event in our own lives—will be necessary for lasting change to occur, be that a renewed civil rights movement, a revivification of coalition politics, or individual commitment to social justice at the cost of social status. Of course, Moore's body, while expressing Cathy's skills at social containment, also carries a literal future event (the birth of her daughter, Liv), and her narratively unnecessary gestures—of effort, of weight, of imbalance—provide, I think, "a hieroglyph in which we can read … this presence of all the absences (memories, lessons, promises) to whose rhythm History becomes both intelligible and desirable" (Barthes 1977, 73).

The film's most hopeful pregnant moment (of which one should be skeptical, because this film is a melodrama) occurs the day after the Whitakers' party. Frank has struck Cathy in frustration at being unable to make love to her, and he leaves a bruise. Raymond spots Cathy crying in the yard outside the house, one hand to her mouth, one to her abdomen. Raymond invites her to visit a nursery to pick up some plants; Cathy demurs at first, but, changing her mind, approaches Raymond, her hands resting atop her abdomen. Walking in a blazingly orange autumnal wood with Raymond, Cathy holds a spray of flowering witch hazel (a gift from Raymond) loosely in front of her, her arms relaxed (figure 3.3). When she asks him what it feels like to be the only one in the room, her hands rest on her abdomen again. Raymond tells her "there's a whole world" in Hartford full of people who look just like him; he invites Cathy to his favorite diner to show her. Cathy laughs and agrees.

Resting one's hands on one's abdomen is not a gesture typical of melodrama. Pregnant women, however, often rest their hands on their abdomens; the gesture is protective or simply convenient. When Cathy first sees Raymond in her backyard, she is crying and ashamed, but she does not turn away; instead, she faces Raymond fully with her body. This kind of body language, "ventral fronting," suggests comfort with another person, even love or security (see Burgoon, Guerrero, and Floyd 2009; Diprose 1994). And although ventral fronting *is* a gesture used in melodrama, it is also typical of pregnant women who likewise feel secure or comfortable with their companions. Cathy is comfortable talking to Raymond; her voice is musical but without the note of restraint. In the woods outside Hartford, Cathy needn't control anything; rather, she's asking questions

3.3 Cathy and Raymond walk in the woods.

and learning—being the Cathy that probably earned her the nickname "Red." Although their relationship will undoubtedly end sadly, that Cathy and Raymond can speak together at all indicates hopefulness about the future; meanwhile, the movement of Moore's hands and body suggest a time scale that exists beyond the narrative on-screen.

Collaboration, Feminism, and the Pregnant Body

Moore tells a story about letting Haynes know she was pregnant, just as shooting on *Far from Heaven* was about to begin: "He was great about it, but the one thing he would do as I got bigger and bigger was that he'd never look down. I'd show up on the set and he'd be like [she looks up and imitates his voice], 'hi, how are you!? You look great . . . You look wonderful today.' He wouldn't ever look down" (Knegt 2009). Haynes's refusal to look down is somewhat unbelievable, especially because he noticed and commented on Moore's breasts; but considering how long Haynes contemplated making this film and how long he pictured Moore as the star, we can imagine that to watch his collaborator undergo significant physical change would be jarring. Ironically, in so much feminist film theory, including that which inspired Haynes's reimagining of Sirkian melodrama, the female body typically functions as a metaphor rather than as a reality, and it barely exists in discussions of acting at all.

In her 2006 study *The Actress: Hollywood Acting and the Female Star*, Karen Hollinger notes that seventies feminist film theory was not particularly helpful for studies of women and acting. The woman character was viewed as a construction—never crafted, just a symbol—or a fetishistic object of spectacle. Although star studies paid more attention to the woman as an agent, the study of stars has largely been separate from the study of acting. A further complication, Sharon Carnicke points out, is that academic inquiries into performance often assume that an actor's training in a particular mode—such as Stanislavskian or Brechtian—translates to a single style of acting across the actor's oeuvre; such inquiries cannot capture the full complexity of an actor's work, in particular an actor's creative collaboration with a given director (2004, 46–48). And of course, most studies of female actors and male directors do not have as their models a feminist queer director so aware of the idea that must be made concrete, or an actress so aware of how to embody abstractions within the frame.

Successful actor-director collaborations have long intrigued film reviewers and scholars, but few studies investigate how a given director and actor work out the intricacies of performance, especially the performance of a character that is intended to be more abstract than realistic.[6] In relief against those few studies, however, Haynes's collaborations with Moore still emerge as the more complicated: their collaborative genius notwithstanding, the changing female body can never entirely be controlled by either director or actor.

NOTES

1 As an example from Brecht's epic theater, Barthes recalls how, "when Mother Courage bites the coin offered by the recruiting sergeant and, as a result of this brief interval of distrust, loses her son, she demonstrates at once her past as tradeswoman and the future that awaits her—all her children dead in consequence of her money-making blindness" (1977, 73). In Mother Courage's distrustful gesture, itself an example of gest, "a whole social situation can be read" (74).

2 Barthes distinguishes the actor's command of the gesture-in-context that can be read as a gest and thus can convey an idea from acting that calls attention to itself or to the actor. He thus dismisses the "facial affectations" of the Actors Studio and Method acting (Barthes 1977, 75).

3 Many of Moore's more crafted gestures in the scene of confrontation between Frank and Cathy recall the gestural repertoire of François Delsarte; see Baron and Carnicke

(2008), Dyer (1998), and Hollinger (2006) for genealogies of Delsarte's system of gestures for performers on the melodramatic stage, and the history of how Delsarte's system remained a training tool for actors in Hollywood's studio era.

4 Babak Ebrahimian (2004) explains that Brecht, in his 1948 essay "A Short Organum for the Theater," calls for actors to learn their parts through a kind of "montage": one scene at a time and out of order. Through this method, Brecht theorized that actors would be "amazed by the inconsistencies" of a given character and understand the intended impact of each tableau; in turn, audiences would experience a play that was not like a flowing river, but rather like "a game of hopscotch," with each scene complete and distinct from the next (Ebrahimian 2004, 57–58).

5 Roland Barthes uses the term *pregnant moment* to identify a concept common to aesthetic theory. The term was coined by eighteenth-century German dramatist Gotthold Lessing, who asserted that the static representational arts achieve their most significant meaning through the artist's careful selection of a single moment. Taking painting as an example, Lessing states, "Painting . . . can use but a single moment of an action, and must therefore choose the most pregnant one, the one most suggestive of what has gone before and what is to follow" (2005, 92). Lessing's primary example is the Hellenistic sculpture Laocoön and His Sons, arguing that the partial opening of the main figure's mouth represents the pregnant moment just before the action (the figure being attacked by serpents in the temple of Poseidon) begins.

6 For a collection that examines precisely this topic, see Stern and Kouvaros (2006).

4 Oh, the Irony
Tracing Christine Vachon's Filmic Signature

David E. Maynard and Theresa L. Geller

The Creative Producer

No discussion of the work of Todd Haynes would be complete without accounting for the woman who has been present for every one of his major works since *Superstar*: producer Christine Vachon. Through her production company, Killer Films, founded with Pamela Koffler in 1995, Vachon shepherded to the screen some of the most notable independent features of the past three decades, from *Kids* (Larry Clark, 1995) to *Still Alice* (Richard Glatzer and Wash Westmoreland, 2014); produced the award-winning HBO miniseries *Mildred Pierce* (2011); and developed programs such as *Z: The Beginning of Everything* (Amazon Studios, 2015–17) and the Deaf queer comedy *This Close* (Sundance TV, 2018–). Along the way, she launched the careers of many important independent directors, including Mary Harron, Todd Solondz, and Kimberly Peirce. Still, Vachon and Haynes are inextricably linked, instrumental as they both were in the emergence of New Queer Cinema before it even acquired that name; indeed, Vachon has produced more films associated with New Queer Cinema than any other producer, including the earliest titles that founded the movement: *Go Fish* (Rose Troche, 1994), *Swoon* (Tom Kalin, 1992), and Haynes's *Poison* (1991). Vachon has, in fact, served as a producer of every film Haynes has directed, working more with him than any other director on Killer's roster.

This chapter therefore attempts to understand Vachon as a woman central to Haynes's work but also independent of it, with an expansive catalog in her own name. Vachon can be considered a filmmaker with an authorial signature of her own, and we seek to bring to light the meanings and sensibilities of Vachon's work as a producer despite (or because of) that role's obscured nature as a palimpsest beneath films bearing Haynes's directorial stamp.

Both Haynes and Vachon attended Brown University and had made their own student films, but their earliest collaboration came only after graduation and notably started on the production side. In the heady days of Manhattan's downtown art scene of the mid-1980s, Haynes, Vachon, and their college friend Barry Ellsworth started Apparatus Productions, "named in a moment of Soviet-style solidarity" (Vachon and Bunn 2006, 33). The three of them set out to fund, produce, and promote short works by new filmmakers and took on whatever responsibilities were needed at the time; each served as director for their own projects and as producer for the others'. During those early years, Haynes had not fully committed to a place behind the camera and was generally interested in "what the future of counterproduction in film might look like" (quoted in R. White 2013, 148). Their division of labor crystallized, however, after Vachon saw the rough cut of *Superstar: The Karen Carpenter Story* (1987), which Haynes made with Cynthia Schneider, a close friend from Brown who suggested the use of Barbie dolls to tell a story. This film would set the stage for Haynes's future collaborations both large (with Julianne Moore, Maryse Alberti, and others) and small (e.g., with filmmakers Kelly Reichardt and Mary Hestand).

For Vachon, *Superstar* would solidify her role as collaborative partner: "Once the film stopped running and I heard the flapping of the last reel, I knew my days as a director were essentially over. . . . I was taking a side" (Vachon and Bunn 2006, 35). But if, at that moment, she took a side, it was far from a place on the sidelines. As a producer dedicated to developing "movies that matter" (the subtitle of her memoir, *A Killer Life*), Vachon plays a critical role in bringing Haynes's films to fruition and orchestrating how they end up in front of viewers—arranging funding, ensuring distribution, negotiating award eligibility, and much more. Such a profound and diversified role, as Vachon explains, "is why producers are the only ones who go up to accept the Best Picture Oscar: they got the film in the can" (Vachon and Bunn 2006, 8).

This chapter argues for a reconsideration of the authorship of the producer, and of Vachon specifically, not simply for the sake of a more comprehensive understanding of the filmmaking process, but also as a feminist corrective to the tendency toward an overarching (masculinist) auteurism. To bring Vachon's palimpsestic signature into the light, we begin by briefly reviewing some of the literature that argues for critical recognition of the producer—an argument shaped by the discourses of auteurism. Although there is a growing body of literature—if still woefully small—on the producer, the amount of work on female producers is minuscule by comparison.[1] Because of the dearth of material on the figure of the producer, most of it tends to be an account of their successes, mimicking the formula of early auteurist studies. Here we seek to move beyond this descriptive work by mapping Vachon's career in relation to historical shifts and social movements, from the AIDS crisis to the #MeToo uprising. In so doing, we see her career as one responsive to cultural changes, even as her oeuvre has consistently responded to these changes with a perspective of "lesbian irony," casting a gimlet eye on social norms by producing caring and detailed portraits of an array of antisocial figures who reject them.

In the case of Haynes and the discourses that circulate around his work, rethinking his films with and through Vachon redefines queerness as a relation among genders and sexualities, rather than as an identity. Although the queerness of Haynes's films is always at risk of being reduced to the author's own (male) gayness, insisting on the authorial presence of both a gay man *and* a lesbian works against that impulse. In this way, Vachon helps us to return to the definition of *queer* that eschewed stable, positive identities in favor of queer acts and intersections, of *queering* as a constitutive practice that was thoroughly antiassimilationist by "challeng[ing] and break[ing] apart conventional categories, not [seeking] to become one itself" (Doty 1993, xv). The development of Vachon "criticism" also mitigates the prima facie contradiction of centering a feminist study around a male auteur. Whereas most feminist film scholars would see such an objection as spurious, it is still helpful to remember that every feature film *by* Todd Haynes is also a film *from* Christine Vachon. Despite playing such a significant role in producing Haynes's work and bringing it to audiences, much of the academic writing on the director avoids mentioning Vachon at all, and she tends to disappear in critical discussions of his films. Remarkably, she is omitted entirely from the 2007 collection *The Cinema of Todd Haynes*, edited by James Morrison, and does not even merit an entry in the index. She does appear a few times in Rob White's 2013 monograph on Haynes, but only because Haynes himself brings her up during the extended interview that accompanies White's text. These omissions index the numerous challenges to discussing producers in an auteurist context, beginning with the belief that relationship between director and producer is inherently antagonistic—a narrative about the studio system that has never entirely dissipated.

Further complicating matters, as Vachon herself admits, is the fact that "the job of the producer is one of the great mysteries of the moviemaking process" (Vachon and Bunn 2006, 2). Because of this mystery, nearly every critical evaluation of the producer follows the same narrative arc, beginning with claims that they are the forgotten "unsung heroes" ignored by film history "due to the difficulty of determining what the producer does," and that their role has been downsized and marginalized "with the peak of so-called auteur cinema in the sixties" (Pardo 2010, 2). Considerations of the producer are repeatedly framed in auteurist terms, as Matthew Bernstein (2008) models, asking, "Can a film producer be an auteur?"; and even though he rhetorically claims, "on its face, the question seems preposterous," he, like so many others, nevertheless pursues, if equivocally so, a canon of "great" producers (180). Yet such canon formation is clearly far from amenable to a *feminist* consideration of the producer, as the producer-auteur model has proven to be even more male centered than traditional auteur criticism, even while claiming to challenge its hegemony.[2] For instance, in his lengthy study of the creative producer, Alejandro Pardo cannot name a single woman except for Spielberg producer Kathleen Kennedy, despite an extensive list compiled from both sides of the Atlantic and from several sources (2010, 6). If the "creative producer nowadays ... has witnessed an increased appreciation," this newly bestowed recognition certainly does not apply to the women who have fought their way into the field only to be elided from critical considerations other than those connected with identity, such as LGBT and women's cinema (Pardo 2010, 7), which still essentially focus on directors. Vachon is surely a key figure, however, in *any* discussion of the creative producer, as she is an outspoken proponent of such a model of film production: "When you're committed to artistic filmmaking, you've got to behave, in some ways, like an artist" (Vachon and Bunn 2006, 74).

Vachon's creative work cannot be underestimated, as it embodies (quite literally) a significant intervention by a female producer into a male-dominated field; attending to her significance asks us to think *producer*, *woman*, and *lesbian* together in an attempt to deal with the realities of gender in the film industry today. While a few scholars have tried to recognize her importance in contemporary media studies, they have had the awkward challenge of fitting a producer into the critical rubric of auteurism. This is apparent in Ros Jennings's entry in the 2002 anthology collection *Fifty Contemporary Filmmakers*. Jennings is very aware of the unconventional choice of including a producer in a book that defines "filmmakers" as directors—and that includes nearly all men. Because Vachon is the only nondirector (and one of only nine women) discussed in the book, Jennings leans into Vachon's exceptional circumstances, emphasizing the particular historical moment when her career emerged as an opening onto new possibilities for producers generally: "In the 1990s, the kind of publicity and excitement that surrounded both US independent film production and Vachon suggested that there might be the possibility of thinking about producers as auteurs" (2002, 356). Of course, her equivocations here speak to the disruptive force of making this claim in a book series wholly instantiated in the canon-building project of auteur criticism—and possibly in bestowing the title on a woman as well. Jennings, at the time, did "not want to argue this position forcefully, [that] it does make a difference who makes a film," but in the wake of #MeToo and Time's Up, such arguments have become quite urgent (356). David Thomson is correct when he proclaims, "it is a disaster that the theory and practice of production have been so willfully avoided in American film studies," though for reasons he never considered (1982, 39).

A certain, possibly suspicious, synchronicity exists in the rise of auteur theory that would come to dominate both criticism and popular journalism as the studio system edifice began to crack after the antitrust decisions of 1948. Myopic focus on the director provided film culture a heroic narrative opposed to the troubled image of the industry: "Just because it is peopled with cretins, scoundrels, and bigots—if it is or ever was—does not mean that it may not have worked. . . . But film culture has been dismissive of the trade and loyal to the battered, half-hearted artists" (Thomson 1982, 35). Thomson seeks to challenge the caricature of the lascivious, abusive media titan, yet Harvey Weinstein's recent conviction for rape makes those stereotypes hard to dismiss.[3] Indeed, Louis CK (Pig Newton), John Lasseter (Pixar), Les Moonves (CBS), Roy Price (Amazon Studios), and Bryan Singer, among so many others, renew such well-founded suspicions about industry leadership, independent or not. These producers are the most recent "cretins" and "scoundrels" in a disturbing lineage that long predates Weinstein, making claims to "a few bad apples" as specious as it is disingenuous. Although directors, of course, have also been named, the notion of "the male genius-artist" founds "*auteur* apologism—the separation of the art from the artist underpinned by the claim that a problematic identity is a prerequisite for creative genius," which, as Stefania Marghitu argues, "pervades as a power dynamic in popular discourse, ultimately resisting and obfuscating any reckoning for the male genius-artist accused of abuse" (2018, 491).[4]

Vachon herself is no stranger to the cultural fetish of the male-genius artist, having to confront time and time again audiences, critics, and financers who "want to be able to look at one person—usually a man—and say 'Oh, that's the boy genius who made this movie!' That's what people love" (quoted in G. Davis 2010, 42). This narrative of the singular male genius has worked doubly to efface Vachon's labor and creativity as a female producer, rendering questions about her contributions and collaborative practices relatively mute in discussions of the films she and Haynes have brought to the screen. Indeed, a producer succeeds insofar as she is *not* in evidence in the film itself—in direct opposition to the aura of "personality" that marks a director as an "auteur." And yet, the producer looms large in any given film, as Vachon explains: "The production designer on *Camp* did exactly the same job as the production designer on *Cold Mountain*. But 'producer' is a catchall ... they tend to do a little bit of everything, and what they don't do, they have opinions about" (Vachon and Bunn 2006, 9–10). Although these "opinions" carry hermeneutic weight, imprinting Killer Films with the producer's own creative marks, in recent years they have increasingly moved beyond the film frame. Lauding Vachon's ability "to firmly politicize her own sense of the personal," Jennings notes how, in New Queer Cinema's heyday, Vachon became "the public face at the intersection of queer artistic practice and concerns about gender and lesbian identities" (2002, 355). Vachon has increasingly focused on these latter concerns, adopting a different yet equally politicized "public face" in response to the systemic misogyny of the industry. Whereas some may argue this coming-out of Vachon's "feminism" is a recent political shift, we contend that its incipience has long manifested in her film work and is constitutive of her "signature" as a creative producer.

"Taking a Side"

In a piece she wrote for the *Guardian* after the 2016 US presidential election, Vachon urges "film-makers [to] defy Trump": "As film-makers and storytellers we need to use the moment right now to take stock and examine our own practices. Are we inclusive? Are we diverse? Are we telling stories that resonate for people right now? I hope Carol did that" (2017). Yet Vachon's claims for *Carol* in terms of its "resistance" would be complicated, to say the least, several months later when accusations against Harvey Weinstein, an executive producer on the film, came to light.[5] Since the emergence of the Sundance Film Festival in the late 1980s, Weinstein has been the biggest name in independent narrative cinema, working with "maverick" directors such as Quentin Tarantino, Robert Rodriguez, Gus Van Sant, and of course Todd Haynes—Weinstein was an executive producer on Haynes's *Velvet Goldmine*, *I'm Not There*, and *Carol*.[6] The revelations about Weinstein's abuse—sexual and otherwise—have certainly exploded the myth of independent cinema as a haven from corrupt and venal Hollywood studios. Even after Salma Hayek (2017) recounted the degradations she faced while working with the producer, Weinstein would go on to brag about how he has "made more movies directed by women and about women than any filmmaker" (Rosenberg 2019).[7]

Of course, Haynes's films number among the movies about women Weinstein claims for himself. Filmmakers such as Kevin Smith have admitted that they profited as women suffered (D'Alessandro 2017), whereas Haynes has been a little less introspective, despite the fact that the news on Weinstein broke while they were all making the rounds with *Carol*. "I think everyone's trying to point fingers and try[ing] to find complicity," Haynes responded when asked about Weinstein after the news broke, "as if Harvey Weinstein is the exception to a culture that is progressive about these things. . . . That culture doesn't exist. . . . Harvey Weinstein is a grotesque, extreme example in one tiny corner of a much bigger ongoing issue. . . . We all keep letting this happen and pretending that we're past it" (quoted in Ryan 2017). This unified "we" glosses over those *women* (Rose McGowen, Mira Sorvino, Courtney Love, Ashley Judd, etc.) who tried to speak out for decades and who lost artistic and economic opportunities because of Weinstein's blacklist. Vachon and her colleagues sprang into action on behalf of these women when Level Forward and Killer Content (formed in 2014 with Adrienne Becker) pursued acquisition of the assets of the Weinstein Company (TWC), promising to recompense survivors with its ill-gotten gains. They were thwarted by Lantern Capital, a financial group with no history in entertainment, which ultimately won the rights to TWC (Seltzer 2017). Killer Content (2018) responded to this shutout: "Our first commitment is to survivor justice, and as such, we believe that the sale should not be an optical rebranding of management or name. Only a true dismantling of pernicious practices can advance the healing process for our industry and beyond. We want to do our part to ensure that no matter the outcome, the blood money generated from the systemic protection of alleged rape, abuse and a culture of violence against women will soon be allocated to the prevention, the support and advocacy efforts of anti-discrimination and survivor support organizations." What all this points to, particularly after Weinstein's rape conviction, is the complex and crucial significance of the producer in shaping film culture, and the culture at large—a responsibility Vachon did not take lightly even before the #MeToo movement.

Journalists and film scholars must ask how Weinstein's abuses of power shaped films bearing his name, but such questions, in the long run, might well point to the salutary effects of a producer like Vachon, who takes her role as an "intimate collaborator" very seriously (Vachon and Bunn 2006, 2). Vachon's work in "foregrounding underrepresented stories and voices" presents a crucial progressive model of a producer as feminist activists continue to demand change in the media industry and beyond, particularly with regard to its persistent sexism, which Vachon has confronted for years: "The question she often hears from potential investors is: 'Who's the guy?'" (Hole and Jelača 2019, 44). For Vachon there is no "the guy"—even when she is working with Haynes—because of the collaborative nature of the creative partnerships she nurtures. Vachon's body of work might be fruitfully approached, to this extent, in terms of the specifically queer collaborative model Matthew Tinkcom develops in his discussion of Vincent Minnelli's work in the Arthur Freed unit of MGM. Although he focuses on Minnelli, he makes the case that other queer creative workers in Freed's unit shared similar queer-inflected sensibilities in their work for the MGM producer. Tinkcom maps out certain sensibilities in the work of the Freed unit that set its musicals apart from other musicals of the time, and he argues that these differences are not derived "solely from the perceived formal qualities of their mise-en-scene and choreography," but from the situation of production as well (2002, 37). Tinkcom argues that the musicals produced under the Freed banner were marked by a camp aesthetics, which raises the question: "How … do we align camp, which has long been understood as a practice performed by audiences on texts … with the analysis of production?" (41). Tinkcom makes the case that "emerging queer metropolitan subcultures" shaped mass cultural forms, and "that the queer employees at Metro's Freed unit during this period formed a collaborative effort to alter the look of the Hollywood musical through camp" (43). Although these employees were mostly closeted at the time, of course, Tinkcom's claim "that dissident sexualities have a bearing on the final product" would come to be ratified by Killer Films, when a very different emergent queer urban subculture would produce its own stamp on cinema, with its own sensibilities.

Vachon's Archive of Resistance

One of the earliest explorations of the imprint of dissident sexualities on cinema is Judith Mayne's work on Hollywood director Dorothy Arzner. In *The Woman at the Keyhole* (1990) and, later, *Directed by Dorothy Arzner* (1994), Mayne seeks to account for Arzner's lesbian identity in ways previous feminist studies had not. In an industry that remains disproportionately segregated by gender, it cannot go unremarked that Arzner, the American director with the most Hollywood features to her name, and Vachon, the producer with the most independent films to her name, are both, in their own way, iconic lesbians behind the camera. Recognizing that female authorship is irreducible to textual marks, as "women have not had the same relationship to the institutions of the cinema as men have," Mayne forwards an account of female authorship located in "a diversity of authorial inscriptions, ranging from thematic preoccupations, to the designation of a character or a group or characters as a stand-in for the author" (1990, 97). In Mayne's discussion of Arzner, a reading practice emerges suitable for scholars of Vachon, since both "signed" work written and developed by others with their own creative "opinions." Thus, in what follows, we trace Vachon's "authorial inscription" through the motif of "antisocial" and ironic feminism that transects her extensive body of work, and conclude by identifying figurations of the "creative producer" in the films she has "signed."

Whereas the assumption is that Arzner had a more direct impact on the films the studio assigned to her as director, Vachon's ability to choose which projects she develops, often identifying the talent herself, makes the case for a level of authorship denied Arzner by the male-dominated studio system (which may offer one explanation for why she stopped directing films altogether).[8] Mayne provides ways to map the stamp of Arzner's dissident sexuality on works of mass culture within the context of a pre-Stonewall, Fordist studio system—quite a different context than Vachon's, to be sure. Nevertheless, we assert that both share a "lesbian inflection" to their "female signature ... marked by that irony of equally compelling and incompatible discourses" concerning sexual norms and women's social position in patriarchy (Mayne 1990, 115). Indeed, one might well find that Vachon's "signature" also frequently "articulates the division between female communities which do function within a heterosexual universe," as exemplified by Haynes's women's films, "and the eruptions of lesbian [and queer] marginality which do not," which are more evident (somewhat ironically in itself) in her other films, for example, *I Shot Andy Warhol* (Mary Harron, 1996) and *Go Fish* (Rose Troche, 1994) (115). Indeed, several critics (Doty, Ramanathan, and others) have discussed lesbian irony, but it has rarely been taken up outside of discussions of Arzner herself (except in Mayne's work). Lesbian irony allows us to parse two strands central to female authorship in Vachon's career that link up in thematic ways. One strand is Vachon's own reputation as an out queer producer whose "self-promoting, visible" presence in independent cinema ironically ties her to Arzner, who was neither (Mayne 1990, 104).

Like Arzner, Vachon is noted for her butch aesthetic, one she has not compromised for the past twenty-five years as the self-described "face" of Killer Films (W. Mitchell 2020). Although both she and Haynes began their careers during "a crazy time in New York" in the late 1980s and early '90s, when the emerging queer metropolitan subcultural activism of ACT UP and Gran Fury impacted both "film ... and fashion," it is usually just Haynes who is placed in this context in order to frame interpretations of his films (W. Mitchell 2020). Yet it is Vachon who continues to dress the part; in some variation of dark jeans, T-shirts, and black combat boots, she sustains the wardrobe of ACT UP activists (figure 4.1). Yet these are also "elements of lesbian style," which have been interpreted as "striking a blow against the consumerism of a capitalist society as well as leveling class distinctions ... [in their] Levis ... t-shirts, work shirts" (Deborah Wolf, cited in Stein 1995, 476). The political implications of her consistent attire are clear and confrontational. Vachon tweeted in response to the fashion issue of *Out Magazine*, which celebrated men's and trans people's appropriation of highly feminine objects such as high heels and tiaras: "you know what would be REALLY radical? me and my boots in the OUT Fashion issue!" She implicitly challenges the redeployment of fetishized feminine fashion pieces in queer contexts, especially when those contexts efface the political realities of the mandate for normative feminine garb, exemplified in Weinstein's violent abuse of Kate Beckinsale for wearing a suit instead of a tight dress to a film opening, accusing her of looking like a "fucking lesbian"—which, of course, Vachon looks like at every premiere (Wagmeister 2020).

Such "an eruption of lesbian marginality" is of a piece with Vachon's ironic signature, one that is contrary to both normative gender expecta-

Christine Vachon
@kvpi
My red carpet footwear
7:50 AM · May 19, 2015 · Twitter for BlackBerry®

4.1 Vachon's "REALLY radical" antisocial feminism.

tions and supposedly progressive LGBT politics. A coherent thematic of "antisocial feminism," grounded, like her wardrobe, in Vachon's political coming of age during the AIDS crisis, can be tracked across her films with and without Haynes and in her critical relation to normative femininity. Throughout the films she has produced, so-called positive representations are troubled or actively rejected in favor of complex interrogations of sexuality *and* gender. Vachon spells out her modus operandi as a producer when she describes passing on the opportunity to make a movie about Matthew Shepard, the Wyoming teenager killed in a gay-bashing, proclaiming, "That's a movie Killer would never make.... I'd rather make a film about the killers ... their reported meth use addictions, and the speculation that they had known (and maybe even slept with) Shepard" (Vachon and Bunn 2006, 19). Defining what constitutes a Killer film, Vachon opts for the story of the killers over Matthew Shepard's lost life, and indeed, she developed several versions of just such a narrative, including *Swoon* (Tom Kalin, 1992), *Party Monster* (Randy Barbato, 2003), and *Boys Don't*

Cry (Kimberly Peirce, 1999). This "Killer" film profile rejects the idea of a tragic film focused on Shepard for reasons akin to those Lee Edelman (2004) sets out in his discussion of the public discourse that took place in the aftermath of the murder, which worked to mitigate the threat of the sexual practices of the living man by converting him into the figure of the Child in death. As Edelman describes it, the news circulated Shepard's mother's plea for other parents to go home and hug their children, "which even on the occasion of a gay man's murder defined the *proper* mourners as those who had children to go home to and hug, specif[ying] the mourning it encouraged as mourning for a threatened familial futurity" (116). His point is that such a narrative effaces the very reasons for the murder in the first place—the threat "Shepard's *life*" took in political discourse premised on the logic of heteronormative reproductive futurity that "justifies that violent fate in advance" (116). Vachon's films shift focus to those cast out as threats to familial futurity in order to ironize the violent norms of the social discourse that render such persons as threats in the first place.

It may seem strange that an out lesbian would refuse Shepard's story in preference of his killers', but one might theorize she does so because she understands, like Edelman, the limits of compassion: "Whatever its object or the political ends it serves, compassion is *always* conservative ... so irony's negativity calls forth compassion to *negate* it" (Edelman 2004, 89). The ironic move to opt for Shepard's killers' story forces the terms on which compassion would seem to stake its claims—can we feel compassion for his killers? Such is the irony that marks Vachon's signature as a producer, whose films presciently model the refusal of "a new politics, a better society, a brighter tomorrow" to insist "on the negativity that pierces the fantasy screen of futurity, shattering narrative temporality with irony's always explosive force" (31). Explaining why she has remained in the "nightmare" world of low-budget filmmaking in the first pages of *Shooting to Kill* (Vachon and Edelstein 1998), Vachon intimates her allegiance to this sort of negativity: "Unless someone gives me forty million dollars to make a picture about bisexual rockers, or a sympathetic pedophile, or a woman who wakes up one day and realizes that modern society is slowly poisoning her to death, it's the world in which I'll stay" (Vachon and Bunn 2006, 2). While the *New York Times* lauds Vachon as "the godmother to the politically committed film," and her films are hailed as "bold" and "controversial," the content of her politics—what makes them controversial—is rarely named except by Vachon herself.[9] One might well ask: What good are such antisocial stories of sympathetic pedophiles, like *Happiness* (Todd Solondz, 1998); queer child-killers (*Swoon*); prostitute would-be assassins (*I Shot Andy Warhol*); or drugged-up club kids who brag about killing their dealers (*Party Monster*)? Such antisociality aims not at a general "good," however; rather, as Edelman asserts, "the embrace of queer negativity . . . resides in its challenge to value as defined by the social, and thus in its radical challenge to the very value of the social itself" (2004, 6). Vachon's "signature"—from her boots to her choice of film content—consistently poses such a "radical challenge."

The antisocial thesis in queer theory conceptualizes what makes sexuality "dissident," particularly in relation to political discourse.[10] In this way, adopting it to think about Killer Films begs a question similar to Tinkcom's concerning Freed's campy production unit: How do we align antisocial queerness, which has been demonstrated through its critical figuration in texts, with the analysis of production? As Robert Caserio (2006) reminds us, the antisocial thesis did not begin (or end) with Edelman's *No Future*, but emerged a decade earlier. Leo Bersani (1995) queried, "should a homosexual be a good citizen?" the same year that the FDA approved protease inhibitors (and *Safe* first premiered), forever changing the lives of people who were HIV positive, arguably because queers had *not* been good citizens in staging numerous protests to disrupt government, churches, and pharmaceutical companies to demand compassionate and immediate action to the AIDS crisis (quoted in Caserio 2006, 819). While Bersani and others were exploring "queer unbelonging" in scholarship, expressing a "gay rage for normalizing sociality" that had been sparked by the horrifying non-response to the AIDS crisis, Vachon was doing much the same in her own work, producing films that articulate sexuality's "politically unacceptable" opposition to community—possibly more concretely than any "thesis" ever could (819). In 1995 alone, Vachon collaborated with a remarkable roster of creative talent whose work epitomizes politically unacceptable antisociality, producing, for example, Harmony Korine and Larry Clark's *Kids*—a film that to this day represents the shocking negativity of "meaningless" sex, queer or not. She also worked with Rikki Beadle-Blair and Nigel Finch on *Stonewall* (1995), completing the edits herself after director Finch died of an AIDS-related illness. Indeed, her films at that time exemplify radically queer creative challenges to the social; following on the heels of *Swoon* and *Poison* she produced Steve McLean's *Postcards from America* (1994), a film based on artist David Wojnarowicz's writings about his experiences as a hustler during the AIDS crisis; *Stonewall*; and *Kids*.

Moreover, long before J. Halberstam hailed her as "an antisocial feminist extraordinaire," Vachon brought Valerie Solanas to the screen in a film that quite literally focuses on how "she famously turned theory into practice when she took a gun and shot Andy Warhol" (Halberstam 2011, 109). Solanas is just one in a long line of antisocial women Vachon has worked to give a voice alongside male figures of queer negativity such as Wojnarowicz and Leopold and Loeb. These antisocial women incarnate Vachon's feminist prerogatives as Patricia White identifies: "Killer's feminism finds its emblems in Bettie Page and Valerie Solanas, subjects of two biopics by Mary Harron, a key director on Killer's early roster" (2016, 40). Whereas Solanas certainly represents an eruption of lesbian marginality aligned with antisociality, Bettie Page points to a different, albeit related concern with how women function within a heterosexual universe that better fits Vachon's collaborative work with Haynes. Released the same year as *Kids* and *Stonewall*, Vachon includes *Safe* (1995) with her films on bisexual rockers and pedophiles in the examples for why she remains in the world of independent filmmaking. One may well wonder how the story of a suburban housewife suffering from environmental illness fits with queer antisocial figures like Solanas and Wojnarowicz. Halberstam founds claims for a specifically antisocial *feminism*, however, on just such characterizations as Carol White, for whom muteness and a radical masochism supplant access to speech and agency. In Carol's inability to speak and act as she grows sicker, "a radical form of masochistic passivity" emerges that "offers a critique of the organizing logic of agency and subjectivity" (Halberstam 2011, 144).

Recall that it was Haynes's first critical intervention into this organizing logic, via Barbie dolls no less, that impelled Vachon to become a producer. Accordingly, Vachon's lifework, we suggest, can be seen as curating a cinema of resistance and masochistic refusal in which chrono-normative narratives and positive representations are forsaken in favor of the possibilities afforded by negativity and queer irony. A substantial number of Killer Films—including nearly all of Haynes's films—make up Vachon's own "shadow archive of resistance, one that does not think in terms of action and momentum but instead articulates itself in terms of evacuation, refusal, passivity, unbecoming, unbeing," terms Halberstam uses to define "antisocial feminism, a form of feminism occupied by negativity and negation" (2011, 129). We now turn briefly to a film that incorporates both strands—queer irony and antisocial feminism—and whose significance in Vachon's archive is evident in that it inspired the name of her company, Killer Films.

Feminist Dioramas

Office Killer (1997), a campy workplace slasher, was the first and only feature directed by famed photographer Cindy Sherman; recent film school grad Elise MacAdam and *Swoon* director and Gran Fury cofounder Tom Kalin cowrote the script, with Haynes pitching in to advise and write some of the dialogue. The low-budget film was a critical and commercial failure upon its release, although it has slowly gained a cult following. With its female serial killer, *Office Killer* is an atypical horror, all the more exceptional for its pink-collar workplace setting. At the start of the film, the protagonist, Dorine Douglas, is "a skilled but antisocial copy editor who becomes a murderer by chance," but she develops a taste for it, bringing corpses home to arrange in "tableaux morts" in her basement rec room (Meagher 2009, 135, 137). After a round of downsizing at her workplace, *Constant Consumer* magazine, Dorine is forced to work at home, where she lives with her disabled and abusive mother. Conveying an "irony of equally compelling and incompatible discourses," the film is an awkward mix of genres that might be summarized as *Now, Voyager* (Irving Rapper, 1942) meets *Psycho* (Hitchcock, 1960) by way of *Working Girl* (Mike Nichols, 1988). Like Charlotte in *Now, Voyager*, Dorine begins the film meek and dominated by her ill mother, and she eventually goes through a transformation that by film's end allows her be free of her overbearing mother. Her transformation, however, is facilitated not by psychotherapy's normalizing apparatus, which in *Now, Voyager* compels Charlotte to sacrifice her own pleasure for the sake of the Child (Charlotte volunteers to raise her former lover's daughter), but rather by the creative control of the corpses she collects and arranges for her own enjoyment. Dorine epitomizes the radical passivity of antisocial feminism, as her initial masochistic relationship at both home and work "step[s] out of the easy model of a transfer of femininity from mother to daughter and actually seek[s] to destroy the mother-daughter bond altogether" (Halberstam 2011, 131). This rejection of the mother-daughter bond is central to the film's radical feminist project, as it is repeated throughout the film that is populated with women who stand in for her mother, both as nurturer and as betrayer. Indeed, in one of the few voiceovers, Dorine states that "the key to a successful mother-daughter relationship [is the] need to experience independence and adventure," which she gets through the radical negation of mother stand-ins.

Schweitzer (2010) notes, "This is a movie about women, while also remaining inherently misogynist in the sense that there are no real likeable,

4.2 The fulfilling work of Dorine's "killer" dioramas.

admirable, *sane* female characters," but of course positive images of women do *not* define feminist filmmaking in the least. Indeed, this specious liberal feminist criteria (which would bar a significant number of films—from *All about Eve* [1950]to *Zola* [2021]—from the feminist canon) is precisely what is attacked in the film and throughout Vachon's oeuvre. It is also why she has worked so well all these years with Haynes, who prides himself on telling women's "stories that aren't by definition affirmative or heroic" (N. Davis 2015b). It is quite evident from her body of work that Vachon has little interest in likeable, admirable, or even sane characters. Instead, Vachon's media projects redefine feminist storytelling in antisocial terms. "Antisocial" Dorine kills her coworkers and even some random Girl Scouts who show up at her door—reminding us that *Office Killer* was cowritten by the award-winning anatomizer of queer negativity, Kalin (*Swoon*, *Savage Grace* [2007]). Dorine keeps her victims close, conjuring narratives for the corpses gathering in her basement, giving them a conviviality lacking from her office and home life—a conviviality made possible by the absence of male dominance (figure 4.2). Dorine, like Solanas, is an antisocial feminist extraordinaire, orchestrating in her basement "a shadow archive of resistance" that does not imagine women as adversaries under capitalism, as portrayed in the offices of *Constant Consumer*, where they bicker and compete for the top spot on the corporate ladder. Given only the choices of "freedom in [neo]liberal terms or death," Dorine makes the choice for them (Halberstam 2011, 129).

The film depicts the two worlds offered women—work and domesticity—as dominated by men, in this case Mr. Landau and Dorine's father, who was also a founding editor of the magazine; thus, Dorine's low status there is an extension of how he "kept girls under his thumb" in both settings. This synecdoche of male control, the thumb and the male hand to which it is attached, is a key symbol in the film, shown in close-up in what Schweitzer problematically identifies as "Dorine's first intentional execution . . . [of her] father [who] also died by her hand following his own inappropriate behavior" (2010). This inaccurately describes the scene that provides the origin story for Dorine's radical negativity, conveyed through a flashback. The family is riding in their car, and it is clear that Dorine has told her mother before the trip that she has been sexually molested by her father. The truth is revealed as her father's hand caresses Dorine's thigh while her mother dismisses Dorine's complaint against her father, claiming instead (as she betrays her daughter's trust to the girl's father) that Dorine just loves her father and is jealous of her mother.[11] In an act that immediately contradicts her mother's dialogue, Dorine grabs her father's hand to stop his caress and, refusing to let go, causes the car to crash. Far from an execution, this act literalizes the death drive; Dorine opts for the radical negation of the family, including herself, "insist[ing] that the future stop here," especially as that future is premised on her person as the Child (Edelman 2004, 31).

She survives and, as an adult woman, incarnates antisocial queerness (a coworker calls her a "lezzie" and a "fucking freak"), exchanging the self-annihilating masochism of her girlhood with a murderous rage first directed at her father's replacement at the magazine, the sexual predator Mr. Michaels. *Office Killer* thus weds antisocial feminism to queer negativity through the father's incestuous sexualization of the girl child's body, revealing the profound gulf between the figure of the Child as innocent and in need of protection, and actual children whose silence the patriarchal social order demands.[12] When she speaks her truth about her father, her mother labels *Dorine* the sexual one, the one with the dirty mind. Not for nothing is Dorine mistakenly called "Dora" at work, recalling Freud's most difficult case, a teenage girl who developed hysteria as a form of revolt against the men in power who refused to listen to her protests against being sexually traded by her own father to his mistress's husband, and who ultimately refused to be "cured" of her well-founded fury at her father. Dorine, too, escapes being "cured"; instead, she burns down her house with all its bodies to start over again as an office manager in an unnamed city. Hinting that the cycle will start over, Dorine's final voiceover ironically intones that she hopes that she and her new coworkers "can get along," insinuating the probable gory results if they do not.

With the film's chilly reception, we might well ask why Vachon turned to Sherman, an untried novice, in directing. It might have had something to do with the fact that Vachon's father was a respected photographer, or that she wanted to take steps to tell more stories about women, as her films up to that point had rarely addressed women at all. She may have been inspired, having just wrapped Haynes's *Safe*, to develop more films like it and *Superstar* in which femininity is defamiliarized by denaturalizing the cinematic tropes on which it is propped.[13] While Haynes's women's films recall Douglas Sirk and others, their political aims actually share more with Sherman's mock film stills, "capturing the look of 1950s and 60's Hollywood . . . refracted through a layer of artifice—a veneer of representation" (Baker 2019). Like Haynes, Sherman uses artifice to denaturalize the gestures of femininity; akin to Sherman's film stills, Haynes's film work calls forth discourses of femininity from different historical eras to dialecticize them with the present, defamiliarizing both in the process. Vachon's collaborations with both artists illustrate her authorship as a producer. She tends to bring together talented people and give them the opportunity to make new imaginative arrangements (pairing Sherman with Kalin, feminist with queer activist, for example); Vachon, in this way, provides the conditions that enable them to create a world outside of heteropatriarchal oversight, even if this means remaining in the nightmare "rec room" of low-budget filmmaking.

What we are intimating is that other marker of authorial inscription for Mayne: the designation of a character or a group of characters as a stand-in for the producer. Nearly every critic of *Office Killer* reads Dorine as "a stand-in for Sherman," but there are grounds to make the case that she is also a stand-in for Vachon, the more explicitly queer "killer" (Schweitzer 2010). In several of the films Vachon has produced, characters arrange things and people in new, unexpected ways to create queer or feminist forms (or both) of being and knowing. Dorine certainly does so, having arranged the bodies in her basement as an alternative community that she imagines as alive and interacting together as she drives off to her new destination. Vachon's career as a producer is akin to Dorine's more fulfilling work of "assembl[ing] diorama[s]" from (and for) the people in her basement (Schweitzer 2010). It is no surprise that Haynes's films, too, afford figurations for Vachon's artistic production and collaborative work, given their longtime partnership—from opinionated Eleanor Fine, Cathy

Whitaker's rather brusque best friend (who socializes with gay men and organizes art shows), to Mandy Slade's midwifing of Brian Slade's glam rock stardom. We might also see Vachon in a very different film about dioramas—*Wonderstruck* (2017). Young Rose attends the films in which her mother stars, but she is painfully aware of their false images as she sits among the rapt audience. As an adult, Rose contributes to and manages the diorama of New York City in the Queens Museum, where she covertly alters a public artwork with her "own sense of the personal." Beneath the surface of the diorama, Rose slips fragments of her own story waiting to be discovered. So too with Vachon: her authorial signature is there to be found. We need only be willing to peek under the film worlds she helps bring to life to locate the intimate messages she has been leaving all along.

NOTES

We thank Patricia White for her helpful notes on this chapter.

1 Notable critical pieces on women producers include Lyons (2016), P. White (2016), and Christina Lane's (2020) book-length study of Joan Harrison, producer and writer of Alfred Hitchcock's early work.

2 For discussion of auteur theory's male-centered narrative, see Shambu (2018).

3 Among the most noted producers in the studio system is David O. Selznick, whose fights with Alfred Hitchcock came to define the antagonistic narrative defining the producer-director relationship. As the documentary *Hitchcock, Selznick and the End of Hollywood* (Michael Epstein, 1999) portrays, however, both men's misogyny represents the systemic treatment of women in the industry that was normalized for well over a century. Glenn Lovell's 1999 review of the film notes their comparative abuse of women as if they are just "differences in personality and work habits" and not actually forms of sexual predation: "Forget about Hitch's misogynistic dark side; the David O. depicted here makes the corpulent one look like a well-mannered choirboy.... Peggy Robertson, Hitch's personal secretary; and Selznick's assistant and secretary ... recall being pawed and run ragged by their boss." Hitchcock's "choirboy" is disturbingly contradicted by Tippi Hedren's (2016) allegations that he controlled, abused, and sexually assaulted her.

4 Exemplifying this apologism is Margaret Leclere's (2018) defense of auteurism: "The artistic drive and the sex drive have always been closely linked. The adoration of the human form, the fascination with the object of desire, driving the creation of works of art, or simply driving the artist.... To deny this, to attempt to outlaw it, is an act of cultural suicide." Such are the claims of auteur apologists, with the attendant disavowal of the profound differences between the highly debated notion of a "sex drive" and real acts of sexual violence, alongside hysterical fears about the "outlawing culture."

5 Elizabeth Karlsen insists: "This is a frequent and frustrating misrepresentation of Harvey Weinstein and his role—he was a distributor who stole the producing credit (as well as the financial rewards) from the actual producers who sourced, developed, filmed and fully created the work as we did with *Carol*" (quoted in Gilchrist 2018).

6 For an extensive discussion of this history, see Peter Biskind (2016).

7 That Weinstein forced Hayek to include a lesbian sex scene with Ashley Judd, an early accuser, in *Frida* (Julie Taymor, 2002) shows all too well that producers have a direct impact on the content of the films they produce.

8 See Geller (2003) for further discussion of Arzner's abrupt departure from directing.

9 Although she has been called the "godmother" of independent cinema, her persona is anything but maternal; John Cameron Mitchell observes that "Christine doesn't brook fools lightly" (quoted in Vachon and Bunn 2006, 148), whereas investor John Pierson describes her as "blunt.... Unrepentant. Ruthless. A killer even" (xv). Indeed, it might well be because of her intimidating "butch" character that she is seen only as a "god" mother and not a birth mother, as other women have been identified (from Ida Lupino to Josephine Decker). When women have had an inarguable effect on film culture, their impact is frequently described in maternal language, recasting their shaping of public culture in private, familial, even oedipalized terms (see Geller 2006, 155–57).

10 Robyn Wiegman makes the important intervention that the "antisocial thesis is not 'a' thesis. It is an arena of interpretive battle ... because negativity *is* queer theory's most important contemporary idiom" (2017, 220–21).

11 In this way, for all the extensive film citations critics, especially Schweitzer, identify in their discussions of *Office Killer*, none mention David Lynch's *Twin Peaks: Fire Walk with Me* (1992) and the series that preceded it, which was a widespread cultural phenomenon premised on the daughter's experience of sexual violation by her father (see Geller 1992).

12 We might remember here that directly preceding the infamous quote from Edelman, beginning "Fuck the social order and the Child," he presents a scathing indictment of Bernard Law, former cardinal of Boston, for denouncing proposed legislation giving same-sex partners health care benefits. Law claims "society has a special interest in the protection, care and upbringing of children ... the state has a special interest in [heterosexual] marriage," thus justifying the refusal of "health care benefits to the adults that some children become" (2004, 28–29). Edelman is quick to underscore the irony that Law later "resigned for his failure to protect Catholic children from sexual assault by pedophile priests" (29).

13 See, for example, Theresa L. Geller's chapter on *Safe* and Mary R. Desjardins's chapter on *Superstar* in this volume.

5 "The Hardest, the Most Difficult Film"

Safe as Feminist Film Praxis

Theresa L. Geller

—In Memory of Kate Millett

At the 2018 Golden Globes, the Time's Up movement exploded in response to the culture of sexual harassment, intimidation, and assault, as well as unequal pay and discriminatory practices, rampant in the industry. Time's Up followed on the heels of the #MeToo social media outpouring that had erupted in the waning months of 2017, which finally called out a slew of men in the film industry, starting with independent film producer and recently convicted rapist Harvey Weinstein. Indeed, *Time* named "the silence breakers" who were brave enough to come forward about Weinstein and others the "person of the year," while Merriam-Webster declared *feminism* word of the year. Feminist activism went Hollywood—and viral.

Astoundingly, with accusations dating back fifty years, Weinstein inculpated history to explain his behavior: "I came of age in the 60's and 70's, when all the rules about behavior and workplaces were different. That was the culture then" (Kantor and Twohey 2017). In doing so, Weinstein paints one of the most fractured periods in recent history as unitary in its "culture"; yet many others experienced an entirely different "culture" in this era. Only eight years younger than Weinstein, Todd Haynes identifies with a very different sixties and seventies: "I think many of the ideas that opened up in the sixties got implemented in the seventies, and that certain minority voices that were not being heard in the sixties, like women and gay people, were being heard in the seventies" (quoted in Phipps 2014, 94–95). While Weinstein ignored (or aggressively silenced) these voices for decades, Haynes built a career listening to women and gay people, addressing this era's revolutionary promise in his films. Although Weinstein produced several of them, Haynes believes his films are part of the solution: "I've made a lot of films about women in my career and about the limited freedoms women have to maneuver within—and I'll continue to do so and I'll continue to work with women and think very deeply about their predicament in life. And that's my contribution" (quoted in Ryan 2017). And yet, the current heightened milieu of Time's Up and #MeToo, and of Weinstein's role in producing and promoting some of Haynes's most lauded works, invites new questions concerning the efficacy of such contributions.[1]

Although Haynes repeatedly insists on the feminism founding his film work, it does not guarantee that his films are seen in this light, in large part because, as he describes, "misogyny is built into a kind of love or worship of male power and dominance" (quoted in Ryan 2017), a symptom of which, of course, is male-centered auteur theory. In juxtaposing how Haynes's second feature, *Safe* (1995), has been critically received with his statements on the film, I want to make the case for how film critics and scholars can contribute to the larger political conversation by confronting the silence around women's intellectual and creative labor. By reclaiming the feminist filmmaking tradition that inspired and informed this film, we can assess the ways cinema has allowed Haynes and the women who influenced him—filmmakers and theorists alike—to intervene into the culture's pervasive misogyny. While Haynes asserts the possibilities of intervention as a filmmaker to create films that "think very deeply about [women's] predicament in life," I argue for the significance of criticism and the role of the critic in supporting and increasing these possibilities by recognizing and valuing feminist cinema—thus, recuperating it from the margins of film history. In 1974, Julia Lesage outlined the role of feminist film criticism: "Feminists can conveniently use this ready-made journalistic vehicle not only to attack sexism in a film but also to evaluate the social milieu that generates that film" (12). Through a metacritical analysis of *Safe*, I draw on (and out) the film's feminist politics to return to and amplify questions Haynes poses in his film and in his commentary on it—questions that seek to expose cinema's ideological complicity with a culture that silences women and erases their contributions.

Many critics have evaluated *Safe*'s affective register—whether it is emotionally moving or not—as a measure of its effectiveness. Feminist film criticism, however, has different criteria: "When writing about a feminist film, or about any political film," according to Lesage, "the critic must evaluate what effect this film hopes to have on its audience. And what effect it actually has. Does it intend to provoke specific changes in milieu? How?" (1974, 15). Rather than asking what *Safe* represents (e.g., environmental illness, the porous body, AIDS, whiteness—all of which have obvious hermeneutic traction), I posit that what Haynes's film *does* is inherently more radical. In its resistance to spectatorial identification and narrative closure, *Safe* epitomizes what Lesage identifies as "a more radical work . . . shap[ing] the audience's mind, leaving the viewers with structures which go beyond their consciousness prior to viewing"; this provides viewers "tools with which to reevaluate that which they had previously accepted as 'natural'" (15). *Safe* stands as an example of feminist film praxis, confronting the viewer with feminist thought's founding observations about mass culture—centrally, how patriarchal ideology shapes the meanings and pleasures to be found in narrative cinema.[2] Indeed, Haynes sees countering this ideology as his responsibility as "a filmmaker who is gay": "Heterosexuality . . . is an imposed structure that goes along with the patriarchal, dominant structure that . . . conventional narrative form adheres to and supports. . . . For me, it's the way the narrative is structured, the way films are machines that either reiterate or reciprocate society—or not" (quoted in Wyatt 1993, 8). *Safe* remains to this day Haynes's most difficult film because of its adamant refusal to reciprocate patriarchal structures and socially constructed spectatorial desires. The #MeToo movement has shed new light on the culture and content of the film industry, from general reexaminations of the representation of women in the media today to symptomatic readings of the work produced by men named by the movement.[3] As Rebecca Onion (2017) keenly observes, however, "amid the flood of stories about harassment and abuse, there's been a strange scarcity of broader sociohistorical critique that explains how we got here. . . . What we need right now to go along with our '70s style radical rage . . . is some '70s-style feminist social analysis." Returning to *Safe* from the present moment affords the opportunity to reignite such analyses.

False Images

In the years since its release, *Safe* has proven to be an exceptionally transdisciplinary text, generating commentary from an impressive variety of schools of thought, from the literary tradition to the ecological movement. Yet if one unifying theme is to be found in *Safe* criticism across the disciplines, it is that the film's debated meanings center on its protagonist, Carol White. As Carol grows increasingly ill with an unspecified ailment that leads her eventually to identify as a person with environmental illness or chemical sensitivity—interpellated as she is by flyers and television ads—she makes the decision to move out of her home and into the New Age compound Wrenwood, where, by all appearances, she gets worse. The film simply ends with her withdrawal into a "safe" space of isolation, hinting at her ultimate demise.

Safe reflects Haynes's early training in film theory, an education he traces as far back as high school, where he "watched a lot of experimental films" and was encouraged to "create different criteria for how to look at film" (quoted in Wyatt 1993, 4). Nonetheless, compared with *Poison*'s (1991) avant-garde triptych, strewn with abject and fantastic scenarios, *Safe* seems more recognizable as narrative cinema—and yet, as Haynes tells Collier Schorr, audiences were "in for a slow, quiet shock" (2014, 46). Certainly the film's story about a "sad housewife" may well have been jarring for audiences expecting the antihero frisson that made New Queer Cinema popular, but the film was met with something more than disappointed expectations. In an interview some sixteen years after *Safe*'s initial release, Kate Winslet (2011) asks, "What has been the most difficult film for you to let go of emotionally[?]" Noting the strong reaction to the film when it first premiered, Haynes names *Safe*: "We would take it to gay film festivals because it was the second film by a gay director or whatever and people were like, 'What the fuck is this?'" Haynes is well aware of the expectations with which his films are met: "The problem is always in content; we want to define the perspective of a film solely through its content, and not through its form" (quoted in Laskawy 2014, 20). He links the "problem" of content, and "all this anxiety around meaning," to the ideological work of narrative, suggesting that "our narrative relaxation is rooted in a sense of moral certainty" (Haynes 2003, x). Haynes has defended *Safe* against such moral certitude over the years by underscoring its formal experimentation.

Haynes challenged Larry Gross's assumptions about the film, for example, the year of its release: "Relative to *Poison* and *Superstar*, *Safe* would be classified as less of an experimental film. Did you want this to be a more traditional film?" Haynes, usually an agreeable interviewee, rejects this idea out of hand: "No, not at all. And I think it's the hardest, the most difficult film I've made for audiences" (Gross 2014, 62). Undeterred, Gross continues with this line of argument, but Haynes shuts him down each time; Gross asks, "The thing is … you were moving in slightly more 'conventional' territory. Did you say, 'this is going to be my version of a conventional film … ?" to which Haynes responds: "Actually … I was looking at things that were extreme" (63). For Gross, the film's content seems "conventional territory," but Haynes repeatedly refutes this suggestion by foregrounding *Safe*'s "extreme" aesthetics. Yet few critics have heeded this early intervention—even when they directly cite the Gross interview. Roy Grundmann's review of the film epitomizes much of what makes *Safe* such a difficult film for viewers who are disoriented by the juxtaposition of recognizable, even cliché narrative themes with "extreme" formal experimentation. Despite noting Carol's "punishment" by patriarchy, Grundmann does not read *Safe* as a feminist film or even an experimental film, but rather situates it in the Sirkian tradition: "Haynes knows his film history, and, at the end of *Safe*, he attempts to promote Carol to the ranks of the protagonists of Douglas Sirk's melodramas, who achieve substance … even if their stories are told with deliberate false images" (1995, 25). Grundmann's critique introduces certain unspoken criteria of evaluation that are telegraphed through the comparison to Sirk, a master of the realist style of classical filmmaking; one might well ask, however: Is this the proper context through which to frame *Safe*'s "false images"?

If *Safe*'s formal ruptures, as Haynes insists, "result in a film that cannot be read literally," then the hermeneutic habit of finding the "truth" behind its "false images" is a futile task indeed, especially because it circumvents the feminist question of what the film "does" (1995). To get at this question, I want to forward an exemplary "false image" as an analog for the film as a whole, as it figures (and is a figure for) the film's resistance to the protocols of interpretation. *Safe*'s original promotional materials show the mysterious, solitary Lester, the chemically ill resident of Wrenwood we only ever see, always in extreme long shot, wandering the outskirts of the property, face covered in a balaclava and clothed from head to toe (figure 5.1). Rather than provide an image of Carol White, the focus of the film's narrative, the paratextual image directs us to look elsewhere—toward an inscrutable figure whose "truth" is never revealed, his mask never removed, his story never told. The film is not about Lester; yet Lester's privileged image

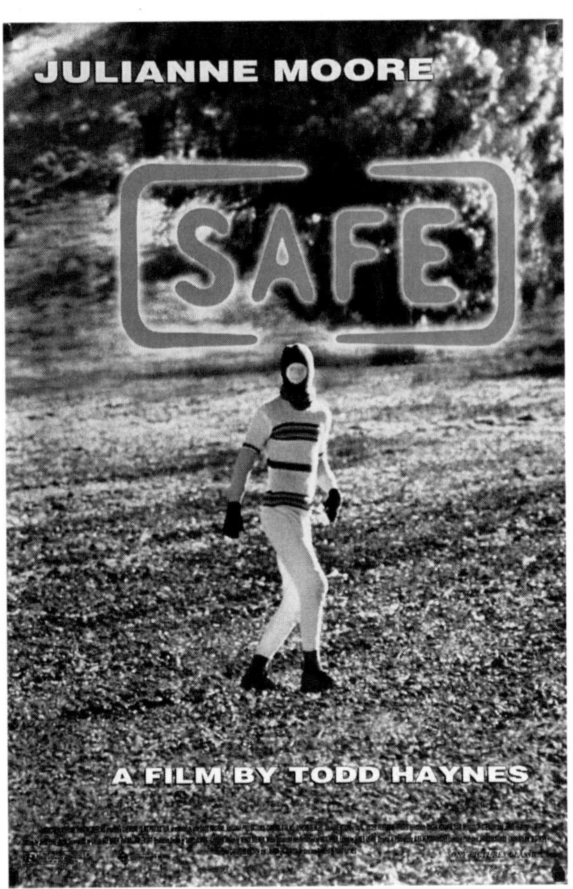

5.1 The poster for *Safe* exemplifies Haynes's "false images," priming the spectator for the film's systematic refusal of identification.

suggests that it is not really "about" Carol either, but rather about the status of the image itself and the promise of identification—and identity—it is supposed to offer the viewer. Haynes explains this promise in the introduction to his "women's films": "Identification has many official definitions, most of them deriving from the psychoanalytic model. . . . [It] connects us to the protagonist onscreen but, at a deeper level, through our implicit understanding of cinematic language, to a basic sense of ourselves as cohesive subjects" (2003, viii). Denying identification with Carol, to this extent, undercuts this "basic sense of ourselves." Haynes states plainly his desire to interrupt "the narrative process . . . its perfect system," by repeatedly frustrating cinematic identification, explaining that by "tinkering or upsetting that process of identification a little bit, people have to think more about what they're seeing, who's telling them what and why" (quoted in MacLean 2014, 55–56). In the case of *Safe*, the question of "what they're seeing"—and "why"—can be traced back to Haynes's knowledge of and admiration for feminist film theory and the film canon associated with it.

Hollywood's "Fucking Lie"

Haynes admits that *Safe*, "like all movies, tells its lies. The difference is that *Safe* lies on purpose. Somehow it lets you know that it doesn't believe in the rules it is bound, nevertheless, to obey" (2003, x). In other words, what *Safe* denotes, contra Grundmann, is that Haynes knows his film *theory*. Haynes seeks to undermine the viewer's ability to "participate in making real or making alive this two-dimensional, technological gimmick projected on the wall," as he describes it (in MacLean 2014, 55). Carol is "made alive" and her illness is "made real" in nearly every review and discussion of the film in order to disavow the "technological gimmick" that the film itself insists that it is. A laudable exception is Susan Potter, who incisively observes that by "refusing Carol any past, and denying the viewer any knowledge of her current state of mind, *Safe* has been criticized for the distance it establishes between protagonist and audience and the emotional flatness of the lead character, as if these were insufficiencies rather than keys to understanding the film's counter-logic" (2004, 138). Haynes's counter-logic is grounded in film theory's criticisms of narrative cinema. "There's this aspect of creating narratives in a commercial sense that I hate," Haynes emphatically asserts, "and you see it in so many ways in movies over and over and over again: the need to create a likeable central character with quirks and interesting things to say. It's a horrible mirroring of the need to affirm who we are through stories. . . . I hate it" (quoted in Wyatt 1993, 5).

Safe conveys this hatred for the "horrible mirroring" of narrative film in what Gross describes as its "exceptionally aggressive" visual style—its uncannily balanced framing, multiple static long takes, eerie synth score, slow tracking shots, and ambient Lynchian sound effects (2014, 65). Its aesthetics point not to Sirk (whose films are predominantly classic love stories) but to Michelangelo Antonioni's *Red Desert* (1964), from which *Safe*'s cinematographer Alex Nepomniaschy drew visual inspiration. The art film's antagonism toward dominant cinema provides a more accurate film-historical context for Carol's "emotional flatness." Challenging critics who pan the film for Carol's "utterly unremarkable personality," Anat Pick equates *Safe* with Barbara Loden's *Wanda* (1970) in their shared "flatness of character ... in defiance of mainstream cinema's realist (humanist) illusion" (2007, 148–50). Pick also calls out Grundmann for failing to discern "the film's powerful feminist critique of a culture that assaults women's bodies" (148–49). In fact, Grundmann accuses Haynes of victimizing his female protagonist, lumping him in with straight Hollywood filmmakers. Still, Pick accepts the premise underlying Grundmann's criticisms, focusing her analysis on "Carol's personal abstractness" (150), even as she asserts *Safe* "locates meaning in the exteriority of filmic surfaces, rather than the psychological depth of the characters" (145). Pick builds her claims about the film around the question of Carol's agency, "making her real" and "alive" in her discussion of the film that goes beyond plot details: "Carol is similarly incapable of *asserting herself* amongst her peers" (150; emphasis added). Indeed, for Pick, Carol not only has agency, she is a "Cartesian subject" (147).

Despite the film's alienating techniques, Pick holds tight to Carol's "singularity," affirming her "transcendental subjectivity" to ground her claims about the film's effects: "By sheer inversion of the norm, remoteness and emotion miraculously coincide.... The result is emotionally engaging ... and ultimately brings us closer ... to the emotional plight of their characters" (2007, 152). For many, of course, such a miraculous viewing experience did *not* take place, borne out by *Safe*'s box office numbers, which remain Haynes's lowest to date. Ultimately, the approbation Pick bestows on *Safe* is just the other side of the coin to Grundmann's and others' opprobrium—and both sides are dependent on the perceived measure of emotional engagement with Haynes's protagonist, asserting identification (or not) with Carol's "emotional plight." These sorts of conundrums are precisely the kind Haynes's films provoke. If *Superstar* proved that spectators could identify with an "ensemble of plastic" because "the power of narrative form ... seduce[d] people into feeling," as Haynes assesses, then *Safe* aims for the opposite effect: "Urged on by these kind of reactions [to *Superstar*], *Safe* proceeds to challenge identification at almost every level" (Haynes 2003, ix). In *Safe*, function follows form. Haynes addresses the chaos of illness *because* it "completely undermines identity" and thus works as a synecdoche for the film's counter-logic (quoted in Schorr 2014, 44).

The absence of mechanisms of identification, attenuation of plot, and baroque aesthetics in *Safe* work to disrupt narrative cinema's "perfect system," impelling viewers to think more about "what they are seeing"; yet, the "why" remains elusive, even when "who's telling them what and why" makes it plain. Following an abstruse question posed by Gross (but not Haynes's response to it), Pick awkwardly asserts: "Yet whatever the authorial intention, there is little doubt that the [film] exercise[s] . . . [a] deliberate fascination over its spectators" (2007, 153). Critics of the film, however, *have* cast doubt on this totalizing claim, and Haynes's intention for the film goes some way toward explaining why. Haynes's authorial intention, in fact, haunts Pick's discussion in symptomatic ways: at times Pick claims others' ideas as Haynes's own, as when she states, "Haynes' concern is . . . with questions of embodiment," and follows it with a citation from Roddy Reid (149). There is a bit of shell game going on in Pick's discussion, with Reid's or others' critical commentary *on* the film standing in for "authorial intention." The director's motivations appear only in a lengthy citation about *Far from Heaven*—a film Pick does not discuss—that precedes her telltale dismissal of authorial intention (152). So what is it about Haynes's intentions for *Safe* that demand disavowal when they are asserted by Haynes directly, or bait-and-switch tactics even when they are not stated? At a different moment in the Gross interview—one that is quite jarring in tone—Haynes adamantly declares his intentions for *Safe*: "If the film is constructed with any kind of target, it targets that unbelievably persistent 'warm feeling' in Hollywood filmmaking that every clumsy narrative is moving towards achieving in the last five minutes, where the central character is really the director, is really the writer, is really you and we're all the guys and we're all in together, and we get the girl and feel so good about life. It's so upsetting to me, I can't tell you. It's such a fucking lie and that's what I wanted to dispel in most of the films I've made" (2014, 71). With such a proclamation (originally published in 1995), it seems truly bizarre that Grundmann would accuse Haynes of the same misogyny as straight male Hollywood directors, not recognizing that this is the very thing Haynes seeks to vilify in the film (1995, 24). It is little wonder, however, that many critics were frustrated with Carol's remoteness; in that audiences don't "get the girl and feel so good about life" by the end, *Safe* pointedly "fails" to provide the "warm feeling" granted by Hollywood filmmaking.

Although critical writing on the film rarely cites this "target," those who criticize the film for Carol's impenetrability seem to apprehend Haynes's intention to dispel this "lie," even if they are reticent to confront what lies behind it, the "gimmick" of cinema itself.[4] A common defense against the ontological unreality of the cinema, of course, is the much-theorized practice of disavowal ("I know very well, but all the same . . ."), evident in the claims concerning Carol's emptiness as *her* punishment rather than their own (in the identification denied them). If most spectators, including critics and reviewers, do not want to have cinema's "gimmick" and narrative film's "lie" exposed, it is because doing so in effect bars them from the very "visual pleasure" Laura Mulvey famously decried in her 1975 feminist polemic, where she condemns, as Haynes does, narrative cinema for creating "a gaze, a world and an object . . . cut to the measure of [male] desire" (Mulvey 1986, 208). Those who laud the film avoid this by endowing Carol with a depth and dimensionality the film otherwise denies them. Notably, though, because *Safe* itself does not provide this depth in its narrative or formal mechanisms, both those who laud the film and those who pillory it frequently prop their claims about Carol by analogizing her with protagonists from other films (and literature), drawing on the film's many cinematic allusions. But in so doing, the "why" of *Safe* is frequently mystified by other directors' objectives, such as the Sirkian context, which is asserted in Pick's chosen citation from Haynes on *Far from Heaven* (but not one on *Safe* itself).

Haynes props *Safe*'s purposeful "lie" on the cinematic lies of "Hollywood filmmaking" in order to expose them; yet this "target," the reason for *Safe*'s different sort of lie, remains unexamined in most discussions of the film's cinematic intertextuality. *Safe*'s allusions are so extensive, in fact, that the film cannot help but be read as allegory, as John David Rhodes avers: "The text that allegorically models itself on an antecedent text is paying homage and declaring a debt to the earlier text, but also attempting to supersede it" (2007, 69). The film's proliferating allusions create a polysemic text that begs the question: To whom is Haynes indebted? Identifying this debt poses important questions about feminist history and its erasure. Pick glosses this debt when she picks up on an altogether different tradition—one that utilized art cinema's formalistic break with dominant cinema to confront Hollywood's "fucking lie": "Haynes' petrified heroines recall a tradition of feminist cinema which has used exteriority and impenetrability strategically as part of its social and cinematic critique" (2007, 150). She turns to Barbara Loden as one example, but by the next page she pivots to Herman Melville's "Bartleby, the Scrivener" to resubstantialize Carol in the comparison, and thus the film's "*cinematic* critique" dissipates. *Safe*'s "social critique" is of cinema itself, lying on purpose in order to refuse to allow this film to be yet another "machine" reiterating and reciprocating heteropatriarchal (cinematic) structures. This refusal, however, depends wholly on the legibility of its image-repertoire.

"A Formative Jolt of Inspiration," or The Influence of Anxiety

As Mary Ann Doane stresses in her discussion of *Safe*, "the force of the image, its legibility, and even its radicality are dependent on its recognizability and its effect of immediacy" (2004b, 13). What Haynes *does* in *Safe* is contingent on the recognition of its debt. That is, its feminist allegory depends on the discernibility of the feminist film praxis that so powerfully influenced Haynes: "I remember Sally Potter's *Thriller* (1979) as a turning point; and I remember *Riddles of the Sphinx* (1977) by Laura Mulvey and Peter Wollen—feature-length, but experimental in every other way.... These films were beginning to work with commercial genres and to make direct references to popular culture using the experimental vernacular" (in MacDonald 2014, 153–54). *Safe* may evoke "commercial genres," but it bears the clear imprint of the experimental vernacular of feminist filmmaking of the seventies, sharing with his previous film *Superstar* a narrative focus on illness set in an "extreme" form of storytelling. *Thriller* clearly influenced both films, which follow Potter's lead in exposing the "lie" of women as romanticized victims through its deconstruction of the function of Mimi's illness and death in Puccini's *La Bohème* (1895). By setting its tale of a woman's "hysteria," as Haynes identifies it, specifically in 1987, however, *Safe* resituates feminist questions about narratives of women's illness in terms of the historical determinants in effect at the end of the millennium (Schorr 2014, 44). "With the economic poverty and precariousness of neoliberalism, the loss of socialist aspiration, and the massive rise of religion of all kinds," as Mulvey observes, "women are newly vulnerable" (2015, 20). It is these "new" forms of vulnerability that *Safe* presciently anatomizes—from an illness directly tied to consumerism (e.g., the black sofa) to its turn to Louise Hay's religion of individual responsibility at Wrenwood that dovetails neatly with neoliberalism's logics. Although most critics take for granted Carol's "privilege" as a beneficiary of global capitalism, the framework of second-wave feminism reminds us of its contingency—that she is wholly dependent on her husband, and that divorce would certainly expel her from Greg's social class if not cast her into poverty, disabled as she is by illness.[5] Haynes has increasingly clarified women's marital precarity in his work, from *Far from Heaven* (2002), in which the dialogue specifies that the Whitakers have little savings and Frank's "job [is] on the line" if he is found out, to *Mildred Pierce* (2011), in which it drives the plot, as Patrick Flanery details in this volume.

Haynes's stylistic evocation of 1970s women's cinema insinuates such second-wave arguments, recalling the first "anti-social" theorists who targeted, if not the figure of the child, then the family itself and women's exploitation within it (see Barrett and McIntosh 1982). By the time of *Safe*'s release, however, right-wing rhetoric had quelled these arguments, and feminist academic communities had dismissed them as essentialist. As Clare Hemmings explicates in her analysis of the temporality of Western feminist narratives, "a common technique of rendering the present more sophisticated and multiple than the past" is to demonize "the 1970s as anachronistic and essentialist," constructing divisions by decade to produce a "forward momentum" that the reader is impelled to identify with or "risk being labeled essentialist or anachronistic[, which is] . . . a more precise anxiety of being understood as racist; this historiographic narrative tactic more than any other ensures a Western feminist disidentification with its imagined past" (2011, 44). Of course, Haynes left the institution in the late 1980s, and thus his filmmaking stands apart from these pressures, if not from the stories told about feminism itself. Haynes's end-of-the-century films, following *Safe* with *Velvet Goldmine* (1998), insinuate what was lost in the dramatic historical changes from the 1970s to the 1990s, as collaborator Jim Lyons explains: "There's a clear nostalgia for [the seventies] when we believed that we were going to have a better and better society, and that feminism would win" (quoted in Taubin 2014, 79–80). Despite *Velvet Goldmine*'s exuberance, for example, the film nevertheless pines for "old kinds of politics pliably reconceived," as Nick Davis contends in his historiography of the film (2013, 246). *Safe* is temporally and thematically contiguous with *Velvet Goldmine* in this way, as both, in their dire representations of the 1980s, adumbrate Haynes's belief that "the seventies were one of the last progressive moments" and insinuate "how things have changed so horribly since then" (quoted in Taubin 2014, 80).

To this extent, *Safe* evokes a very specific set of feminist questions that are not about individual agency but rather its opposite: psychoanalytic feminism and its elaboration of sexual difference. Haynes often evokes Mulvey's name as a shorthand for the theory he had to learn "before you could make a movie," which included, "Marxism, feminism, or psychoanalysis" (quoted in Lantos 2014, 14).[6] The latter two directly impacted Haynes's artwork, which became "deconstructive . . . taking on representation in a semi-antagonistic or investigatory way. A lot of feminist questions were played out against images of women"; Haynes attests that *Safe* was made in much the same way: "It was like, I have a blueprint, a concept, an idea. . . . Films like *Safe* and

Superstar were more conceptually conceived" (quoted in J. C. Mitchell 2014, 88). The concepts behind *Safe* can be traced back to feminist film theory and its turn to psychoanalysis as a weapon used to dismantle the patriarchal structures endemic to narrative cinema. Yet, as Mulvey herself identifies, by the time of the film's release, psychoanalytically inflected critiques of narrative cinema "had lost whatever currency they might once have had. As feminist film theory moved forward to engage with and benefit from ideas associated with the politics of race and queer theory, 1970s film feminism was left looking somewhat white and heterosexual" (2015, 18). *Safe*'s conceptual apparatus predates this move "forward" to "the politics of race," as Jigna Desai and Danielle Bouchard make clear here and elsewhere (2005), but also to "queer theory," reflecting instead ideas Haynes encountered in courses Doane and others taught at Brown. *Safe* and *Superstar*, for instance, fall into the medical discourse subgenre Doane anatomizes in her work on the woman's film. Both center on "the constitution of the female body as symptomatic and hence the vehicle of hysteria," with the woman's illness "threaten[ing] to disrupt the very process of narrativity" (Doane 1987, 48, 58). Haynes amplifies this disruption in his experiments with form and narrative that reject the conventions of the classical woman's film.

In discussing *Safe*, Haynes avers that it "refutes the sense we make of identity, the sense we make of cures," by impelling the spectator to search for a cause or a cure that never manifests (quoted in Gross 2014, 71). This fosters a sense of paranoia in the spectator, borrowing from that other subgenre of the woman's film, the paranoid gothic. In paranoid films, "a certain despecularization takes place . . . , a deflection of scopophilic energy in other directions, away from the female body. . . . The very process of seeing is now invested with fear, anxiety, horror precisely because it is objectless, free-floating" (Doane 1987, 129). Haynes's formal choices are thus enchained to some of the most disruptive narrative tropes of the woman's film in order to render cinematic conventions suspicious and threatening. In describing this mechanism in *Safe*, Haynes admits that "Carol is kept at bay from the viewer. . . . The feeling of removal is furthered by the fact that there are very few close-ups of Carol. It is quietly horrific" (quoted in Schorr 2014, 45). This removal heightens paranoia, which has the effect of transposing the suffering at the core of the woman's film onto the spectator.

This transference of paranoia onto the spectator occurs because, more than any other subgenre of the woman's film, the paranoid gothic evokes "the ever-present sense of being on display for the gaze of a judgmental other," which, as Doane suggests, "is symptomatic of another condition within our culture as well—that of femininity. There is a sense then in which paranoia is only a hyperbolization of the 'normal' female function of exhibitionism and its attachment to the affect of fear" (1987, 126). By attaching fear to the specularization of woman, the paranoid gothic facilitates the interrogation of cinema's dependence on her image. Of course, the classical version ultimately undercuts this critical positioning with the imposition of the Hollywood ending—not so in Haynes's *Safe*, which adamantly refuses it. *Safe* adopts and amplifies some of the most disruptive elements of the paranoid gothic and the medical discourse subgenres of the woman's film of the 1940s, as Doane (1987) identifies them. In so doing, I suggest, Haynes intimates a different sort of lineage for feminist counter-cinema than that traced by Linda Williams: "The most effective feminist films of recent years have been those works—like Sally Potter's *Thriller*, Michelle Citron's *Daughter Rite*, and Chantal Akerman's *Jeanne Dielman* . . . — that work *within and against* the expectations of female self-sacrifice experienced in maternal melodrama" (2000, 500, emphasis in the original). These films are foundational to the canon of feminist counter-cinema, but not because they repurpose the "self-sacrifice" of the maternal melodrama. Rather, they create anxiety for the spectator around the specularization of the woman and thus redirect paranoia back on to the cinema itself—and onto the spectator's "visual pleasure." Indeed, Potter's *Thriller* exemplifies this paranoia as it reframes Mimi's illness and death not as "self-sacrifice," but as a murder to be investigated (and she is not a mother).

Whereas the idea driving *Safe* is a rightfully paranoid interrogation of cinema's reciprocation of patriarchal ideology so that we may begin to question "narrative film's . . . most frightening" and "worst aspects," Haynes found his "blueprint" for doing so in Akerman: "A Chantal Akerman film is a real inspiration because it's so restrained and resistant. . . . It creates a suspense and curiosity, and a huge role for the viewer in the telling" (quoted in MacLean 2014, 56). Certainly *Thriller* is foundational to both *Superstar* and *Safe*, yet *Safe*'s primary "antecedent text" is inarguable; Haynes has repeatedly avowed that Akerman was his "formative jolt of inspiration" (2015). Doane, who introduced Haynes to *Jeanne Dielman, 23 quai du Commerce, 1080 Brussels* (1975) and other "extreme" experimental cinema, observes: "There are multiple ways in which *Safe* resembles Chantal Akerman's portrait of a housewife in *Jeanne Dielman* but preeminently, perhaps, in its tone and relation to duration. Both films have a flatness of tone leaving the central character virtually without affect" (2004b, 8). It is this flatness that evokes Akerman's masterful minimalist work, with its tension and anxiety transferred to the spectator with every slight glitch in Jeanne's routine. In its "extreme" hyperrealism and formal experimentation, *Safe* follows the path carved out by Akerman, whose work "venture[d] into the highly risky business of redefining aesthetic and formal knowledge" (de Lauretis 1987, 134). This risk, however, is at the very least mitigated if not quashed outright if the feminist image-repertoire *Safe* cites remains elusive or, worse, is actively suppressed. At the New York Film Festival in 2015, Haynes dedicated his screening of *Carol* to Akerman: "The weight of [Akerman's] loss is still being understood if it can be. But everyone who knows her work and has seen *Jeanne Dielman* [can remember] what that first experience was. It was profound ... and so inspiring.... Certainly, when it came to *Safe*, it was a seminal film I couldn't *not* think about" (quoted in Laffly 2015). The crucial point here is that her loss is significant only to those "who *know her work*" and the work of other feminist filmmakers who took such risks.

She's Not There: A Feminist Plea for *Safe* Spaces

Reconsidering the film today, this loss is more bitter still, as many who made *Safe* possible in their innovative feminist filmmaking have recently passed away, including Barbara Hammer, Agnes Varda, Carolee Schneeman, and Yannick Bellon, and knowledge of their films grows increasingly obscure. Despite Haynes's insistence on Akerman's influence, for example, she has been disturbingly absent from some of the most canonical criticism on *Safe*. This absence is not simply an oversight on the part of critics—which, with the wealth of interviews with Haynes in which he names Akerman, seems more like willful ignorance—it is part and parcel of the continued excision of women and their contributions to culture. In this way, the paranoid woman's film is truly "meta-textual" in its "narrativized paranoia" in stories about men gaslighting or even murdering women; feminist counter-cinema builds on these narratives to allegorize the "anxieties linked to the muteness of the woman, her exclusion from language," and thus her exclusion from culture (Doane 1987, 126, 148). Exclusion and muteness define women within film and within the discourses produced about film and media, realities epitomized in the iconic image from *Thriller* of Mimi, artist Rodolfo's "muse," with her hand over her mouth in fear and horror. In the wake of the Weinstein revelations, many are now calling "time's up" on the ways women in media industries are rendered mute as artists, relegated only to "muse" or "inspiration" (Moore 2018).[7] Haynes, of course, has declared Akerman an "inspiration" on more than one occasion, and so Eric de Kuyper, Akerman's collaborator, may be thinking of *Safe* when he notes how she "has been copied in many ways and there are some pseudo-Akerman films around," begging the question of how to begin to repay the debt owed to her (de Kuyper and van den Oever 2015).

De Kuyper underscores the conditions that support filmmakers like Akerman: "What is needed is just that one voice welcoming a new talent.... Only recently, an important Flemish critic, Patrick Duynslager, admitted that he had not recognized the talent of Chantal at the beginning. That's a shame. He should have! That was his job, as it was my job" (de Kuyper and van den Oever, 2015). The role of the critic is a crucial one—it can sustain and support feminist filmmakers, or relegate them to the margins of film history. This important role of the critic is precisely why Lesage proposed that part of the project of feminist film criticism was to feed "the growing appreciation of long-neglected women's films," but its goals were more ambitious than this: "Such criticism should have an effect on other institutions as well, hopefully especially on the production and distribution of films ... feminist criticism can bring neglected films to our attention and also demythologize some of cinema's traditional heroes and themes" (Lesage 1974, 12–13). As feminist film criticism waned, however, evinced in the brief three-year life span of *Women and Film*, the hoped-for effects also dissipated. Film criticism, like the industry itself, is notoriously male dominated. Although it can be a space for "combat[ing] sexism in the established cinema [and can] help create a new place for women in film," it continues not to be, which is why feminist film journals and organizations such as Women Make Movies arose in the 1970s to fill this void (Lesage 1974, 13). Directly impacted by these institutions and ideas, Haynes continues to fight for this discursive space despite critics' resistance.

Setting the precedent is Gross's interview with Haynes, who protests the interviewer's repeated insistence that *Safe* is more "conventional" than previous films by countering, "Actually, I was looking at movies like *Jeanne Dielman* by Chantal Akerman," to which Gross's tersely responds: "The margins" (2014, 63). Ignoring Haynes's remonstrations, Gross situates *Safe* in "strands of regular filmmaking ... like Hitchcock, Cronenberg, and Polanski" (63). The question of *why* Haynes was looking at *Dielman* is skirted entirely; rather, Akerman is relegated to "the margins," too *ir*regular to merit discussion (66). By repudiating *Safe*'s indebtedness to Akerman's "extreme" filmmaking, the feminist baby is thrown out with the experimental bathwater. Although Haynes counts Hitchcock among the male filmmakers whose works have influenced him, his is an expressly feminist reinterpretation of Hitchcock: "Certain Hollywood films that were made by Cukor or Sirk or Hitchcock are, for feminists, strongly feminist works, although they weren't created by women" (quoted in Laskawy 2014, 21). This difference is a critical one—and one made possible by feminist criticism. Haynes gets at the crux of the difference, protesting that Hitchcock took pleasure in torturing his actresses, that "he got off on it ... [and] made the viewer get off on it and parallel that to what is innately pleasurable in watching movies" (Gross 2014, 64).[8] *Safe*'s target is precisely this "innate" pleasure, evident in the number of critics who panned *Safe* for what amounts to be frustration at Haynes for *not* allowing them to "get off on it," to "get the girl."

Emulating Akerman's distant camerawork in *Dielman*, *Safe* rejects cinematic conventions in its "restrained coverage and distance from the character" (Haynes, quoted in Gross 2014, 62). Yet even critics who recognize *Safe*'s indebtedness to "extreme" seventies cinema often ignore Akerman and the feminist counter-cinema after which Haynes modeled *Safe*. Rhodes, for instance, provides one of the strongest arguments to read *Safe* as allegory through its expansive cinematic allusions: "When we look at an image or a shot from Haynes's films, and in particular in *Safe*, we are also looking through them: either to shots from other films by other directors, or else to other fields of reference" (2007, 68). Yet, for Rhodes, these fields are entirely male, name-checking everyone from Quentin Tarantino to Dante, whereas the "feminists" he nods to remain nameless—except for Mulvey, whose analysis of Sirk he dismisses out of hand: "The interpretive answers offered by Sirk and Sirk criticism may not be the same answers required by *Safe*" (72). While Rhodes is the only one actually comparing Sirk to *Safe*, in fact, Mulvey's "no longer tenable" reading of Sirk, that his "organization of narrative and point of view around the woman's experience" stands as a corrective to male-centered cinema, is precisely the motivation for *Safe* that Haynes repeatedly gives interviewers (cited in Rhodes 2007, 71). In Rhodes's "film historical exegesis," *Safe* transcends "a mere pastiche of Sirk or Fassbinder, of Kubrick or Antonioni," but he neglects the one director Haynes actually repeatedly names—Akerman (76). His discussion of Fassbinder signals his unwillingness to engage with feminism directly (or "other directors" who happen to be women): "Fassbinder's interest in Sirk was the same interest, one shared by feminist film theorists of the 1970s, in the domestic melodrama as a mode of cultural production that lay bare the contradictions of patriarchal ideology and consumer capitalism" (71). Suspiciously, feminist film theorists only "share" with Fassbinder and Sirk (named, individualized) an "interest" in "patriarchal ideology"—anachronistically applied to Sirk here and speciously identified as an "interest" of Fassbinder's, who openly declared, "I don't make feminist films," in *The Wizard of Babylon* (Dieter Schidor, 1982), and whose sadism toward women is well documented in Rosa von Praunheim's *Fassbinder's Women* (2000).[9] Such a claim is all the more egregious in light of the fact that filmmaker and author Kate Millett (who died a month before Akerman) is rarely ever credited for being the first to "lay bare the contradictions of patriarchal ideology," although the very concept emanates from her groundbreaking feminist work, *Sexual Politics* (1970).

Rhodes's thesis concerning allegory in the circulation of previous images in *Safe* is inarguable; however, he misses the key film history that inspired Haynes's, and one much more accessible (and ubiquitous) in the film than the shot of the drive up to the house before the title credits he discusses. Because this shot vaguely references *Chinese Roulette* (1976), Rhodes insists that Haynes is "letting us know that we must see this film through Fassbinder" (2007, 71). Must we? Rhodes might have picked up "the exegetical gauntlet" *after* the opening credits, which offers an immediately identifiable scene to those familiar with *Dielman* (71). Few films portray heterosexual sex with as much critical and formal distance as the scene that finally reveals Jeanne in bed with one of her regular afternoon clients—and ends with her act of murder. By beginning the story, if not the film, with a scene that mirrors Akerman's penultimate shot of Jeanne's "break," *Safe* announces its feminist counter-logic, one inherited from *Dielman*, which "provid[ed] a radical alternative to traditional narrative cinema's representation of women, and also to conventional cinema itself . . . [signaling] the context of '70s feminist politics" (Margulies 1996, 5). Introducing his feminist allegory with the image of Carol lying beneath her husband, patting his back distractedly while he finishes climaxing, Haynes, like Akerman before him, links women's sexual alienation to the enervation of narrative form.

There may be no need to see Fassbinder in *Safe*, but not recognizing *Dielman*, and its feminist disquisition, "through" this establishing scene comes at a price. Murray Pomerance's (mis)reading of the scene exemplifies the stakes: "The woman hardly stirred to animality by her mate's eager thrusts but instead coddled and protected by a strong and active body that mediates between her and the world" (2007, 81); and Pomerance returns again to it, describing how "Carol's 'safety' under her naked husband is presumably a pleasurable one" (84). One might well ask: Who is presuming this "pleasure"? Pomerance turns a blind eye to the fact that Carol's sickness provides the grounds for her rejection of any further "pleasure" and "protection" her husband offers, to the point of actually vomiting when he touches her, and gives her the excuse by which to flee marriage bed, home, and husband. He passingly mentions that the film may be about "the perils of being a woman in a man's world," but he never puts any stock in this, as he is too preoccupied with chastising Carol for the social class she represents—despite the fact that she has no income or resources of her own (80). Pomerance sees in *Safe*'s "charming yellow flowers" a literary allusion to "lotosland" rather than the 1892 feminist short story by Charlotte Perkins Gilman the film quite literally cites, *The Yellow Wallpaper* (1997) (Carol at Wrenwood: "I remember yellow wallpaper"), a novella famous for articulating the perils of being a (sick) woman controlled by her doctor husband (86). Only by systematically ignoring the many feminist references in *Safe* can Pomerance insist that Haynes wants us "to see the copulation as 'erotic' and 'pleasurable'" (85–86). Certainly, no viewer who looks "through" this image to its obvious field of reference, Akerman's *Dielman*, would ever make such a tendentious claim, because the latter's identical scenario ends with Jeanne stabbing with a pair of scissors "the strong and active body" that was just "coddling" her.

Pomerance's thesis is that Haynes is uncritical of the bourgeois world he portrays, that the filmmaker "is socio-politically naïve in his authorial stance," "seduced" by the very class privilege he films, and therefore betrays a "lack of critical reflection upon the dangers he systematically depicts" (2007, 86). Yet Pomerance, I would suggest, "being himself a blithe inhabitant of the same zone" which Greg occupies—that of "salient [straight] masculinity"—would rather accuse Haynes of ignorant complicity than take the film's "masculine-phobic" critique of heteropatriarchy at face value (85, 82). Akerman sketches out the invisible topography of this zone in *Dielman*, in which she carefully details the affective labor and sexual economies required of women in order to maintain some semblance of middle-class respectability. Jeanne and Carol are just so many "Garbos" in Pomerance's glib dismissal, but Akerman, and Haynes following her, understand that "they have become exquisitely sensitive to the slightest nuances of pressure, social and biological," because their precarious position in heteropatriarchy—their lives and their livelihoods—depends on it (82). Central to the social analyses produced by 1970s radical and lesbian feminism was the recognition that this "sensitivity" is the result of a lifetime of threat, deprival, sanction, and constraint—from the denial of secure income to the fear of sexual harassment and violence—frequently interconnected, as the revelations of the #MeToo movement reveal anew.

Refusing to laugh at Greg's friend's misogynist joke, which arguably is the first sign of her "illness"; expressing no desire for her husband and rejecting his advances; and suffocating when a child is near her renders claims to Carol's "sexual normativity" suspect (Bouchard and Desai 2015, 370).[10] *Safe*, however, critically reflects not on same-sex desire but on the ideology that renders such desire unthinkable, especially for women. Adrienne Rich identified the "nuances of pressure, social and biological," shaping women's lives as the interlocking structures constitutive of the political institution of compulsory heterosexuality: "the pervasive cluster of forces, ranging from physical brutality to control of consciousness, which ... have convinced [women] that marriage, and sexual orientation toward men, are inevitable—even if unsatisfying or oppressive components of their lives" (1980, 640). *Safe* is "hetero-phobic" *because* it is "patriarch-phobic," indicting compulsory heterosexuality, defined in part by "the economic imperative to heterosexuality and marriage" that leaves few alternatives for women (e.g., Jeanne's prostitution) (634). Michael DeAngelis argues that "Haynes has developed narrative strategies ... to express something integral to a uniquely queer experience" (2004, 42); yet his queering of "heterosexual, mainstream narrative cinema by making whatever might be familiar or normal about it strange" is not "new" or "unique," but rather owes much to the radical praxis of women's cinema, which arose two decades earlier with the aim of creating "new times and spaces that exist apart from, and in opposition to, dominant, patriarchal culture" (42). Jeanne's "biological" response (having an orgasm) and Carol's social "sensitivity" (rage at the sexist joke) symbolize how the slightest shift in pressure threatens to expose the extensive repressions and oppressions (desire, anger) required to maintain women's compliance in heteropatriarchal capitalism—a system sustained by Hollywood's "fucking lie," which reifies the ideology of heterosexual romance ("getting the girl") that mystifies compulsory heterosexuality.

These shared feminist themes are conveyed in visual parallels that occur throughout *Safe*, as Haynes insists: "*Dielman* ... is so much about the power of the small action. I was trying to do that with *Safe*—reduce the level of activity and crisis, so that smaller things would have a bigger impact" (quoted in Lim 2014, 106). With scenes of Carol sitting, staring, often drinking milk in inexplicably static long takes, *Safe* replicates shots of Dielman sitting in her kitchen or, especially, the extended sequence following the murder which concludes the film (figures 5.2 and 5.3). The

5.2 *Safe* cites *Jeanne Dielman* in its wealth of cinematic allusion, doubling shots from Akerman's masterwork of "extreme" filmmaking in its feminist allegory.

5.3 Chantal Akerman's hyperrealism allows for the formal interrogation of cinematic language.

much-discussed ending of *Safe*, with Carol speaking to herself in the mirror of her sterile igloo, completes the homage to Akerman, although it is most prey to interpretations of content precisely when the formal allegory reaches its apex. Carol looks in the mirror in an extensive static long take, evoking Akerman's first film, *L'enfant aimé ou je joue à être une femme mariée* (1971), in which a young wife examines her body in the mirror—a scene so important to Akerman that she would revisit it in her installation piece, *In the Mirror* (1971/2007). At the same time, Carol also looks directly into the camera at "us," alluding to another work by Akerman: "*La Chambre* (1972) is a ten-minute silent . . . in which a camera surveys a small apartment [occupied by] . . . a young woman . . . who looks directly at us (the visual field occupied by the camera)" (Bergstrom 1999, 27). This direct address harkens back to a privileged moment in seventies feminist film theory—the pivotal scene in Dorothy Arzner's *Dance, Girl, Dance* (1940) in which the protagonist Judy O'Brien, a ballerina forced to dance in a burlesque show, addresses the camera under the guise of confronting her diegetic audience "and has the effect of directly challenging the entire notion of woman as spectacle" (Johnston 2000, 31). Carol's bruised, gaunt, and affectless face staring back at us is offered in lieu of Judy's accusation, but much to the same end.

Whereas Arzner's scene provides a momentary rupture in the classical Hollywood form, it is Akerman who fulfills the promise of feminist counter-cinema: "It is not enough to discuss the oppression of women with the text of the film; the language of the cinema/the depiction of reality must also be interrogated, so that a break between ideology and text is effected" (Johnston 2000, 30). The conclusion of *Safe* mimics *Dielman* in its formal interrogation of cinematic language. In the latter, the murder stands as a hackneyed element imported from narrative fiction film intruding on Akerman's minimalist art cinema. *Safe* follows suit by awkwardly evoking that other narrative cinema cliché, the final "I love you." In her aptly named *Nothing Happens*, Ivone Margulies unpacks the role of cliché in Akerman's work: "The notion of cliché is helpful in understanding the subversive powers of cinematic hyperrealism. . . . [It] refers to a platitude, a phrase flattened out by repeated use. . . . Its potential effectiveness in film lies in the recognition of the difference that the cliché can meaningfully suggest" (1996, 84). Like the murder, Carol's "I love you" is a narrative platitude confronting us with the banality and stultifying violence of narrative cinema's representational systems (the final "I love you" signaling getting the girl), including identification—the "horrible mirror." Its indebtedness to *Dielman* is clear, as it bookends its opening scenes of affectless sex with the final scene of Akerman's film in which Jeanne just sits doing nothing (after the murder) for more than three minutes. After Carol's final line, the script concludes: "Nothing happens. Hard cut to black" (Haynes 2003, 180).

If *Safe* is Haynes's "pseudo-Akerman" film, it surely exceeds "mere pastiche." Rather, it reminds us of the profoundly important interventions of feminist counter-cinema and of Akerman's redefinition of aesthetic and formal knowledge specifically. "She changed non-commercial, avant-garde, and experimental cinema," de Kuyper insists, and in doing so, "her impact was evident," but when Akerman is ignored by film critics and erased from film history, her impact is diminished; fewer and fewer get to know her work and what it accomplished (de Kuyper and van den Oever 2015). *Safe*'s homage to feminist counter-cinema and the film theory it embodied leads us unremittingly back to Akerman, who models, as de Lauretis characterizes it, "the project of transforming vision by inventing the forms and processes of representation of a social subject, women, that... has been all but unrepresentable" (1987, 145). Film criticism needs to aid in this project—and can start by *listening* to filmmakers like Haynes, as it is too late to listen to Akerman herself; as de Kuyper admonishes, it is "a shame" more critics did not "recognize" her work while she was alive. Feminist film criticism first emerged to recognize and extend the project of women's cinema, being shaped by and contributing to the broader social critique developed by seventies feminism. As Lesage explains, "feminist film criticism, in attacking sexism and promoting women's films," as I have tried to model with this metacritical intervention, "will hopefully have a favorable effect on the milieu" (1974, 13). It undoubtedly had a significant effect on Haynes, as he stresses in his many discussions of the film—discussions that repeatedly articulate *Safe*'s "patriarch-phobic" meanings while promoting the contributions of women such as Akerman and Potter to film culture. In doing so, Haynes adjures film critics to do their "job"—to be part of those "processes of representation" that make unrepresentable social subjects visible. This requires doing the work of learning marginalized or repressed film histories and recognizing the work of visionary filmmakers such as Akerman (preferably while they are still alive). "In the context of a broader public awareness" generated by today's feminist activist movements (e.g., #MeToo and Time's Up), my hope, following Lesage, is that once again "we can see an anti-sexist perspective in the work of both men and women critics" and a "criticism [that]... can aid feminist activity" at the present moment and in the feminist future to come (1974, 12–13).

NOTES

1 Although Haynes says he heard little over the years, he knew of Weinstein's predation as early as *Safe* (and continued to work with him anyway): "I heard some stuff before I started working with Harvey. On my second feature film, I had an assistant director who had come from Miramax, and she left. She was an assistant for Harvey Weinstein. That was the first time I ever heard anything" (Montagne 2017).

2 I discuss the history of this intervention and its cultural persistence elsewhere (Geller 2018).

3 See Wilkinson (2017) for an insightful analysis of *Wonder Wheel*.

4 I have seen this quote only in Grossman (2015), who fails to recognize it as a translation of Mulvey's anatomization of primary and secondary identification in the patriarchal ordering of cinematic *form*. Grossman erroneously sums up Haynes's quote as his "attempt to pass judgment on *this aspect* of *ameliorative* mainstream film" (123; emphasis added), circumscribing the scope of his Mulvey-esque argument to plot structure: "We do not identify with Carol White because there is no heroic teleology embedded in her character" (124).

5 See Cunha (2016). After a separation, 27 percent of women fall into poverty; in fact, Cunha's lead example is a woman who becomes impoverished because her husband leaves her due to her medical issues.

6 Freud continues to be an important figure for Haynes, whose "real passion project ... where my heart and soul are anchored"—is a "multi-part, episodic" miniseries on the father of psychoanalysis for Amazon (quoted in Rowin 2019).

7 Akerman was painfully aware of this catch-22; when contacted by an admirer who told her he was inspired by *Jeanne Dielman*, she responded that she should be paid for her inspiration, poignantly asking why "so many people told [*sic*] me that I had influenced them and I don't see a penny" (Emily 2015).

8 "Female fear is apparently arousing: think of Hitchcock or Roman Polanski" (Moore 2018).

9 *Fassbinder's Women* was originally titled *Fassbinder Was the Only One for Me: The Willing Victims of Rainer Werner F.* Fassbinder's films are beloved by feminists, but he was certainly no friend to women (or to many men), as Ryan Gilbey (2017) details in his interview with Hanna Schygulla, who tells of Fassbinder pressuring actors into sex and personally intervening to ensure *she was paid less* than her male costar on his 1981 wartime melodrama *Lili Marleen*.

10 In her painfully attenuated access to language, and in the ways her illness forces viewers to confront the meaninglessness of the death drive, Carol incarnates an antisocial queer femininity, "one that does not speak in the language of action and momentum but ... in terms of evacuation, refusal, passivity, unbecoming, unbeing" (Halberstam 2011, 129, 144). For an elaboration of this argument, see Maynard and Geller in this volume.

PART II

Intersections and Interventions

6 "Toxins in the Atmosphere"
Reanimating the Feminist *Poison*

Jess Issacharoff

Todd Haynes's first feature, *Poison* (1991), is generally cited as a foundational entry into New Queer Cinema. The body of work Haynes has produced since *Poison* is marked by a persistent and overriding attention to the place of women under patriarchy, as seen in films like *Safe* (1995) and *Far from Heaven* (2002), and in the HBO miniseries *Mildred Pierce* (2011). With the benefit of hindsight, then, we can recognize that *Poison* represents a crucial step in the development of Haynes's feminist film practice. Resituating Haynes's first film in the history of feminist film criticism and practice requires a restaging of Haynes's work and a consideration of its theoretical and political contexts and concerns, some of which have been obscured by its canonization in New Queer Cinema. This process means both recovering the often-overlooked female characters central to *Poison*'s three-part narrative and developing a critique of the erasure of women from prior critical engagements with the film.

In reframing *Poison* in this context, I would like to consider the film alongside feminist film theory and queer theoretical texts from the same period, which work with and through its feminist foundations. Situating *Poison* as a theoretical text in conversation with and highly influenced by feminist theory requires a reconsideration through close reading. In departing from the dominant New Queer Cinema reading of *Poison*, with its focus on "Homo," one of the three segments in the film, and the only one without female characters, this chapter only briefly rethinks "Homo," focusing centrally on the other two segments, "Horror" and "Hero." In reading these segments in particular, this chapter reanimates the feminist themes of the film and the under-investigated considerations of the female body and its relation to the domestic space, constructions of femininity, and patriarchal power structures. *Poison* both highlights these turbulent relations and offers modes of resistance, particularly through a model of cross-identification and collaboration between the figure of the mother and the queer child.

In retracing *Poison*'s queer critique alongside feminist influences, I hope to recover in *Poison* a queer theory that does not, as Janet Halley (2006) suggests, take a break from feminism, but rather stages a return to feminist foundations and those foundational figures who straddle the apparent divides separating film theory, queer theory, and feminist theory: B. Ruby Rich, Biddy Martin, and Mary Ann Doane. *Poison* also models an important feature of queer histories—the partnership between gay men and women, both lesbian and straight. In tracing Haynes's relation to feminist theory, his extensive work with Christine Vachon, and the partnerships and cross-identifications portrayed in *Poison*, I resituate the film not only as building on the previously established commitment to feminist filmmaking practice in Haynes's work, but moreover as crucially exploring the familial relationship between feminist and queer theory writ large, through an ethics of cross-gender identification.

Poison at the Box Office: Context and Reception

Although Haynes gained some recognition with *Superstar: The Karen Carpenter Story* (1987), it was *Poison*, his first feature film, which brought the initial wave of critical attention to his work. *Superstar* remained essentially a footnote to the splash that *Poison* made, both popularly and critically, cementing his status as an avant-garde filmmaker. The film was the subject of a particularly intense protest by the American Family Association (AFA) because of its partial federal funding, NC-17 rating, and brief depiction of homosexual sex—though Donald Wildmon, founder and former chairman of the AFA, admitted he had not in fact seen the film. The salacious attention garnered Haynes increased visibility and attendance, guaranteeing *Poison*'s place as a crucial text in the critical canon of queer film theory, and strengthened the film's association with New Queer Cinema.

B. Ruby Rich's inclusion of *Poison* in her foundational piece "New Queer Cinema" emphatically situates Haynes within a particular queer movement in avant-garde filmmaking. Rich's article in *Sight and Sound* heralds 1992 as a "watershed year for independent gay and lesbian film and video" (1992, 31). In particular, Rich celebrates a queer panel she hosted at Toronto's Festival of Festivals, which included Haynes as well as his contemporaries Jennie Livingston and Tom Kalin and newly appointed queer elders Derek Jarman and Isaac Julien. The panel presented a noteworthy confluence of the queer avant-garde and the mainstream film festival circuit. The commercial viability of films like *Poison* and the popular attention it received, partially because of antigay protests, positioned Haynes as a central figure in what would from then on be canonized as New Queer Cinema.

Rich's attention both heightened the queer significance of Haynes's work and inadvertently dampened attention to Haynes's feminist foundations, despite his own emphasis on the importance of feminist theory in his work. In a 1993 interview, Haynes credits the growing body of what would become queer theory with emphasizing for him the importance of feminism, noting that "in a way it wasn't until gay theory was ushered in by people like Diana Fuss, identifying the essentialist versus social-constructivist perspectives, that I realized how significant and important feminism is" (Wyatt 1993, 29). Significantly, Wyatt does not pick up on this thread and follows this answer with a quote from the gay magazine *The Advocate*, dubbing *Poison* "the most important gay American film since [Gus Van Sant's 1986] *Mala Noche*" (30). The abrupt shift from feminism to gay film signals the level of attention paid to this aspect of Haynes's archive. Rich pointedly notes a distinct emphasis on "the boys" in the popularization and distribution of the "New Queer Cinema," despite the presence of work by and about lesbians and the influence of figures like Vachon, who coproduced several of the films represented at the panel in Toronto, including *Poison*. Vachon, an out lesbian and prominent figure in independent film, has been a long-term collaborator with Haynes. She has produced all of Haynes's feature films to date as well as many other canonical films of New Queer Cinema by filmmakers such as Tom Kalin and Kimberly Peirce.

Because of the combination of increased interest in Haynes as a queer filmmaker and a simultaneous emphasis on "the boys" as more commercially viable subjects and artists within New Queer Cinema (and cinema as a whole), the women involved in Haynes's work (both behind and in front of the camera) are easily obscured in critical accounts. Thus *Superstar* is relegated to a charming footnote, whereas *Poison* is known as a celebration of violent and aberrant masculine sexuality and a metaphorical rebuke to the stigma of AIDS, both of which it certainly is. Yet this shorthand assessment is not entirely representative of the film's multilayered structure, which takes the form of three interwoven narratives of vastly differing plots and generic styles. "Homo" is a Jean Genet–inspired prison romance shot in dark, almost monochrome, interior shots interspersed with Technicolor flashbacks to outdoor scenes from the narrator John Broom's sojourn at a boy's reformatory. "Horror," which opens the film, is a black-and-white, mad scientist tale of a doctor who discovers a secret potion for "the sex drive" and then, distracted by his attractive female co-worker, accidentally ingests it, causing him to become visibly disfigured and marked a "leper sex murderer." The last narrative, "Hero," is a pseudo-docudrama account of a shocking patricide in a suburban community and the mother's "extraordinary" claim that her son flew out the window after murdering his father. While critical responses to the film rarely treat "Hero" in any depth, presumably because of its perplexing ending and lack of clearly queer contexts, this chapter takes up its narrative as central to a potential restaging of the relationship between gay men and women, and furthermore, between feminist and queer theory.

Early critical accounts of *Poison*'s three-part narrative focus on the erotics of "Homo" and interpret the apparent AIDS parable by way of 1950s sci-fi camp in "Horror" (while ignoring its key character, Nancy Olsen), yet most express mystification when faced with the true crime, news report account of patricide in "Hero." A review by Jonathan Romney (1991) in *Sight and Sound* proclaims "Hero" the "most fascinating section by virtue of its elusiveness" (57). Seemingly confounded by its presence in the triptych, Romney asks, "How does this domestic anecdote relate to the two other stories of sexuality?" (57). This question draws a distinct line between narratives that deal with the domestic and those that deal with sexuality. This delineation, along with Romney's subtle distinction between the "stories" of "Horror" and "Homo" and the "anecdote" of "Hero," make for a troubling portrait of the place of the domestic and the feminine in these queer "stories." Not coincidentally, of the three parts, "Hero" features the most central female character and deals most clearly with feminist themes of domestic abuse and patriarchal subjugation.

Norman Bryson (1999), in a later piece on the film, again deals mostly with the section "Homo," though he also cites the AIDS allegory in "Horror" and the queer child of "Hero." Bryson mentions Nancy Olsen precisely once, referring to her as "Graves's loyal intern." Felicia Beacon, as the witness to Richie's final flight and his abuse at the hands of his father, receives slightly more attention; however, Bryson never names her and refers to her merely as Richie's mother. Jon Savage's (1991) article "Tasteful Tales," also published in *Sight and Sound*, neglects to mention the presence of women in the film at all, apart from a single reference to the "mother" in "Hero." Despite citations of *Superstar*, a film explicitly concerned with women, and *Poison*'s own inclusion of two female protagonists, both pieces focus on the potential of Haynes's work rooted in an explicitly masculine resistance to heterosexual norms, aligning Haynes with what Savage terms "the new hostile homosexual politics" (17).

The themes of antinormative and anti-assimilationist politics were central to queer cultural production in the 1990s. The work of ACT UP in particular influenced theoretical work and prioritized opposition to social norms as crucial to radical political projects. The AIDS crisis of the 1980s lent both queer social movements and theoretical concerns a political urgency. Although AIDS was at first politically construed and largely experienced as a gay man's disease, lesbians were active in ACT UP, and the history of debates over women's health and feminist theories of power and bodily autonomy were significant influences in the development of rhetoric around AIDS activism and in theoretical responses to the crisis. In the introduction to the influential collection of essays *Fear of a Queer Planet*, Michael Warner (1993) recalls, "Feminism has made gender a primary category of the social in a way that makes queer social theory newly imaginable," and he cites the work of Gayle Rubin, Adrienne Rich, Eve Kosofsky Sedgwick, Judith Butler, Iris Marion Young, and others as central to theoretical work on sexuality (viii). Here Warner echoes Haynes's own assertion of the significance of feminist work in his filmmaking. In addition to highlighting the significance of feminist theory, Warner's citations emphasize the feminist credentials of many of the foundational figures of queer theory. *Poison*, however, is frequently read into a queer theory framework that either elides feminist work (even that of Todd Haynes himself) or constitutes itself in opposition to feminism as a fixed and stagnant past.

Poison and Feminist Film Theory

Feminist film theory has long been concerned with the problem of the gaze. Laura Mulvey's foundational essay "Visual Pleasure and Narrative Cinema" (1975) framed the filmic gaze as one that inherently figures the feminine as passive object of scopic pleasure and the only avenue of identification in classical cinema as through the male gaze, which is united with that of the camera. Claire Johnston, on the other hand, argues that the woman is not just passive on the screen, but absent: "Woman represents not herself, but by a process of displacement the male phallus. It is probably true to say that despite the enormous emphasis placed on woman as spectacle in the cinema, woman as woman is largely absent" (1973, 25). This idea poses a significant problem for the potential of feminist filmmaking, to say nothing of the lesbian spectator. Rich comments on this problematic construction in a 1978 discussion of feminist aesthetics with Michelle Citron, Julia Lesage, Judith Mayne, and Anna Marie Taylor. Rich highlights the paradoxical position in which the feminist filmmaker finds herself in light of these critiques: "According to Mulvey, the woman is not visible in the audience which is perceived as male; according to Johnston, the woman is not visible on the screen.... How does one formulate an understanding of a structure that insists on our absence even in the face of our presence? What is there in a film with which a woman viewer identifies? How can the contradictions be used as a critique? And how do all these factors influence what one makes as a woman filmmaker, or specifically as a feminist filmmaker?" (Citron et al. 1978, 87). Woman as both the receiver of the male gaze and in fact absent altogether from representation of the feminine leaves the feminist film project in something of a double bind, unable to formulate a resistance to either the negation of the feminine or the overrepresentation of it as static receptive object of visual pleasure. This double bind can in part explain why *Poison* is so often read into a male-queer project and out of a female-feminist one. This singular reading does a disservice not only to Haynes but also to queer theory, which, along with feminist theory, has a history of structural critique that goes beyond simple identity politics. Haynes has demonstrated, through work like *Superstar* and *Domestic Violence* (discussed further below), a sustained interest in feminist projects that are critically engaged in both feminist subjects and formal experimentation. Although *Poison* is often read out of this history, it should be more properly seen as predicated upon it, in its complex reworking of both feminist and queer approaches to the problematics of identification.

One early moment of both connection and divergence between feminist and queer theory occurs in Eve Sedgwick's influential *Epistemology of the Closet* (1990). Sedgwick marks the closet as structuring signifier in western social formations and in her own life, but she maintains the specificity of its constitutive effects on the lives of queer people. She highlights the signifying force of the coming-out narrative as a broadly structuring metaphor in western epistemology, but she maintains the difference of the queer coming-out as one that does not, according to Sedgwick, maintain a system of gender subordination. For Biddy Martin, this distinction allows Sedgwick to distill a form of sexuality that evades the problem of gender. In her reading of Sedgwick's construction of the closet, Martin problematizes Sedgwick's oppositional reading of gender and sexuality, which signals her desire to distance herself from feminist theory:

> The lack of conceptual clarity in our efforts to distinguish between sex and gender lead her to collapse those two terms. Yet she reacts to the irreducibility of sexuality to gender by making them more distinct, even opposed to one another. This will have the consequence of making sexuality, particularly homo/hetero sexual definition for men, seem strangely exempt from the enmeshments and constraints of gender (read: women), and, thus, even from the body. The result is that lesbians, or women in general, become interesting by making a cross-gender identification or an identification with sexuality, now implicitly (though, I think, not intentionally) associated with men, over against gender and, by extension, feminism and women. Crossing becomes preferable to passing for women, at least in the context of antihomophobic analysis and its challenge to normative feminist identifications. (1994, 107–8)

Martin highlights the one-sidedness of Sedgwick's cross-identification as a de facto position for women seeking to escape the constraints of gender, whereas the same does not seem to be true for gay men.

In fixing sex and gender as entirely distinct and lending to the masculine all the possibility of sexual ambivalence, the feminine remains mired in a fixed gender system. This formulation, according to Martin, recapitulates to the very problematic it sought to escape. In a coauthored piece, Martin and Judith Butler (1994), dealing explicitly with cross-identifications, introduce an alternative model:

> To take cross-identification as a site of departure is precisely not to take for granted the pregiven status of the terms that identifications are said to relate. Even when these terms have, over time, acquired specific forms or contents, processes of identification make what we imagine to be preconstituted forms or contents irretrievable.... Rather than offer a pluralist panoply of "difference," we aim to offer a set of intersecting analyses that work ... to reconsider cross-identification as a critical point of departure and to explore the way in which these fields are mutually implicated in one another. (3)

This point of departure, which figures cross-identification as central while maintaining a critical ambivalence of identity and the instability of the object and the drive of identification itself, is precisely the form of identification *Poison* offers. Keeping this theoretical model in mind, with its potential crossings and yet its constant slippages, I turn to a close reading of the film and its own formulation of this theoretical site of departure. In doing so, I revisit, in particular, those moments and characters that have often been elided in favor of highlighting and canonizing the overtly male-queer content of *Poison*.

Identifying (with) the Feminine: Queer Cross-Identifications

Although this chapter is less concerned with "Homo," I recognize several ways the narrative hinges on gay male identification with the trappings of femininity. The first scene of "Homo," set against the musical score that returns at the end of the film and serves as a leitmotif, follows John Broom as a child running his hands over objects in a room that is presumably not his own. John lingers on a chest of drawers in which he finds an assortment of silken and lacy fabric, which he caresses lovingly. The close-up of his hands in the drawer highlights the forbidden pleasure of this caress. After discarding several other objects, John finally picks up something from the drawer and at that moment gets caught. The mother accuses him of "stealing from her drawers," making clear that the crime of theft is also one of perverse identification with the feminine. This instance of cross-identification is only the first in the film, a relation that seems central to the way it deals with gender and sexuality as both fundamentally unstable and ambivalent and yet mutually constitutive and necessarily in conversation.

John Broom frames prison as a world of masculine and revolutionary potential, proclaiming, "In submitting to prison life, embracing it, I could reject the world that had rejected me." There are no women in this space; however, there are many references to femininity and instances of ritual shaming and sexual play based on feminization. The words *faggot* and *bitch* are used interchangeably, always to describe the receptive "bottom." Furthermore, the dominant and penetrative man (although these are not always necessarily aligned, they absolutely are here) is jokingly told to marry the submissive man, making the latter the presumptive wife. In a flashback sequence to his childhood, we see a mock marriage ceremony in an Edenic garden setting, with John Broom as the bride, complete with lacy veil, recalling the first scene of the narrative described above, in which Broom as a child is caught handling lacy garments, the crime for which he is permanently branded a thief and figuratively marked as homosexual.

In another flashback scene, Jack Bolton is forced to kneel and receive the boys' saliva as they spit into his mouth in a mimicry of ejaculation. The climax of the scene is a shot of Jack eyes closed, mouth open, covered in the boys' semen-like spit. Jack's expression is simultaneously pained and ecstatic as he accepts this treatment with open arms. The shot is both disturbing and erotic. Jack's Christ-like pose, his absolute submission, and the Edenic scenery figure Jack as an almost sublime object of abjection. The chain of signification that links the feminine, the receptive, the abject, and the sublime subtly shifts the simplistic identification of the feminine with subordination into a more complex relation. This cross-identification offers a masculine alternative to Sedgwick's unidirectional cross-identification, framing the feminine as the site of erotic possibility while maintaining its slippery ambivalence as a signifier.

Unlike "Homo," which cites a femininity absent any female-identified character, "Horror" is centrally concerned with the female body, though little critical attention is generally paid to its female characters. The narrative hinges on Nancy Olsen, the doomed assistant and lover of Dr. Thomas Graves. Graves's sexually transmitted disease clearly evokes tropes of AIDS and its representation, though the specificity of Nancy's narrative demands a more complex reading than the B movie–style parable seems to invite. Literalizing the AIDS parable and focusing solely on Graves erases the (dead) bodies of Nancy and the other (nameless) women who bear the brunt of this narrative. "Horror" opens with a narrator's booming voice, trumpeting Graves's lifelong scientific ambitions: "Ever since he was a child Thomas Graves had been hungry for knowledge, hungry to discover all the secrets of the universe. Science, man's sacred quest for truth, was his first and only love." This rationalist and manly pursuit brings Graves to the discovery of the chemical formula of the sex drive, which he claims will revolutionize medicine in several fields other than the sexual. As he succeeds in this momentous discovery, despite the disbelief of his colleagues, his musings on his own success are interrupted by a woman, suggesting immediately the trope of woman as seducer—her love supplants his love for truth and scientific inquiry, leading him to madness and untamed sexuality. The woman is, however, to Graves's surprise, a fellow scientist who wishes to assist him in his work, though it is initially suggested and eventually confirmed that she is a potential romantic partner as well. Nancy Olsen congratulates the doctor on his success and leaves him to record his work. As Nancy walks away, the viewer and Graves are treated to a sustained view of her backside, which is, we are led to believe, what causes Graves, the rational scientist, to be so distracted as to drink from the wrong cup and dose himself with his own concoction of the distilled sex drive.

Nancy, however, has disappeared from view by the time Graves drinks from the fateful cup. Or rather, she should have. The shot of Nancy walking away that plays while Graves reaches for his cup is not the original shot but a looped repetition of it. It is not the filmic body of the woman that is the impetus of the tragic crescendo of the film, but rather its image, summoned up and erotically reiterated from the perspective of the male protagonist. As Graves drinks what the audience knows is the sex drive formula, the camera offers a close-up of his eyes, marking Graves's gaze, rather than the original diegetic narrative, as the conjuror and consumer of Nancy's image. "Horror," which begins with an explicitly masculine quest for truth, interrupts itself not through the body of a woman, but by framing an explicitly male fantasy of a woman. In her conversation with Michelle Citron, Julia Lesage, Judith Mayne, and Anna Marie Taylor, Rich wondered, "How does one formulate an understanding of a structure that insists on our absence even in the face of our presence?" (Citron et al. 1978, 87). In my reading of *Poison*, Haynes posits one solution to Rich's dilemma in this sequence from "Horror," which both insists on the presence of woman while also portraying her absence in the passive object of the gaze. Nancy Olsen is here represented as both character and fantasy. This sequence breaking down the mechanics of the male gaze is followed by a close-up of Graves's eye, along with several shots of the doctor examining his own body. Although his sexed body, and particularly his mouth, is represented as the pathway of the disease he will spread to several women, Graves's eyes are highlighted here, framing as dangerous not just his diseased body but also his gaze.

Nancy finally discovers that Graves is the infamous "leper sex murderer" when a reporter advises people to "be on the lookout for a dark-haired man with intense eyes and a badly infected mouth." The mouth is obvious, though the intense eyes are marked first. As Nancy accuses Graves and then apparently accepts his love, they embrace, and the scene cuts back and forth between close-up shots of their eyes. Throughout the scene, their gazes fail to meet; Nancy first realizes the secret that has eluded her and then fails to see the beginning of the infection that will eventually kill her. Graves, however, does see the infection, though he doesn't tell Nancy as she finally flees, needing space "to think."

6.1 Nancy, dead in her negligee, appears as an eerie apparition of the idealized wife.

When Graves goes after Nancy he passes by a store window and is distracted by his own reflection, in which his face appears smooth and unmarked by the disease. The reflected face turns to an image of Nancy and kisses her, strengthening Graves's resolve to find her. It is this hallucination, compounded by his own fantasy of kissing Nancy, that convinces him they can have a relationship after all, underscoring heterosexuality as the projection of normalcy and the essentially constructed nature of the heterosexual couple. Graves's image of himself is a fantasy projection, just as it was his fantasy vision of Nancy that caused the "accident." Graves finally leaves Nancy dead in her home in a white negligee, an eerie apparition of the idealized wife: domestic, virginal yet sexy, and perfectly passive in death (figure 6.1). The two versions of Nancy, as female subject and as passive object of Graves's fantasy, finally converge in the spectacle of Nancy's corpse. Upon returning to his own home, Graves smashes all reflective surfaces he sees before confronting the mob gathered outside his house. These reflections had previously allowed him access both to the fantasy version of Nancy and his idealized relationship with her, as in the store window, and to the reflection of his face, indicating the death of that fantasy. Graves refuses both in his destruction of the reflective surfaces in his home, paradoxically uniting the two as mirror images of a violent heterosexual domesticity.

Graves as "the leper sex murderer" is explicitly tied to connotations of sexual violence against women, his main victims. The first woman he kills does not die of the disease: he strangles her in order to silence her. Later, when Nancy discovers that Graves is the murderer, the reporter mentions that "counts of sexual violence are also on the rise." The next segment of the narrative portrays Graves running through the nighttime streets seeking Nancy. He sees from afar a man berating and holding onto a blonde woman and approaches, thinking it might be Nancy. The setting of a dark alleyway and the suggestion of intimidation by a stranger conform to scenarios of sexual violence as conceived in the public imaginary, despite the fact that domestic violence and acquaintance rape are far more common. As the couple turns around, however, it is revealed that they are both infected, and the two laugh in Graves's face. This visual trap suggests both a critique of violence inherent in the heterosexual relation and the refusal of the "dark street" cliché as the primary site of this violence, rather than that of the home, where Nancy eventually dies and, as I discuss in the next section, where Felicia and Richie Beacon are abused by the patriarch in "Hero."

Nancy, confirming her scientific prowess, reveals in her final moments that it was "toxins in the atmosphere" that rendered the disease contagious; this discovery radically shifts the source of threat in the narrative. It becomes apparent that it is not exposure to illness through sexual contact with Graves but in fact her environment that kills Nancy Olsen. Although "Horror" contains several hints at a more recognizable or easily policed violence in public spaces, it is the allegedly serene space of the home that is the final scene of Nancy's death, prefiguring Haynes's next film, *Safe*, in which the protagonist is allergic to her environment, as well as later work with Christine Vachon outside his feature films.

In 1996, Vachon and Haynes cocreated an exhibition titled "Domestic Violence," which was displayed at the Wexler Center in Columbus, Ohio. B. Ruby Rich describes the show:

> *Domestic Violence* was a provocative video intervention. . . . Approaching the television set from behind as viewers were required to do, one en-

countered an inexplicable barrage of soundtracks that slowly clarified into excerpts from a canon of famously violent movies. . . . Once on the sofa however, visitors were ambushed by the discovery of a television screen filled, not with the familiar actors in their signature roles, but with a substitute cast of performing cats, dogs and babies. . . . *Domestic Violence* ambushed its audiences at the intersection of sentimentality and outrage, splicing discourses of violence and innocence onto a screen the two were never meant to occupy simultaneously. (2013, 72–73)

Rich describes the shock of viewers at the idea of "innocent" infants and domestic pets being implicated in the violence of these scenes. Rich reads the Vachon and Haynes piece as posing the question, "Does violence really come from outside or within?" (73). Furthermore, this provocation questions not only the sanctity of the family as a social institution, but also the space of the home as well. The title, punning on domestic violence and the domesticated (unthreatening) animals cast in the rewritten scenes of violence, hints at the essential violence of the living room space itself, regardless of the actors in it. The violence is not marked by the domestic, but rather the domestic by violence. Rich connects the title to the violence visited upon queer children in the home, recalling *Dottie Gets Spanked* (1993), though *Poison*, *Superstar*, and *Safe* also highlight feminist critiques of the domestic sphere and its potential as a site of violence. This exhibition further exemplifies a sustained and piercing critique of domestic violence and patriarchy throughout Haynes and Vachon's long partnership.

This emphasis on the violence of the heterosexual domestic scene also marks a shift in the representation of the diseased body. Doane discusses the discursive confluence of disease and the figure of the woman in what she terms "the medical discourse film" of the 1940s: "Disease and the woman have something in common—they are both socially devalued or undesirable, marginalized elements which constantly threaten to infiltrate and contaminate that which is more central, health or masculinity. There is even a sense in which the female body could be said to harbor disease within physical configurations that are enigmatic to the male" (1987, 38). But unlike in the woman's films of the 1940s in which medical discourses blur the boundaries between the (female) body and the somatic, "Horror" upsets the initial visual impression of Graves's diseased body as the site of infection by placing fault on the "atmosphere." In the cultural context of the film's release in 1991, the diseased body most significant within the public imaginary is that of the person with AIDS, generally pictured as male. Leo Bersani (1987), however, similarly draws on the significance of the feminine in medical discourse, noting the "startling resemblance" of "the public discourse about homosexuals since the AIDS crisis began ... to the representation of female prostitutes in the nineteenth century 'as contaminated vessels, conveying "female" venereal diseases to "innocent" men'" (211). "Horror" refuses the pure parity of diseased vessel and innocent victim, stressing instead a diseased *social* body, in which Graves can be both perpetrator of masculine violence and figural victim of AIDS paranoia. Likewise, Nancy's death is neither purely symbolic of the gay male experience of AIDS nor individualized, but rather representative of the death of a victim of a toxic social atmosphere.

The final section, both in this chapter and in the film, likewise takes up a critique of toxic domesticity. "Hero" is the least discussed section of *Poison* and, perhaps unsurprisingly, is the most obviously concerned with a feminist critique of patriarchy and the violence of domestic space. In "Hero," Richie Beacon, whom we can only assume is the hero referenced by the title, murders his father in defense of his mother. The narrative is less overtly queer than the other two sections in that it does not include explicit reference to homosexuality or represent an obvious parable of contemporary queer politics. In recovering a feminist critique in "Hero," however, I also want to highlight its particular queerness. Specifically, in "Hero," which closes the film, *Poison* offers an explicit pact between a mother and her son, whom I read as a manifestation of Kathryn Bond Stockton's (2009) queer child who violates the patriarchal bonds of father and son. This refusal of patriarchal inheritance and its grounding in a feminist critique of the domestic as a space of violence and trauma offers a vision of queer theory that takes its mothers seriously, and one that does not, as Martin (1994) worries, foreground "antifoundationalist celebrations of queerness [that] rely on their own projections of fixity, constraint, or subjection" and read these projections onto the female bodies and feminist theory, designating "queer" as its opposite in both its implicit masculinity and its performative and playful capacity (107). The danger of this maneuver, Martin argues, is that "in the process, the female body appears to become its own trap, and the operations of misogyny disappear from view" (107). *Poison* instead figures a queerness that does not surrender all the possibilities of queer to the masculine, or that at least attempts to allow for potentially multidirectional identification and cooperative bonds between the masculine and feminine.

"Hero" opens with a tracking shot of a suburban neighborhood, overlaid with the voiceover of a news reporter who declares, "The quiet residential community of Glenville was stunned" by the "strange death of Fred Beacon." As the scene transitions from the black-and-white backdrop and campy, anxious instrumental music of "Horror," the cut is marked by a booming drum that sounds distinctly like a gunshot, both foreshadowing the murder revealed by the voiceover and lending the ensuing shots of suburbia an oversaturated and claustrophobic air. Doane characterizes this shot as one of two "signature shots" in Haynes's work, which "appear in *Superstar* (US, 1987) and *Poison* (US, 1991) and functions as the opening shot of *Safe* (US/UK, 1995). A long tracking shot, sometimes marked as originating from inside a car, traces row after row of classic suburban houses—all basically the same with only slight differences, all overly familiar. . . . The suburban house in its many incarnations is the site of both the familiar and its etymological kin, the family, the site of the potentially explosive repressions and power structures so carefully delineated in each of these films" (2004b, 1–2). In all three films, the establishing shot anticipates a critique of the suburban mythos as a nexus of power relations. This image is grounded in feminist critiques of the family and the domestic as sites of patriarchal domination.

At the end of this tracking shot there is a sound bridge in which the voiceover ends; as the camera continues to travel over the houses, another voice cuts in: "It gave everybody the creeps." Although the film edit quickly catches up to the sound edit, cutting to an interview segment, for a brief moment it is the visual image of suburbia itself that also gives the viewer "the creeps." The creepiness of the suburban landscape is echoed by the violence that permeates the domestic space of the house. All the scenes that take place in the Beacon home are marked by alternatively muted and oversaturated color schemes, which lend Felicia a washed-out, sickly pallor and a wide-eyed, almost vibrating intensity as she recounts her "extraordinary" tale. The colors and lighting of the interviews emphasize the disembodied voiceover's characterization of Felicia's narrative as unreliable, though by the end of the film this perspective is overturned as the voiceover disappears and Felicia's voice supplants it as the author of her own narrative.

In Felicia's first narration of Richie's discovery of her affair—the catalyst for the eventual murder of her abusive husband at the hands of her child—the discovery is narrated but not seen by the audience. Instead, through Richie's perspective, the camera moves through the house, ending on a shot of the empty bedroom where the affair takes place and is later shown. Through these shots of the empty house and specifically the marital bed, the home itself is imbued with intimations of the violence that will occur. The camera lingers on the bed, the shot accompanied by piercing musical score reminiscent of that of a horror film. As when the nondiegetic music in a horror film indicates a killer's invisible presence, the domestic scene itself here becomes murderous. The home proves to be more destructive, and perhaps more poisonous, than even the prison, which John Broom reads as a potential space of queer antinormative refusal in his Genet-inspired fantasy. The home, however, remains the scene of violence, particularly for women—Nancy Olsen, who dies at home, and Felicia Beacon, who is abused and almost murdered in her bedroom. The home is also a site of violence and trauma for the queer, in this case male, child, who is constantly under threat of abuse or abandonment for his failure to live up to masculine norms. The overwhelming hazard of the domestic sphere, and the common threat of patriarchal violence, is a link uniting mother and queer child, a bond that is literalized in "Hero" when Richie saves his mother by killing his abusive father.

The drastically different accounts of Richie from those interviewed closely follow tropes of the gay child, alternately described as sensitive, creative, and strange. He doesn't quite fit, but nobody seems to know why, or at least no one is capable of uttering their suspicion. Whereas a social worker describes Richie as "extremely gifted, imaginative, telling elaborate stories," the school nurse deems him "evil," and a teacher calls him "a chronic liar" who drew other children into his stories and "liked controlling people." As Sedgwick notes in a reading of Foucault, as knowledge and sex become "conceptually inseparable," homosexuality becomes constituted as *the* secret (1990, 73). Felicia recalls that Richie was "always doing these private things, private games," again gesturing at the secrecy of the closet. Richie's unspeakable strangeness and the incoherence of the narratives surrounding him produce him as an inescapably queer child.

Richie, as we discover through several interviews, has a habit of manipulating or seducing other children, one boy in particular, into spanking him, reenacting the trauma of abuse by the father in a ritualized and controlled setting. The spanking scene, like the panning shot of the suburban landscape, is another favorite of Haynes; as Doane points out, such a scene appears in *Poison*, *Superstar*, and *Dottie Gets Spanked*: "It is in all cases a resolutely subjective shot, located deep within memory or dream or as the object of desire. It is directly evocative of Freud's well-known essay on masochism, 'A Child Is Being Beaten'" (2004b, 3). Richie's repetition of the trauma through his seduction of a classmate, however, and the strange bond he shares with his mother reconstitute Richie's spanking as a refusal of the patriarchal power of the father.

Stockton reads the queer child as a masochist, one who reframes the abuses of the home and turns them, through delay, into a site of perverse pleasure: "Masochism does not seek to overtake the father but rather to humiliate the father and his law" (2009, 78). Bond Stockton cites Deleuze and his rereading of the Freudian oedipal scene as an undoing of the father's law in the stylized repetition of it: "Hand in glove with this disavowal [of the world as we know it] is the masochist's suspension of laws by his making absurd contracts with them—especially the sexual laws conventionally mapped for men and women. In other words, by his submission to the law, the masochist undoes it. Whipping ceases to punish erection. Rather, it produces it. Moreover, when the masochist through his punishment literally atones for his resemblance to the father, he seeks in its place a maternal symbolic, both nurturing and cruel" (78). This analysis of masochism demonstrates how it restages and thus undercuts the father's law; it also bears striking resemblance to Felicia's own reading of the scene of her son's spanking, as well as the circumstances surrounding it as recounted by Richie's doctor and the voiceover.

The testimony of the doctor implies that Richie has been sexually abused, most likely by his father. The voiceover remarks on Richie's treatment for injuries to the thighs and lower back, and an interview with Richie's doctor mentions "other strange circumstances" including a "genitally secreted infectious discharge." The implied specter of sexual abuse is followed by a stylized scene of spanking, in which we can only see Richie's backside, Felicia's face, and the mechanical movement of the father's hand coming down on Richie (figure 6.2). Richie's face is turned toward his mother as she describes the look he gives her, the same one she sees when Richie discovers her in bed with the gardener. This look, unlike those between Nancy Olsen and Thomas Graves in "Horror," is truly a shared moment in which something is communicated between mother and son. Felicia recalls the look "like some oath in some other language. His face was so weird. It made me feel ashamed." This recollection of the spanking, itself a repetition of the act, stages an undoing of the father's law, as in Bond Stockton's reading. Despite the physical manifestation of the father's symbolic word-as-law, Richie refuses the symbolic realm and forms with his mother a bond that cannot be spoken in the language of the patriarch and that reframes

6.2 The specter of sexual abuse haunts the spanking scene.

6.3 Felicia appears sickly and strange.

sexualized shame as a performance that connects mother and son. The look also refuses to be incorporated into the gaze of the camera. We see it only obliquely in Felicia's reaction shot and hear her description, which fails to capture its otherworldly quality, but we are never given the shot-reverse-shot that would signal our inclusion in the shared look, seemingly emphasizing Felicia's affirmation that the look signals an oath that the audience cannot understand or experience.

It becomes clear as the narrative of the docudrama progresses that Fred Beacon has also been abusing Felicia. Presumably after discovering her affair with the gardener, Fred tears up Felicia's garden and eventually threatens to kill her, first with a gun and then with his hands. As they are struggling in her bedroom, Richie comes in with the hidden gun, shoots his father, and then flies out the window like the angel Felicia calls him. In this final scene, Richie betrays the bond of heteropatriarchal lineage, killing his father to defend the life of his mother and then fleeing, negating his own narrative to allow for her survival. The generic form of the piece is crucial here—the obvious artifice of the documentary and the constructed nature of its claim to reality emphasize the artifice of the suburban landscape, the constructedness of the domestic sphere, and the "natural" nuclear family.

Finally, however, "Hero" violates the documentary altogether, refusing the reality of the supposedly neutral voiceover and handing over the narrative legitimacy to Felicia. Early during the segment, the voiceover and talking heads paint Felicia as unstable, setting up a clear binary between the rational narrating voice and the incoherent narrative of Felicia's mysterious son. The lighting and mise-en-scène of her first appearances highlight her strangeness; shot from behind as she drives home, Felicia appears initially cloaked in shadows, her eyes guarded by sunglasses and her face turned away from the camera, as the voiceover introduces her "extraordinary account of her son's disappearance." Already the audience is prepared to take Felicia's word as suspicious. The next shot cuts to Felicia in her kitchen, where despite the natural light from the window behind her, Felicia appears sickly and strange, her skin tone almost perfectly matching the Pepto Bismol pink of her dress, which is too large on her thin frame (figure 6.3). The unsettling color scheme, along with her wide-eyed assertion that Richie "was a gift from god," completes a first impression of Felicia as unhinged.

In the final scenes, however, the voiceover disappears and Felicia takes over; her version of the story, formerly framed as unreliable, becomes the official narrative. As Felicia assumes ownership of the narrative, the camera occupies Richie's perspective, uniting the voice of the mother and the gaze of the queer child. In the final shot of the film, portraying Felicia's narrative, the camera fades to white, leaving a bright, visually blank screen and Felicia's voice, fading into the musical leitmotif from the film's opening shot of John Broom. The significance of this moment cannot be overstated, particularly given the erasure of women from the film in many readings. Richie, after murdering the patriarch in defense of his mother, removes his own body from the film, taking the camera with him, allowing her voice to survive without the invasive gaze of the camera or the audience. This final shot produces Richie as the "angel of judgment" his mother claimed him to be and the titular hero. Richie's heroism is constituted in his violent refusal of the father's law and his absenting his body as a potential vessel of that law (though, crucially, through a queer ascendance rather than death) in a pact with the mother, whom his actions allow to survive, both diegetically and narratively as the last spoken words of the film, reiterating her bond with Richie, "my little boy."

Conclusion

This chapter has resituated *Poison* in the context of Haynes's sustained investment in feminist critique. In this context, the film speaks to both queer and feminist theoretical aims, potentially reenvisioning a relation of cross-identification and collaboration between two unstable objects. Through the complex identifications with the feminine in "Homo," the way "Horror" and "Hero" frame the very atmosphere of suburban domesticity as poisonous, and how "Hero" positions a queer bond between mother and son that undercuts patriarchal inheritance, *Poison* places queer and feminist theory in conversation and refuses to reduce queer to a merely retaliatory relation to feminism.

Rather than differentiate between the Haynes of New Queer Cinema and the later Haynes that reconfigures the woman's film of the 1940s, it is fruitful to recognize the thematic and formal elements in *Poison* that anticipate his work, also with Vachon, in *Safe* and *Far from Heaven*, and to recognize a continuity of feminist critique that began with *Superstar*, in which *Poison* is a link rather than an aberration. Conversely, this allows *Poison* to do queer work that does not necessitate a burial or refutation of the feminine or feminist theory.

Recognition of the film as part of a sustained feminist praxis places the theoretical work of *Poison* alongside the material cooperative work of its production by Haynes and Vachon, and calls on a history of partnerships between gay men and women, both queer and straight, in queer theory. In looking back at these figures, crossings, and foundations, *Poison* can offer a way forward that takes up Butler and Martin's ethical call for cross-identification as a site of departure, reframing the contested sites of feminist and queer theory as working "in concert though not in unison" (1994, 3). Reading *Poison* as a site of departure rather than a fully theorized text of a particular moment allows it to take a place in an ongoing conversation, not only in Haynes's body of work, but also in the often anxious familial relationship between feminist and queer theory.

7 "All the Cake in the World"
Five Provocations on *Mildred Pierce*

Patrick Flanery

Moments of Crisis: Historical Dialectics

The original film adaptation of James M. Cain's 1941 novel *Mildred Pierce* (Michael Curtiz, 1945) spoke to postwar anxieties about women in capitalist American society as it emerged from the financial crisis of the Great Depression and the geopolitical crises of the Second World War.[1] In this chapter I ask how Todd Haynes's five-part miniseries *Mildred Pierce* (HBO, 2011) is legible as a dramatization of energies attendant on the financial and foreclosure crisis of the late 2000s, a crisis whose social corollaries with the 1929 crash are as obvious as they are often invisible.[2] Rather than reading Haynes's new *Mildred* as an updated but naturalistic period melodrama, or as a more "faithful" adaptation of Cain's novel,[3] I argue we should regard it instead as an example of what Lauren Berlant, in her 2011 book *Cruel Optimism*, calls the *situation tragedy*, a genre attuned to the affective discontents of our neoliberal present (176), and one that wears its seriality as integral to its form. Doing so suggests that Haynes's adaptation offers a salutary and urgent diagnosis of the impossible traps late capitalism sets for women in particular.

By illuminating the ways fantasies of the "good life" are set in order to trap women across society, Haynes's series allows us to see such gendered experience intersectionally, by offering portraits of lives differently circumscribed by class—whether waitresses, domestic employees, entrepreneurs, or some of the many women whose work is in the home.

Mildred herself occupies all of these categories at various points, her own position one of rollercoaster circularity that returns to origins (a narrative patterning congruent with and formally reflecting the adaptation's seriality), while other characters' experiences suggest more linear processes of professional ascent, even as it remains clear how gender and class delimit opportunities. For Mildred, her successful fulfillment of maternal domesticity limits her employability outside the home; even other women assume she is good only for analogous roles in the public workforce. At one time employed as a waitress, Mildred has to manage the unwanted sexual attention of male customers, as she does the sexual aggression of male partners; in a way that anticipates the #MeToo movement, her experiences demonstrate how women are forced into transactional sexual objecthood in both the public and the private spheres.

Just as in 1945, under the Production Code Administration, Mildred's daughter Veda could not get away with murder, so Haynes's Mildred (Kate Winslet), refracted through the lens of late capitalism, cannot hope to escape her gendered class position as a single, working mother: the system simply will not allow it in either case. We might ask, however, what it says that monstrous Veda is punished in the earlier adaptation but allowed to get away with (figurative) murder in Haynes's series, in which Mildred, rather than Monty, is Veda's victim. The answer might be that if, in the 1940s, Veda's ruthless pursuit of her own material and social advancement is framed as analogous to parricide, in our era, Haynes allows the aspirations of his Veda (Morgan Turner and Evan Rachel Wood) to function as fantasy engine and enforcement machine, ensuring that Mildred remains stuck in cycles of hopeful self-delusion that inevitably plummet into realist despair (only to rise again). This situation leaves Mildred in a volatile state of impasse, while Veda—the one character whose belief in the good-life fantasy never visibly wavers—surges forward in solidarity only with herself.

Part of what makes Haynes's treatment of Cain's story inescapably feminist is its focus on Mildred's being stuck in an agonistic relationship with gender norms, while Veda, caught in her own way, uses such gender-normative expectations instrumentally to power her ascent. This focus is also what ensures that the adaptation is utterly in conversation with the sociopolitical energies of its moment of production, complexly attuned to the vulnerability of women for whom the promise of the good life is an ever-receding horizon, and whose rhythms are reiterated in the form of the series itself. Haynes's long-standing commitment to telling women's stories allows him to make of what Berlant calls the situation tragedy a specifically "women's genre," and one that engenders a historical dialectic by mobilizing older texts—Cain's novel, even arguably Curtiz's film—in a new form. The historical allegory offered by Haynes's *Mildred* is therefore a specifically *feminist* interpretation of the failed fantasy of the good life made manifest in Berlant's diagnosis of an emergent genre, here reflected in Haynes's embrace of the rhythms and restrictions of serial television to create in the viewer affects of failure and impasse that are key structures of situation tragedy.

Situation Tragedy

Whereas the first adaptation of *Mildred Pierce* is one of the great camp texts of midcentury American film, blending melodrama, crime, and Grand Guignol scenery chewing, Haynes's miniseries largely evacuates camp from its seemingly naturalistic and unironic take on Cain's novel.[4] It returns the setting to the 1930s, hewing more closely to the novel's dialogue and scene descriptions than did the first adaptation, as Pam Cook notes (2013, 381). Just as the 1945 adaptation united the contemporaneously urgent genres of noir thriller and melodrama, Haynes's *Mildred* is uncannily synchronous with the emergent genre of situation tragedy that Berlant aligns to our own moment of neoliberal precarity. In *Cruel Optimism*, Berlant develops her analysis of the retrogressive attachment to fantasies of self-sufficiency in the age of post-Fordist precarity through her reading of films by Belgian directors Jean-Pierre and Luc Dardenne, particularly *Rosetta* (1999). A *situation*, Berlant writes, constitutes "a state of animated and animating suspension that forces itself on consciousness," generating "a sense of the emergence of something in the present that may become an event" (2011, 5). Distinct from situation comedy, *situation tragedy* is among the "new aesthetic forms" that "emerge during the 1990s"—Berlant argues—"to register a shift in how the older state-liberal-capitalist fantasies shape adjustments to the structural pressures of crisis and loss that are wearing out the power of the good life's traditional fantasy bribe without wearing out the need for a good life" (7). The genre is characterized by "the marriage between tragedy and situation comedy" in which subjects "are fated to express their flaws episodically, over and over, without learning, changing, being relieved, becoming better, or dying" (176).

Rosetta's title character, Berlant writes, maintains her sense of "optimism about the prospect of becoming … 'a good worker,'" supporting herself as a cleaner and seamstress before seeking employment (and eschewing welfare) "to earn her value the way 'normal' people do" (2011, 163).

This step up to the status of employed allows Rosetta to fantasize "about spaces of the good life or good times ahead" (163); as Berlant sees it, in Rosetta's case "the affects" in operation are those "of aspirational normativity" (164). As Rosetta longs for "a *sense* of something rather than something" itself (in Berlant's formulation, my emphasis), we are certain the character will fail, even though she might *survive* while being drawn into repeating cycles of that "generic hybrid, *situation tragedy*" (176). It comes as no surprise that Haynes might produce a work legible as situation tragedy given his long-standing concern with the gendered nature of pathos and pathology, as Mary Ann Doane (2004b) has suggested. We can productively read Berlant's analysis of cruel optimism alongside Doane's observation that "[p]athology is only possible, in Haynes's cinema, when viewed by those who cling to their status as normal" (15) and her suggestion that Haynes's "focus on the pathological is not simply an elaboration of the processes of social marginalization but a challenge to the persistent denial of the inextricability of the sensible and the intelligible" (18). Haynes's sustained investment in producing work that evokes sympathy, as well as his interest in depicting pathological states and conditions associated with characters' aspirations to normativity, recur in Mildred's own situation tragedy.

Melodrama, of course, focuses on "the trials and tribulations of family life," is "characterised by an extravagantly dramatic register" and "overtly emotional mode of address," and "use[s] the family and the social position of women as [its] narrative focus" (Mercer and Shingler 2004, 1–2). In Veda and Mildred's relationship we can see how "lining up life with fantasy" (to use Berlant's phrase) requires a significant quantum of cruelty (2011, 166), but in Haynes's hands, this connection is articulated in a generic mode less beholden to melodrama than to what is recognizable as the repetitious form of situation tragedy. Haynes's orchestration of the cruel mechanics required to align the fantastic with the real also recalibrates the risks and rewards of the mother-daughter relationship by expanding it from the domestic to the public sphere. What is at stake for Mildred begins as a domestic problem but turns into an economic one, and the visual aesthetic of the series, which recalls documentary photographs of the 1930s and '40s, is critical to establishing a sense of the characters being constrained by gender and class, and caught in a moment of economic crisis. Cinematographer Edward Lachman said he "felt close to a documentary attitude" reminiscent of Robert Frank's and William Eggleston's photography, and he eschewed "expressionist lighting" (which is integral to the 1945 *Mildred Pierce*), instead modeling the visual aesthetic on Farm Security Administration photography by

Ben Shahn, Walker Evans, and producer Christine Vachon's father, John Vachon. Moreover, the visual style of the series references the aesthetic of 1970s New Hollywood films like *Chinatown* (Roman Polanski, 1977) and *Klute* (Alan J. Pakula, 1971), suggesting less a sensibility of lush stylization (as with Haynes's 2002 *Far from Heaven*) than one that is, as Lachman says, what a film in "a more documentary" style would have looked like had it been "shot in the 1930s" (Ciment and Niogret 2014, 35, 38; my translation). Haynes himself has said that shooting on Super-16 provided an image with "grain . . . and sensuality": it is "a rougher format, rawer, with dust or hairs on the edge of the frame" that suited the depiction of the 1930s as an "age of conflicts" (Ciment and Tobin 2016, 20; my translation). This attempt to depict reality as it might have been captured during the period focuses in particular on the realities of economic precarity for women—realities that demonstrate the perilous artifice of neoliberal postfeminist fantasies of the good life, and the toll when they fail. Haynes, in fact, equates realism with artifice, as Dennis Lim (2011) remarks: "it's no surprise to hear him describe the naturalism of the series as itself a kind of . . . throwback to what he called the 'dressed-down' style of the American cinema of the 1970s, when films like *The Godfather* and *Chinatown* were revising genres and, often, revisiting earlier eras." Haynes emulates such films' style to similar ends, revising the maternal melodrama and updating it to situation tragedy in the process. Having read Cain's novel in 2008, "with the Great Recession looming and conversations about class in America taking on renewed significance," Haynes found in it, he says, a way to "[link] potential pathologies in maternal desire with potential excesses in middle-class yearning"—the very stuff of situation tragedy as Berlant conceives it (Lim 2011).

"All the Cake in the World"

That Haynes's rendering of Mildred's story revisits an earlier crisis (the Great Depression) suggests how exhausted fantasy bribes of the good life myth are in the moment of the series' production, too, while dramatizing the absolute need for *a* good life of some (other) kind. How appropriate that the plot begins with the financial frustrations of a speculative housing development, how fitting that Mildred's downfall is precipitated by her borrowing so extravagantly that she uses two sets of books to cover her tracks. These narrative elements speak with particular force to a contemporary audience, itself living in what Berlant calls "catastrophic time" and watching in *Mildred* an allegory of its own experience, as "a paralyzed but aware spectatorship of its own demise as a public" (2011, 290n18). As for Mildred, as for the viewer: the pursuit of a good-life fantasy is destined to disappoint because its object is an endlessly retreating horizon of possibility. Those who pursue it are doomed to find that their desires repeatedly outmatch the capital at their disposal, almost always in ways that produce downward mobility in the very moment that fantasies of a better life valorize both aspiration and the laborious struggle to ascend, consume, and acquire. Mildred relies on fantasy as she rises from the ruins of Bert's business failures, baking pies and cakes to keep the family afloat in a war of attrition against both the deterioration of the material conditions of daily life and the fantasies of a better life that might have been. When Bert leaves the family home, and though he was not obviously contributing to the household expenses, Mildred is thrown into crisis, as if the absence of a husband erodes her already precarious social standing.

In the trajectory of Mildred's ascent from unemployed pieceworker to owner of her own business we see a dynamic analogous to what Berlant identifies as exemplary of the situation tragedy protagonist's cruelly optimistic investment in the fantasy of the trappings of a middle-class good life. At the beginning of part 1, the upbeat song "Milenberg Joys" accompanies close shots of Mildred's hands making pies, her limbs disarticulated from the rest of the body, all the camera's focus on her labor so that this making (essential for the family's survival) is initially presented as a pleasurable, even sensual craft. Before we see Mildred's face, the gaze of the camera travels outward, through the textured glass windows of the fussily decorated mission-style bungalow and onto a suburban world aestheticized by those distortions of the aspirational home's fabrication. What might appear to middle-class viewers in the present as a comfortable life, the light golden as it streams through those textured windows, is for Mildred a monument to the failure of Bert's business.[5]

When we finally see Mildred's face, three minutes after the opening credits, her preoccupied expression is visibly out of synch with that upbeat music. Reminders of what has been lost abound in framed images: a formal pen-and-ink portrait of Bert; blueprints and photographs of Pierce Homes, the housing development with which he was to make his fortune. These reminders—glimpsed in a slow pan as Mildred and Bert argue offscreen in a fight that launches Mildred into the first cycle of situation tragedy—both decorate and serve as remnants of a hope disappointed. Lachman has noted that no dolly shots were used (Ciment and Niogret 2014, 38), and we might see this choice as structurally replicating, or offering a formal metaphor for, the refusal of movement out of a state of impasse. Later, even when Mildred moves through public spaces, the camera pans but remains fixed, suggesting that her range of motion is always constrained by forces outside her control.

Following Bert's departure from the home, Mildred's first instinct is to turn to an employment agency, but this leads to a series of situations revealing the precariousness of her class position in ways too painful to bear. Herbert Hoover's portrait hanging in the agency recalls the existence of the Hooverville shantytowns (a feature of American urban life in this period), but the series never zooms out from Hoover as metonym for the moment's rampant poverty and social precariousness to represent the gritty realism of homelessness and shack living, as if Hoover himself, gazing at Mildred from the wall behind her, is the most she can bear to see (see Harvey 1987).[6] This visual citation is enough, however, to suggest what fate awaits Mildred and her daughters if she were to lose the house, and the threat is real: Mrs. Turner, owner-operator of the employment agency, tells Mildred that without secretarial skills she has no chance of finding a job as a receptionist.[7]

An advertisement for work in an upscale tearoom offers hope, but when Mildred watches a waitress serving two sophisticated and imperious older women before scrutinizing the poor tip she receives, Mildred realizes she cannot do that particular job. We see her looking through glass (the tearoom doors), observing the exchange between waitress and patrons. Then, in a reverse shot, the waitress's perspective on Mildred, the waitress's own reflection approaches and coincides with Mildred's face on the other side of the glass. Haynes's use of glass and windows in which reflections of individuals and the passing world are juxtaposed against Mildred, often revealing her inability to see herself or her own position clearly, suggests failures of a working-through of the kind Berlant describes as integral to the experience of subjects caught in the cycles of situation tragedy. Although Cook (2013) notes Haynes's "copious use of reflections in mirrors and windows," she sees this in terms of such tropes "[making] it difficult to read spatial relationships," the "views through windows and doorways . . . curtail[ing] vision" in a way that "denaturalizes the spaces: rather than give the illusion of transparency, as with naturalism, it produces a sense that characters are constricted by their surroundings" and "an appearance of surface rather than depth" (384–85). In my reading, however, Mildred looks away because she cannot place herself in the position of *that* waitress in *this* context; ultimately, however, it seems her reservations are less

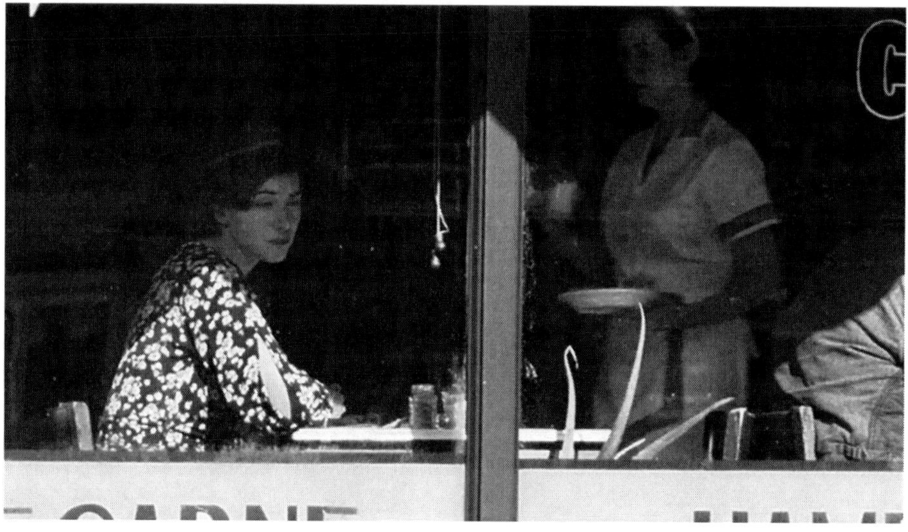

7.1 Haynes's use of glass and windows in which reflections of individuals and the passing world are juxtaposed against Mildred.

about wearing a uniform and taking tips than having to serve in a space marked by such stark class difference.

After abruptly terminating an interview to be housekeeper for a patronizing wealthy woman, Mildred stands on a bus we see a moment later reflected in shop windows as it comes to a stop across the street from a parked car, as if to suggest her ongoing incapacity to see her position clearly (riding a bus rather than driving a car), just as she was unable to see at the tearoom the equivalence of her class position to that of the uniformed waitress.[8] As a newsboy shouts headlines about the Scottsboro Boys, reminding us of the wider social and historical context of Jim Crow racism even as the series' focus remains on forces of class and gender, Mildred retreats to Cristofor's Restaurant. She takes a table by the window through which we have watched her approach before the camera returns to the street so that we see her from outside, framed by the window—a dime store across the street reflected in the glass, pedestrians and vehicles passing as Mildred gazes out in a composition that recalls photographs by Ben Shahn (who captured store-window reflection to great effect) and John Vachon (figure 7.1).[9] Cristofor's is closer to Mildred's natural habitus, a space where she is not made to feel out of place. Cutting back inside, the camera pans across the modest restaurant, coming to rest on the body of waitress Doris, framing her from the waist down so our focus is on her sensible shoes and white uniform, the parts of her body that labor to live in a moment of crisis, just as we focused earlier on Mildred's own laboring body at home. When Doris wipes a table, covertly slipping a tip into her apron pocket (because waitressing does not pay enough to ensure survival), we understand that such labor disarticulates the body into parts that struggle to become a whole person, a whole life.

Nonetheless, for Mildred, a job in *this* place can be borne, even if it requires wearing a uniform and taking tips, because it is a zone without obvious class difference between those served and those serving. Yet, waitressing reduces her to an object, a laboring body: the framing in a montage of Mildred waitressing often focuses on arms and hands carrying dishes, cutting off her head and legs (she is rendered the object of aggressive sexual attention, too, when a male customer pinches her). This job might be better than starvation, but it remains far from the good life. Payoffs for working in a milieu less marked by class difference and economic inequality are, the viewer realizes, not worth the costs to Mildred's agency or subjectivity, as the emotional costs of this labor are vividly apparent: telling her neighbor Lucy about the job makes Mildred vomit. She protests that she "can't wear a uniform" or face the "awful" customers; if anything, she feels she ought to be able to look down on *them*. As much as Mildred hates it, she has no other option, and yet the shame is overwhelming: the girls cannot know about it, "Veda in particular," because her eldest has the "pride or nobility" Mildred thought she herself possessed; she wants for her daughters "not just bread" but "all the cake in the world," the impossible dream that fantasy insists is possible.

The Wages of Sin Is Death

Why is optimism cruel? Berlant explains that "the *affective structure* of an optimistic attachment involves a sustaining inclination to return to the scene of fantasy that enables you to expect that *this* time, nearness to *this* thing will help you ... become different in just the right way" (2011, 2). It becomes "cruel when the object/scene that ignites a sense of possibility actually makes it impossible to attain the expansive transformation for which a person ... risks striving," and "is cruel insofar as the very pleasures of being inside a relation have become sustaining regardless of the content of the relation, such that a person" becomes "bound to a situation of profound threat," which is nonetheless "profoundly confirming" (2). Mildred's optimism operates in two simultaneous and often hopelessly intertwined currents: one pursuing the good life; the other, the good *love* (an aspect of the good life, as good love is integral to the hoped-for happiness and security—emotional and affective—central to the good-life fantasy). Although chiefly concerned with women-authored middlebrow texts, Berlant's earlier work, *The Female Complaint* (2008), suggests that such texts as those arising from the "intimate public" of "women's culture" endure not least because their "central fantasy . . . is the constantly emplotted desire of a complex person to rework the details of her history to become a vague or simpler version of herself, usually in the vicinity of a love plot" (5, 7). Within this archive of "women's culture's stories," Berlant says, operate "many kinds of bargaining women do to stay in proximity to the work of love at the heart of normative femininity" (16). Mildred's romantic life, her serially disappointing romances with Bert, Wally Burgan, and Monty Beragon, mark her story as one of inescapable repetition and locate the series generically in a cultural archive of women's romance (whether authored by women or men), even as Haynes's series is also legible as a feminist critique of that genre's tendency toward "sentimental realism" (5) precisely because it so unmistakably illuminates what Berlant describes as "the circularity of the feminine project": an inescapable "sphere infused with activities of ongoing circuits of attachment that can at the same time look like and feel like a zero" (20).

For Mildred, return to the scene of fantasy operates first in the zone of romantic attachment, starting from a locus of disappointment that is *also* about the fantasy of the good (material) life. Bert fails the family economically and affectively; in the wake of his abandonment, Mildred lurches to his former business partner, Wally, in whom she invests hope for *both* romantic solace and material security. Although she does not wish to be kept, neither does she want to have to worry about being able to feed and house her children, or endangering Veda's exorbitant fantasies. Haynes signals the nature of Mildred's pursuit of fantasy in his use of the vaudeville song "I'm Always Chasing Rainbows" (which remains a half-submerged allusion in the novel, "the song about rainbows that had been Mildred's favorite") (Cain 2002, 262). The quest for the beautiful, ephemeral pot of gold, always vanishing at the horizon, both sustains Mildred affectively in the face of serial rejection—by Bert, by Veda, by Monty and Veda together—and prevents her from escaping cycles of optimistic pursuit in a way that might save her from the bleak future suggested at the series' end, in which she returns, once again hopefully, to Bert.

As propulsive force behind the expansion, consolidation, and incorporation of a business she nonetheless reviles, Veda drives Mildred's pursuit of more than ordinary happiness. Even though Mildred slaps and spanks Veda for calling her waitressing degrading, the defeat is Mildred's, and yet she presents her degradation as strategic, saying she needed to learn the restaurant business in order to open her own. Veda's response, disingenuously reconfirming her love for Mildred, temporarily reseals the relationship: Mildred kisses her daughter and takes her to bed in a manner that suggests codependent seduction. But the erotics of the relationship can never entirely satisfy Mildred because they are so deeply antinormative. This is the point when Monty enters as exogamous proxy, providing a socially acceptable outlet for Mildred's unsatisfied desires, but one instantly punished with the death of her younger daughter, Ray; the simultaneous striking of Eros and Thanatos thus frames Mildred as having failed her family by indulging her desire for Monty.

Faced with the ways Veda's and her own fantasies are marked by "instability, fragility, and dear cost," Mildred clings to them nonetheless; fantasies of wealth and "enduring reciprocity" provide a mechanism to "hoard idealizing theories and tableaux" that tell her she really does "add up to something" and is not just a laboring object (Berlant 2011, 2). A small measure of success (affective, material), notwithstanding those fantasies' great cost, is enough to keep Mildred bound to their pursuit. Significantly, each of the series' five parts ends on a note of darkness, with Mildred brought low, producing a rhythm in the seriality that begins to recapitulate the cycle that is the impasse of the neoliberal moment: every happiness paired with loss, every loss propelling Mildred toward the next cycle of fantasy. She returns repeatedly to the fantasy, as if "*this* time, nearness to *this* thing" (Monty) will allow her "to become different in just the right way" (2)—to secure either an enduringly reciprocal romantic attachment or a filial one (in Veda). Essential to this operation are the ways that Wally, Veda, and Monty each raise the ante of Mildred's fantasy, pushing the end of the rainbow farther beyond the horizon, promising a larger pot of gold—whether a more sustaining emotional connection, greater economic success, or loftier social status. Mildred's repeated capture by fantasy requires an ongoing and mutable process of torsion, twisting back and forth between Monty and Veda. Here, the economic and interpersonal are inextricably contorted and contorting, so it is never entirely clear which of the two forces Veda or Monty might be wielding in any particular moment, and the stakes always verge on the tragic: the loss of a child or the violation and dissolution of the self.

Your Money or Your Love

If seriality and repetition without insight are markers of situation tragedy, then Haynes's *Mildred Pierce* embodies these at the level of both character and form. Mildred is doomed to repeat the same genre of error, and we see these errors lived out episodically during the course of the series, and ultimately through a mini series of returns to origins in part 5: first house, first branch of Mildred's restaurant, the café where she first wore a uniform and met Monty. Even the multiple locations of Mildred's restaurants and the cookie-cutter suburbs of mission-style bungalows function as geospatial mirrors for the adaptation's seriality and the seriality of the situation tragedy it constitutes, as if tragedy were situationally playing itself out in Laguna and Beverly Hills and Glendale, its everyday horrors visible to Mildred even as she averts her gaze (as she did at the department store tearoom) from her own decline. Having lost Veda, Mildred recognizes in Monty an opportunity to regain the object of her greatest desire and so announces her plan to move to Pasadena. For Mildred, the goal of winning back Veda drives her acquisition of Monty's mansion, but Mildred's own larger desires (for secure social status, for Veda herself) are ultimately as unsatisfiable as Veda's own, even as they are "not reducible to the Oedipal/castration model" of mother-daughter bonds, as Amber Jacobs (2014, 165) has argued.[10] If Veda is the locus of Mildred's affective needs, Veda herself must compel Mildred to internalize her lofty fantasies of social ascent and to work (even in legally and personally compromising ways) to transform those dreams into realities. Visually reinscribing how social and familial roles and cycles trap these characters and how the seriality of situation tragedy is a structuring and constraining genre for *both* Mildred and Veda, part 1 of the series concludes with a panning shot that ends frozen on Veda framed from behind, facing a privacy fence, her head centered in the spiraling wrought-iron filigree hearts of a window in the family's Glendale home (figure 7.2). This image suggests her early capture by two opposing forces: the constraint of her middle-class suburban origins (the enclosure of the fence) and her own destructively vicious cycles of aspirational fantasy. Here the wrought-iron ornamentation of that suburban house is marker of its petit-bourgeois class pretensions and anxieties (the wrought iron is legible as a home security measure), but that spiraling ornamental form (a series of six mirrored heart shapes) also suggests a metacommentary on the temporality, structure, and rhythm of the series itself: in place of the feature-film melodrama's tendency toward linear chronolo-

7.2 Formal motifs reflect processes of cyclical repetition that are integral to the structure of situation tragedy.

gies, situation tragedy repeatedly spirals back to origins to recommence another iteration of the cycle.

Cook (2013) has suggested that Haynes "elides [the novel's] focus on Mildred's incestuous desire for Veda" (383), but the incestuous energies remain unmistakable in the series and drive the machinery of its cyclical narrative. When Veda returns for Mildred and Monty's wedding reception, Mildred sneaks into Veda's room at the end of the evening, leans over her bed, and kisses her sleeping daughter on the lips.[11] In the torsions of situation tragedy, this desire for Veda functions as private relief from the sustained external pursuit of what the good-life fantasy promises; Veda, also the engine for this pursuit, stands apart from that world of material acquisition, and she becomes the focus of Mildred's desire in those moments when the outside world overwhelms. Haynes's series thus frames Mildred's desire for Veda as an allegory for the ways contemporary patriarchal neoliberalism offers women a pathological intensification of affect within the home as compensation for various forms of marginalization in the public sphere. For Mildred, her desire for Veda is—if nothing else—entirely her own, not subject to the objectifying desire of Veda or Monty themselves, as everything else she possesses is. But in desiring material wealth and social advancement, Veda repeatedly forces Mildred to instrumentalize her incestuous desire in pursuit of capital, redirecting that desire outside the home and family.

In Mildred's ultimate return to origins, remarried to Bert, living in the same house in Glendale, having lost her business but hearing that her first boss is looking for a new source of pies, we see the cycle of situation tragedy spiraling back: a hope resurges that things will be better *this* time. Nonetheless, the series reminds us how misplaced hope for the good life—even the ordinarily good life—might be. After a final confrontation with Veda, Mildred and Bert turn to the bottle, and we can easily imagine their new life together beginning yet another cycle of tragedy for Mildred, if not necessarily for Bert, and the story spiraling on in perpetuity. That the male characters survive largely outside the constraints of the situation tragedy machine, never susceptible in quite the same way to those good-life fantasies, reminds us how invested Haynes is in portraying the effects of socioeconomic forces and social myth on women especially, and the ways such forces may structure and affect their affect. As Haynes said early in his career, "films are machines that either reiterate and reciprocate society—or not" (1993, 8). It is clear that his *Mildred Pierce* is deeply invested in refusing acts of uncritical social replication and reciprocation as it mobilizes historical allegory to critique its present.

Affect, Berlant suggests, "registers the conditions of life that move across persons and worlds"; its "saturation of form" reveals "a poetics, a theory-in-practice of how a world works" (2011, 16). This saturation is capable of demonstrating "the conditions under which a historical moment appears as a visceral moment, assessing the way a thing that is happening finds its genre," so that "the aesthetic or formal rendition of affective experience provides evidence of historical processes" (16). To approach Haynes's HBO production of *Mildred Pierce* as an instance of situation tragedy is thus to recognize in its treatment of narrative, renovation of genre, and a working-through of what Berlant calls the "corporeal, intimate, and political performances of adjustment that make a shared atmosphere ... palpable" (16) a new and profoundly engaging conversation with cycles of hope, fantasy, and disappointment as they operate in our difficult, ongoing historical moment. If postwar adjustments to the position of women in society found their genre in the melodrama of Curtiz's adaptation, Haynes's *Mildred Pierce* frames current and ongoing happenings in a new genre that allows his feminist and left-oriented politics to direct our attention to the operations of affect and the traps laid by fantasy, for women especially, that remain in place for the next cycle of situation tragedy lived out in real—catastrophic—time.

NOTES

I am grateful to Theresa L. Geller and Andrew van der Vlies for their very helpful reading and suggestions. The final edits on this essay were completed in the weeks following the death of Lauren Berlant, whose ideas were so important for its genesis. I remain indebted to her work and grateful for its generosity and ongoing urgency.

1 For a survey of readings of the 1945 adaptation, see Jurca (2002).

2 Haynes himself has suggested the connection. See Cook (2013, 381–82).

3 Cook (2013) argues that "viewers were urged to forget Michael Curtiz's noir classic and appreciate Haynes's respect for the melodrama at the heart of the book" (378).

4 Ruptures in the naturalism, however, appear in the performances of Morgan Turner and Evan Rachel Wood, and of Guy Pearce, all of whom seem to be acting in *Mildred Pierce* (1945), not *Mildred Pierce* (2011). Pearce's Monty remains so consistently in the mode of camp that it is difficult to know with certainty what the character feels or desires. Haynes's subversive and insistent redirection toward Berlantian situation tragedy might also be regarded as a camp parody of the maternal melodrama.

5 The novel is clearer about the class signifiers of the house and its decoration.

6 There was a Hooverville in Watts, in Los Angeles County, in the early 1930s; it was demolished in 1932.

7 In Cain's novel, the threat of defaulting on mortgage payments and losing the house propels Mildred to seek a job.

8 Doane's (2004b) well-known analysis of Haynes's use in his earlier work of recurring tropes—tracking shots of "classic suburban houses" (1), a marked emphasis on the subjectivity of a female protagonist's perspective (often involving quotation of midcentury melodrama's mobilization of windows as visual metaphor for the gendered structuring of space), scenes of a child being spanked—and their relation to an engagement with gendered pathos and pathology are equally pertinent for reading *Mildred Pierce*, in which all of these tropes occur.

9 For Farm Security Administration color photographs, including work by Vachon, see Hendrickson (2004). For Ben Shahn photographs, see Mora and Brannan (2006, especially 51, 55).

10 See A. Jacobs (2014) for an argument that Haynes's series "transforms *Mildred Pierce* into a feminist work that . . . completely breaks with the pessimism of Lacanian film theory and psychoanalytic feminism regarding the apparently bleak possibilities of representing femininity outside the concepts of objectification, symptom and lack" (164). Jacobs analyzes Haynes's structuring of the Mildred-Veda relationship through a close reading of the series' use of sound as a spatiotemporal "conduit" of communication between mother and daughter (173).

11 Cook revisited her argument in a less categorical mode; see her video essay and discussion of the kiss specifically (Cook 2015).

8 The Politics of Disappointment
Todd Haynes Rewrites Douglas Sirk

Sharon Willis

Condensation and Displacement

Far from Heaven (2002), Todd Haynes's lush, lurid, strikingly amplified homage to Douglas Sirk, bristles with reworkings of Sirk's signature effects as it consistently evokes his 1950s melodramas of heterosexual longing and disappointment. In the almost electrifying network of condensation and displacement that structures it, *Far from Heaven* also amalgamates elements drawn from Sirk's films: *All That Heaven Allows* (1955), in which suburban middle-class widow Cary Scott (Jane Wyman) falls in love with her gardener, Ron Kirby (Rock Hudson); *Imitation of Life* (1959); and *Written on the Wind* (1956). Cinematically, *Far from Heaven* shares with these Sirk productions an obtrusive score, a meticulous attention to color, strikingly truncated interiors, and a rhythm of hysterical eruptions. As it consistently elaborates its difference from Sirk's universe, however, this film opens onto a social and historical perspective that explores the shaping effects of the 1950s on the contemporary culture.

Far from Heaven deftly filters heterosexual disappointment and failure through Cathy's (Julianne Moore) scandalous relationship with her black gardener, Raymond Deagan (Dennis Haysbert), reframing the drama of the suburban middle-class wife and mother through a "racial angle" (figure 8.1). Thus the film also borrows the terms set up by *Imitation of Life*, which stages its twin maternal melodramas within the framework of intra- and interracial difference. That film turns on parallel mother-daughter conflicts. Ambitious

8.1 Julianne Moore plays Carol Whitaker alongside Dennis Haysbert as Raymond Deagan in *Far from Heaven*.

single mother Lora Meredith (Lana Turner) pursues her acting career while remaining consistently indifferent to the concerns of her daughter, Susie (Sandra Dee). On the other side of the film's structuring racial divide, Lora's maid, Annie (Juanita Moore), as overattentive to her child as Lora is inattentive to hers, remains painfully and futilely hopeful that her "mulatta" daughter, Sarah Jane (Susan Kohner), will eschew the desire to pass as white and accept her blackness. As *Far from Heaven* thus refracts the plot of *All That Heaven Allows* through the concerns of *Written on the Wind* and *Imitation of Life*, in a process that resembles nothing so much as filmic "dreamwork," it furnishes its viewer with a rich generational cinema archive.

To highlight the richness of this layered archive, we might remember a moment of striking self-reference in *Imitation of Life*: when Lora declines to appear in David Edwards's next comedy, the genre for which he is known, and opts instead to do a drama, the author protests: "And that 'colored'... angle in it. It's ... absolutely controversial!" Thus winking at its audience, Sirk's film calls attention to the status of its own "colored" angle as potentially a mere artifice or prop, a backdrop of "authenticity" that highlights Lora's fakeness, just as the diegetic play's "colored angle" endows it with a frisson of controversy and helps to code it, or package it, as "serious drama." By similarly playing on this "angle," Haynes invites his viewer to wonder whether race may be at risk of becoming a dramatic device for his film as well.

Set in a network of displacements and transfers of energy and affect, the status of this film's racialized representation remains unstable. We must read race through this film's intense attention to repression, both in Sirk's melodramas and in the 1950s popular discourse of euphemism, which renders gay cruising, for instance, as "loitering." But we must also understand the film's representational work on the visual and theoretical planes. If we look at its striking technical departures from Sirk's cinematic vocabulary, we notice, for example, that *Far from Heaven* often abruptly introduces a canted frame. Such angles, drawing our attention back to the frame itself and disaligning us from the character occupying screen space, remind us of the film's interpretive distance—and agency—at the level of the visual. Likewise, as the film articulates its sequences together with a strong inclination toward dissolves and fades, it suggests both film history and its own artifice. Its dissolves continually render a visual analog to its overlapping intertextual references—a montage of memory—so that the editing itself evokes the structure of condensation and displacement.

In this regard, *Far from Heaven* is as much an homage to film theory, and in particular to feminist film theory, as it is to Douglas Sirk. It reads the 1950s melodrama (and beyond it, the 1950s in popular memory) through the lens of 1980s and 1990s feminist film theory. This feminist work cast Sirk into renewed prominence, as his films opened up new angles on the spurned genre of women's melodrama.[1] Furthermore, in the moment when feminist concerns and approaches took over the study of this genre almost completely, feminist theory also turned to explore the 1950s as something other than a regrettable post–World War II regression in gender ideologies intent on luring women back into the home; it began to reconfigure the period as one of intense contradiction around femininity, particularly in its relation to popular culture, especially television and consumerism.

The 1990s witnessed an explosion of scholarship examining the period of the 1950s as conflicted and animated by shifts in racial and gender politics and in sexual identity formations. Cathy Whitaker appears as the perfect icon for contradictions and shifting social relations. Much like the television set itself, she smuggles public struggle into the domestic environment, where it transmutes into haunting "family secrets."[2] Because Haynes's film elaborates on the social pressures that Sirk's films—like their historical milieu—repressed, marginalized, or "euphemized," we could describe its project as both archeological and fantasy driven: archeological because it seeks to restore the social subtext whose anxieties the films captured in their exquisitely overwrought dramas and decors; fantasy driven because *Far from Heaven* lavishes an obsessive attention upon moments when the 1950s "unspeakables"—the loves that dare not speak their names, homosexuality and interracial sex—body forth in all their scandalous effects. Inviting the repressed to return, the film represents the past as trauma. Both the archeological and the fantasmatic come together as *Far from Heaven* searches out those tensions—homoerotic, racial, and social—that Sirk's films held in check, or displaced, in order to disclose them and to restore them to their "proper place."

It is indeed the question of proper place that incites such tensions, for this film is intent on imagining what would happen if "mother" deviated from her popularly assigned tasks. What if she dropped the task of strictly regimenting masculinity into the form of properly virile heterosexuality? What if, instead, she sought not just to support equal rights in the abstract, but to make an actual connection across racial lines? And what if all these things were linked and her personal "politics" exploded the heavily guarded boundaries of suburban middle-class convention? What if she refused to collaborate in the management and repression of what lay just beneath the surface of her home and her culture? What if she made representable what Sirk's films could only hint at? Such a project of re-elaboration or transcoding suggests a dream of filling in the gaps, of exposing underlying textual architecture, and ultimately of retrieving the fullness of the films'—and their period's—meanings. Can the dream of restored plenitude ever be far from maternal metaphors?

In its fantasy of restoring maternal plenitude, *Far from Heaven* seems to me a film that poses the question, What kind of mother does the cinema of the 1950s make? More specifically, what happens if we understand 1950s film melodramas as offering oblique but active contestation of the world of television family sitcoms? Surely, Cathy Whitaker functions as an icon for such contradictions, as all her personal "proclivities" elaborate a certain politics. As Haynes reworks Sirk, de-oedipalizing the melodramas that inevitably turn on intergenerational conflict, he does so from a particular historical perspective. Born in 1961, Haynes comes from a generation for which his film's period, 1957–58, represents the historical moment just before his birth. Thus, we might imagine that period to function as a kind of historical primal scene for the filmmaker.

The year 1957 saw the founding of the Southern Christian Leadership Conference and it witnessed the integration struggle at Little Rock Central High School, which began in August 1957 and continued into 1959. Significantly, the film's very precise historical detail centers on this crisis. For all the TV images we see in the film, the one instance in which we actually see and hear a television broadcast features President Eisenhower's September 23, 1957, appearance on national TV to announce that he was sending federal troops to Little Rock Central High School. At that point, the school remained surrounded by the Arkansas National Guard troops that Governor Orval Faubus had posted on September 2 to prevent its integration.

This isolated televisual event in a text for which Hollywood and television are centrally organizing figures tells us much about the film's angle of view. We can set this moment alongside the emphasis the film puts on *The Three Faces of Eve* (Nunnally Johnson, 1957). That drama of a small-town out woman's shifting identity—between mousy Eve "White" and sultry Eve "Black," in the role that propelled Joanne Woodward to stardom—opened in September 1957. Thus *Far from Heaven*'s studied historical accuracy carries significant political weight: this reference to film history displays the tense vibration during the period between the visibility granted both consciously and unconsciously to race relations in the public media and the rigidly segregated boundaries that conditioned private life.

In its obsession with the image landscape of the 1950s, *Far from Heaven* engages its viewer in the "retrospectatorship" Patricia White so brilliantly analyzes in *UnInvited: Classical Hollywood Cinema and Lesbian Representability* (1999). For White, "all spectatorship, insofar as it engages subjective fantasy, revises memory traces and experiences, some of which are memories and experiences of other movies" (197). Thus retrospectatorship allows us to find in our repeated viewings of the classical Hollywood cinema to which we are personally attached new angles of view on our present media culture. White describes the importance of this process: "Although its modes of production and reception have been historically superseded, it preserves a structuring role culturally and frequently marks individuals and subcultures with its texts and characteristic modes of consumption" (197).

In its own retrospectatorship, *Far from Heaven* entertains the "public sphere" of film and engages with sexuality as a social—rather than a familial—difference. This transformation of the sexual from a familial to a social issue, from a private to a public question, depends heavily on the parallels this film establishes with racial difference.

Extending Sirk: Television as Icon and Agent

Significantly, because *Far from Heaven* deploys television and the movies as technologies for introducing difference into the homogenized world of white suburbia, the period 1957–58 registers as the peak of anxious rivalry between Hollywood and television. Hollywood studios struggled to regain ground from television—and *on* television in the form of the newly evolving genre of "telefilm," films released for TV broadcast. TV's crisis in programming, which is clearly related to the medium's negotiations with Hollywood, can also be connected with cinematic representations of telephobia that abound during the period. Sirk himself appeared systematically hostile to television. In *All That Heaven Allows*, he savagely abases the medium in the memorable scene where Cary's children offer her a TV set as a replacement for the love relationship they have demanded that she relinquish.

Television figures powerfully in *Far from Heaven* as a dead zone within the living room and as a haunting symbolic presence that governs both the Whitaker family's own economy and its iconicity, and that reminds us of the world outside its suburban interior. TV secures a dense network of intertextual resonances, among which are, of course, the connection between television, advertising, and consumer culture that *All That Heaven Allows* so aggressively criticizes. In *Far from Heaven*, by contrast, TV is much more basic, as it is literally constitutive of the family's economy on account of Frank's (Dennis Quaid) position as an advertising executive for the television manufacturer Magnatech. Frank and Cathy embody precisely the consumer nexus that *All That Heaven Allows* and other Sirk films reject.

Television and advertising may be the ground on which *Far from Heaven* operates, but they are never simply taken for granted. For example, TV anchors a sharply telling sequence in the master bedroom, where we see, through Cathy's three-paneled mirror, Frank in bed. As she probes him about his therapy, he resists discussion, asserting his right to privacy. The television playing at the margins of the scene marks the erotic impasse, a substitute for sex and an icon of dysfunction. As the characters speak, we see at least two images of Cathy, from in front of and within the mirror. As in Sirk's films, this split image disorients us as it displaces Cathy in relation to herself. Frank, on the other hand, is mirrored between her images, as though he is confined or framed there. Significantly, this scene is the only one in which the film explicitly references the public-private divide, as Eisenhower's speech about Little Rock imports the most spectacular social conflict of the moment into the bedroom itself. This scene is also the *only* moment the TV is illuminated for the viewer, as we both see and hear Eisenhower; elsewhere, we only ever hear the TV. Yet, because neither character acknowledges the television, it constitutes a kind of ghostly voice-off invading from the public sphere.

But TV also acts as a catalyzing and binding force that actively organizes the film's condensations and displacements. It literally defines Cathy as corporate "wife and mother." Mrs. Leacock, of the *Gazette*'s society page, has, after all, come to interview Cathy as "Mrs. Magnatech." Frank's professional position thus defines her as a "poster" wife and mother explicitly in relation to television. It is this interview that structurally propels Cathy's encounter with her gardener into public view. As the *Gazette* article and its author shadow the couple, the television again propels civil rights to the foreground.

Later on, when Cathy entertains Mrs. Leacock among her many guests at the annual Magnatech corporate party, the television set emerges again as a central object and consumer icon, for both the family and the film, with its broadcast content and its news reporting function. A woman announces that "what's happening in Little Rock couldn't happen in Hartford." Someone suggests that the reason might be that there is no Governor Faubus in Connecticut. But another man chimes in to assert that it's because "there are no Negroes here." In a stunning cut, the film offers us a canted frame, showing the black waitstaff arranging the buffet and being momentarily arrested by this startling comment. When Dick Dawson then intervenes to indicate that, still, "there are some rather dangerous pro-integration types here in Hartford," provoking general jocularity with an allusion to what in this tight community has become a running joke about Cathy's "proclivities," the scene retreats from the visible evidence of white blindness and disavowal.

Dawson thus reminds us of the interview that has generated this characterization of Cathy: "a devoted wife and mother" who is "kind to Negroes." This moment links the TV set to mirrors, screens, and surveillance in a dense condensation of its images and effects. Unilluminated television consoles, like oddly placed mirrors, objects that are *not* for viewing, emphasize the film's ongoing interest in ways of seeing and *not* seeing. In a sequence that is overloaded with mirrors, Mrs. Leacock sneaks up on the Whitakers in their home, thereby recalling the ways that Sirk's mirrors act insistently to deny privacy, to guarantee surveillance. As we watch Cathy and Frank's morning goodbye kiss—in a pose reminiscent of sitcoms and commercials of the period—we hear the camera's shutter click and see the flash as the photographer takes a "candid." This candid image suggests that it is a pose that makes Frank and Cathy a family at all.

As the characters exchange pleasantries in the hallway, we first see Mrs. Leacock in the mirror, flanked by her photographer and by Sybil (Viola Davis), the Whitakers' maid. In a radical departure from the position of black servants in Sirk's films, Sybil is coded early on for an active interpreting gaze: we frequently watch her observing the family around her. During the interview, Cathy sits beside the dark TV set, which is placed awkwardly in a corner, between the couch and the fireplace. Above her head hangs a poster image of Mr. and Mrs. Magnatech by their own TV set. This image clearly bears a schematic resemblance to Cathy and Frank; in other words, it abstracts them. At the same time, it also echoes this film's own work of "abstracting" from Sirk. The Whitakers' relationship is entirely mediated by TV; they are constituted by Frank's professional identity as its advertiser. In a sense, the couple is *only* this image and thus exists only for and through advertising.

Embracing the 1950s obsession with feminine definition, and with it her role as an advertisement for television and for the family, Cathy declares: "My life is just like any other wife and mother's." She continues, elaborating: "I don't think I've ever wanted anything ..." Her sentence trails off at this point as something offscreen catches her interest. We follow her gaze to the window, but its object remains obscure.

After a cut, we follow her outside, where we discover the object of her curiosity and concern, Raymond Deagan. A shocking incongruous detail in the suburban yard, he punctuates Cathy's impossible sentence. He may just be the "anything" she doesn't think she's "ever wanted." When he informs her that he is replacing his dead father as her gardener, Cathy apologizes for her confrontational response to him. She then places her hand on his shoulder and offers condolences. We see this image framed through a pane of glass in the door and from Mrs. Leacock's point of view. Framed through glass, a picture that emblematizes Cathy, this tableau will be frozen and publicized by Mrs. Leacock's article, which describes her as "a woman who is as devoted to her family as she is kind to Negroes." Thus the article creates a kind of slogan that verbally echoes the advertising poster image.

If television underwrites and occasions Cathy's performance as wife and mother in this sequence, it also calls our attention to the actual structure of the model family that surrounds the console. *Far from Heaven* rewrites the central generational conflict of *All That Heaven Allows* in a drama of parallel universes. Most stunning in the parent-child negotiation that constitutes the melodramatic center of *All That Heaven Allows* is, of course, the famous television set that the children offer Cary as a Christmas gift in compensation for the love she has relinquished.

In that key scene, a salesman wheels the console into Cary's living room. As the camera moves in to frame the set, we see her face reflected on its surface. Across her ghostly image we see the evanescence or maternal iconicity to which her children would condemn her. The ghostliness of the darkened screen on which Cary's image floats reminds us that for her children, she is most useful as an image, one borrowed from the idealized repertoire of television.

Sour Notes and False Details

If we can describe Haynes's film as "turning up the volume" on Sirk, exceeding Sirk's excesses, we can see this effect in its proliferation of just such false details and moments of embarrassing strain. These are cast as frequently on the aural plane as on the visual one. Haynes has restored the fullness of the *melos* to his reworking of Sirk. Elmer Bernstein's score provides a more nuanced musical palette than we are accustomed to finding, even in Sirk; it alternates among distinct solo piano, woodwind, and full orchestral passages. Likewise, in its volume, it often obtrudes aggressively into the affective tonality of the unfolding sequences. Much the same effect obtains in this film's dialogue. Where Sirk's characters may rely on euphemism and suggestion, rarely are they inarticulate or strained in expression. By contrast, Haynes's characters experience regular verbal blockage and bypass.

Far from Heaven picks up on this structure at its own conclusion: it ends on a pronounced false note, as an isolated sour note floats free of the piano solo that punctuates the move from the last shots into the ending credit sequence, holding long enough to disturb. A kind of aural pun, this tone reminds us that Sirk specialized in tingeing his happy endings with sour notes, even as it recalls the abundance of false details that shape Haynes's own film, whose false notes—like Sirk's—provide ironic punctuation or retreat from the texture of sentiment and affective charge that composes the melodramatic environment.

Specifically, these details help to mark Frank's "deviance," his affiliation with a subcultural world. We may think of the hideous salmon-orange bird-shaped lamp that his secretary quizzically presents to him on his arrival at his office one morning. We know, of course, that this broken lamp was smashed during his lover's panicked flight after Cathy's interruption of their office tryst. Frank has stuffed it in the *closet*, where the inquisitive secretary has found it. This false note structure carries across and mediates between the specific and punctual embarrassments of private life and the more global scale of public discursive circulation and scandal, as when Mona Lauder spots Cathy getting out of Raymond's truck. On the level of the film's thematics of social difference/deviance, the false note structure effects a transfer between two zones of transgression—homosexuality and interracial relationships.

Among the richest of these false notes are those that mark the central sequences of this classically structured drama, propelling its conflicts into a crisis. In a shockingly revelatory master stroke of performance, Frank disrupts Magnatech's celebration of its new line of televisions, organized by Cathy and her closest friend, Eleanor Fine (Patricia Clarkson). In reply to a vacuous compliment about Cathy's beauty from one of the male guests, Frank erupts with hysterical force. Contorting his body back onto the couch, and affecting a tone lifted directly from Paul Lynde, arguably TV's favorite unacknowledged queer of the 1970s, Frank blurts out: "It's all smoke and mirrors, fellas." Wrinkling his nose and baring his teeth in a signature Lynde grimace while allowing his hands to hang limp in an additional flourish as his body convulses in disgust, he delivers this blow: "You should see her before she puts her face on!" This hideously exquisite moment of stupefying embarrassment and inappropriateness is one of the many tense scenes that anchor and advance the film's plot.

With the fifties housewifely poise exhibited by June Cleaver and Harriet Nelson, Cathy diffuses the shocked silence of the guests: "No, he's absolutely right. We ladies are never what we appear. Every girl has her secrets." Of course, at this point, Cathy's well-guarded secret is her husband's sexuality. But soon the film provides her with an "open" secret of her own relationship with Raymond, with the community of hostile gazes around her fixing the erotic "meaning" of this relationship even before Cathy herself discovers it.

After the party that occupies the film's temporal center, we find Cathy tidying up, crossing the dark living room, where Frank lurks crumpled in an armchair, to stand by the television set near the picture window. We follow her gaze as she turns abruptly. Frank enters the frame, a predatory look contorting his face. Embracing her aggressively, he leads her to the couch and begins to make love to her. When he breaks off brusquely, his discourse mimics the sexual impasse, as he exclaims, "Jesus! What's happening? I can't even . . . God!" Cathy's attempts to reassure him are desperately stilted, and her tone reminds us of the therapeutic discourses that treat homosexuality as a pathology to be cured by "adjustment": "It's all right. The important thing is to keep trying." Frank replies by taunting that perhaps she wouldn't mind if Dick Dawson "could lend his services from time to time." This sequence ends with Frank striking Cathy in frustration. And this moment of violence diffuses itself into the mise-en-scène and across the relay of "false notes" that the film consistently strikes.

The "Color" Angle: Cathy's Clothes

Just as *Far from Heaven* pays scrupulous attention to melodrama's musical signature effect, it also insists on the primary importance of color to the genre, as Sirk handles it. As the literal and figural meanings of color continue to slide into each other, we can begin to read the elaborate effects of condensation and displacement that structure this film's reading of Sirk and of the historical period in which his films emerge.

A key moment produces an abrupt shift in *Far from Heaven*'s color coding. The morning after the Magnatech party, after Frank has struck Cathy, she has rearranged her hair to cover the telling mark. As she puts it brightly to Eleanor, "I experimented." In the film's marvelously economical universe, this slight remark reminds us of Frank's "experiments," both with men and with the failed pose of heterosexuality, and it anticipates Cathy's future cross-racial bonding. What renders this detail so arresting for the spectator, as opposed to Eleanor, however, is that we can't see the bruise. And we never do, despite continued reference to it. Instead, the effect that we *do* see is a startling—almost sickening—chromatic dissonance.

This scene is the first time that the women's clothes don't match or harmonize in a pattern of analogous colors. In her mustard colored coat, brown pants, and green, gold, and brown leaf-patterned blouse, Eleanor rhymes with the autumnal trees behind her. Cathy's attire, however, introduces a striking visual discordance—a cacophonous note. She wears a lavender sweater over a minty green dress. Not only does her dress clash with Eleanor's, but it introduces a new tonal range into the centrally important thematics of women's clothing, as her colors suggest a more 1960s palette. These colors also recall, by contrast, an earlier scene of almost claustrophobic feminine harmony.

Cathy's outfit, with its striking contrast of near complementary color, echoes her signature lavender scarf, a key signifier in the film's metonymic and figural economies (figure 8.2). One especially gorgeous scene—regularly

8.2 Cathy's lavender scarf clashes with the autumnal palette of her friends' outfits but serves as a central signifying knot within the film's political and representational worlds.

referenced in popular critical response to this film—takes shape around the lavender scarf. Cathy's friends have come for lunch, and the four women standing outside the house display across their harmonizing outfits a stunningly coordinated range of warm reds through oranges to gold. These colors blend with the foliage around them and create an exaggerated replica of a common Sirkian effect: keying a woman's clothing to the setting, Sirk merges her into her environment.

One element interrupts the seamless texture of analogous colors here: Cathy's scarf. This cool accent stands out as the false note in the red-orange palette that unites the group and their surroundings. But it rhymes beautifully with the scene's narrative text. Eleanor reads from the *Gazette* article. Her tone turns ironic as she delivers the line that will haunt Cathy throughout the film: "Wife and mother and Mrs. Magnatech herself, Cathleen Whitaker . . . is as devoted to her family as she is kind to Negroes." Eleanor goes on to mention that Cathy has always been a liberal, "ever since she played summer stock in college with all those steamy Jewish boys"; that's why they called her "Red." As Cathy jokes about Senator McCarthy, her lavender scarf blows off and over the roof, leaving her clad entirely in red. So this scene offers not one but two color puns. As the red links Cathy to communists, the lavender suggests her sympathy for homosexuals. Thus Cathy comes to function as a central signifying knot within the film's political universe and its representational one.

After the friends' departure, we next see a close-up of the lavender scarf in Raymond's hand. We hear his voice: "I had a feeling it might be yours." Cathy alludes to her absentmindedness. But Raymond is thinking something else. He has a feeling for "her color": "It was the color . . . it just seemed right." This "feeling for her color," of course, produces another chromatic pun. Beyond the metaphoric reference to race here, not only is Raymond right about Cathy's palette, but he also registers this color as her signature. She will wear a scarf this color to see him off at the train station in the film's poignant final moment, and her appearance in lavender and green, clashing with Eleanor, structurally precipitates her daring expedition with Raymond into the public sphere, where color is also a central issue. That expedition will generate the gossip that forces an end to their contact.

Cathy's sartorial palette consistently produces hyper-signifying effects. Her color spectrum both encodes her centrality to the film's structure and establishes her alternating relations to the diegetic world. Often, the striking contrasts of her outfits seem to speak to her surroundings, but they also lift her out of them by recalling another scene. A dramatic example is her emerald-turquoise blue coat over the russet red dress in which we first see her. Significantly, the basic complementary structure of this red-green ensemble relates to some of the film's most lurid effects of lighting and to the spaces it establishes beyond the home and the office. The movie theater lobby is cast in red and green lights, and both the gay bar and Eagan's Restaurant, the black "club" to which Raymond takes Cathy, are dramatically defined in reds and greens. As Frank hesitates on the threshold of the gay bar, he passes through red and green light, which creates an uneasy effect and anticipates the bar itself.

Likewise, as Cathy and Raymond enter Eagan's, they pass through a pronounced red-green light shift. This garish red-green combination of lighting and interior seems to mark disciplinary or *disciplined* spaces: the movie theater as protected space for furtive private acts, the gay bar and the black club as spaces closed off from the heterosexual and white worlds. These zones of semiprivacy carved out from the public sphere provide a certain privatized sanctuary at the expense of a protective segregation that consolidates difference in a site that is readily policed. Cathy's red-green ensemble, then, helps to establish a link between the spaces that attract and confine Frank and the space of African American leisure and entertainment, thus casting the latter as a zone of furtiveness as well.

Whereas Cathy's palette is defined by its vividness and its extensive range, and by its volatile relationship to the environment, Raymond's and Frank's remarkably restrained wardrobes are no less powerfully engaged in the film's chromatic metaphors. Frank appears only in shades of gray and blue—until Miami, that is, where the film's palette emphasizes the contrast of pink to blue in a gendered pun. He is most frequently shot in blue light, which perhaps suggests a pun on his "perverse" sexuality, recalling a contemporary term for pornography: *blue movies*. Raymond, by contrast, appears entirely clad in earth tones and muted warm colors, as in the red-orange-yellow plaid wool shirt he wears with brown corduroy trousers for gardening. His uniform attire fixes him in his place as a man centered in his own inner confidence, but also visually static and resolutely bound to nature.

Stammering

Cathy's wardrobe secures her status as the film's captivating visual center. Rare are the moments when a scene does not focus on Cathy, and most telling are those moments when the film's attention wanders from her or becomes urgently drawn away from her. As she alone traces a path connecting Frank's secret world and Raymond's invisible world, her presence and absence condition what we see, and this conditioning amounts to a narrative limitation. Although we see Cathy herself almost continuously, often we do not see what she sees; just as often, our view exceeds or anticipates hers, as in the scene where Eleanor phones to warn her about the gossip surrounding her and Raymond. Before Cathy notices, we see Frank tensely approaching, tightly framed by the verticality of the hall doorway off the kitchen. The displacement of our view from Cathy's produces dramatic consequences that reverberate in camerawork and framing as they shape encounters of impasse, blockage, or bypass among the characters.

Striking displacements also emerge in the montage. Among the most stunning of the film's dissolves is the one that propels Cathy out of her kitchen and into the revolving door of Frank's office building, where she will discover him with another man. This expressionistic image matches the rate and direction of Cathy's passage across the kitchen onto the flurry of the door's revolution, literally precipitating her toward a moment of discovery and out of the illusory closure of her conventional domestic life. Here, both montage and camerawork operate with an interpretive force and an obtrusiveness that rival the work of the film's imposing and fraught mise-en-scène. Shallow focus forces the figures to stand in sharp relief against blurred backgrounds. Such an effect obliges continual reexamination of figure and ground relations, and metaphorically destabilizes the characters' relation to their contexts.

In two-shot compositions, which Haynes strongly favors for Cathy's and Raymond's interactions, rack focus pulls one figure into crisp definition while blurring the other. Frequently, one of the two figures dominates the frame as a blur or a blob, as the camera shoots from behind the back or shoulder to capture the other figure frontally in a medium shot. Thus, we could say that in *Far from Heaven*, *angles* of view predominate significantly over *points* of view, meaning that subjective shots are largely replaced by distinct angles on the characters and their interactions—the view of a deeply interested and always interpreting third party.

Frank and Cathy's scenes are marked by distance, by noncommunicating space, almost never supported by shot–reverse shot techniques of spatial continuity. Rack focus casts one into relief, while the other fades into the background, as if to inscribe their inability to inhabit the same plane. Their encounters often begin with the audience realizing, along with Cathy, that Frank hovers nearby, just out of frame. Equally important, Frank and Cathy's dialogue could best be described as haltingly inarticulate, stammering in bypasses.

Perhaps the most striking example emerges when Frank "comes out" to Cathy. After her shocking discovery at the office, she sits in darkness beside the dark TV set at home until Frank arrives. Dazed, she resorts to household small talk about a roofer's estimate, until the following "exchange" ensues:

CATHY I can't . . .
FRANK I don't . . . uh, I don't . . .
CATHY What?
FRANK You see, uh . . . once a long time ago, a long, long time ago, I had, uh . . . problems. . . . I just figured that was . . . that was it. I never imagined . . .
CATHY You had problems?
FRANK (*anguished*) Yes.
CATHY You never spoke to anyone? . . . A doctor?
FRANK No.
CATHY No? . . . I don't understand.
FRANK Neither do I.
CATHY What if? . . . I mean, there must be people . . .
FRANK I . . . I don't know.
CATHY Because, otherwise, I don't know what I . . .

In this last line, Cathy applies the same locution she uses when expressing exasperation at her son's refusal to heed her instructions. And Frank finally capitulates to her unspoken demand: "All right." Hearing the densely charged silences that bear the meaning between the words here, one might imagine the "closet" as equipped with a revolving door.

By contrast, the film tracks the development of intimacy between Cathy and Raymond through a shift from embarrassing and sputtering conversations to more "naturalistic" dialogue. And transition is significant, because the film thereby establishes a parallel between the increasingly stalled articulateness between Cathy and her husband and the growing fluency of her exchanges with Raymond. As Cathy's ignorance underpins this structure, the film equates her heteronormative wishfulness with the naïveté that feeds her racial curiosity about, as she puts it, "being the only one in a room."

After their first awkward meeting on her porch, Cathy and Raymond come together again at Eleanor's art show (figure 8.3). Spotting Raymond, Cathy crosses the gallery to ask with surprise, "How on earth did you find out about this show?" Raymond replies with irony: "I *do* read the papers," prompting Cathy to offer the following "account" of herself: "No, of course you do. I just meant that it's such a . . . it's a coincidence. Because, you know, . . . I'm not prejudiced. . . . My husband and I have always believed in equal rights for the Negro and support the NAACP." "I just wanted you to

8.3 Cathy encounters Raymond and his daughter at the art show.

know," she continues. Raymond rescues her with a wildly inappropriate, "Thank you."

This conversation, captured at weirdly oblique angles—as Cathy's view of Raymond amounts to a take on the "race angle"—suggests again the importance of angles throughout this film. As Raymond and Cathy speak in her yard after he has found her lavender scarf, for example, the couple is framed together from varying angles. A low angle on Cathy alternates with a high angle on Raymond, and subsequent shots offer a low angle on him and a higher one on her. Our sense of perspective, of size, and of relations of power keeps shifting, suggesting an overall instability or indefiniteness to this relationship.

Canted frames function similarly, and they likewise puncture the diegetic surface. As such, they introduce a trauma around the emergence of "deviance" or transgression in the public visual field. The abrupt dislocation of the frame and with it of our perspective suggests the trauma the transgressive figure or couple fears or experiences in public; it also suggests the traumatized hostility of the white or heteronormative public sphere when interrupted by the spectacle of its "others."

Because *Far from Heaven* provides us with few conventional point-of-view shots, we spectators confront a universe where characters uneasily inhabit ambiguous spaces. In two-shot structures that largely replace shot–reverse shot conversations, we read mostly through reaction shots. Notable point-of-view shots do occur, however, and they form a striking pattern. When Cathy enters Frank's office on that fateful evening, a swish pan follows her inquisitive gaze as it picks up the men's kiss. Can the choice of a "swish" pan be neutral?

Frank's visit to the Ritz Theater provides the most sustained and particularly stunning derailment of the film's attention to Cathy. The only sequence in which we see him alone creates a particularly pointed—poignant—and dense intertextual kernel. Days after his arrest for "loitering," Frank leaves his coworkers after a business dinner, drunk and careening. He ducks into the theater, where he catches a sequence from *The Three Faces of Eve* and also observes a very dandified young man who has descended from the balcony for a smoke. Later he follows two men from the balcony outside the theater. Under lurid blue light reflecting on the wet pavement, Frank scuttles along, framed in a sharply canted angle that marks his "wrong turn," the altered perspective that leads him to the gay bar, where he picks up the fellow with whom Cathy will later catch him.

Switch Points

Far from Heaven carefully constructs a sort of symmetry within its own architecture between racial and sexual oppression, bringing together the violent repressions of both racial mobility and sexual choice. Not surprisingly, to render oppression in the visual, the film recurs to the forbidden couple: on the one side, the homosexual couple, "unnatural" because of its nonreproductive erotics; on the other, the interracial couple, which scandalizes because its sexuality might reproduce the "wrong" children.

In this transfer from invisible to visible "vice" or difference, Cathy becomes the film's switch point, the central fulcrum through which the film constructs its parallel worlds. This function emerges strikingly during an exchange with Eleanor, who reminds Cathy to attend the art show she has organized, while gossiping cattily about Mona Lauder and her uncle, Morris Farnsworth, a New York art dealer. Eleanor muses at length: "A bit flowery for my taste.... A touch light on his feet?... Yes, darling, he's one of *those*.... Of course, I could be mistaken. It's just an impression I got...." This pause allows a beat in which the scene's delicious and aggressive irony asserts itself, because it highlights the ignorant knowingness that makes Eleanor such a comfortable inhabitant of her era, while it simultaneously underlines Cathy's discomfort and alienation.

Cathy indicates that she's done some reading on the subject of homosexuality (just like the good liberal that she aspires to be and, of course, in keeping with the 1950s popular appetite for analyses of deviance). Eleanor remarks that Cathy is taking an interest in "another civic cause" and imagines society page copy about "Cathy Whittaker and her kindness to Negroes and homosexuals." Meanwhile, Eleanor's confident assertion of her ignorance about homosexuals counterpoints her anxious policing of Cathy's public interaction with Raymond at the art show and her horrified concern to deny the gossip Mona circulates about Cathy's interracial dalliance. Her carefully guarded ignorance forges another link—albeit one of disavowal—between Frank's and Cathy's transgressions, which in turn contributes to a growing parallel between their bad object choices.

Of course, both of Cathy's object choices are "bad." Each of the film's men is condemned and endangered if he finds himself in the wrong place—takes a "wrong turn," in the vocabulary of the boys who harass Raymond's daughter. And the wrong place is, respectively, the segregated space of the art show and the company of a white woman, or the gay bar, the cruising zone, or the arms of another man. The striking difference between the two men's positions, however, is that Raymond is continually contained and surveilled by the social gaze, whereas Frank becomes "visible" only if he enters a gay zone or appears coupled with a man. Only when Raymond enters the black club, the one space in the film where we see a population of black characters, might he shed his hypervisibility. But he cannot, because he has brought Cathy along with him, thus reproducing as inversion the same effects he encounters in the white world. Signally important here, this scene reminds us of a black parallel universe that this film imagines but also segregates. We never gain access to Raymond independent of Cathy's presence or agency. By marked contrast, we do see Frank in the key sequence that "outs" him to us, which also takes place in a culturally segregated bar.

As the film produces striking incidents involving social difference, it becomes especially attentive to gaze structures, both introducing its relatively rare subjective point-of-view shots and emphasizing the collective gaze. In *Far from Heaven*, an especially poignant moment links imposed homosexual furtiveness with racial segregation: when Frank and Cathy are reclining by the pool in Miami, a little black boy runs out of the hotel and dips his foot in the pool. Horrified white women desperately urge their children out of the water and scramble away from the poolside, demonstrating the kind of visceral terror of contamination that a Jim Crow system built and sustained. As a man dressed in hotel livery, who appears to be the boy's father, berates the child aggressively, the incident introduces a brutally realist cast into the melodramatic texture.

But this scene also recalls the discourse of pathology and contamination surrounding homosexuals, that other group segregated out of Frank and Cathy's world of white suburban families. So, we must read the awful incident that ruptures the idyllic and luxurious Miami scene by revealing its structural subtext, the segregation to which it is hysterically bound, in terms of another subtext, as Frank visually tracks the movement of the pretty boy (Nicholas Joy) he had spotted the night before. We follow Frank's gaze across the pool to the young man's family, and we watch as the boy goes lazily to join them, overhearing with Frank his claim he was looking for them "on the other side."

After spotting the young man, Frank volunteers to go back to the room to fetch Cathy's forgotten book, her "Miss Mitchell," as she puts it. The reference to *Gone with the Wind* reverberates: it recalls the book's romanticization of segregation via plantation life, and it suggests the kind of conventionally escapist literature the suburban lady of leisure might pursue, in place of Cathy's "civic issues." When Frank reaches the room, we see him captured in an oblique angle through the mirror, from a point just outside the door, which stands ajar. In the next shot, from a vantage point just behind Frank's shoulder, the camera reveals the pretty young man's face in an opposing oblique angle through the mirror. In addition to deploying Sirkian play with mirrors to indicate indirection, violations of privacy, and structures of both revelation and masking or distortion, this shot retrospectively places us in the spot the young man is now occupying. And the slow movement of his hand across his torso and down into his trunks constitutes what is unquestionably the film's most erotic gesture, as this scene offers the film's most intense sexual charge, along with the most sustained shot–reverse shot structures that are not hostile. This scene reminds us of the absence of eroticism between Cathy and Raymond. And it reminds us that Raymond is systematically deprived of point of view.

But this furtive erotic connection takes place against the background of the brutally interrupted connection between black and white at the pool. Thus, the visible and public violation of social rules sets the stage for the unseen private violation. Significantly, moreover, the seriousness and erotic charge of this scene may be undercut by the young man's classic resemblance to all-American white boy Troy Donohue, whose character beats Sarah Jane in *Imitation of Life*. When, later in the film, the lover for whom Frank has left Cathy turns out to be this very same impervious, flat, superficial character, his blank indifference assures us that Frank will not live happily ever after; his story will end in disappointment.

Disappointments and False Analogies

Like Sirk's work, this film exploits the layered texture of melodramatic form to elaborate both affect and irony. And like Sirk, Haynes understands that the imposition of affective tonality native to melodrama guarantees and embeds ironic potential that the structure itself can never fully control. But, as in Sirk's work, it is the moments of referential "breakthrough," those instances where the film incorporates contemporary social issues of race and sexuality, that remain problematic and that trouble—or disappoint—the logic of *Far from Heaven*.

Raymond and Cathy's final meeting at the train station mobilizes a surprising level of pathos within the film's generally cool tonality. This wordless scene, filmed in shot–reverse shot, offers the spectator sustained subjective views as it captures the exchange of looks upon which it turns. And the scene does turn, literally, as the camera pivots to follow Cathy's gaze on Raymond as the train pulls past her, and then turns to frame her against the yellow wall of the station, maintaining a fixed distance from her as Raymond recedes. Thus establishing point of view to control the scene, and then withdrawing, like Raymond, the film emphasizes Cathy's solitude, as it highlights the actors' performances in facial expression and body language. But this is also the only time Raymond's point of view is not limited to inscribing a reaction to hostility.

This compelling moment, however, also gains force by its contrast to other less successful moments of pathos. One such moment is when Cathy breaks off her relationship with Raymond, after Eleanor has announced the scandal it is causing and Frank has flown into a rage about the damage Cathy is causing to *his* reputation. Cathy delivers her decision to Raymond in the tone of bland, superficial politeness that has characterized most of her discourse throughout the film: "You've been nothing but kind to me, and I've been perfectly reckless and foolish in return," concluding, "It's just not *plausible* that we should be friends." Here we remember the film's continual play on plausibility and verisimilitude in its extended reflection on melodrama.

Raymond's response bears all of the scene's affective force: he asks whether people "can't manage for one fleeting moment to see beyond the surface, beyond the color of things?" When Cathy replies that she herself cannot get beyond the surface, we are reminded that, as a figure, Cathy is all external appearances, her clothing a dazzling carapace. Raymond—who, by contrast, asserts enigmatically that he "has no choice" but to see beyond the surface—is also the character who is confined, constricted, and policed purely on account of the visual surface of things. In the distance between its characters here, the film forces a question it cannot answer: What draws Raymond to Cathy? Is it desire? Identification? Is he attracted to what she is, or what she has? Is his attraction erotic or pedagogical? Does he pity Cathy, or does he identify with the social circumscription of her life? Tellingly, because the film never clarifies Raymond's motives, it limits the story it can tell about him to the allusive set of vague analogies that Cathy provides.

As Cathy turns to leave after her pronouncement, Raymond places his hand on her arm to detain her. At this point, the film interrupts the couple: a white man across the street yells to him, "Hey, boy, hands off." Subsequent shots frame groups of white spectators in canted angles, as if shifting the balance of the world, leaving everyone else on one side of the frame, opposing Cathy and Raymond. But this canted angle also suggests potential violence in response to this sudden reorientation of their perspective as they see something that shouldn't be seen. Here, as elsewhere, the film emphasizes the displacement of erotic tension onto the aggressive responses of those who witness the couple's interaction. The violence of diegetic spectator response inscribes a displaced intensity, eroticism coming on the rebound, so to speak, since it is utterly suppressed between Cathy and Raymond.

In other words, no tension emerges *between* Raymond and Cathy, though it emerges all around them. Conversely, nothing but tension marks Cathy and Frank's interactions, in the barely suppressed aggression just below the surface of Frank's voice and expression. Thus, *Far from Heaven* offers a distinct displacement of interest from Sirk's films. Whereas in Sirk's films women tend to function as sites of tension, both in relation to men and between men, in this film men remain the primary site of erotic interest, and they establish the sharpest contrasts.

In contrast to the men, Cathy, bustling purposively through her household, like Donna Reed or June Cleaver, is the model 1950s "wife and mother." She is obtrusively, but indifferently, attentive to her children's and husband's health and hygiene—physical and mental (figure 8.4). Her alternately therapeutic and managerial style with her family produces an

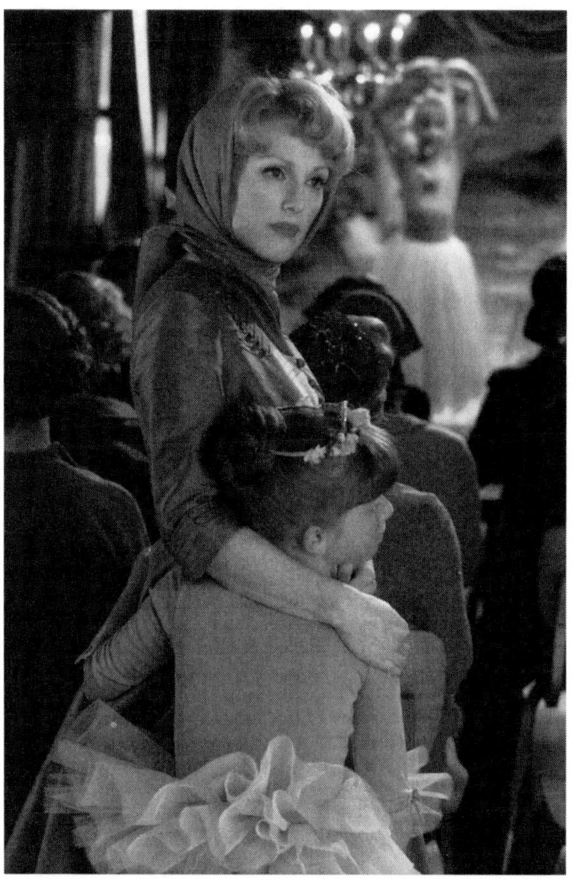

8.4 As a typical 1950s housewife, Cathy is obtrusively, but indifferently, attentive to her children and husband.

image of the 1950s mom caught in a web of discourses of expert advice and saddled with the task of managing everyone. In this world, Frank's eruptions reveal the false details in the smooth Hallmark greeting card picture the family is expected to uphold.

This film constructs Cathy as the image of a mother the 1950s dreamed of: herself having internalized the repression that she imposes on the family, she is a force charged with maintaining domestic stability and boundaries. Because she consistently disappoints her role even in its performance, she might appear to be the ideal figure for feminist sympathy, alignment, or projection. But in *Far from Heaven*'s world, within the fragile, tenuous moments of potential identification this film offers—and they are limited by its paucity of point-of-view shots, its preference for reaction shots, and its commitment to aesthetic distance—Frank is the character who displays and deploys the uncontrolled rage, the uncontainable erotic energy, and the affective protest that we wish to find in Cathy.

If the film stages the decline of Cathy and Frank's marriage to its final breakdown in the strangled inarticulateness of their dialogues, by contrast, Raymond stands out as the most fluent character. He is the one who stimulates the flow of Cathy's speech and thought. Eloquent as he is, however, Raymond can only *tell*. Unlike Frank, who can *show* us his most private world, Raymond never appears without Cathy in this film. Because she is the switch point, effecting a transfer between the two men and their worlds and establishing a parallel in their respective opacity for her, Raymond, in the end, remains the film's mystery.

Raymond has spoken explicitly about his other world, a world that the film inadvertently constructs as a kind of parallel to Frank's "secret." This world is one to which Cathy has had no previous access, and which seems indeed not to exist for her. In this connection, we might say that Cathy's exchanges with blacks inevitably reach an impasse. Her encounters with all but Raymond are disappointed, disappointing, or failed.

But Cathy is also continually both disappointed and disappointing in her knowledge of Raymond's world. Significantly, the film disappoints on this point as well: Raymond's world is, for the film, even more invisible than the gay subculture whose margins Frank haunts and with which it strikes a false structural analogy. When Raymond notices Cathy's bruise and makes the connection to the secrets she wishes to hide—domestic strife and, behind it, Frank's sexuality—she deflects his concern: "I guess we all have our troubles.... I'm sure you do yourself ..." She trails off, indicating that she means to suggest an awkward analogy. But seeing his interrogative look, she ventures: "I keep wondering what it must be like to be the only one in the room ... colored or otherwise." In response, Raymond describes a life that remains a "secret" to Cathy: "There *is* a world where everybody does indeed look like me.... Trouble is, most people never leave it."

This exchange brings them to Eagan's, an implausible combination of restaurant and midafternoon nightclub—as if all the community's entertainments had to be condensed into this one space. Nowhere is Raymond's inability to *show* rather than tell more evident than during this ethnographic visit to a "black space." And the fact that he must keep telling and explaining suggests that in *Far from Heaven*'s universe, "blackness" requires explanation, whereas gayness does not.[3]

But Cathy troubles the sealed world of black leisure. She troubles it just as she and Raymond, by alighting from his truck together, disrupt Mona Lauder's world, as a canted frame captures her shocked—and smug—reaction. As they enter Eagan's, Cathy and Raymond are greeted by a range of hostile gazes. This building tension culminates when an older male customer speaks to Raymond: "What the hell you doing, boy?" At this point, the film seems intent on suggesting that black and white hostility to interracial couples are precisely analogous. Perhaps most significantly, this forced comparison seems to hinge on the word "boy," which the white man outside the movie theater will later echo. But of course this is a false echo: the white man uses the word as a racial epithet, whereas the black man uses it generationally. To the implausibility of this implied analogy, the scene in Eagan's adds other false notes.

Eventually, as Raymond and Cathy begin to dance to a full jazz ensemble (which is, again, implausibly playing to a midafternoon dance crowd), the couple is isolated at the center of the frame, a pure spectacle for the now invisible black spectators. This sequence in the uncomfortable but safe refuge of the all-black space ends with a utopian, fantasmatic image. Posed as an ethnography, this scene, riddled with false details, strikes us primarily as a suburban white fantasy about segregated black spaces.

A similarly facile analogy between black and white hostility and violence makes the last dialogue between Cathy and Raymond also ring false. Having learned belatedly about the white boys' attack on a little black girl, Cathy rushes to Raymond's house. In a striking parallel with the use of the service entrance sometimes required of blacks, Raymond asks Cathy to meet him at the side door of the house. He explains that his business has been ruined by the scandal of their relationship—plausible enough, since he relies on white patronage for much of his livelihood. What he tells her next, however, is starkly implausible. He declares that the rocks that have broken his windows "were thrown by Negroes" and concludes that "that's one place that whites and colored are in perfect harmony."

Although this scene strives for a tragic pathos here, it derails on this stunningly unlikely premise, failing to acknowledge, let alone capture, the historical complexity and nuance of African American communities' responses to interracial relationships. As it strains for a racial analogy here, the film stumbles on its referential breakthrough. It cannot, in other words, consistently rely on the referential force of the civil rights movement in the years 1957–58 and then go on to strike an unbelievable parallel like this one. In this moment, the tensions between realism and melodrama reach their most extreme. At this point, perhaps more than at any other, one is aware that the film aligns itself with Cathy, persists in relaying an identification with her. But here, its viewpoint seems to slide into coincidence with hers, believing for a moment what Cathy herself might want to believe.

In a world where everyone's longings and desires are disappointed, Raymond's is surely the harshest fate: he must liquidate business and property and move to Baltimore to start over. He is expelled from his world—both the white world of his business and the black one of his community. Although Frank is expelled from his family and from heteronormativity, and Cathy is expelled from suburban wifely normalcy, neither ends up as bereft as Raymond. He is literally pushed off the film's map, and off his own map as well: by his account, he has never even been to Baltimore.

Gradually, but consistently, *Far from Heaven* effects a certain displacement of difference, transferring and articulating the "invisible" vice of Frank's homosexual desires onto the transgressive scandal of "visible" difference in the interracial couple. Because the film builds its parallels around Cathy, her fascination with the mystery and inaccessibility of both men introduces an equivalency between them. Perhaps more to the point, it constructs the men as the "secret," the mysterious depth to be investigated and penetrated, and leaves Cathy as a vehicle for the spectator's, and its own, interest in the men.

This web of fascination, secrets, and disappointments splits into two parallel universes around Cathy. All the sexuality and desire coalesce in the homosexual sphere, while the interracial couple is drained of erotics. Equally important, racial difference becomes accessible only through an analog structure founded on coupling, by which we return to the lens of heteronormativity. Ultimately, the film disappoints its own logic because its structural analogy between racism and homophobia fails through its very visual organization. It cannot go beyond the boundaries it has set for Cathy in terms of racialized geography and spaces. And it can't grant Raymond the independence it permits Frank because it has not endowed him with a point of view.

Race, then, is *dis*placed into the interracial bond and *re*placed by the white-black couple. Thus, the film's "racial angle" fades into a white perspective of fascination with the ongoing mystery of a black world elsewhere. Perhaps, like the protofeminist 1950s mother whose complex and contradictory political plenitude the film seeks to restore, and proceeding by the analogies that she might have favored, *Far from Heaven* is condemned, by the very project it so lovingly elaborates, to disappoint. But, like Sirk's characters and Haynes's own, this film is a lovely and compelling disappointment.

NOTES

This chapter originally appeared in *Camera Obscura: Feminism, Culture, and Media Studies* 18, no. 3 (2003): 131–75. An edited version is reprinted here.

1 To name just a few of these important interventions: Doane (1991); Doane, Mellencamp, and Williams (1984); L. Fischer (1991); Gledhill (1987); Penley (1988).

2 On the liminal status of television in US culture, see Joyrich (2001). In arguing that television is both conceptually and structurally bound to the logic of the closet, she contends that "by both mediating historic events for familial consumption and presenting the stuff of 'private life' to the viewing public, the institutional organization of US broadcasting situates television precisely on the precarious border of public and private, 'inside' and 'outside.' Here it constructs knowledges identified as both secret (domestically received) and shared (defined as part of a collective national culture)" (445).

3 In this connection, Haynes's film is negotiating ongoing exchanges and tensions between race and sexuality that shape many popular representations. Lynne Joyrich finds that, on TV, contemporary queer sidekicks have come to occupy much the same place to which African American secondary characters have often been relegated. Within these specific roles, she finds a distinct vacillation at what she calls "epistemological nodal points." "Television's queer characters," she writes, "may not necessarily play the (still often common) role of obscure objects, loci of mystery, scandal, and uncertainty; instead they may be figured as devoid of all mystery (and thus potentially of all dramatic interest), more pedagogic than puzzling . . . [ultimately] constructed as epistemological nodal points" (Joyrich 2001, 456).

9 All That Whiteness Allows

Femininity, Race, and Empire in *Safe*, *Carol*, and *Wonderstruck*

Danielle Bouchard and Jigna Desai

Todd Haynes's 1995 film *Safe* not only marked a certain moment of arrival for this esteemed filmmaker, but also offered sophisticated and timely commentary on a confluence of late 1980s/early 1990s political events and social formations. In the figure of Carol White, the film's main protagonist, we get a deep reflection on the neoliberal, imperial, and white-ascendant undertones of progressive discourses that tout self-help and consumerism as the "safe" methods of social change. *Safe* is set in 1987, and through affluent homemaker Carol's slow decline due to a seemingly undiagnosable illness, the film critiques the mutually constitutive relationship of whiteness and compulsory heterosexuality informing certain contemporary renderings of the AIDS crisis. *Safe* clearly indicts the fetishization of individual suffering white bodies, which served to hide both the blatant instrumentalization of this illness in order to attempt to consign queer people of color to death *and* the intersectional organizing that brought HIV/AIDS to light and demanded both resources and love for those affected by it. The film also, for us, importantly troubled an ongoing event in the formation of feminism itself: a white sense of entitlement to the study and practice of feminism, expressed in a centering of the white self precisely through the appropriation of others' work.[1] *Safe* came on the scene at a key moment of feminist institutionalization, when feminist of color scholarship, creative work, and indeed labor were being simultaneously called on and covered up by whitened renditions of gender and sexuality.

In the early 2000s we wrote about *Safe* after learning of our mutual love for this film (Bouchard and Desai 2005). Although Haynes's work has been the subject of a rich body of feminist and queer analysis, his films also, in a notable but less commented on set of thematics, often gesture toward the fraught relationships between racial formation, empire, and the regulation of public and private life through gender and sexual norms. US wars of empire, for example, are often hinted at as the subtext of the gender and sexual trouble Haynes's main characters face: the US War in Vietnam in *Superstar: The Karen Carpenter Story* (1987) and *I'm Not There* (2007); the so-called Cold War in *Far from Heaven* (2002) and *Carol* (2015); the forced migrations of people from places subject to US military "intervention" into Carol White's suburban enclave in *Safe*. Yet these themes remain underexplored, perhaps most explicitly so in regard to the status and uses of whiteness that are so abundantly apparent in the patterns and themes that have come to define Haynes's body of work: the choice of fictional narratives, cultural figures, and artistic works that predominantly feature white people or who are themselves white; the consistent casting of certain actresses for whom whiteness has become one hallmark of their careers (Julianne Moore most notably, but also Cate Blanchett); and sometimes the more explicit thematizing of whiteness as a multilayered signifier that deeply conditions femininity and sexuality within the larger context of US empire.

Of all of Haynes's films, *Safe* is the one that perhaps most directly explores and even centers the latter kind of approach. In this chapter, we thus revisit themes explored in our 2005 article in order to examine how whiteness, racial normativity, and US empire deeply inflect the rendering of queer or feminist analysis in Haynes's work. Of the six features Haynes has directed since *Safe*, we focus on *Carol* and *Wonderstruck*, the two most recent that also have the least amount of scholarship written about them. (The pivotal film *Far from Heaven* serves as a significant reference point for us, particularly with regard to *Carol*.) *Carol* was heralded as a work of aesthetic and technical perfection and a landmark film of the "LGBT" genre (Brown 2016). Precisely because of the way it has been figured as simultaneously beautiful and a timely political statement—it was released not long after the US Defense of Marriage Act was struck down, and it features two women falling in love—*Carol* calls for further discerning considerations, ones that detail the sorts of queer aesthetics and politics it both allows and forecloses.[2] So does *Wonderstruck*.[3] Adapted (and not by Haynes) from Brian Selznick's award-winning novel, *Wonderstruck* actually revisits what could be said to be key "Haynesian" themes—the domestic and public geographies produced by differential mobilities, the relationship between seeing/looking and power in the visual arts—yet it routes these through the eyes of white childhood innocence in a largely uncritical way. Haynes did not write the screenplays for either of these movies, making them a departure from his previous films. Yet as he has earned deep respect and admiration as an independent film director, "Todd Haynes" has come to be a meaningful signifier in its own right, and many have taken up his films as defining contributions to what a queer or feminist representational politics (or both) should be. Haynes himself has from very early on thoughtfully complicated the labels and framings applied to his films, for example, in articulating a commitment to a queer film practice not confined to the question of gay identity (Laskawy 2014, 21). It thus seems that questions regarding the particular characteristics of the queer and feminist analyses informing and created by these two films surely are in the spirit of Haynes's own intellectual, political, and artistic commitments.

Visual and Spatial Architectures of Whiteness in *Safe*

When we first wrote about *Safe*, we highlighted its complex rendering of the emergence of heteronormative femininity within the processes of racialization particular to US empire. Whereas some writings about the film emphasized the theme of women's entrapment within married domesticity, we saw Carol White more as a thoughtful critique of white feminine mobility, entitlement, and ownership. Here, to frame our readings of *Carol* and *Wonderstruck*, we focus our discussion of *Safe* on its exposure of the production of whiteness and of the technological, aesthetic, and ideological forms through which it has come to be normalized within dominant cinematic practices. In *Safe*, whiteness is made visible as a force that obscures. It makes certain people and spaces, and the relationships among them, difficult to see. It impedes understanding, of both oneself and others. It fails to yield safety precisely because it produces risk and harm. It ensures Carol's continued decline despite all her efforts to "get clear," not least because it relies on precisely that which is making her sick—namely, the domestic consumerism through which she undertakes her self-fashioning. Another way to say this is that *Safe* imagines and images a breakdown of

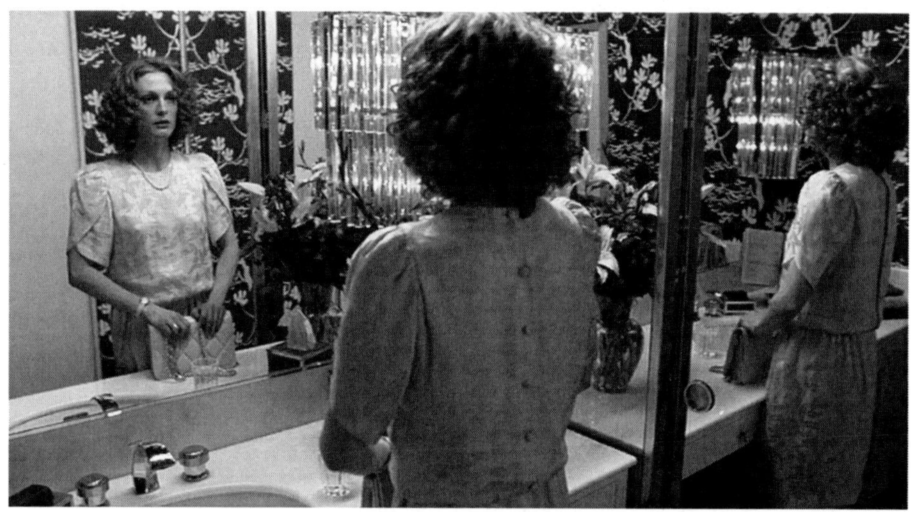

9.1 At her friend's baby shower, *Safe*'s Carol White begins to show outward signs of illness. In the bathroom mirror, Carol is confronted with the breakdown of her whiteness; meanwhile one of her friends remarks to another friend, "Is there something wrong with Carol? 'Cause her skin looks kinda ..."

the standardized cinematic relationship between whiteness, looking, and the spatial configurations of the imperial, settler colonial state.

It is worth considering how whiteness looks in *Safe*. On Carol in particular it looks neither healthy nor natural. Moreover, the film makes clear from the beginning that whiteness is something that is in constant active production through a wide array of specific bodily practices—the intake of certain foods, the creation of a specific body shape, the choice of particular hairstyles, the comportment of one's body in specific ways with specific people, and meticulous clothing choices (figure 9.1). In one very early scene, in the locker room after an aerobics class, Carol's friends—all of them seemingly white, though none of them as hyperwhite as Carol—discuss various forms of self-maintenance (diet, exercise, emotional "health"). One of them pauses to remark, "You know, Carol, you do not sweat." Carol replies, modestly, "It's true," but even this seemingly natural and effortless quality is revealed to be fleeting as Carol's aesthetic "perfection" is compromised by the onset of her illness. In contravention to conventional cinematic lighting, staging, makeup, production, and other standards, *Safe* exposes the numerous efforts whiteness requires. Not the least of these are Carol's interactions with a variety of other characters, including, and perhaps most importantly, those whose service work Carol and her cohort rely on, almost all of whom appear to be people of color. The film's tracking of Carol's movements through and placement within the spaces of the home, the city, and later the desert retreat (Wrenwood Center) makes visible the processes through which white inhabitation of such spaces is made to *seem* natural—even as it relies on the production and continued existence of racial, ethnic, and geopolitical differences.

In a thoughtful reading, Nicole Seymour (2011) considers the way certain shots allow a purposely compromised view of people who are quite literally marginalized by and in the spaces that Carol White and those like her own and freely move through. In one example, Carol sits in her living room drinking a glass of milk while the soundtrack and a slow dolly zoom focused on Carol's largely still figure convey a sense of dread; this scene is a pivotal one, the first in which Carol is portrayed as not feeling well. In the background, in the right-hand corner of the frame and through a cutout in the wall, we see two painters, though their faces are obscured and we can only see the top halves of their bodies. They are painting the kitchen cabinets, thus being exposed to compounds with much more deleterious health effects than milk, as Seymour points out (28). Indeed, Seymour invites us to read *Safe* as primarily about "the sovereignty of the visible, and how the visible *becomes visible*" (30; emphasis in the original), noting that the film's focus on Carol is meant to draw attention to the many deletions that such a focus requires. What Carol herself is unable or unwilling to see, or perhaps both, is often suggested through such cinematic choices; for instance, when we see domestic worker Fulvia instructing another domestic worker (in untranslated Spanish), we hear but do not see Carol (who herself cannot see Fulvia) calling for Fulvia over and over from another room.

Considering such examples provides a somewhat different reading of an oft-noted characteristic of *Safe*: Carol is in almost every shot, but very often she appears off-center in long or medium-long shots, her placement in the frame unconventional for a film so focused on one character. Although this has often been discussed as representing Carol's alienation from and circumscription by the gendered spaces and roles she is forced to inhabit, in our view the camerawork is more about revealing the architecture and organization of these spaces, namely, just how very ordered and managed they are, and the social structures that imbue them with meaning. In this way, *Safe* reveals the normative modes of positioning white characters in space and in relation to light that have become so naturalized as to be difficult to see. According to Richard Dyer in his book *White* (1997), this involves not just lighting practices that favor lighter skin tones, but "a whole culture of light" (84) that includes (among other standards) the positioning of individual white characters as standing out from the background to highlight "the unique and special character of the individual" (102).

Through Carol's placement, movement, and appearance, *Safe* traces a geography of empire, the attempted ordering of the space not just of the US but of the entire globe. It thus reveals how looking is, under this ordering regime, organized as a constant attempt to reinscribe the white heteronormative self at the center of the frame, so to speak, whether through the settler colonialist tactic of figurally absenting Native peoples who are in fact *still there*, or through the trope of the globe inhabited by a supposedly unified humanity. This reinscription becomes devastatingly apparent as the setting of the film shifts from blatantly conservative suburbia to the Wrenwood Center, with its ostensibly progressive approach to recovery and recuperation.[4] As she comes to recognize herself as environmentally ill, Carol is forced to abandon some of the methods through which she had previously reproduced her body as a white and straight one (makeup, an exercise routine, expensive clothing). One set of self-management techniques is replaced with another, as she shifts her focus to the practice of "getting clear." The twin methods of bodily purification (fasting, eliminating toxic and infectious agents from one's environment) and psychological control define health as the complete mastery of the self over and against potential contamination. The implication of this logic, in true neoliberal form, is of course that if one is or remains sick, one only has oneself to blame. Various informational sources and authority figures exhort Carol and the other denizens of Wrenwood to "focus inward," to "throw away every negative, destructive thought we have," and, finally, to see illness as a gift precisely because it allows a recentering of focus to where it should ostensibly be: the self. In the words of one Wrenwood authority, Claire, it was precisely the fact that everything "in the material world" (supposedly) got taken away from her that she was able to heal because "what was left, was me."

The final, deeply chilling shot of the film, in which Carol's white face is finally the main subject in the frame, the one thing toward which the eye must go, suggests the many deaths and forms of death that the (re)production of whiteness requires. In the concluding scene, Carol, looking terribly ill, enters a safe house at Wrenwood she has just moved into. Not incidentally, the safe house co-opts the form of the "igloo"—one of the film's many instances of visual commentary on the imperialist cultural and geographical appropriations that appear in New Age practices and the racist logics that are so deeply entrenched within certain progressive movements and discourses. Carol is completely surrounded by and clothed in white, but the space is poorly lit. She sits on the bed, desperately tired, breathing from an oxygen tank. Then she looks up, toward the camera; she stands and shuffles painfully toward the object of her gaze, which turns out to be a mirror. The very last shot is a direct extreme close-up of her face using a very slow zoom, during which she says several times into the mirror, haltingly, in a very weak voice, "I love you." Her face is lit only dimly while a strong glare from the overhead light creates a very thin halo around the top of her head, contrasting harshly with her diseased-looking skin. Given its suggestion of Carol's continued decline despite her performance of the individualist self-management techniques promoted at Wrenwood (various forms of abstinence, "giving herself to love," isolation from potential contaminants), this shot offers a powerful conclusion to the film's general denaturalization of contemporary whiteness and its attendant gender and sexual norms.

Carol: Expending Whiteness, Expending Wealth

Carol, as has been widely noted, is based on a 1952 Patricia Highsmith novel, originally published under a pseudonym as *The Price of Salt* and reissued later under Highsmith's own name and with the new title of *Carol*. Highsmith purportedly was inspired to write the novel when, working at the counter of a department store, she had an experience very similar to the depiction of Therese Belivet and Carol Aird's first meeting. Highsmith was immediately smitten with a beautiful woman who, in her words, "'seemed to give off light'" (M. Anderson 2015, 114). Indeed, in the film, both Carol and Therese seem to give off light. Their illuminated faces stand out against the otherwise muted color palette of the film, becoming its aesthetic and interpretive focal point. Light and whiteness have a deeply intertwined history. For Dyer, light is an "aesthetic technology" that has been foundational to the social construction of whiteness and indeed has been equated with whiteness (1997, 140). Whereas *Safe* clearly denaturalizes white compulsory heterosexuality, in part through techniques that make the whiteness of Julianne Moore's skin look unnatural, unhealthy, and damaged, *Carol*'s aesthetic and narrative form seems to renaturalize whiteness even though it forwards a distinctly queer femininity. More than this, *Carol* arguably renaturalizes implicitly racialized practices of looking. Indeed, *Carol* is all about looking, about the discovery and intensification and fulfillment of queer desire through practices of looking. Although this feature of the film is commonly read as mostly indicating the characters' lack of a language to describe and understand themselves in a profoundly homophobic time (N. Davis 2015b; Smith 2018), we cannot rest with this explanation if we are to understand the work of this film from a queer intersectional perspective.

Lest we forget, institutions structure racialized, gendered, and classed practices of looking. In the case of *Carol*, the institution structuring the initial gaze between Carol and Therese, and gazes between other women, is the department store. The film sets their first encounter at Frankenberg's, whose thriving business epitomizes the postwar economy of upward class mobility and the accumulation of consumer goods. Women were not only shoppers but also, as sales clerks, custodians of the objects, and were themselves objects on display—gendered consumers but also commodities. The department store creates for Carol a public space that links consumption, whiteness, and gender. Moreover, it is a space in which she is sanctioned to gaze liberally because of her classed consumption. The white bourgeois woman shopper establishes the power of looking as she appraises luxury goods and clerks equally. The desires of the bourgeois white woman were enveloped, according to Anne Friedberg, in "a system of selling and consumption that depended on the relation between looking and buying, on the indirect desire to possess and incorporate through the eye" (1993, 37). Clad in rich furs, kid gloves, and red lipstick, Carol appears in and cruises the store as a luminescent presence distinct from the other shoppers, who are washed out and wan in comparison.

On the other hand, under the surveillance of the floor manager and the gazes of the bourgeois women, Therese is on constant display. She participates in the workforce as a sales clerk and thereby is able to live independently while also accessing modest consumer goods herself. The class distance between the two women is relayed through the relations of looking within the space of the department store. Therese's gaze, like the viewer's, is drawn to Carol as she glides around the store. We understand that when Carol leaves her luxurious kid gloves (often a symbolic token of love) on the counter and then later, when Therese returns them, invites Therese to lunch, she has crossed class boundaries to initiate contact with the youthful, white, seemingly heterosexual, working-class shop girl. This encounter sets the stage, blurring the line between erotic and consumer desires, and ties white bourgeois same-sex female desire to capitalism. Therese appears a desiring subject and desired object. And the relationship that progresses is imbricated within the racialized and classed consumerism and propertied citizenship that brought it into being.

Carol is framed largely from Therese's perspective, and the fact that she is a photographer plays a key role in the narrative and in the film's rendering of queer desire and self-fashioning. Therese's photography is both empowered by and empowers her realization of queer possibility. In one key scene, a friend attempts to seduce Therese by playing to her interest in photography, showing her his office at the *New York Times* (where she hopes to work) and asking her what her photographs are like. Therese seems reluctant to speak about them and to have general doubts about their quality, noting that she does not like to take pictures of people, though she cannot articulate why, and indeed her friend finishes her sentence for her. This interaction suggests that the possibilities for her to look at others are heavily circumscribed by her position within compulsory heterosexuality, as further underscored by her friend's attempt to parlay this discussion of vision and art into a come-on. But when Therese starts to take pictures of Carol, she quickly begins to gain a sense of confidence. Carol purchases a camera for Therese; later, Therese's photographs of Carol are featured as a means to represent the sense of self and place in the world she has developed through her relationship with Carol. Indeed, Therese gets that job at the *Times*.

Certainly, the emphasis on vision in *Carol* hearkens to the limited opportunities for women characters and spectators alike to engage in a variety of practices of looking within standard cinematic forms (Smith 2018; P. White 2015b). Given, however, the wealth of scholarship that has long questioned the representation of white women's right to look as a feminist achievement,[5] we need to ask: Who can look at whom, with desire and even queerly, with a degree of safety? Who can experience being so looked at as enabling self-discovery, fulfillment, and pleasure in a way that does not require the negotiation of different and perhaps competing meanings and orientations? As Patricia White puts it, "Lesbian representability encompasses social and historical discourses, and the corresponding aesthetic and narrative structures, that make desire between women and its consequences recognizable in both film texts and the subjects who decode them" (2015b, 10). Following this, what are the racial discourses and structures that make queer desire in *Carol* recognizable, particularly given that during the period in which *Carol* is set, looking was both a main target and a technique of deadly state-sanctioned violence?

Far from Heaven, Haynes's other film set in the same decade and addressing themes of sexual transgression similar to those in *Carol*, also deals heavily with looking—but in *Far from Heaven*, looking is deeply troubled and troubling, the site of complex racial dynamics. The black characters in the film are never not seen, even when they are being described by fragile white people as not there, highlighting the centrality of black policing to the white social fabric. Raymond Deagan (Dennis Haysbert), the black male object of Cathy Whitaker's (Julianne Moore) affections, cannot in the end risk the violence that would surely be the outcome of a relationship with Cathy, a relationship that would be always already visible. Meanwhile, Frank Whitaker, as a white businessman, is not subject to routine public scrutiny, which enables him to engage in clandestine sexual relationships with other men and even, in the end, run away with his lover.[6]

The whitened way in which *Carol* portrays looking as at the heart of queer self-fashioning is of concern because it is constituted on the basis of a double omission: a nonthematization of the role that whiteness plays in enabling Therese and Carol's relationship to looking, and a nonconsideration of more complex antiwhitened relationships to looking. In *Far from Heaven*, even the underwritten character of Sybil, the Whitakers' maid (played by Viola Davis), gets to look; her looks partially index the existence of another viewpoint and another life than Cathy's sometimes sympathetic, often solipsistic one. Yet *Carol*'s cinematography seems designed to aesthetically center and locate almost all interpretive possibilities within the confines of Therese and Carol's looking relationship. Interviewer Nick Davis foregrounds this when he asks about Haynes's decision to "make the film's surface less conspicuously 'legible'" (2015b, 32). That multiple sources describe the cinematography as purposely "grainy" and even "soiled" takes on racialized implications when we consider the long-lived equation of racial "difference" with interpretive difficulty (Smith 2018), the resistance to meaning or knowledge. Ironically, what Haynes describes as the "cleaned-up, shiny, Eisenhower-era Fifties" look of *Far from Heaven* seems to be mobilized toward a troubling of Cathy Whitaker's thoughts and commitments (Davis 2015b, 34), not least in her acknowledgment to Raymond that she is unable (and, it is implied, unwilling) to "see beyond the surface" of white heteronormativity. Cathy is not necessarily meant to be identified with; Therese and Carol are. Their luminous faces seem to rise up out of the dirty illegibility of their surroundings, distinguishing Therese and Carol and giving the viewer at least some access to the quality of their psychic interiorities.

In affording Therese and Carol both a kind of meaningful depth and access to the privacy of self-definition,[7] the film engages in a kind of prediction after the fact: in locating the possibility for queer life in the realm of the interior and the private, it arguably plays out the sanitized and whitened version of same-sex love that formed the ideological foundation of the *Lawrence v. Texas* ruling (which finally, in 2003, struck down sodomy laws) and the *United States v. Windsor* ruling (which struck down the Defense of Marriage Act in 2013). In fact, Carol's wealth suggests that of Edith Windsor. The *Windsor* ruling in particular emphasizes how arguments for marriage equality have been grounded in claims about rights to transfer of property and capital through marriage; white lesbian desire gets articulated in its contemporary manifestation as strivings for white propertied citizenship. This legalization of narrowly defined versions of queer desire, sex, and sociality was predicated on an ejection of people of color from the realm of appropriate sexuality,[8] a history that seems to go unacknowledged in the common understanding of *Carol* as a sign of progress. Haynes's own thinking is more complex and critical than this: he is skeptical of progress narratives and of the codification of queerness as a productive part of the neoliberal economic order.[9] At the same time, *Carol* and the way it has been commonly taken up call for such a critique.

One brief scene in *Carol* offers an intricate view of the relations between US empire, heteronormativity, and the class status required to be white. Carol and her ex-husband, Harge, sit with Harge's parents during a meal, after Carol has decided to try to at least appear committed to straightness so that she can see her child. When asked by her former in-laws about how things are with her "doctor," Carol immediately retorts that "actually he's not a doctor, he's a psychotherapist," but then she seems to remember the performance of "normalcy" she is attempting to put on and alludes to the fact that he has been very helpful (presumably in getting over her queerness). The television is on, and Dwight D. Eisenhower is giving his inaugural presidential address (which places this scene in early 1953). Interestingly, this scene echoes a similar one in *Far from Heaven*: Cathy and Frank are in their bedroom at night, and Frank watches Eisenhower give a televised speech about his decision to send troops to deal with the school integration crisis in Little Rock, Arkansas (S. Willis 2015, 126). Cathy ignores the television and attempts to engage Frank in conversation about the psychiatrist he is seeing for conversion therapy; Frank responds that "it's private" and refuses to tell Cathy anything about it, while Cathy maintains the cheery attitude upon which her performance of white heteronormativity is predicated. Here the year is 1957, during the McCarthy era's conjoining of homophobia and anticommunist securitization. And Cathy's role as participant in the pathologiz-

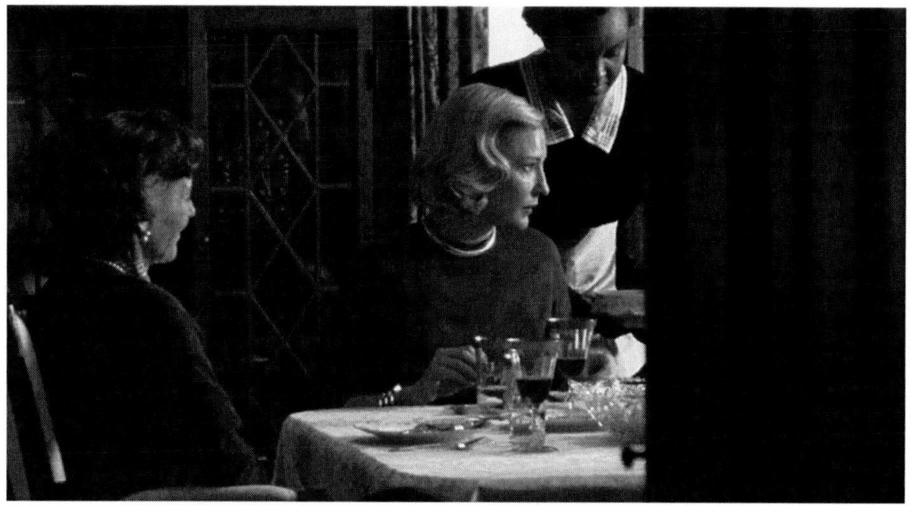

9.2 Racialized domestic labor provides a backdrop—in the form of blackness as an absent presence—for white heteronormativity in *Carol*.

ing of queer sexuality is, in this scene, compounded with the US state's ramping up of racialized securitization (as indexed by the reference to Little Rock). In *Carol*, Eisenhower's speech similarly offers a reminder that this is a "post–World War II" moment that is not actually postwar: the US is deeply involved in the Korean War, and "homosexuality" is increasingly codified as a mental illness within the fields of psychology and psychiatry, rapidly growing in scope and influence precisely as a result of the support of military dollars. With the focus on Carol's attempt to play the part in order to regain access to her own daughter (a part that she indeed later refuses), this scene subtly suggests that proper femininity within the heterosexual family structure might be partly determined by the politics of imperial statecraft. But another presence exists in this scene, a servant, someone who appears to be a black woman, attending to the white people at the table. We see her standing behind Carol, looking down as she serves mashed potatoes (figure 9.2); soon she walks off the set, through a doorway and directly in front of the camera, during which her image becomes blurry and distorted. She never looks up, and she has no lines. Unlike in *Far from Heaven*, the staging of marginalized black presence is brief and superficial: the fact that this character's absented presence is necessary to consolidate the white family as sexually normative is portrayed as an unremarkable part of the scenery.

Wonderstruck: Visual Plenitude and Settler Curatorialism

Julianne Moore makes her fourth appearance in a Todd Haynes film in *Wonderstruck*, and in two different roles no less. We first see her as the disembodied head of famous silent-film actress Lillian Mayhew, exuding the "glow of the [white] woman" that was such an explicit cinema aesthetic at the time this story line is set, 1927 (Dyer 1997, 84). Indeed, one of the first deployments of this standard lighting technique was used for Lillian Gish in *The Birth of a Nation* (1915), in which the white woman's aesthetic luminosity became the focus of not just a gendered gaze but a racialized national one; and Gish herself is directly referenced in *Wonderstruck* through Lillian's appearance in a silent film.[10] The image of Lillian Mayhew's white face against dark backgrounds is lovingly cut from magazines and newspapers, collected, and gazed at by a young girl, Rose. Rose is deaf, and she is fierce in her determination not to conform to the verbal/aural dictates of the nondeaf, as indicated by the textural richness of her visual world. She flees from her home after her strict father hires someone to teach her how to speak and read lips, and she seeks out Lillian in a New York theater, at which point we discover that Lillian is in fact Rose's mother. The meeting is profoundly disappointing, for Rose and perhaps for the viewer, as Lillian expresses a mixture of concern for her daughter and a sense that she represents the confinements of the heteronormative home she herself is trying to escape. This disappointment is, in part, indexed by the distinction between Lillian's silent image within Rose's curated, visually dominant world and her actual speaking self, who wants to impose a particular way of being on Rose just like everyone else does. It is also arguably represented by a shift in the quality of Lillian's whiteness. In still images and in the film that we see her in, Lillian's face appears as radiating beauty and goodness. In person, she appears unnaturally white in full and very pale stage makeup and a white wig and light-colored dress; she is sweet to her daughter in front of others, but in private reveals just how constructed her "whiteness" is (visually referenced by the quite literal layers of whiteness that dress her face and body) (figure 9.3).

Yet in contravention of this potential critique, *Wonderstruck* goes on to valorize the visual and the access to a self-defined life of curiosity, wonderment, and human connection that it can provide. This valorization is, to be sure, in the interest of honoring the functional diversity of the film's two main characters, both of whom are deaf; Haynes has stated that this is "a

9.3 Lillian Mayhew's cosmetic motherhood is revealed.

film about deafness" (Gray 2017, 15). As such, the scenes focused on Rose are accessible to deaf and hearing viewers alike in that they evoke silent cinema, the narrative unraveling through action and intermittent written text to relay a heightened visual experience. During the 1920s, oralism was the dominant and ableist modality that imposed normative hearing standards on deaf persons; the film's emphasis on visuality and American Sign Language (ASL) is a counterpoint to the mandate of oralism and advocates for Deaf culture rather than assimilation. And yet, although it would be problematic to indict the visual in and of itself, its particular staging in the film is of concern. Whereas the film rejects, and rightly so, equations of monstrosity and disability, Rose's deafness along with her white bourgeois femininity allow her to claim and access a place within natural history. Rose's access to Deaf education in turn gives her access not only to ASL but to repronormativity itself as she marries and has a child with another deaf student, Walter. Deafness (and therefore visuality) is a heightened experience, but it does not impede heteronormativity and repronormativity. Indeed, although the young Rose is played by the deaf actress Millicent Simmonds, Haynes casts Julianne Moore as the older Rose. Consequently, the one actor whose primary language is ASL does not sign throughout the film, while Moore stands in for the possibility of Deaf culture. That Haynes was willing to cast a deaf actor for young Rose but not older Rose reinvests in Moore's whiteness over her deafness.[11]

If the department store structures the racialized, gendered, and classed relations of looking in *Carol*, then in *Wonderstruck* it is the museum that organizes our visualities. In *Wonderstruck*, vision provides a fuller way of perceiving the world: vision is what defines deafness as a state of plenitude. More specifically, practices of curation characterized by aesthetics and techniques of quasi-scientific and historical realism become the privileged site of visual wonderment. The film's narrative, which begins by moving back and forth between two distinct times (1927 and 1977) and a child protagonist in each (Rose and Ben, respectively), eventually focuses only on the latter timeline as Ben and now-adult Rose (who turns out to be Ben's grandmother) meet. The two museums that serve as the staging grounds for key plot points, the American Museum of Natural History and the Queens Museum, are haunted places, sites of compounded US settler colonialism and broader empire. As Donna Haraway (1984) brilliantly argues, the American Museum of Natural History is at its base a civilizationist project; a purveyor of racial, sexual, and gender taxonomies and normativity; and a technology of western ownership. The visual splendor, perfection, and enlightenment it offers are predicated on the disavowed exploitation and death of others. The Queens Museum, presented specifically in terms of its role in the 1964 World's Fair, hearkens to the escalation of the US War in Vietnam, a critical year in the civil rights movement (and the violent US state response), the Cold War cultural apparatus of the US Space Program, and the continuing depredations of western imperialism in a supposedly *post*colonial time (Queens Museum 2018).

Wonderstruck erases the multiple violences underlying the practices of collecting, curating, and displaying that are central to the museum and the forms of knowledge production that have sustained the US imperial project. As such, the film frames Ben's and Rose's fascination with the museum as something wondrous. Ben, in particular, simultaneously demonstrates a fascination with the physics of the universe and a fear of its fauna, namely, wolves. The dioramas of animals and humans emerge out of shadows in the museum, as we encounter the exhibits while Ben chases his new friend Jamie throughout the various halls. Although the film captures the haphazard play between the two boys, the museum is in fact organized into halls reflecting taxonomies with long histories grounded in eighteenth-century colonialism. To imagine all the world's living things as connected and classifiable into a holistic taxonomy required an epistemology of the visual. In *Imperial Eyes* (1995), Mary Louise Pratt describes the emergence of a scientific imperial visuality that is the basis of the classificatory science of natural history. Carl Linnaeus developed this system, which was instrumental to imperialism in that it created a visual hermeneutic through which Europeans understood their relationship to the living world as one characterized by distance, omniscience, and separation. These imperial classifications within natural history extended to racial, sexual, and disability categorizations as well. Identifying what was supposedly natural about natural history meant also identifying what deviated from the norm as monstrous, deviant, or freakish. As differences of disability, race, and sexuality were intimately connected, queer intersectional critique must take into consideration how natural history produced knowledge linking the three.

What devastations must be disappeared in order for Rose and Ben to participate in "the joys of looking, of negotiating the world as an adventure in perception" (Pinkerton 2018, 59)? For whom is the visual field of the natural history museum, or of the World's Fair display, perceivable as characterized by *plenitude*? Haynes notes, "Once upon a time, queerness meant you stood outside dominant culture, and there's a lot to be gained from looking at culture from oblique angles. Both Rose and Jamie, Ben's friend (played by Jaden Michael), are cast out in specific ways, so they perceive the world differently" (Osenlund 2017). Whatever oblique view Jamie has, however, seems to be completely instrumentalized in order to fulfill Ben's reconnection with family, his discovery of a new sense of self, and indeed his ability to curate. Although Jamie appears with Ben and Rose at the end of the film, his proto-friendship is put into the service of reuniting the family. Whereas his presence might disrupt the naturalness of natural history and allow us to imagine other epistemes that are in excess of family and kinship, we do not get that opportunity. Jamie might represent the queer intersectional potential of the film, but Ben rejects his friendship precisely because Jamie did not reveal information regarding the possible identity of Ben's father immediately during their second encounter. In short, Ben rejects Jamie's queer overtures because he did not prioritize the familial. That one of the very few main characters of color in any of Haynes's films appears here, in the character of Jamie, largely in order to facilitate a white child's (Ben's) self-discovery and unification with a surrogate mother figure (at the site of the museum, no less), is concerning.

Two moments of possible critical disruption of the museum exist in *Wonderstruck*, but they are both subverted by its resignification as a site of healing. In the first, when Ben encounters the wolf diorama at the American Museum of Natural History—for what he thinks is the first time—he cannot make sense of it. His vision blurs, and he relives his recurrent nightmare of being chased by wolves. This destabilizing vision is, metaphorically speaking, resolved when Ben learns that it was his father who constructed the diorama, that it was this project that led to Ben's conception, and that in fact Ben had seen the diorama at his father's funeral but he was too young to remember. This potential troubling of the knowledge and pleasures offered by the museum is immediately undermined, as any recognition of the violence of white settler colonialism is sublimated in favor of the psychodrama of the heteronormative family, for which the museum functions as the site of reunion, potentiality, and mastery. To create the wolves for the diorama, Ben's father traveled to Gunflint, Minnesota, where he met Ben's mother. That region of Minnesota is the traditional territory of the Ojibwe (Anishinaabe and Chippewa) people. Moreover, wolves remain a highly visible and contentious issue between the white settler state and tribes of Minnesota, who have designated many areas under tribal laws as wolf sanctuaries. Although this portion of the film is set in 1977, actual contestations over white settler state–supported wolf hunting impacted the region in the early 2010s. Robert Des Jarlait of the Red Lake Ojibwe-Anishinaabe Nation comments, "If you take the fur of ma'iingan [wolf], you take the flesh off my back" (Nienaber 2012); he challenges the colonial taxonomies that undergird natural history, creating strong distinctions between human and animal, as well as the politics of the white settler colonial state that consequently targets the wolf for leisure game hunting. Ben's discovery of his father's "virtuous" death (of a congenital heart condition, not as a soldier in the US's doomed effort in Vietnam) seems to allow him to realize that the wolves hunting him are in fact also dead, never really a threat; the resolution of Ben's familial rupture thus requires the erasure of ongoing contestations over imperial knowledge.

In the second possible moment of disruption, Rose exposes her hidden personalizations of the diorama of New York at the Queens Museum. Tucked into the tiny buildings and structures are intimate mementos that signify her memories of her son. She attempts to break the omniscient perspective presented by the large-scale miniaturized diorama by investing individual components with personal, rather than natural, history. She attempts to disrupt the objective and distant aerial visuality required to see the diorama, but she replaces it with repronormative familial history. In this way, although both Ben and Rose may seem to trouble colonial white ways of knowing and classifying life, in part because of their deafness, ultimately they literally insert themselves into, rather than outside of, the tableaux of natural history. For both Ben and Rose, healing not only happens at the site of the museum, but is made possible by the act of curation—a collection of the right objects of knowledge, put together in the correct way in order to reveal a solid, stable, true understanding.

Coda: All That Whiteness Does Not Allow

When considered in relation to each other, each individual film becomes something other than it is on its own. Indeed, reading these films in the context of each other produces lingering questions: What does it mean to not question whiteness and its entanglements with empire and racial capitalism? And even when it is done in the mode of critique, what are the stakes of continuing to center white characters, whitened story lines, and even the failures of whiteness in the service of a queer and feminist project? Using *Safe* to frame a critical analysis of many of Haynes's subsequent works also provides new grounds from which to ask questions of *Safe* itself, questions that emerge within and about Haynes's body of work taken as a whole. As productive, critical, and insightful as *Safe* is, there are many things it is not, and indeed cannot be, about. Our concern about those people and things that Haynes's films never seem to be about is partly about Haynes's work and about the work the invocation of "Todd Haynes" does for various scholars, but it is also about queer and feminist filmmaking and film analysis in general. This concern is a disciplinary one as well as a political one. What is visible as queer or feminist, or both? And how might we continue to insist on examining the constitution of such concepts and what and who they can or cannot accommodate?

NOTES

1 In our 2005 article "'There's Nothing More Debilitating than Travel': Locating US Empire in Todd Haynes' *Safe*," we discussed this in regard to Laura Donaldson's (1999) work. See also Ann duCille's (1994) brilliant commentary on this problem.

2 We thank Theresa Geller for pointing out how often film critics connect *Carol* and the striking down of the Defense of Marriage Act. See, for example, M. Anderson (2015), Gilbey (2015), and P. White (2015b).

3 Whereas *Carol* was met with seemingly universal acclaim, *Wonderstruck* has received more mixed reviews. Some have found it to be an emotionally effecting and technically masterful film (Gray 2017; Koresky 2017; Pinkerton 2018); others have found it to be less compelling than Haynes's other work (Gilbey 2018).

4 For a more thorough and extensive discussion of what we see as *Safe*'s examination and critique of the way New Age discourses rely on orientalist, imperialist, and racist logics, see our earlier article (Bouchard and Desai 2005).

5 See Jane Gaines's (1986) essential callout of the white presumptions driving feminist critiques of the filmic gaze; Fatimah Tobing Rony's (1996) work on the development of

cinematic technologies in the heart of western colonialism and the looking practices of those who have mostly been thought of as only to-be-looked-at; and Jennifer Nash's (2014) paradigm-shifting consideration of the perilous assumptions made in some feminist theory about black woman cinematic subjects.

6 Whereas some scholars have read *Far from Heaven* as mostly conflating or analogizing racial normativity and sexual normativity (see, for example, Scherr 2008), we see the possibility for a somewhat more complex (if still imperfect) attention to the emergence of racial and sexual norms as fundamentally intertwined.

7 We thank Sarah Cervenak for providing insight and clarity on this point.

8 For this argument, see, for example, Eng (2010) and Shah (2005).

9 In his interview with Haynes, Ryan Gilbey (2015) asks, with regard to *Carol*, "With equal marriage suddenly being a reality, is the film saying: 'Don't forget how we got here'?" Haynes replies: "That somewhat superior position of pointing out that things are so much better now doesn't really interest me creatively. It's more that the hidden corridors and secret modes that minorities and subcultures had to create to survive are really interesting, and we've lost those" (20). Haynes also offers a critique of the "monetizing" of queer identity through alignments with whiteness (20).

10 We thank Theresa Geller for pointing out the reference to the film *Orphans of the Storm* (D. W. Griffith, 1921).

11 We thank Marie Coppola for her assistance on this point. See also McDougall (2017).

PART III

Intermediality and Intertextuality

10 Written on the Screen
Mediation and Immersion in *Far from Heaven*

Lynne Joyrich

Recently, while partaking in a favorite form of procrastination—using my computer to search for midcentury modern bargains on eBay rather than to engage in more rigorous, or at least more legitimated, intellectual pursuits—I came across an interesting listing: one "'FAR FROM HEAVEN' red '50's Eames era purse," described as looking as though it had been taken right from the set of the film. This was a lucky find, not because of the object itself (however lovely), but because of the ways in which it encouraged me to reconsider assumptions about what might operate as a legitimate intellectual pursuit and how that operation occurs, specifically with regard to the media, consumer, and (given the cultural coding of both purses and melodramatic films) gendered pursuits both representative of and represented within Todd Haynes's *Far from Heaven*. Although I didn't bid on that item (nor on another purse, this one in black patent leather, also listed under the heading of "Far from Heaven"), one might say that it gave me purchase in helping me crystallize my thoughts about Haynes's work, especially concerning what that work reveals about how we, as viewers and consumers, relate to and through mass-mediated culture—a culture that has both been determined by and, in turn, helped to determine gendered, sexualized, classed, and raced meanings. For here was an instance of a media text providing a language with which to express a particular identity, whether a gender, consumer, aesthetic, or fan identity:

a film producing semiotic and epistemological cues for recognition. (And indeed, achieving the status of key word on eBay is a sign of approving recognition in today's mediated universe.) The fact that the phrase *Far from Heaven* was used to signify not an actual item from the film but a "look" presumed to be known and appreciated by viewers (of both computer and film screens) suggests how deeply cinematic and other media texts enter our consciousness, providing us with objects in which to invest—whether materially, as for the bidder who bought the purse, or, more elusively, as for spectators such as myself who simply invest emotionally and epistemologically in the film.

Of course, as scholars have long argued, there is nothing simple about investing in a text. More to the point of my argument, this notion of investing in cinema is not only something others (whether eBay buyers or film critics) enact on a film like *Far from Heaven*: given the text's link to films past, it is already fully enacted and inscribed in *Far from Heaven* itself. The film's narrative traces the dissolution of the marriage of characters Cathy and Frank Whitaker as they attempt to escape the confines of their 1950s white, middle-class, suburban environment by exploring other social and sexual yearnings—yearnings that the characters see as problematic, if also somewhat mobilizing, in terms of race, class, gender, and sexuality. Yet this narrative is supplemented by one that traces the problematic, if also sometimes mobilizing, confines of cinematic and media texts as well. Indeed, these issues—of mediation and of sociality, subjectivity, and sexuality—are inseparable. In light of how formations of media and consumer culture have historically been understood and enacted through formations of gender, race, class, and desire—figuring the quintessential twentieth-century consumer as a white, middle-class, suburban female (precisely the position to which Cathy Whitaker has been assigned and against which she chafes) and the quintessential media fan as an overinvested, emasculated pervert (precisely the position that Frank Whitaker fears publicly inhabiting)—*Far from Heaven*'s engagement with media and consumer culture is intimately interwoven with its engagement with gender, sexuality, race, and class. This interweaving, I suggest, makes Haynes's media reflexivity a feminist and queer project.

The claim that *Far from Heaven* addresses cinematic *and* social issues, yoking the two together (and revealing how mediatized and social formations are always so yoked), is hardly a startling one. For example, practically all critics writing about it have noted that the film, in its articulation of social issues in and through domestic and romantic entanglements (and, as I will argue, in and through media entanglements), stands as a kind of homage to, or reworking of, the melodramas of director Douglas Sirk. It references most clearly Sirk's 1955 film *All That Heaven Allows* (with its story of an upper-middle-class woman who scandalizes her social circle through her romantic involvement with her gardener), but it also brings in key elements of the 1956 text *Written on the Wind* (with its emphasis on frustrated sexuality and appropriate class, gender, and familial performance) and the 1959 text *Imitation of Life* (with its emphasis on tensions of race and, once again, appropriate class, gender, and familial performance). By referencing these texts—and heightening even further their already high-pitched intensity—Haynes calls attention both to the issues that these films engage and to issues with which Hollywood film was, at that time, unable to deal. This attention is registered through *Far from Heaven*'s treatment of interracial romance (marked in the film by Cathy Whitaker's relationship with African American gardener Raymond Deagan) and same-sex romance (marked by Frank Whitaker's desires for men). The two are connected through the switch point of performance: namely, the substitution of Haynes's gardener, played by Dennis Haysbert, for Sirk's gardener, played by Rock Hudson, who, with his textual history as leading man in Sirk's texts and his extratextual history as a closeted gay man in Hollywood, serves, in his structural absence, to signify all manner of appropriate and inappropriate romantic fantasies.[1] By alluding to Sirk's films, style, and stars, *Far from Heaven* thus reminds us of media history in addition to, or as interwoven with, the history of social and identity struggles.

But, again, this use of cinematic convention to comment on the possibilities and limits of Hollywood is not something enacted only on Sirk films: Sirk's texts themselves are notable for how they call attention to Hollywood cinema, using dramatic mise-en-scène to elevate viewers' awareness of cinematic textuality.[2] Indeed, one might argue that, as a whole, the genre of family melodrama insists that viewers see, rather than just see through, cinematic form.[3] Through their stylistic, narrative, and performative excess, these texts reject or subvert Hollywood's usual "invisible" practices, opening the possibility that viewers might question not only the topics treated in the films but also cinematic treatment in and of itself. This effect is that of the critical distanciation that many film scholars have attributed to melodrama: the way that its formal elements might produce ironic, doubled, and "hysterical" texts so that the contradictions and distortions of cinematic melodrama expose the contradictions and distortions of both the diegetic worlds presented and the very bases of cinematic representation, undermining (even if inadvertently) the patriarchal, bourgeois ideology of consumer culture as they undermine the naturalization of Hollywood's realist conventions.[4] In this manner, Haynes's reworking of Sirk's reworking of melodrama's reworking of classical Hollywood film (and the social and personal issues it narrates) enacts a complex attitude toward, and position within, mediated culture. Such immersion indicates a deep involvement with mass culture that is also highly analytical. In other words, *Far from Heaven* demonstrates how media immersion—which has historically been seen as gendered and sexualized, and disparaged accordingly—need not be opposed to critical distanciation. Rather, media critique can arise with and through exactly that immersion, yielding a particular kind of queer feminist approach.

This interest in the possibilities and limitations of media, mass cultural, and a gender-coded consumer involvement inflects all of Haynes's work. From *Superstar*'s and *Safe*'s examinations of women who are literally sick of consumption (in the former, Karen Carpenter starves herself even as her image is consumed; in the latter, Carol White seems to be allergic to the very space of mass-produced life), through *Poison*'s experimentation with various film traditions and media genres that have historically been used to mark and manage "deviancy" (with segments that recall a Genet-inspired sordid romanticism, a B movie horror flick, and a bit of tabloid journalism), to *Dottie Gets Spanked*'s and *Velvet Goldmine*'s explorations of the pleasures and dangers of media fandom (whether of TV sitcoms or glam rock music), Haynes's work impels its viewers to consider our complex relations to mass-mediated culture. It thus demands that we think about not only film and media history "proper," but also the mediation of our own personal histories: the ways that our desires and anxieties, identities, and positions are imbricated with those of the media.

Likewise, the more engaged a spectator is with popular media history and conventions, the more engaging is Haynes's work. Haynes rewards the cinephile, not to mention the television and pop music lover, by peppering his texts with media citations and allusions that gratify in-the-know viewers and incite others to become more knowledgeable. In this way, Haynes thinks through the media, making media forms not only objects of analysis but modes of analysis, mediums of thought and reflection themselves.[5] It may be this very construction (or exposure) of media technologies as also "epistemological technologies" that has incited such critical interest in Haynes's work. By marking film and other media texts as themselves analytical discourses, Haynes invites complementary analytical discourses by film, media, and cultural critics (including centrally, as this volume demonstrates, feminist and queer critics). Such thinking through the media is clear in *Far from Heaven*'s aforementioned use of the vocabulary of 1950s cinematic melodrama. Yet movies and other media are central to the film in other ways too. Indeed, many mediums are represented in, and representative of, *Far from Heaven*'s mode of thinking: film, television, telephony, painting, photography, print, and performance are all crucial to the narrative—used as focal points for the film's diegesis even as they also help focus the film's form and structure.

While Sirk's films clearly provide a reference point for *Far from Heaven*'s style and story, they are nowhere mentioned in Haynes's film itself; others, however, are explicitly referenced in the text, and what those films are, as well as when and how they appear, is thought-provoking, providing viewers with an opportunity for fascinating reflection. Specifically, at two points in *Far from Heaven* we see characters at a movie theater, and the camera makes a point of lingering on the marquee that advertises the double features so that we, as viewers of this film, know just what is playing in the diegetic world. My interest here is, in fact, how these films "play" in and across the narrative, for they are truly "double" features in more ways than one: film pairings that mark the conflicted world in which the characters live, and texts that mark the conflicted nature of the characters' own hopes for pairing. Both scenes that occur within or just outside of the Ritz Theater are key moments in *Far from Heaven*, providing opportunities for the characters to recognize their desires and/or the impossibility thereof, and such tension is externalized onto the film texts themselves.

This externalization might be most obvious in the first scene when, after a business dinner, Frank overlooks a female prostitute to head instead for the greater pleasures (visual and sexual) to be found at the Ritz (figure 10.1). On the screens are the films *Miracle in the Rain* (a 1956 melodrama starring Jane Wyman, one-time leading lady for both Douglas Sirk and, extratextually, Ronald Reagan, as a lonely woman who deteriorates mentally and physically when the soldier with whom she has fallen in love is taken from her), and *The Three Faces of Eve* (the famous 1957 "true life" story of a woman with multiple personalities—two of whom are [not so] subtly coded by race: Eve White, the good housewife and mother, and Eve Black, the seductive good-time girl).[6] Perhaps not surprisingly, Frank chooses to watch the psychiatric drama *The Three Faces of Eve*, at least until his attention is diverted by two men who go off to the balcony (or restroom) together—the same men he follows, after the flick, to a gay bar. Although tellingly dis-

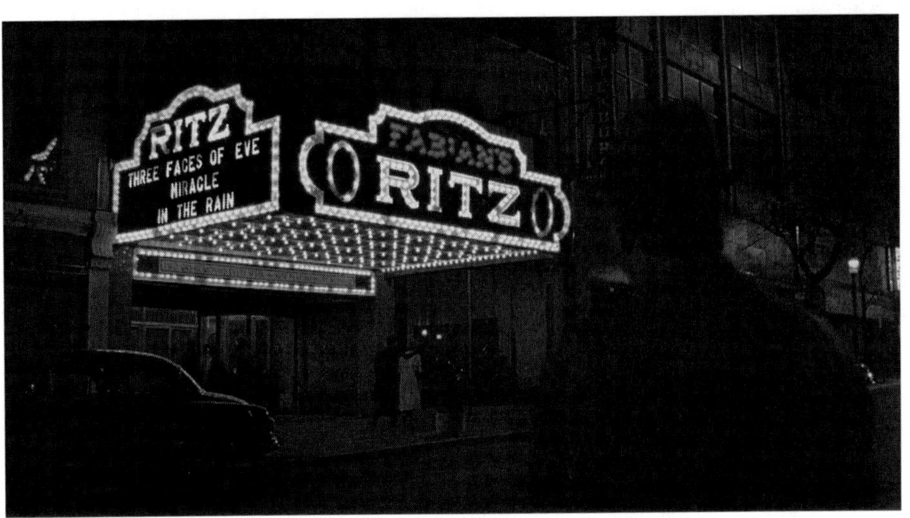

10.1 Frank explores cinematic pleasures and possibilities at the Ritz.

placed through terms of gender and race, the dilemma posed within Frank's cinematic choice (good domestic urges versus bad sexual appetites) and even the dilemma posed between the two possible cinematic choices at the Ritz (wasting away from desire versus a reintegrating yet medicalized cure) nonetheless resonate with Frank's own dilemmas in a way that is quite revealing.

This resonance, however, produces an echo with a difference, particularly regarding *The Three Faces of Eve*. It is precisely because closure attained through a psychiatric reintegration into dominant, heteronormative society is presented here as a cinematic option—a story that Frank can watch, consider, critique, or simply ignore (as he does when he chooses to step out from the theater to watch the two men instead)—that *Far from Heaven* is able to differentiate its own closure (or lack thereof) from that of melodramatic medical films. Later in *Far from Heaven*, Frank does consult a psychiatrist to help him with his "problem" (his own split identity as a closeted gay man), yet because the Ritz scene has allowed us to perceive the process of mediation involved in such stories and their dissemination, opening a gap between spectator and film both diegetically and extradiegetically, we need not see this trajectory as a necessary or compelling one—however powerful and overdetermined it historically has been for countless gay men who, given the pathologization of homosexuality, have opted for (or were forced into) it.

The second Ritz Theater scene is no less suggestive. After hearing that she has been the subject of malicious and racist gossip, Cathy reluctantly decides that she must stop seeing Raymond—a decision she communicates as the two stand beneath the Ritz marquee. The two films now listed are *Hilda Crane* (another melodrama, this one about a woman with "a past" and the problems of divorce, notable for the tagline "I want to live like a man . . . and still be a woman!") and the war film *The Bold and the Brave* (once advertised as a "guts and glory story boldly and bravely told"). Although both of these 1956 films are relevant to Cathy and Raymond's situation—marking the choice between love or war, independence or marriage, and spilling one's guts or gaining social glory—it would also be interesting to imagine a diegetic reversal in the pairings of films and protagonists. Rather than a commutation of actors (as I previously suggested in my comment about Haysbert and Hudson), one might imagine a substitution of the characters and film titles under which they (literally) appear, with Frank having to choose between "feminine" or "masculine" objects of visual pleasure via the film he might pick and Cathy and Raymond having to face the polarization of Eve White and Eve Black.

In their scene at the Ritz, Cathy and Raymond do not enter the theater as Frank did; they thus do not directly engage with the cinema (or actively choose to disengage) as he does. Yet Cathy and Raymond reproduce a distancing cinematic discourse within their dialogue. Indeed, the articulation of their relationship is striking for how it sounds like what a critic might say of a film. Informing Raymond that "it isn't plausible for me to be friends with you," Cathy describes their situation in terms more of narrative credibility, character motivation, and diegetic consistency than of interior emotion. That is, she reads their relationship through a discourse of realist narrative that positions her as merely a spectator rather than an active participant in her own life. Instead of going inside the theater to watch a film, she treats herself as an image to be watched for credibility and verisimilitude—as someone acting in a film instead of enacting a life. She extends this position to Raymond as well, treating him as almost a film image as she exclaims, "You're so beautiful." The passersby, however, are not so taken with the image of the two and seem determined to enforce the "implausibility" that Cathy notes. Those viewers gape at the scene and "critique" it through a racist lens, with one calling out, "You, boy; hands off!"

Something similar happens in Cathy's dealings with the press and TV, again revealing how social and subject positions are here also always media positions. In each case, Cathy is figured less as a media consumer than a mediated image: we don't see her watching television or reading the paper but framed as sights for both. How Cathy is doubly transformed from "daily-life performer" to media performer and from spectator to spectacle is perhaps most pronounced in *Far from Heaven*'s portrayal of the press and photography. In the narrative, a local society paper, the *Weekly Gazette*, is doing a story on Cathy as the wife of a prominent executive at the television and electronics company Magnatech and as a prominent hostess in her own right. Twice we see Cathy surprised by the flash of the *Gazette* team's camera bulbs, which surprises us as well because the diegetic cameras emerge from offscreen space: first, when she's kissing her husband goodbye as he goes to work on the morning following his arrest for "loitering" (i.e., cruising), and later when she's at a modern art exhibition. In the first instance, a mobile time of domestic disruption is turned into a static scene of idealized domestic bliss; the *Gazette* reporter exclaims, "The candid view is always the best," even as she goes on carefully to pose Cathy at the family hearth, defined by fireplace, television set, and framed advertisement of Frank and Cathy as "Mr. and Mrs. Magnatech." In the second instance, Cathy goes from enjoying the art exhibit to being the exhibit—not only for the *Gazette* team, who once again startle her with flashbulbs, but for the entire crowd at the art show, who are scandalized by seeing her talking with Raymond.

I will return shortly to *Far from Heaven*'s engagement with visual mediation to continue this point about how Cathy is prevented from appreciating the imagery around her as she instead becomes the imagery. But first let me take a brief detour, related to the mention of Cathy's conversation with Raymond, through the film's engagement with aural mediation as well—specifically, its engagement with the telephone. Certainly, as the aforementioned "scandalous" encounter exemplifies, there are numerous face-to-face conversations in *Far from Heaven* that serve as narrative pivots. Yet the number of telephone conversations that take place throughout the film, and the way these conversations are arranged, is striking. To be sure, an emphasis on the telephone as both a diegetic source of information and a loaded sign for viewers is typical in melodrama. Think of the cliché, seen in many films and television soap operas, of a close-up of a telephone ringing with no one there to answer, or the reverse, a shot of a silent telephone as our heroine waits for a call. This cliché allows the text to comment on the interruption of communication that so often plagues melodramatic characters.

In that sense, the use of the telephone in *Far from Heaven* is only to be expected in a film so attentive to melodrama's conventions. Yet the phone does more than register *Far from Heaven*'s attention to melodramatic mise-en-scène, for phone calling itself (telephony as a communication medium, not simply the telephone as object) plays an important role in the text, occurring at transitional moments and both enabling and emphasizing turning points for characters' relationships.[7] In *Far from Heaven*, telephone usage thus supplements that most definitive form of aurality in the melodrama: the use of the musical score to highlight and even supplant diegetic emotion. What is interesting about the pattern of phone calling in *Far from Heaven* is the way these two melodramatic tropes connect, as the arrangement of telephone calls functions almost as a musical score, composed in a sequence that forms a rhyming structure.

We witness eight telephone calls in the film; additionally, news of another call is crucial to the narrative, but it's one that we neither see nor hear. Let me begin with the eight overheard calls:

1. Cathy receives a call from the police after Frank's arrest, one that results in Frank being put into Cathy's custodial care (he is, in effect, under "house arrest").
2. When we next see Frank at work following his arrest, he asks his secretary to place a call to his wife. We see Cathy take this call (interrupting her *Gazette* photo session), and Frank tells her he'll be working late—though in fact he goes to the Ritz Theater and then to a gay bar.
3. During dinner with her children on a subsequent evening, Cathy receives another call from Frank, and again he tells her that he is working late. The children express dismay that their father "never wants to come home," and Cathy decides to surprise Frank at the office by bringing him a meal; there she comes upon him kissing a man (whom we recognize as a patron from the gay bar).
4. Shortly after a now-distraught Cathy befriends Raymond (and after a particularly bad evening with her husband and friends at the party she throws for his work and social set), she receives a call from a woman in her kids' carpool. The woman requests a change in driving days, which frees Cathy to spend the afternoon with Raymond, as she can now accept an invitation from him she had previously declined.
5. On returning from her outing with Raymond, Cathy answers a call from her best friend Eleanor, who has phoned to report the "vicious talk" she heard about Cathy being spotted with "a colored man." This call once again prompts Cathy to reconsider her relationship

with Raymond. She goes on to tell Frank (who, apparently, has also been told the "vicious" gossip through a phone call of his own) that she's already fired "that man" (though this, in fact, isn't true). She thereby reestablishes Raymond as a servant (and not even hers anymore) rather than an equal friend or partner.

6 Later in the film (after Cathy and Frank have gone to Miami to try to solve Frank's "problem" and rekindle their romance), Cathy phones the National Association for the Advancement of Colored People to ask about volunteering. This call is interrupted when Frank comes home to confess that, despite all efforts to resist, he's fallen in love with a man.

7 Soon afterward, Cathy calls Eleanor, whom she then goes to see. While confiding in her, Cathy divulges both the situation with Frank and her feelings for Raymond. As viewers might expect, Eleanor is shocked and disapproving on both counts.

8 Finally, near the end of the film, Frank calls Cathy and they make arrangements for their divorce, in effect ending their marital (again, one might say custodial) relationship.

What we have, then, is almost a series of reversals or mirroring sets of telephone "call and response" pairs—one that follows the sequence of an envelope (or "kissing") rhyme scheme (here, the octet ABBCCDDA). The first call (A) puts Frank in Cathy's "custody" whereas the last releases them both from this bond. Between those enveloping calls we have the two calls that Cathy receives from Frank informing her of his impending absence (B). These are united in that each impedes Cathy's desires for domestic time with her husband and children, but opposed in their results for Frank's desires: the first frees him to go to the movies and then the bar where he meets the man with whom he has a romantic liaison; the second exposes that liaison to Cathy, causing a break to both of those relationships (as first the lover and then Cathy run out of Frank's office, leaving him alone). The next set (C) also involves telephone calls that Cathy receives, though these calls pertain more to her own desires (and their difficulties): one liberates her from a domestic duty, enabling her to spend time with Raymond and so to begin a relationship with him, and one presumes a social duty, warning her about that time with him and so seeming to put an end to that relationship.

The final set (D) is created by the two calls that Cathy herself makes (or tries to make), both of which mark the difficulty or interruption of communication. This interruption is explicit in the first instance (in that Cathy is waiting on hold but hangs up the phone when Frank enters with the news that he's in love) and implicit in the second (in that it yields a break, or at least tension, in Cathy's relationship with Eleanor, who, while sympathetic about Frank, expresses amazement and chagrin over Cathy's feelings for Raymond, especially when Cathy states that Raymond has been the only one with whom she felt she could talk, thus verbalizing a failure in her relationship with Eleanor as well as with Frank). These two calls from Cathy rhyme—or, perhaps more accurately, invert one another—in another way as well. When Cathy calls the NAACP, she displaces her feelings for Raymond, disavowing her personal involvement with him by staging it as simply a social involvement with others; at the same time, this action suggests that Cathy desires more diverse and expansive human relationships. Conversely, when Cathy talks to Eleanor, she throws some relationships in doubt (detailing the end of her marriage to Frank and risking her friendship with Eleanor), while at the same time acknowledging the seeds of yet another connection—now avowing her feelings for Raymond with no displacement (figure 10.2).

As I've described it, then, the series of phone calls makes a neat pattern of relational and communicative possibilities opening and closing, all framed by the authorization and then deauthorization of white, middle-class, heterosexual marriage as a privileged, controlling institution. But the pattern is actually not quite so neat, for, as noted above, the film includes one additional telephone call, though it is one to which we, as viewers (and auditors), are not directly privy.[8] Between calls 5 and 6 (or sets C and D)—that is, after Cathy hears the gossip from Eleanor, leading her to deny her relationship with Raymond, and before she attempts (in displaced fashion) to reach out to the possibilities he has shown her via the NAACP—Cathy phones Raymond himself. During a brief scene at the Deagan Garden Shop, a worker comes to tell Raymond that "there's a lady on the phone for you." Presumably, this lady is Cathy, for the next scene is the one in which they meet (at a place and time that have clearly been prearranged) and, as the scene proceeds, decide, at Cathy's instigation, to meet no more (the news that she delivers under the Ritz marquee, as previously elaborated).

This call therefore complicates the pattern that I've mapped not only because it is withheld from us. It also breaks the rhythm—or perhaps accentuates it—by incorporating and imploding the opposites that the other calls pose as reversals. Rather than signaling either conversation or lack of

10.2 Eleanor is on the line: the possibilities and limitations of mediated communication in *Far from Heaven*. Photo courtesy of Killer Films.

10.3 Sybil, Cathy, and Raymond play out raced, classed, and gendered dynamics of looking and appearing/disappearing.

conversation, either recognition or repudiation of a relationship, either the formation or the breaking of ties, either a connection or a disconnect, it does all of these: Cathy initiates contact with Raymond but only so as to end that contact, acknowledging their relationship through her call just to call it off. In that sense, this phone call blends all the options, becoming an impossible (precisely because it is an all-possible) communication—which is perhaps why, as a sort of absent center, it cannot actually be shown or heard. As with its treatment of cinema and photography, *Far from Heaven*'s representation—or, in this case, refusal to represent—phone calling enables the film to hint at both the potential and limitations of (necessarily mediated) communication.

Of course, even though Cathy's heavily mediated relationship with Raymond is ultimately deemed "implausible" by *Far from Heaven* itself and so bound to fail, one very significant relationship that Cathy does manage to maintain—and, arguably, another absent center in the film—is the one that she has with her housekeeper, Sybil. The importance of this bond—particularly for considering the feminist, queer, and antiracist implications of the film—is initially suggested during the film's opening phone call. While Cathy is speaking to the police about Frank's arrest, Sybil (who first answered the phone) stands nearby; during the conversation, Cathy and Sybil gaze with emotion into one another's eyes. Sybil is represented as having a keen ear and penetrating gaze at other points in the film as well. For instance, after Cathy first spots Raymond in the garden during her *Gazette* interview, Sybil comes outside to report yet another telephone call (an unseen one from the party caterers) and watches their encounter with a concerned expression, almost as if she knows the likely outcome of the introduction of this new character (figure 10.3). Later (after call 3), she attempts to dissuade Cathy from bringing dinner to Frank at his office, again as if she knows that this action can only lead to trouble.

Sybil is privy to other important information too. For instance, after call 4, she watches (again with a look of concern) as Cathy and Raymond drive away for their day together; she acts as Cathy's agent by signing her up with the NAACP (neglecting the telephone once more ringing in the background—a call, we can infer from Cathy's later conversation with Eleanor, attempting to report Cathy and Raymond's outing, about which Sybil already knows); and she is the person who informs Cathy that it was Raymond's daughter who was the victim of the racist attack about which Cathy heard when she returned from Miami (thus instigating Cathy's renewed, even if short-lived, contact with Raymond and eliciting the only instance of Cathy's anger in the film when she yells at Sybil for not sharing her knowledge sooner). Sybil thus seems to have a kind of epistemological authority in the film, having access to knowledge that other characters lack—even if she is powerless to act on that knowledge. Indeed, in many ways she operates as the spectator's stand-in, watching and listening silently yet reading the film's signs so as to predict the narrative's outcome.

In other ways, Sybil functions as yet another loaded sign, for, through her, *Far from Heaven* references several other media texts. Perhaps most notably, her very name suggests the well-known 1976 TV movie *Sybil*, the film that surpassed *The Three Faces of Eve* as the definitive mass cultural text on "split personalities." Like *The Three Faces of Eve*, *Sybil* is based on a "true story," but *Sybil*'s title character has more than "three faces" (being split into as many as sixteen personalities). Haynes's use of this name, in a film already referencing the problem of fractured and mediated identities, thus alludes to the even greater degree of multiplicity defining a character like *Far from Heaven*'s Sybil than other (even more narratively elaborated) characters in the film. Other characters in the film do not seem to recognize this multiplicity and complexity (Sybil's intersectional position as a single, black, female domestic worker), a point that leads to another intertextual reference: Cathy's surprise when she hears that Sybil belongs to several community organizations, which mirrors a comparable scene in Sirk's *Imitation of Life*, when Lora Meredith expresses surprise that her maid/partner Annie Johnson has friends and belongs to several organizations.

Yet just as *Imitation of Life*'s Lora and Annie form the primary "couple" in that text, so do Cathy and Sybil in *Far from Heaven*. At the end of the film, after the final phone call and after Cathy has recognized the impossibility of her relationships with both Frank and Raymond, Cathy and Sybil maintain the household on their own: at one point, as Sybil does housework while reminding Cathy to pick up food on her way home, Cathy exclaims, "I don't know how on earth I'd ever manage . . . ," trailing off before she can voice the expected "without you." This scene is the only one in which Cathy wears a plain tailored suit, in contrast to her previous feminine, nipped-waisted, embellished dresses, recalling the shift from feminized visual object to phallic powerhouse, also marked by a wardrobe change to a plain gray suit, that defines the character Marylee Hadley in Sirk's *Written on the Wind*. Yet however much these intertextual cues tempt us to read Cathy and Sybil as the true couple here (in fact, as the successful "marriage" in the film), *Far from Heaven* is unable to narrate this possibility. As an absent center, this possibility would include, in a single pairing, the variety of issues the film addresses (same-sex, interracial, and cross-class relationships) through its other couples. The truly "multiple identity disorder" that this pairing would represent (how it would surely threaten to disorder the limits of even this narrative through its very multiplicity) makes this relationship one that can be approached only by allusion—allusions that depend on *Far from Heaven*'s references to and thinking through other media formations.

It is thus through mass mediation that, in this film, the mediation of identity itself is conveyed, and it is through media moments that character bonds are negotiated, revealing that it is precisely via media reflexivity that Haynes's feminist and queer interventions occur. Yet if *Far from Heaven* suggests the instructive, affective, and communicative value of the cinema and the telephone for both characters and viewers, it appears much less sanguine about the value of that other major tele-technology: television. The difference between telephony and television, of course, is that telephones embody the possibility of two-way communication that commercial television simply promises, substituting an illusion of immediacy, "liveness" and interpersonal discourse for "the real thing."[9] I am not trying to suggest that television permits only passive reception or that the power dynamics it involves are unidimensional, with viewers as powerless victims; indeed, much work in television studies has documented the active use viewers make of TV texts and how television can provide a basis for creative exploration, self-expression, and negotiated empowerment.[10] The investments one might make in television—identificatory, political, erotic, semiotic, epistemological—therefore go beyond the merely consumptive (or, more accurately, consumption is never "merely" limited to a financial transaction, as it necessarily involves a transaction of meaning and affect as well), and the risk of "viewer victimization" emerges not because of TV (or any medium) per se but because of how it might be engaged and read (or not). Haynes's texts that address fandom, such as *Dottie Gets Spanked* and *Velvet Goldmine*, make this same point through their own creative explorations of the powers and pleasures of media involvement and mediated interaction.

Such interaction, however, is not an aspect of *Far from Heaven*'s characters' relationship to television. Certainly the film interrogates other media forms such as, as I've discussed, film, photography, and the press. These forms offer some benefits for Frank—the newspaper story about his family seems designed to boost Frank's stature, and movies allow him to distance himself from pressures in his life even as he can also choose to distance himself from the types of closure that Hollywood films pose as appropriate solutions—but *Far from Heaven* details how Cathy is more plagued than empowered by the media around her, caught in their sights, as in the sights of a gun, rather than able to "re-view" or take aim at them herself.[11] Still, the most dismal and damning exposure of how Cathy becomes framed as image, instead of enjoyer of images, occurs through *Far from Heaven*'s treatment of television.

I previously mentioned how Frank and Cathy are figured as "Mr. and Mrs. Magnatech"—an image used in advertising for the TV set manufacturing company for which Frank works as a sales executive. Indeed, this image of the two of them not only appears in their house, hanging just over the television set itself. It also is positioned right outside of the elevator near Frank's office, where the characters must confront it whenever they enter—or try to escape from—this scene of corporate conformity (for instance, when Frank arrives at work after his arrest, or when Cathy later runs out of his office after discovering him in the arms of a lover). This placement of the ad, at the very sites of public and private repression, within the heart of both domestic and corporate culture, is telling: it is in the home, where it directs attention to and competes with the TV set below, and at the Magnatech elevator doors, where it operates to mark the "ups" and "downs" of the Whitakers' lives.

The "Mr. and Mrs. Magnatech" image also marks the literal incorporation of the Whitakers into media and commodity culture, offering an even more pointed commentary on the danger of being absorbed into television than the one Sirk offered in *Far from Heaven*'s template film, *All That Heaven Allows*. In a 1988 essay titled "All That Television Allows," I discuss a scene from that film in which heroine Cary Scott is given a TV set as a gift from her children after they've pressured her into ending her relationship with gardener Ron Kirby. As the now socially isolated Cary listens with dismay to a TV salesman exclaim, "All you have to do is turn that dial, and you have all the company you want right there on the screen—drama, comedy, life's parade at your finger tips," the camera closes in on Cary's face, tightly framed and reflected in the screen—"literally collapsed onto the picture of her misery . . . [her] very subjectivity incorporated into television" (129). My purpose in that essay was to trace the multiple ways that the melodramatic mode itself became incorporated into the (at the time of Sirk's film, relatively new) media form of American commercial television. In addition to investigating the relationship between TV's pervasive production of melodrama and its consumer function, not to mention TV's relationship to the possibility of women's misery, I also suggested how the critical potential of melodrama that's been linked to texts like Sirk's may still operate within television itself.

Nonetheless, it is difficult to find evidence of such critical potential in *Far from Heaven*'s representation of television—or, perhaps more accurately, of the discourses around television. For although the TV set has a place of prominence in the Whitaker home, we see more evidence of the texts that accompany television (such as the Magnatech ads or the *TV Guide* that Frank flips through after returning from Florida) than television texts themselves. In fact, we see something on the TV set only once. That is not the only time, though, when we know the set is on: at one point, Cathy is distracted by the offscreen noise of her son watching what sounds like a TV Western; she makes him turn it off and go to bed, at which point the film cuts to Frank trying to satisfy his urge for visual and narrative pleasure at the Ritz, watching, as I noted, not a Western but the medical "woman's picture" *The Three Faces of Eve*.

It is also Frank who is the one watching TV for that singular instance in the film, the sole moment when we watch a character watch television. As Cathy tries to talk to him about his doctor (to whom Frank, perhaps inspired by his film viewing, has turned in an attempt to find a cure for homosexuality), Frank unsuccessfully attempts to keep his attention focused on the television set, on which we see and hear President Eisenhower discussing his deployment of federal troops. One might argue that Frank is caught between one discourse of compliance (that of medical normalization) and another, more aggressive one (that of armed intervention)—but it's not so simple. The military pacification of which Eisenhower speaks is not one involving a battle against an external threat but rather a domestic conflict: the troops sent on September 24, 1957, to Little Rock, Arkansas, to ensure, against the initial actions of the state's National Guard, that the orders of the federal court demanding school desegregation be duly executed. This topic comes up again later in the film when, at the Whitakers' Magnatech party, some of the guests discuss the situation in Little Rock. One man says that such a thing could never happen in their town of Hartford, Connecticut, stating, "the main reason: there are no Negroes"—at which point we cut to an image of a black servant, as invisible to the guests at the party as are TV signals traveling through the airwaves.

Perhaps both Frank and Cathy would have done well to postpone their conversation and listen to President Eisenhower, thereby acknowledging how national and domestic issues, political and personal problems, and social and intimate relations are necessarily intertwined through the

10.4 Steven watches television (and redraws its boundaries) in *Dottie Gets Spanked*. Photo courtesy of Killer Films.

complex connections forged by television as it publicizes private lives and brings political events into the home. Or—not to be too flip—perhaps they would have done even better by switching the channel to *I Love Lucy*.[12] I reference *I Love Lucy* not simply because it was the most popular show of the period, nor because of the detail that, within their own televisual diegesis, Lucy and Ricky had just moved to Westport, Connecticut, only fifty-six miles from the Whitakers' town, but rather because of Haynes's own exploration of the pleasures to be had (or relinquished) from *I Love Lucy*.

I'm speaking, of course, about Haynes's brilliant film *Dottie Gets Spanked*.[13] In that short piece (which itself aired on television as part of a PBS/ITVS series on TV families), six-year-old Steven Gale is obsessed with both *The Dottie Show*, a television program that's clearly modeled on *I Love Lucy*, and its producer and star, Dottie Frank, the lead both on and off the set (figure 10.4). Despite the disapproval that Steven's gender-atypical viewing preference provokes—ranging from the girls at his school labeling him a "feminino" to his otherwise supportive mother suggesting that it might be better for Stevie to try watching something that "Daddy likes" instead—the TV program and his fandom nonetheless serve to help Steven articulate fantasies that move him away from middle-class heteronormativity into something that seems like a "proto-queer" identity—even if these fantasies must be temporarily buried. At the end of the film, Steven carefully folds a drawing he's made of Dottie into a tiny tin foil–enclosed package and buries it in the garden, where it might someday take root in all its queerness. In other words, *Dottie Gets Spanked* demonstrates how love of a television program and star might also allow one to begin to come to terms with other (and othered) kinds of love as well—exactly the problem plaguing the characters in *Far from Heaven*.

Whereas Frank Whitaker arguably follows the advice given to little Steven Gale (watching something "manly," like real events on the news, rather than displaying "feminino" tendencies by tuning into a sitcom or, worse, a melodramatic soap opera or movie on TV), this may obscure, rather than clarify, the terms of his reality. That is, the problem may not be that the Whitakers are too absorbed into television but that they're not absorbed enough—or, perhaps more accurately, they're absorbed in the wrong way, framed only as televisual spectacles and not as television spectators, posed with and against the TV set and thus set into place themselves, rather than being engaged readers of the texts. For no filmmaker has done more than Haynes to reveal the sometimes quite surprising—and surprisingly feminist and queer—implications of media engagement. From his treatment of television in *Dottie Gets Spanked* and music in *Velvet Goldmine* to his own obvious love of cinema displayed in *Poison*'s, *Velvet Goldmine*'s, and *Far from Heaven*'s homages to Sirk, Fassbinder, Welles, Roeg, Genet, and old horror films, Haynes has shown us that deep involvement in mediated culture need not mean thoughtless conformity. Indeed, even when something such as *Far from Heaven* seems to conform to the model of 1950s Hollywood, this appearance can be deceptive, because "conformity" may reveal the differences that lurk within the mainstream. In this way, Haynes's work thinks through the media to incite us to think through them carefully ourselves. His work thus demonstrates how mass-mediated texts, far from being only objects of knowledge (and improper objects at that), might also be feminist and queer mediums of knowing, epistemological assets for viewers rather than simply financial ones for studios (or for eBay sellers marketing their wares).

I opened this essay on *Far from Heaven*'s intermediations with an anecdote about eBay, a trivial story about the way that trivial things, such as fashion accessories or movie memorabilia, enter our lives. I hope I have demonstrated, however, that such things are not trivial: not only are media and mass cultural objects crucial to appreciate and understand, but such objects and texts themselves might provide us with new means to appreciate the significance of the issues they raise. Haynes's work is interestingly positioned in this nexus, enacting at one and the same time both a loving and a critical attitude toward media and consumer culture (perhaps the sort of critical gaze that one can direct only at something loved so much, and vice versa). This loving critique is apparent in all of Haynes's films, but it is especially pronounced in *Far from Heaven*.

It could be for that reason that I found the "Far from Heaven" eBay listing so provocative. Its attempt to appropriate a film that itself appropriates consumer culture seemed, at one and the same time, incongruous and expected, both ironic and instructive as a way of interacting with the film. One might argue that appropriating the film for an advertising slogan is not a particularly productive mode of interaction, or productive only in the narrow sense of producing business—an added irony, given the scathing look at just those sorts of advertising slogans in the film's treatment of the Magnatech ads. In that regard, one might say that it ignores the film's social concerns to capitalize only on its consumer ones (which is why the fact that the eBay item is a purse—the gendered, sexualized, and classed object par excellence—is so striking). Yet the film itself gets at social issues, not in place of but precisely because of its consumer engagement: it thinks through its social questions by way of the media and mass cultural ones, revealing in the process how the two are always intertwined and how feminist and queer interventions thus necessitate media interventions, and vice versa. Through such intertwining, *Far from Heaven* sheds new light on our involvement with the media, providing us not only with things we might want to purchase but with a valuable sort of purchase on our culture itself.

NOTES

This chapter originally appeared in "Todd Haynes: A Magnificent Obsession," special issue, *Camera Obscura: Feminism, Culture, and Media Studies* 19, no. 3 (2004): 187–219. It is reprinted here in altered form.

1 For analyses of Rock Hudson's star image with regard to sexuality, see Dyer (2002), Lippe (1987), and Meyer (1991).

2 For some of the founding texts on Douglas Sirk's films, see Mulvey (1977–78), Neale (1976–77), and Willemen (1971, 1973). The journal issues *Screen* 12, no. 2 (1971) and *Bright Lights* 6 (1977–78) are both special issues devoted to Sirk. See also L. Fischer (1991), Halliday (1972), Halliday and Mulvey (1972), Klinger (1994), and Stern (1979). For an analysis of *Far from Heaven* that insightfully addresses the relationship between Haynes's and Sirk's work, see S. Willis (2003).

3 Useful discussions of melodrama include Bratton, Cook, and Gledhill (1994), Byars (1991), Elsaesser (1972), Gledhill (1987), Landy (1991), and Schatz (1981). Special journal issues on melodrama include *Film Reader* 3 (1978), *Wide Angle* 4, no. 2 (1980), *Movie* 29–30 (1982), *Screen* 25, no. 1 (1984), *Film Criticism* 9, no. 2 (1984–85), *Screen* 27, no. 6 (1986), and *Screen* 29, no. 3 (1988).

4 These questions of excess, distanciation, hysteria, and irony arise in the aforementioned texts on melodrama. For a specific debate on the subject, see Pollock, Nowell-Smith, and Heath (1977).

5 I have found Pendleton (1993) very productive for my own thoughts about how one might think through the media (though the piece itself does not address Haynes's work).

6 From diegetic temporal references it is clear that the narrative of *Far from Heaven* occurs between the fall of 1957 and the spring of 1958, and most of the films seen playing at the Ritz Theater are from 1956. The release date of *The Three Faces of Eve*, however, was September 23, 1957, just one day before President Eisenhower's famous national television address in which he announced his decision to send federal troops to Little Rock, Arkansas, to ensure compliance with a federal court order striking down racial segregation in public schools. Not only is this event referenced in the film, but one of Eisenhower's televised press releases concerning the situation is seen on the Whitakers' television set. In light of *Far from Heaven*'s acknowledgment of the crisis over school desegregation, its hints concerning *The Three Faces of Eve*'s contemporaneous engagement with such issues as sexuality and race, identity and difference, and deviancy and compliance become only more salient and suggestive.

7 For interesting readings of other films that also make heavy use of the telephone, see Crane (2002) and McCallum (1999). In the former piece, in particular, Crane applies a strategy of reading the structural arrangement of phone calls across the film that's similar to my strategy here.

8 There are also times when we hear telephones ringing in the background—for instance, on secretaries' desks at the Magnatech office and, more significantly, at the Whitaker home when Cathy is running out to pick up her daughter after her outing with Raymond. The latter, presumably, is an attempted call from Eleanor to alert Cathy to the gossip; when Eleanor manages to reach Cathy, she states that she's been trying all day. Apparently, Frank's phone, too, has been ringing; he comes home early to confront

Cathy about the news. Although these unanswered or offscreen calls (or both) do not affect the structural pattern of phone calls across the narrative that I discuss, they do emphasize the significance of the telephone as a medium for communication (or missed communication) in the film.

9 Numerous scholars have analyzed broadcast television's illusions of "liveness" and discourse. For just some of the founding work, see Ellis (1982), Feuer (1983), and Morse (1986).

10 Many television studies scholars have argued that TV viewers should be conceptualized as active producers of meanings, pleasures, intertexts, viewing communities, and so on, rather than simply as passive receivers. For just a selection of some of the founding arguments on this, see Ang (1996), Fiske (1987), H. Jenkins (1992), Morley (1992), and Seiter et al. (1989).

11 This is not to say that all modes of media, communication, and entertainment operate at Cathy's expense. For example, hints about her history in amateur theater suggest that performance is something that has opened possibilities for her in the past, even though the main way in which we see her "perform" in the film's present is in limiting roles and scenes not necessarily of her own choosing—as the model wife, as the object of gossip, as the spectacle for others to gape at disapprovingly, and so on.

12 *I Love Lucy* ended its original six-year run in May 1957 (when it was still the highest rated program), just four months before Eisenhower's decision regarding Little Rock—though, because of production company Desilu's practical creation of television syndication (and thus the TV rerun), the program has nonetheless been almost continuously available since its inception.

13 *Dottie Gets Spanked* itself aired on television as part of the 1994 PBS/ITVS series *TV Families* from producer James Schamus. For a wonderful analysis of *Dottie Gets Spanked* in terms of what she calls "retrospectatorship" (the way a viewer's reception of a text engages fantasy, memory, and past experiences, including fantasies, memories, and experiences of other media texts), see P. White (1999), in particular 197–202.

11 It's Not TV, It's *Mildred Pierce*

Bridget Kies

Intermedial Readings

Following the three-week run of Todd Haynes's version of *Mildred Pierce* as a miniseries for premium cable channel HBO in 2011, film scholars and reviewers were quick to compliment Haynes for his faithful adaptation. Originating as a novel by James M. Cain in 1941, *Mildred Pierce* was first adapted in 1945 as a film directed by Michael Curtiz and starring Joan Crawford. Much of the praise given to Haynes rewards him for the luxury of time that the miniseries format grants him to remain faithful to the Cain novel, extend takes, and revel in his formalist cinematography. This praise often attempts to link Haynes's auteurism with his appreciation for feminist film theory and his use of slow narrative pacing, which allows for a rich characterization of Mildred (Kate Winslet). This auteurist approach, however, tends to draw heavily on film theory at the expense of reading *Mildred Pierce* through the history of the television miniseries and HBO programming. Rather than seeing *Mildred Pierce* as the product of singular, auteurist vision that is also feminist, this chapter concentrates on its intermediality and intertextuality as a miniseries. In doing so, I argue that Haynes's feminist vision for the project can be read through the history of the miniseries, its relationship to other HBO programming, and other incarnations of *Mildred Pierce*. This reading is essential to understanding how the project exhibits and refashions our understanding of Haynes's feminism.

The five installments of *Mildred Pierce* are labeled as "parts" in the opening credits, but they could just as easily be understood as episodes. The opening credits pointedly describe the project as a "film by Todd Haynes," yet HBO Miniseries is also credited as a production company. These multifaceted ways of understanding what *Mildred Pierce* is have led some critics and film scholars to applaud Haynes for finding malleability in the film form or for pushing the boundaries of television. Noting that the credits list *Mildred Pierce* as a "film by Todd Haynes," Amelie Hastie cautions that "this mini-series is very much television" (2011, 26). Nonetheless, she finds that it has a "more cinematic emphasis on a singular thread of narrative focus (our heroine) rather than the multiple strands of a conventional serial form" (28). Citing Haynes's studies in semiotics and feminist film theory while at Brown University, Hastie argues that his *Mildred Pierce* is not so much an homage to Curtiz's 1945 version, "but rather that it's influenced by the subsequent feminist reading of the film" (32). Pam Cook's (1980) essay on the Curtiz film is part of that feminist legacy, arguing for a reading of *Mildred Pierce* that recognizes the gendered implications of its favoring of film noir (and masculine) elements over its melodramatic (and feminine) elements. Hastie goes so far as to describe the Haynes miniseries as "a welcome resolution of two strands of 1970s feminist film theory that are too often divided from one another: a critical attention to classical narrative film and a focus on experimental women filmmakers" who influenced Haynes's style (2011, 32). In other words, though Hastie acknowledges the miniseries as television, her reading of it cannot be divorced from the previously released film or from feminist film theory in general.

Cook's reading of the miniseries takes a more nuanced approach to understanding it as "decidedly transmedia" yet neglects any significant excavation of the history of the television miniseries and *Mildred Pierce*'s possible place in that canon (2013, 379). Cook's assessment of the project as transmedia results from its adaptation of form and from the credits: "announced as a film on the credits, made for television, based on a book—signaling the convergences characteristic of contemporary media and the variety of potential consumer experiences" (379). After an assessment of Haynes's announced fidelity to the Cain novel and his own cinematic style, Cook concludes that the textual universe of "Mildred Pierce" is best described as a palimpsest onto which Haynes has written his own notes or a "fluctuating point of convergence between fragmented texts and media" rather than a "static, finished object that can be recovered whole" (387). Despite her insistence that Haynes's *Mildred Pierce* cannot be understood if divorced from the larger textual universe, Cook also understands Haynes as an auteur who inscribes his vision onto said palimpsest.

Haynes's style throughout the five-part miniseries is "dominated by frames within frames and views through windows and doorways" (Cook 2013, 384). This aesthetic, which Cook describes as an "aesthetic of exclusion" (386), reduces the sense of naturalism to the miniseries, reminding the viewer at all turns that they are watching a mediated narrative unfold; in doing so, it alludes to the other mediated narratives already in existence. For Cook, this stylistic choice "contributes to confirming the miniseries as a product of Todd Haynes's singular vision" (387). A singular vision, however, implies an auteurist and, in this case, male perspective on what Cook herself describes as a series of fragmented texts. On the contrary, Haynes's iteration of *Mildred Pierce* is not the singular vision of an auteur but rather the result of collaborative processes with several people, from cinematographer Edward Lachman and producer Christine Vachon to executives at HBO Miniseries and star Kate Winslet, shaped as well by an assortment of preexisting texts to which Haynes simultaneously pays homage and reinterprets: the Cain novel, the 1945 film, and other HBO miniseries.

The Feminine Medium and "Quality" Cable Programming

A closer look into the history of HBO Miniseries and the miniseries' history on American television gives a much broader framework for situating Haynes's feminist approach to *Mildred Pierce*. By thinking of the 2011 miniseries as television first and miniseries second, despite Haynes's proclamation that it is a film, we can see Haynes as contributing to a domestic form of entertainment that finds its legacy in stories about women for women (if not *by* women). Television's historical theorization as a "feminine" medium has stemmed from several points of origin, most notably television's relationship to consumption and television viewing habits. As Andreas Huyssen has shown, a "masculinist and misogynist current within the trajectory of modernism" sought to distinguish modernist art from the contemptibility of mass culture and its emphasis on consumption; as a result, mass culture has long been correlated with the feminine (1986, 49). Television's place in the home, the site of women's domestic labor, and its traditionally advertising-driven revenue model have required television to encourage consumption. During its early years, this goal was achieved through advertisements that presumed women to be the primary household consumers and programming that encouraged better performance at household labor, usually through consumption of newfangled products and appliances (Spigel 1992, 73–98). In the 1980s, as middle-class women migrated to the workforce, television executives and advertisers sought them as the new "quality" audience because of their disposable incomes (D'Acci 1994).

Television's association with femininity has also been understood through its formal differences from film. The notions that television requires less concentration from its audience (because of its place in the home) and that it has historically relied on sound and dialogue over image (because of its low resolution) lead John Ellis to characterize television watching as a passive, distracted "glance" compared with the active and attentive gaze required by the cinema (1982, 24). Lynn Joyrich interprets Ellis's glance as a "domestic, distracted, and powerless look . . . a 'feminine' look that is too close to the object to maintain the gap essential to desire and full subjectivity" (1996, 74). By creating *Mildred Pierce* as a miniseries instead of a two-hour theatrical film, Haynes intervenes in this historic conceptualization of television as a feminine, and lesser, medium to give the television audiences a story centered on a female protagonist.

With large budgets, greater emphasis on cinematography, and complex storytelling that commercial-free broadcast can make more intelligible to the viewer, premium cable series are widely regarded as the new "quality" television, even with acknowledgment that such a description is problematic. Twenty-first-century "quality" (cable) television asserts its difference from "feminine" (broadcast) television in its focus on male protagonists, its "cinematic" style, creators and showrunners who are nearly exclusively male, and a prized audience of men (Mittell 2015, 233–51; Newman and Levine 2012, 80–99). In 2011, there were few exceptions to the hegemony of the male melodrama.[1] *Mildred Pierce* disrupted the landscape of male-centered "quality" programming with a story of a woman's struggles: to provide for her family when her husband leaves, raise her children, overcome the tragedy of losing a child, come into her sexual awakening, and lose her empire through setbacks and betrayals. With five episodes and more than five hours of content, the sheer amount of time the viewer spends with Mildred is one reason Hastie credits the miniseries as giving the viewer "the time to care for Mildred" in a way that the Curtiz film cannot (2011, 28).

Beyond centering Mildred in the narrative, Haynes privileges Mildred's point of view to grant the audience access to her emotional world. Numerous medium shots and close-ups revel in the carefully composed yet emotionally layered expressions Winslet uses to show Mildred's complexity. As an encore to her first concert as a coloratura soprano, her daughter Veda surprises Mildred by singing "I'm Always Chasing Rainbows," a song that Mildred loves but that is a great departure from the concert lineup of operatic arias. As Veda sings, Mildred is first seen in the center of a shot with other audience members, then in a medium shot that slowly zooms to close-up. The camera exploits her emotions, first surprise and doubt and then joy, so touched is she by this gesture from her usually selfish daughter (figure 11.1).

Other scenes are presented from Mildred's emotional perspective, if not her visual point of view; the most notable of these are the sex scenes. Unlike Curtiz's film, which could only mildly insinuate sex in accordance with the Hays Code, Haynes's version appears on HBO, a network that revels in the delight of showing subscribers that which cannot be shown on broadcast and even basic cable networks. Sex scenes are requisite for programming on HBO, whose provocative tagline, "It's not TV, it's HBO," reminds subscribers that they pay a premium to access content that is different from the rest of the television market. In other words, HBO "stakes its reputation on consciously violating codes policing the illicit" while "asserting the importance of the creative contribution it believes it is making to modern television drama" (McCabe and Akass 2007, 69, 70). By insisting upon its own respectability, HBO "sanctions the obscene and coarse in language and deed" through discourses of "quality" (76). By establishing itself as "not television," HBO has "cultivated expectation that watching certain television series requires and rewards the temperament, knowledge, and protocols normally considered appropriate for encounters with museum-worthy works of art" (C. Anderson 2008, 24). A central way HBO drama series achieve this end is through the exploitation of nudity and depictions of sex. The sex scenes in *Mildred Pierce* remind viewers that the miniseries is part of HBO's brand. The difference in the presentation of sex between Curtiz's film and Haynes's miniseries is less a distinction between Code-era and post-Code-era Hollywood; it is a distinction between the demands of Code-era Hollywood and contemporary premium cable, which not only allows for nudity and sex scenes but in fact requires them in order to fulfill audience expectations.

Although HBO series occasionally depict male nudity, nude women's bodies are far more common, though representations of sexual gratification tend to be exclusive to men. Sex scenes in HBO miniseries are rarer, and, for this reason, the scenes in *Mildred Pierce* might be understood as

11.1 A touched Mildred mouths the words to her favorite song while Veda sings.

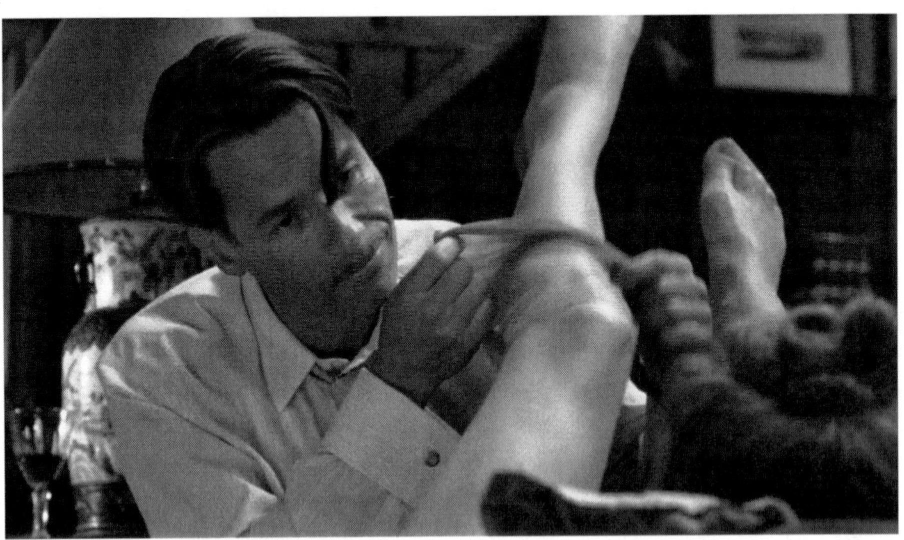

11.2 Monty may reveal Mildred's body to the viewer, but it is Mildred's pleasure that drives the scene.

subversion of "quality" television sex in their emphasis on Mildred's pleasure and her economic gain. The first time Mildred has sex in the miniseries, the event occurs off-screen and results in a rent-free space for a restaurant she wants to open. The second time, she and Monty have escaped to the seaside on her last day as a waitress before opening the restaurant. When they have sex, Mildred tops. Her naked breasts are visible, but it is her orgasm, not Monty's, that punctuates the scene. In part 5, Mildred and Monty discuss the possibility of marriage, which will allow Monty to save his decaying mansion with Mildred's money. For Mildred, the marriage means a bigger house that she can invite Veda to live in; she knows Veda will be impressed with her wealth and status. Once the arrangement is settled as a business proposition, Mildred lies back on a couch while Monty performs oral sex on her (figure 11.2). There is no hint that she reciprocates.

Only the bodies of Winslet as Mildred and Evan Rachel Wood as adult Veda are seen nude, arguably perpetuating the male gaze of "quality" cable series that exploit women's nudity. In the climax to the miniseries, for example, Mildred discovers that Veda, now an adult, has been having an affair with Mildred's husband Monty. As Veda slithers out of bed, fully nude, the audience's perspective is very much Mildred's, looking on with horror but not turning away from the inappropriate spectacle. The viewer witnesses Veda's nudity from Mildred's point of view, and the scene is intended to be more horrifying than arousing. Mildred's partial nudity, on the other hand, occurs in sex scenes that foreground her pleasure, and her sexual experiences always occur in tandem with her economic gain. Like HBO itself, *Mildred Pierce* links sexual enjoyment with economic success. Haynes's *Mildred Pierce* therefore challenges the ways premium cable has traditionally relegated women to supporting (and primarily sexualized) roles. Its narrative emphasis on a singular protagonist who appears in every scene, its investment in her sexual satisfaction, and its exploration of her hopes, dreams, and traumas as told in a miniseries on HBO provide a feminist counterpoint to much contemporary premium cable programming.

The Television Miniseries and HBO

Mildred Pierce premiered on HBO on March 27, 2011, with a two-part installment that saw Mildred through separation from her first husband, Bert, to her success as a restaurateur and the death of her younger daughter, Ray. The subsequent Sunday night the third episode aired, and the fourth and fifth parts were shown together the week after. The double airing during the first and final weeks gave viewers an overwhelming amount of story to digest in one sitting, creating a tightly compacted experience of seeing Mildred through numerous conflicts, successes, and setbacks. That the miniseries was stretched across three weeks, rather than aired on successive nights, also gave viewers an expanse of time to digest each week's material before encountering the next. Thus, the broadcast model for *Mildred Pierce* was both temporally compact and expansive, creating a sense of binge-watching during the first and final weeks while also capitalizing on dramatic climaxes to sustain viewer interest between segments. Each episode, including those that aired back-to-back, ends with Mildred taking decisive action or suffering the consequences of those actions. These dramatic ends to each episode are not cliffhangers; the viewer is not in doubt as to how a scene will resolve. Haynes and cowriter Jon Raymond break up the narrative so that each episode feels complete but encourages further viewing in order to see what repercussions there might be in future installments. This structure is a trademark of the miniseries that extends as far back as *Roots* (ABC, 1977), which led Leslie Fishbein to declare that the "narrative structure of the miniseries is highly satisfying" because of the thematic coherence across episodes and the tidy resolution to the theme's conflict by the end of the episode (1983, 283). In structure, then, *Mildred Pierce* resembles most television miniseries far more than it resembles most Hollywood films.

Histories of the television miniseries are rare, often bound up in textual and industrial analyses of prominent miniseries like *Rich Man, Poor Man* (ABC, 1976) and *Roots*, which were iconic of the "Golden Age of the Epic Miniseries" from 1974 to 1989 (DeVito and Tropea 2010). Most brief histories of the miniseries concur that its origins on American television lie in the success of programs like the *Forsyte Saga*, which aired on the BBC in 1967 and on the American PBS in 1969–70. Programs like *Masterpiece Theatre* on PBS brought installments of British serial drama into American homes, and the success of the serial narrative led to the creation of numerous American-produced miniseries. According to many accounts, the idea of broadcasting the miniseries in segments on consecutive nights was the brainchild of television executive Fred Silverman, who saw consecutive, segmented broadcasting as a way to prevent a ratings failure for an entire month if the miniseries was unpopular (DeVito and Tropea 2010, 40; Fishbein 1983, 280). The record-breaking success of the adaptation of Alex Haley's *Roots* that was broadcast on eight consecutive nights paved the way for the "limited miniseries in lieu of open-ended weekly series," which "allowed television to achieve the thematic power and narrative sweep ordinarily reserved for film" (Fishbein 1983, 280). The expansion of cable and satellite programming in the late 1980s and 1990s, however, made the miniseries a riskier proposition for broadcast networks.

At the same time, cable networks began airing miniseries, limited series, and made-for-TV movies—programming inspired by the early successes of the broadcast miniseries. HBO's commitment to such programming was apparent in its establishment of HBO Miniseries, a division separate from HBO's more commonly known television programming. Kary Antholis, who had been named division head in 2008, announced *Mildred Pierce* as early as 2010, declaring a shift from "big, sweeping Americana series" (the epic miniseries) to a story with "one of the great actresses of our generation playing a woman trying to raise two kids in tough economic times" (Kronke 2010). Antholis believed the Depression-era setting of *Mildred Pierce* would resonate with audiences during the Great Recession. Paratexts included on the DVD of *Mildred Pierce* emphasize its contiguity with contemporaneous HBO miniseries such as *John Adams* (2008), *Grey Gardens* (2009), *Temple Grandin* (2010), and *You Don't Know Jack* (2010) about the infamous euthanizer Dr. Jack Kevorkian. All these miniseries are stylishly dramatic and centered on eccentric, melodramatic protagonists whose stories the five- to eight-hour miniseries promise to tell in rich detail. Like *Mildred Pierce*, many of these miniseries are adaptations from other literary and media forms; all include casts with big-name stars from television and film.

Historically, one of HBO's most ambitious miniseries was the television adaptation of Tony Kushner's two-part play *Angels in America*. Originally airing in 2003 after years of development, the HBO version of *Angels* was six hours long and aired in six installments spread across two weeks. Like *Mildred Pierce* and many of the HBO miniseries that followed, *Angels* finds its origins in other media—in this case, theater—but provocatively styled itself as literature through the label of "chapter" for each of the six episodes. Kushner had worked for years on a film adaptation but found it too difficult to cut the intricate plot down to two hours. The amount of time needed to cover all the plot points, plus the central story line connecting the AIDS epidemic with the end of the millennium (and perhaps the world), likely meant the project would be unviable as a mainstream motion picture. As Gary Edgerton describes, "*Angels in America* proved to be just too long, too artsy, too political, and too gay," a "constellation of unconventional or controversial components" that would have made traditional film studios hesitant to produce it (2008, 146). For HBO, however, the project demonstrated the network's willingness to pursue risky forms and controversial subject matter, a signal that "bolder projects had a far greater chance of being produced on TV than ever before" (146).

Angels' success with critics and audiences had a large impact on subsequent offerings from HBO Miniseries. A project like Haynes's *Mildred Pierce*, a lavish period piece requiring a reported budget of $20 million, was not unheard-of for a network that had already dedicated $62 million for *Angels in America*. The adaptation of *Mildred Pierce* from novel to film to miniseries and the presumption that the viewer has some familiarity with the previous incarnations of the narrative established the pattern other HBO miniseries would follow. Although the subject matter of *Angels* is explicitly political in its anatomization of the impact of the AIDS epidemic and internalized homophobia, *Mildred Pierce* offers a story about a single mother's economic struggles in the 1930s, which has implicit but evident political significance in light of the 2008 financial crisis and the Great Recession that followed. Yet Haynes's established position as a queer director in the New Queer Cinema canon, often working with queer subject matter, also fit quite well with HBO's desire to follow up on the specifically LGBT accolades for *Angels in America*. It is not by chance, then, that *Mildred Pierce* shares many of the key characteristics of several HBO miniseries: a cast with esteemed actors known for their work in theater and prestige film rather than television, and a historically centered narrative inspired by, adapted from, or working across other media forms such as print literature, theater, and film. The center of *Mildred Pierce* is the title character whose life the audience is supposed to want to watch. Although Mildred Pierce is a fictional character, this structure nonetheless sets up the miniseries as a pseudo-biopic of some famous persona (such as John Adams or Jack Kevorkian)—which, given the rich history of Cain's novel and Curtiz's film, perhaps she is.

Melodrama and Women's Stories

Compared with the sweeping epic of *Angels in America* or the historical gravitas of *John Adams*, *Mildred Pierce* is a quiet domestic story about a housewife-turned-entrepreneur. The banality of Mildred's life belies the mythic nature of the way she refashions herself from housewife to single working mother to business mogul to middle-aged nobody as a result of successive crises. Forever conscious of his miniseries' position as an adaptation distinct from

Curtiz's film, Haynes was quick to emphasize in pre-broadcast publicity that he was remaking not the noir version but the novel itself. Many feminist film scholars, like Cook, certainly "appreciate[d] Haynes's respect for the melodrama at the heart of the book" (Cook 2013, 378). Yet Sarah Churchwell (2011) argues otherwise, seeing Haynes's reverence to Cain's novel as an "object lesson in authorial ambivalence about a central character and her desires," in that his fidelity to the novel and careful attention to detail create a "proto-feminist epic saga about power struggles between mothers and daughters" that ultimately falls short because Cain's novel itself cannot decide whether Veda's snobbery and treachery are worse crimes than Mildred's obsessive love for her daughter.

Filmic maternal melodramas follow much the same structure as *Mildred Pierce*: The woman, for one reason or another, loses her child and fights to get the child back. She often fails, but her daughter is free to pursue life in a better world. It is through this inevitable outcome that the "maternal melodrama presents a recognizable picture of woman's ambivalent position under patriarchy that has been an important source of realistic reflections on women's lives" (Williams 1984, 23). While Mildred is expanding her restaurant empire in part 4, Veda feigns pregnancy in order to extort money from the family of the boy she names as the father. When Mildred learns the truth, she and Veda have a falling out. In part 5, Mildred dedicates herself to reclaiming Veda's affection and, as a result, neglects work, squanders her fortune, and eventually loses her position as the head of her own company. She is seemingly punished for attempting to combine work outside the home with her duties as a mother (Kaplan 2000, 468). But Veda's corruption is not a result of Mildred's work outside the home; Haynes shows Veda eavesdropping on adults and using what she hears against them as early as the first episode, when she is still a small child. If Veda is and always has been a self-absorbed brat, even when Mildred was a housewife, then Mildred's career cannot be to blame.

Most scholarship on spectatorship and the melodrama uses a psychoanalytic approach to show how the female spectator is neither prefigured by nor permitted identification with the central character. In the Curtiz film, for instance, Crawford's aloofness and coolness, combined with the film noir storytelling style, make it difficult for viewers to identify with Mildred. Worse still, by the conclusion of Cain's novel, Mildred is described as fat and drunk. In Haynes's miniseries, however, Winslet portrays Mildred with a soft-spoken voice and timid demeanor. Her hairstyles change as the years advance, but she ages only minimally, and she certainly does not become fat or drunk. Haynes's framing and Winslet's performance discourage audience ambivalence despite the basic story similarities with Cain's novel. We feel Mildred's pain as she marches up and down the streets of Los Angeles looking for a job, stopping only to ease the pain of a blister on her heel. We share Mildred's excitement at watching her restaurant business grow. And when Veda's ultimate betrayal with Monty is enacted, the focus becomes "Mildred's loneliness and emotional suffering," which hinges on "Winslet's highly charged, physically expressive performance" (Cook 2013, 382–83). Haynes's/Winslet's Mildred is a woman whose primary quality is her struggle to find her place in the world as a divorced woman in the 1930s. This tonal shift helps the audience empathize with Mildred and reclaims *Mildred Pierce* as a maternal melodrama.

For Thomas Elsaesser, the protagonists of melodrama must "emerge as lesser human beings for having become wise and acquiescent to the ways of the world" after a narrative of suffering is concluded (1987, 55). Mildred makes a financial, geographic, and marital return to the film's beginning: having lost Veda, Monty, her business, and her wealth, she is remarried to Bert and back in their first, tiny family home. But it is not an emotional or intellectual return to the innocence of the past. When Bert suggests in the concluding scene, "Let's get stinko," we understand that Mildred and Bert may well be drinking to all that they have learned about the cruelties of the world, as embodied in their daughter Veda. It is not unusual for contemporary television series with female-centered narratives to depict "deeply threaded connections between women's work and personal lives to the point that they are entirely conflated" (Lagerwey, Leyda, and Negra 2016). Mildred's downfall, however, casts a different light on this conflation, as it troubles the celebration of resilience that usually attends it. Instead, the tragedy of Mildred's end is in keeping with the maternal melodrama genre, Cain's clear disdain for the character he created, Haynes's tendency to portray malaise rather than happy endings, and, finally, HBO's preference for indeterminate, if not tragic, endings.

Conclusion: Haynes and Feminism

A 2015 *Elle* magazine "listicle" names Hollywood's top feminist male directors and gives brief descriptions of how they contribute to feminism (Zemler 2015). Included in the list with Pedro Almodóvar ("the loyalist") and Jonathan Demme ("the drama student") is Haynes, described as "the auteur." The description under his name credits Haynes for casting Cate

Blanchett as one of several actors playing Bob Dylan in *I'm Not There* and describes his "perceptions on gender" as "nuanced," citing *Far from Heaven* and *Mildred Pierce* as examples (Zemler 2015). But other than name-dropping and describing *Carol* as a "lesbian drama," Zemler does not provide an exact explanation of how Haynes's feminism is being measured or interpreted. The short blurb implies, as do more extensive film critiques and academic essays, that the mere selection of projects about women, especially lesbians, indicates a director's feminism. A more nuanced analysis of Haynes's selection of projects and adaptations of existing media, such as those addressed in this volume, is necessary to show how the director might be viewed as a feminist director.

This chapter has attempted to reconcile Haynes's *Mildred Pierce* with contemporary cable programming; the history of the miniseries, particularly those produced by HBO Miniseries; other melodramas; and other iterations of *Mildred Pierce*. By reading Haynes's *Mildred Pierce* across media but with special attention to its status as television, we gain a more complete picture of how the miniseries fits in his growing catalog of feminist work. In his collaboration with HBO, Haynes recovers *Mildred Pierce* the narrative from its 1945 adaptation; in his collaboration with Kate Winslet, Haynes recovers Mildred Pierce the character from the distaste even Cain had for her. The miniseries also redirects HBO, steering it away from its trajectory of programming focused on male characters and male perspectives. Despite the miniseries' opening credit as a "film by Todd Haynes" and this chapter's sardonic title, *Mildred Pierce* is very much a television text. This fact does not denigrate the miniseries' significance; instead, regarding *Mildred Pierce* as intermedial television allows us to appreciate more fully Haynes's contributions as a feminist director across media platforms.

NOTE

1 One notable exception is *Enlightened* (2011–13), a series about a woman rebuilding her life after a breakdown and for which Haynes himself would direct an episode. I thank Theresa Geller for pointing out the premiere of this HBO series was the same year as *Mildred Pierce*.

12 The Incredible Shrinking Star
Todd Haynes and the Case History of Karen Carpenter

Mary R. Desjardins

Critics have consistently characterized the films of Todd Haynes within the terms of what B. Ruby Rich described in 1992 as the "new queer cinema"—films whose style displayed traces of "appropriation and pastiche, irony," and a social constructionist understanding of history. Not surprisingly, most of these critics, as well as Haynes himself, have sought analytical explanations for his directorial choices in relation to the genre (the woman's film, the star biopic), auteur cinema, and film theory antecedents cited in his body of work (see DeAngelis 2004; B. Rich 1992). Haynes's authorship is constituted in the repetition of his particular citations of past forms. The ironic recontextualizations of these forms evidence a social constructionist historiography and assert Haynes's directorial agency as resistant to the norms of conventional cinematic representation and spectatorial identification.

This essay does not seek to overturn these models of authorship or those of the new queer cinema. It examines the construction of Haynes's authority as it emerged from the material practices that produced and surrounded *Superstar: The Karen Carpenter Story* (1987), a film biography co-written with Cynthia Schneider of the singer Karen Carpenter, who died of anorexia nervosa in 1983 at age thirty-two.. This forty-three-minute, 16mm film using dolls to enact the life of the 1970s singing star was not Haynes's first work, but it was the one that authorized him as a promising

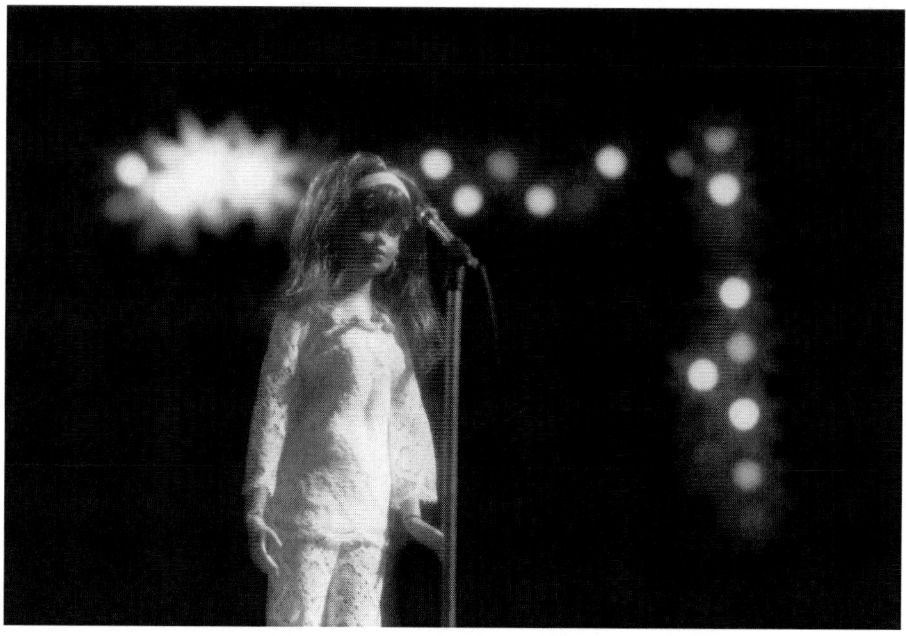

12.1 Shot on 16mm film, *Superstar: The Karen Carpenter Story* (1987) runs for forty-three minutes and uses dolls to enact the life of the 1970s singing star, who died of anorexia nervosa at age thirty-two.

director of alternative cinema. Film festivals and critical reviews served as the vehicles of Haynes's ascension as director. But his decision to shape the narrative around the placement of a number of Carpenters songs also resulted in a losing legal battle with A&M Records and the Carpenter family over the question of who was authorized to represent Karen's life and her voice. Defining Haynes's emerging authority at this time only in the contexts of his trajectory to critical fame or of his legal troubles with *Superstar*, however, would prove insufficient in answering key questions about Haynes's authorial choices that produced a particular version of Karen Carpenter's life within its historical and cultural context. For that reason, this essay explores the degree to which *Superstar* affirms and reproduces the norms of conventional cinematic representation and spectatorial identification—even as its citations of the woman's film and star biopic deploy irony, distanciation, and hybridization to question and critique those norms. Haynes's self-conscious recontextualizations of generic conventions of the woman's film and the star biopic, as well as his infamous use of dolls, do not necessarily result in an escape from either the fantasy potentialities or epistemic foundations of those genres, which promise the recovery, the plentitude, of the biographical subject. The film's threat to A&M Records and the Carpenter family plausibly came as much from its forceful evocation of this desired plentitude (expressed through the voice) as from its parodic critique and the illegal soundtrack.

The generic, cultural, and historiographic work that *Superstar* performs, and the constraints in which it operates, are made clearer by comparing and contrasting the film not to one of its antecedents but to one of its successors, *The Karen Carpenter Story* (Richard Carpenter and Joseph Sargent, 1989), the made-for-television movie authorized by the Carpenter family. It could be argued that the films should be discussed together if for no other reason than that the subsequent television movie offers the Carpenter family's version of Karen's life that was produced after Haynes's version had been legally silenced through their efforts. The films do, however, share remarkable similarities in their contexts as biopics: they were released during a period in which there was an explosion of media-produced biographies; they share similar representational challenges in narrating, visualizing, and vocalizing a well-known public figure; and their actual content occasionally—and uncannily—overlaps. In some ways, the films arrive at—even resurrect—the same Karen.

Both films participate in the biographical genre doing the work of history at a time when biography-as-history was big business. Although the biopic never completely disappeared from Hollywood theatrical feature production, the decades of the 1980s and 1990s, starting with the critically acclaimed *Raging Bull* (Martin Scorsese, 1980), were arguably high points in the genre's status since the decline of the studio system in the 1950s. Furthermore, the popularity of many biographically oriented television programs at that time, including A&E Channel's *Biography* series, not to mention the many print biographies on best-seller lists, attests to the profitability of and presumed public appetite for understanding the historical past through the life stories of celebrities. The use of biographies to organize historical narrative during this period sometimes became the subject of heated discussions about the value of so-called great men narratives in public education and museum exhibition. This idea held especially true for biographies of nontraditional historical figures and members of marginalized racial, ethnic, or sexual groups. A focus on such figures made apparent the tendency of traditional biographies to assert which lives are acceptable as they narrate which lives are exceptional.[1] *Superstar* and *The Karen Carpenter Story* may focus on a mainstream media star, but Karen's story and its contexts raise questions about how certain figures become representative, idealized, and claimed.

Superstar and *The Karen Carpenter Story* share representational challenges that are both basic to the genre and particular to their specific star subject. They struggle with similar conundrums about how to represent the anorexic body, how to represent the star body and voice, and how to negotiate the possibilities of agency for an adult woman still being guided by her parents while contracted to a business circulating mass-produced images of femininity. Both films are examples of contemporary star recyclings that use the biographical form, or what is assumed to be an audience's knowledge of a star's life story, to explore implicitly (*The Karen Carpenter Story*) or explicitly (*Superstar*) the relationship between stars as idealized embodiments of cultural ideals and the body as enacting the staged performance of identity in contemporary capitalist, patriarchal culture. The legal battles over who was authorized to tell Karen's story serve to highlight the extent to which these two films might provide exemplary texts and contexts to explore the performance of (feminine) identity in patriarchal, capitalist culture. The star body, the scandal of anorexia, and the authorization/ownership of biography are terms so interrelated and overdetermined in these films that what follows here repeatedly returns to them, as each section of the essay explores a different facet of their interlocking relations.

Stardom, Biography, and Ownership

If the production of "meaning in biographical form is a powerful force in shaping and reshaping cultural memory," then biographies can provide crucial sites of contestation over historical meaning (Rhiel and Suchoff 1996, 3). Because the body is the "material embodiment for ethnic, racial, and gender identities, as well as a staged performance of identity," it is central to those contestations of history and identity politics in biography (Balsamo 1996, 3). Much of the machinery of star making at the industrial level, as well as at the level of reception, has affirmed the role of the star body in constructing the star as a cultural ideal. It is not surprising that many film, television, and video star biographies foreground how stars literally and figuratively embody cultural contestation over identity, or even reveal the similarities between stardom and the construction or performance of the body.

Stars perform identity through corporeal signs that constitute idealized embodiments of cultural values and norms. William H. Epstein (1987) writes of biography as a modern "gospel" of the body, tracking and disciplining its "godliness in the rising eminence of the professional career" (147). If Epstein's biography of biography was relevant in the late twentieth century, then traditional biographies of media stars would tend to naturalize this process of identity production and the media industries that profit from them. In these narratives, obstacles to or interruptions of the subject's stardom are usually presented as accidental or as the culture's temporary misrecognition of the subject's talent, rather than as the star's failure to obey the culture's injunction to be a particular kind of subject. However, a recent subgenre of experimental films or videos relying on stars' biographical narratives (Sheila McLaughlin and Lynne Tillman's 1984 film about Frances Farmer, *Committed*; Mark Rappaport's 1992 *Rock Hudson's Home Movies* and his 1995 *From the Journals of Jean Seberg*; Joan Braderman's 1993 video *Joan Sees Stars*) recognizes the ideological instabilities in the star biography genre—its reliance on scandal and its simultaneous criticism of and participation in surveillance of the star body. These experimental biographies focus on stars whose ailing, aging, or transgressive bodies fail, exceed, or "defy the injunction by which . . . [their identities] are generated" (Butler 1990, 145). If biography has been "appropriated by the nation-state of industrial capitalism as an articulation of its knowledge-power," these star bodies trouble the process by which biography has traditionally plotted the trajectory of the body in cultural discourse as a support for patriarchal, capitalist culture "administering the body and controlling its insertion into the machinery of production" (Epstein 1987, 147). Works like *Superstar* interrupt the success story trajectory by exposing the way the star body engages in staging identity in response to culture's requirements for certain kinds of subjectivity.[2] The film's use of dolls and dollhouses suggests that the staging of identity can simultaneously reify the subject and engage her in a death-in-life process.

Superstar and *The Karen Carpenter Story* expose the tensions under which the star body in biographical representation performs its work in capitalist, patriarchal culture and becomes visible in history, although they do so to varying degrees and with their own specific effects. These tensions become evident in the variety of thematic and formal concerns the films raise: the necessary substitution of another performing body for the body of the star–biographical subject in the dramatized or staged biographical text, the conflicted terms of ownership of the biographical narrative or star image, the linkage of star body norms to the ideological and metapsychological implications of the classical Hollywood film image and the narratives in which it is typically embedded.

As Epstein argues, the traditional biography's collection of facts introduces the "natural event" into the cultural text, turning the nonnarratable, unlimited semiosis of the body (birth, growth, reproduction, illness, death) into a narratable text, but "textualizing the 'natural' inevitably involves a loss, a falling away from some posited ontological state of wholeness and order" (1987, 42). Although Epstein is writing about the development of biography of the eighteenth and nineteenth centuries, his argument seems to address what are inherent representational problems for traditional film biographies of well-known media stars. They must represent, rather than present, the aura or uniqueness of their star subjects. In other words, they must convince us of the star's worthiness for biography, while another star or performer portrays the star subject of the narrative. Biopics have their ways of compensating for this "lack": having a major star with their own aura of power play the star subject (e.g., Barbra Streisand playing Fanny Brice); having the star subject dub the singing voice of the actor playing them (e.g., television biography of Judy Garland); casting an actor who bears a close physical resemblance to the subject (James Franco playing James Dean); or, in rare cases, having the star play themselves in the movie (as Sophia Loren did in the made-for-television movie about her). *The Karen Carpenter Story* and *Superstar* not only share these representational challenges but expose their problematics by attending to the ailing, dying, or corruptible star body and by evoking sadness that this body can no longer be present.

The right to revive or represent the star presence through evidentiary material—such as the traces of recorded voice and photographed image—is central to the production of many biographies. It is well documented that many biographers working in the literary mode or in traditional Hollywood film and television have legal problems with estates cooperating in terms of access to letters, manuscripts, photos, and the like, yet those estates are rarely able to prevent biographies from being written or filmed at all. These issues have become so heated in recent years that books and articles have appeared about conflicts between biographers and estates. In her book examining biographies of poets Sylvia Plath and Ted Hughes, Janet Malcolm has compared the negotiations between biographers and the subject's relatives (often the owners of the estate) to the tensions and skirmishes between an imperialist explorer and hostile tribes guarding territorial resources (1994, 10–11). If Malcolm's metaphors are overstated and perhaps self-serving (she is clearly on the side of those guarding territorial resources), it is significant that she makes the family's tendency to claim ownership of the famous figures central to the exercise of estate and copyright power. Recent extensions in copyright ownership have, in fact, been spearheaded by the widows of dead celebrities Fred Astaire and Sonny Bono. Their efforts to strengthen the rights of heirs to block unauthorized use of images of dead celebrities through copyright extensions have contributed to the increasing inaccessibility of some media images and sounds to cultural reworkings.

Recent experimental film and video star biographies are products of media practices and biographers possessing unequal access to the images and sounds of public figures because these practices and their ideological underpinnings have not been supported by economic capital or given legitimate symbolic capital. For that reason, the question of who is imperialist exploiter and who is the victim guarding the resources of meaning is left open, or is posed in order to lead us to conclude the reverse of Malcolm's frame of reference. For example, Mark Rappaport, writer-director of *Rock Hudson's Home Movies*, would see Hollywood institutions as the imperialists: "My excuse in a court of law [for using clips from Hollywood-produced films] would be that these images have corrupted us and it's our turn at bat" (1996, 22). Joan Braderman, writer-director of and actor in *Joan Sees Stars*, also used clips of stars from Hollywood films and asks in the voiceover of her video, "How can MGM own what is a part of me?" *The Karen Carpenter Story* was produced in alliance with members of the Carpenter family and a television network—uniting rights to the image and the voice with economic and cultural capital—whereas *Superstar* is a product of industrially and culturally marginalized media practices allied with performance art, critical theory and academic institutions, and traditions and economic support associated with alternative, even subversive, cultural production. This kind of economic marginalization made it impossible for Haynes to fight back when A&M Records and the Carpenter family prevented him from distributing *Superstar*, which used audio clips from Karen Carpenter's performances.[3] Haynes and Schneider's film foregrounds the issue of representation of the star body or likeness and elicits understanding partly through assuming the spectator's extratextual knowledge about the star and production contexts of biography. Reliance on this audience knowledge encourages a reception context in which questions are raised not only about ownership of film images and star bodies but also about spectatorial identification with narrative film images and star bodies.

Stardom, Disciplining the Body, and the Scandal of Anorexia

In a *TV Guide* article published the week *The Karen Carpenter Story* was broadcast on CBS (January 1, 1989), producer Hal Galli is quoted as saying, "We're not really making a movie about anorexia. It's a story of Karen Carpenter and her career of 20 years" (Littwin 1988, 29). But if Karen Carpenter had not died of anorexia nervosa, it is unlikely that Galli would have produced this television movie biography. Stardom and anorexia, as both disease and social scandal, overdetermine Carpenter's story. The processes and achievement of stardom and anorexia each involve discipline, surveillance, and hypervisualization of the body; the conceptualization of perfection; and the attainment of ideals. It is the intersection of these two modes of identity—star and anorexic—in Carpenter's story that makes it the subject of two very different film biographies and biographical practices: *The Karen Carpenter Story*, with its made-for-television movie framework of "disease of the week," and Todd Haynes's controversial *Superstar*, which uses dollhouses as sets and casts Barbie dolls to portray its characters.[4] This intersection allows the films to resonate with contemporary struggles over the meaning of the female body and female agency—discursive categories and lived realities for women in society after the women's movement. The films' willingness to enter this particular contradiction-ridden topical arena is perhaps obvious. After all, modern women are supposed to exercise agency yet are constantly encouraged to idealize what they do not have—the body of the female star. The female star seemingly has cultural power, but she is constantly exposed as pressured, manipulated, and disciplined by others. The filmmakers must have known that Carpenter's story would generate viewer interest because of the ubiquity of these messages throughout contemporary culture. But if we have already established the biopic's difficulties in representing the star subject, how can it represent the anorexic star body?

The representational problems that plague star film and video biographies in relation to the substitution of the star body—what Jean-Louis Comolli (1978) calls the "body too much"—would seem to be especially pertinent to a biography of an anorexic star whose defining physical characteristic is a lethally thin physique. When the star subject has a visible physical affliction or a body that changes radically over time, convincing makeup is necessary at the very least. Within a Method-acting approach, Robert De Niro in *Raging Bull* can gain seventy pounds to play Jake LaMotta in his later years, but to portray an anorexic within a parallel understanding of authenticity in performance would require an actress to lose weight to the point of jeopardizing her life. Although there are precedents of actresses risking death for filmic authenticity, threats to life and limb usually exist as the outmost limits of truth in performance.

The producers of *The Karen Carpenter Story* widely publicized their casting of a thin, small-boned actress (Cynthia Gibb) as Karen, claiming she wore padding during the scenes depicting Carpenter's years before the onset of anorexia. Carpenter's emaciated body is mostly suggested through dialogue and reaction shots of characters looking horrified when they hold or touch her. In *Superstar*, the dolls are altered to represent the passage of time and the progression of the disease during the course of Karen's self-starvation. Haynes carved into the Karen doll's plastic face to suggest emaciation and partially burned the doll playing Mrs. Carpenter to suggest age and horror. In the last section of this chapter, I discuss some important implications of the director's choice to cast dolls in the film in relation to the biopic genre's epistemic and fantasy status. But a crucial point about the choice should be made here in this context of female agency and stardom: the female child is encouraged to play with dolls as a way to narrativize adult identities for her future self. Although this play is suffused with potential resistance to patriarchal roles, girls are usually encouraged to play with dolls as a rehearsal for them (e.g., playing "mommy"). In ironic contrast, Haynes's use of dolls rather than human beings allows him unlimited powers over the bodies of his female "performers." This particular and unusual directorial power seems to simultaneously call attention to and critique how little power female stars have, at the same time as it authorizes Haynes to somewhat aggressively (cutting, burning) and fantastically assert his directorial status over them.

The avoidance of using an actual anorexic body is not evidence that the films have forsaken a politics of authenticity, presence, or biographical "truth." The use of Karen Carpenter's singing voice to structure the narratives of both films and assert an authorial and authorizing voice for their producers indicates their investment in presenting traces of the singer's presence. The effect of Karen's voice is an issue to which I will return when I discuss both films' relationship to the promise of fullness and recovery that melodrama offers. However, both films have an investment in another register of authenticity in relation to stardom—authenticity in relation to scandal. This register is crucial to the films' ability to draw audience interest, and it demonstrates, again, the interrelatedness of stardom and anorexia as terms that offer constructions of femininity on which the films rely or comment. Here the frameworks of scandal and sensationalism also provide opportunities for cultural players to claim ownership of the definitions of femininity, anorexia, and stardom.

George Custen (1992) has argued that the entertainer biography film of classical Hollywood presented stardom as a ritual of democracy—a person with talent is given a "fair hearing on a popular stage" and, after the ups and downs of a career, is taken into the hearts of the diegetic audience that represents the historical audience of that entertainer's time (175). Knowledge of the star's career authenticates the popular judgment of both diegetic and viewing audiences. Contemporary biopics associate authenticity with knowledge of scandal. The possibility of scandal has existed as an underside of star discourse since it began in the 1910s to focus on the star as a private individual (see DeCordova 1990, esp. 117–51). Scandal erupts when the constructed discourse is unable to contain the visibility of the private within socially acceptable parameters. Of course, what is judged as acceptable about the private concerns sexual or other behavior indicating sensual desires, such as excessive consumption of drugs, alcohol, or food. Scandal, in its assumption of giving the audience a glimpse behind the image, gives the sense that what one is seeing is "real" biographical "truth."

Changes in moral standards and in obscenity and libel laws, the decentralization of the origins of star discourse, and the rise of new media as sites for new proliferations of star discourse have all contributed to increasing revelations of star scandal in the past fifty years. The increasing and repeated revelation of star scandal changes what can be considered scandalous—for example, heterosexual activity outside of marriage, except when involving murder, abuse, or incest, is rarely scandalous now. Drug addiction and eating disorders, especially when they end in death or near death, are still relatively scandalous. The latter behaviors suggest deviance from what is considered to be "natural" or healthy behavior with regard to recreational consumption of mood-altering chemicals or eating. To a person who does not have anorexia, anorexia as self-starvation speaks a taboo death wish. From this perspective, the narration of Karen Carpenter's stardom cannot be disarticulated from the scandal of her anorexia, and television movie producer Hal Galli's remarks seem either naive or disingenuous, or political vis-à-vis his dependence on the cooperation of the Carpenter family in making the telefilm.

The narratives of stardom and self-starvation have their similarities—they are about the construction of an image as fantasy ideal; they involve

12.2 The narratives of stardom and self-starvation are about the construction of an image as fantasy ideal, struggles over agency and control, and the subject's discipline, especially discipline of the body to meet the ideal image.

struggles over agency and control; and they involve the subject's discipline, especially discipline of the body to meet the ideal image. Both stardom and anorexia narratives have gained currency as speaking to and about political and symbolic gains and losses for women since the women's movement. Some of the contemporary interest in such stars as Marilyn Monroe, Judy Garland, Rita Hayworth, and Frances Farmer, for example, revolves around their putative lack of agency, their victimization by the studio system, and the latter's repression of their rebellious feminine desires. Feminist writers routinely use female stars or images from music videos, films, television, or magazines as examples of how all women are constructed by the patriarchal imaginary. Feminist cultural critics, as well as clinical researchers, psychiatrists, and psychologists, emphasize the statistical evidence of anorexia as a female disease—90 percent of its sufferers are women. Despite disagreeing about the significance of various determinants, they concur that women with anorexia experience a feeling of powerlessness and impose on their bodies a regime of discipline in which the choice between eating and not eating is a way to control one essential thing about their lives.

Thus Karen Carpenter's story, as it combines narratives of stardom and self-starvation, becomes an overdetermined story of femininity in contemporary culture since the women's movement. The particular ways in which CBS's *The Karen Carpenter Story* and Todd Haynes's *Superstar* express an interest in femininity can be analyzed, in part, in relation to their production contexts. Critics and industry insiders generally agree that the typical made-for-television movie is addressed to a female audience defined by the industry as a valuable consumer market of women between the ages of eighteen and forty-nine. The film's depiction of anorexia reflects the industry's use of topical issues and "real" people to continually resecure audience interest in a genre that offers women a chance to watch the stories—usually traumatic (sometimes triumphant)—of other women. Critical interpretations of this status of the made-for-television movie have ranged from claiming it taps into all the political right's fears about the collapse of the family to designating it as one television form that has consistently provided a sympathetic look at female gender roles in flux (see Feuer 1995; Rapping 1992; and Schulze 1990).

Superstar uses the made-for-television movie as a template for its own narrative. It follows the form's focus on individual trauma and family crisis, showing all of Karen's achievements and problems as a star as influencing and relating to her parents and brother. It seems to share with *The Karen Carpenter Story* what Elayne Rapping has identified as the television movie's assumption that the "relational self" defines femininity (1992, 103). The film also evidences, however, a relation to experimental, independent cinema. Applying an artisanal mode of production, with "found" and handcrafted objects as props, the film plays with the conventions of the documentary, biopic, and woman's film, and combines live action featuring "real people" with what appears to be doll animation (actually the dolls are moved by people offscreen, not animated in the traditional sense). Like many experimental films since the intervention of feminism in media studies, *Superstar* cites past films or genres to expose the degree to which strategies of narrative cinema depend on the representation of the female body. These production contexts suggest that the struggles over the meanings of the female body take place across modes of filmmaking and reading communities, even when the relationship between authorial sources and feminist discourse varies.

Balancing the promotional advantages of sensationalism with a desire to avoid lawsuits, television movies based on the lives of real people are usually made in cooperation with the subjects or their families. As we have seen for *The Karen Carpenter Story*, cooperation with the Carpenter family was essential in order to secure music rights and to gain access to aspects of Karen's life not in the public record. Consequently, the television movie has to negotiate the meanings of Karen's life not only across the various registers of signifying activity that operate around any television movie—the industry's production and marketing practices, the textual practices deriving from genre conventions of the woman's film and biopic, and the reception context of an assumed female, middle-class audience—but also across the authorial prerogatives of family and copyright. From this perspective, Galli's contention that the film is the story of Karen's career rather than her anorexia is a fictive construct that recognizes the version of Karen's life authorized by the Carpenter family, especially Richard Carpenter, Karen's brother, former music partner, and executive producer of the film. In interviews immediately after Karen's death and right before the film aired, Richard Carpenter expressed skepticism over the social and cultural analyses of anorexia, claiming it was genetically determined and had little to do with family dynamics or show business. Although made-for-television movies tend to negotiate social and cultural problems through an emphasis on individual afflictions, cures, and recoveries, they typically assume a pedagogical or even therapeutic role by having diegetic characters and recognizable authorities spell out in promotion the causes, symptoms, and cures of the disease or disaster of the week.

The influence of Richard Carpenter's beliefs about Karen's anorexia—that it is "genetic in the same way talent is"—would seem to mitigate this overtly prosocial function of the made-for-television movie in its intimation that anorexia is genetically unchangeable (Littwin 1988, 29). In the *TV Guide* article that ran the same week as the movie first aired, actress Cynthia Gibb is reported to be so afraid "the family won't accept [her]" if she concedes a typical psychiatric conclusion that people with anorexia tend to come from families that avoid "honest, direct communication about feelings" or tend to be controlled by authoritative parents that she leans over and shuts off the writer's tape recorder when this issue is broached in the interview (29). The actress's complicity with or fear of the family prevents her from performing one of the typical roles of television-movie performers playing ill characters: spokesperson in the public service announcement touting curative solutions. The term *anorexia nervosa* is mentioned only in the last twenty minutes of the film itself, during a scene depicting Karen's psychiatric treatment; scenes of her early life are careful to show her once healthy relationship to eating (a scene near the beginning

12.3 Richard stands by as Karen collapses on her dressing-room table: *Superstar* and *The Karen Carpenter Story* share a primary target of blame for Karen's disease: the family, especially the mother.

of the film, for instance, has her yelling "yippee!" when a pizza dinner is announced). There is also a noticeable lack of emphasis on the industrial, promotional, and fan community configurations of the recording business and the pressures of stardom. Producer Herb Alpert and other A&M Records executives are portrayed as benevolent businessmen and the perfect connoisseurs of Karen's vocal abilities.

It is the experimental film *Superstar* that is invested in clearly defined explanations of anorexia. For example, a voiceover narration breaks into the narrative story world of Karen to historically contextualize women's relation to food and body ideals in postwar America. Such hybridization of the documentary and narrative functions in a prosocial pedagogical role is missing from *The Karen Carpenter Story*, even as such displays remind us of *Superstar*'s relation to the anti-illusionist, nonclassical mode of alternative cinema. The nonnarrative discursive modes of explanation used in these segments contrast sharply with the narrative segments depicting the music executives as causal agents. The film renders their banal commentary about Karen's voice menacing by slowing down the soundtrack so that the actors' voices are deep and their speech slurred. Despite *Superstar's* multiple, hybrid strategies for causal explanations, and despite Richard Carpenter's stated beliefs about the origins of anorexia, the two films do share a primary target of blame for Karen's disease: the family, especially the mother. The two films most powerfully overlap in their act of bringing together the underlying fantasies of the biopic and the maternal melodrama.

Maternal Origins: Recovering Bodies through Vocal Presence

The Karen Carpenter Story's adherence to mainstream narrative and genre conventions positions dramatization of conflict as a necessary representational strategy in the depictions of Karen's life and eventual demise, even as it avoids controversy over the workings of the culture industries. Conflict has origins, and because popular contemporary psychological categories such as the dysfunctional family suggest the family and romantic love as credible sites of conflict, it is not surprising that *The Karen Carpenter Story* traces Karen's search for an ideal in the need for demonstrations of love from family and the right romantic partner. While the emphasis on family honors the Carpenters' own understanding of the familial context for events in their lives, it also contradicts Richard's belief that family relationships had nothing to do with Karen's anorexia.

In other words, the film's need to have a topical, dramatic, and, as we shall see, fantasy origin for Karen's anorexia wins out over Richard's beliefs about the lack of connection between the disease and family dynamics. This need ultimately displaces all of the cultural determinants of anorexia onto the mother, Mrs. Carpenter. This struggle over the authorization of Karen's starvation is crucial to understanding how the film participates in contemporary notions of the female body and in the biopic's depiction of the female star body. *The Karen Carpenter Story*, like so many melodramatic narratives, conceptualizes feminine identity in terms of its closeness with the maternal. In this theorization, women are assumed to be too much body, doubled as they are with the bodies of their mothers not completely relinquished in the movement out of the oedipal moment. Melodramas often focus on the conflicts between mothers and daughters.[5] While the threat this closeness poses to heterosexual attachments can be viewed as subversive, this conceptualization of the mother-child dyad can also depict the mother as possessive and suffocating. Until a social constructionist, historiographic feminist perspective became influential, such oedipalizations were also common in sociological and medical literature on anorexia. Joan Jacobs Brumberg (2000) suggests that when a parent is implicated in the causes of a young woman's anorexia in this literature, "it is almost always the mother ... [who] is unable to see and reflect her daughter as an independent being" (31).

Not surprisingly, Mrs. Carpenter is depicted as loving but as controlling every aspect of Karen's identity. She sews Karen's clothes, resists her move into her own place—though she finally consents when Richard suggests Karen live with him in a house not far from the parents' home—and disapproves of Karen playing the drums because it is not ladylike. When Karen finally seeks psychiatric help, her mother refuses the psychiatrist's pleas to tell Karen she loves her because "Karen knows we love her." Mrs. Carpenter's assumption, based on a belief of mother-daughter closeness that can take a fundamental love for granted, thus enables her to wield a powerful psychic hold over Karen. The casting of Louise Fletcher as Mrs. Carpenter accentuates the phallic associations of this maternal construction—Fletcher is best known as Nurse Ratched in *One Flew over the Cuckoo's Nest* (Milos Forman, 1985), a character who tyrannizes a group of male mental patients with sadistic psychological disciplinary practices.

Placing all of the origins of anorexia onto the suffocating closeness between Karen and her mother has implications for how the film depicts stardom. On the one hand, the film makes stardom a narrative catalyst for Karen's literal starvation. Her constant visibility to the public, resulting in press commentary on her weight and derisions of her clothes, underscores the paucity of her resources to experience a sense of self and receive love from others, which is ironic because stardom supposedly promises that love. On the other hand, the film's combination of the biopic with the maternal melodrama depicts stardom as the ultimate space for Karen to have a body. Musical stardom is shown as an avenue for Karen to express her separation from her mother. The slender body becomes Karen's self-imposed ideal to make others love her more as a star, and to separate from her mother's smothering body. The psychiatrist—in one of those quick television-movie diagnoses—explains that anorexia is symptomatic of Karen's need for love and attention. Mrs. Carpenter, at the family's last Thanksgiving together before Karen's death, finally tells Karen she loves her. Karen hears the message, fulfilling melodrama's fantasy of a possible utopian relation of closeness between mother and daughter, and the biopic's fantasy that the subject will be recognized and approved of for the unique star she is. However, the mistiming of realization and expression functions as a defining element of the melodrama: at this point the anorexia has already damaged Karen's heart and she dies, intertitles tell us, a few months after this touching moment.

Are the melodramatic tensions and poignancy between mother and daughter, in which bodies are assumed as too close, another substitute for the film's inability to actually show us an anorexic body? Perhaps they displace the problem of both anorexia and the film's inability to really show us evidence of the disease onto the problem of a daughter having a visible identity separate from the mother. Significantly, the film also substitutes Karen's voice for her body. All of the biographical materials circulated after Karen's death designate her voice as the defining element of her stardom—to remember it or hear it again, claim record promoters, critics, biographers, and family, is to understand why she was a great star. The recorded voice acts as a fetish that signifies presence in the absence of the loved one (see Lawrence 1991 and Silverman 1988). Karen's special phrasing, claimed to simultaneously express irony and vulnerability, constitutes the "grain" of her voice, what Roland Barthes argues is "the body in the voice as it sings" (1977, 188). *The Karen Carpenter Story*, with authorized connections to the legal and familial ownership of Karen's voice, claims to recover the fullness of Karen's body, now not only gone but "shrinking" or fading during the last years of Karen's own lifetime.

Despite its maverick status as an unauthorized film, *Superstar* shares with *The Karen Carpenter Story* the challenges of representing the anorexic body and its attempted resurrection through the star's voice. Its citation of the family melodrama could also be read as a citation of the simultaneously utopian and dystopian fantasy of maternal plentitude and serves as an explanation for its similarly negative portrayal of the mother. We see here, too, Mrs. Carpenter sewing Karen's clothes, making comments about the antifamily values of show business life, and resisting Karen's move into autonomy. The parents' Downey, California, home, just as in the television movie, is a crucial setting in which to portray Karen's life as enmeshed in a claustrophobic relation to her family.

But Haynes and Schneider trouble any claims to both realism and melodramatic sincerity by using dolls to play the characters and mixing live-action doll performance with dramatizations and documentary sequences using real actors. Haynes has been quoted many times as saying that he wanted to use dolls for actors so that viewers would be conscious of how conventional narratives coax us into identifying with characters and their ideologies.[6] The portrayal of Mrs. Carpenter as tyrannical phallic mother is not based on the film's assumption that mothers and daughters are psychically or essentially close. *The Karen Carpenter Story* expresses this assumption by representing the mother as both controlling and desirous (however late) of a loving, accepting relation to the daughter. The bad mother is centralized in *Superstar*, however, because it is a genre convention of the melodrama and the female star biopic (e.g., *Mommie Dearest* [Frank Perry, 1981], *Frances* [Graeme Clifford, 1982], *Gypsy* [Mervyn LeRoy, 1962]) to have a controlling maternal figure as the prime impetus for the star daughter's rebellion, resulting in little dramatic depth in the portrayal. Although this convention potentially exposes the figure as an obvious stereotype, *Superstar*'s investment in critique of genres and character types does not circumvent its conveyance of the sexist notion that mothers are often the worst, albeit unwitting, purveyors of patriarchal ideology. This idea is most evident in how the doll representing Mrs. Carpenter appears monstrous—the plastic face has been burned, and she is often shot in low-angle close-ups, as if she is looming threateningly over Karen. She is prone to pivoting quickly so that her body—matched to an actress whose voiceover is performed in condescending or whining tones—turns to look at Karen in a show of disbelief at her daughter's meager attempts at asserting agency over her own life. She continually spouts clichéd, conservative laments about the immorality of show business culture as a way to prevent Karen from emerging as a sexual being.

The film offsets problematic aspects of this contradictory imaging of the mother's role in the daughter's anorexia—as both patriarchal mouthpiece and stylized element in the film's strategic self-reflexivity—by using other strategies to depict and explain the twin narratives of stardom and starvation that overdetermine Karen's life. Although also problematic, these strategies align the film more closely with some of the explanations of anorexia offered by feminist theorists that refute simplistic condemnation of the maternal figure. Susan Bordo (1993) positions the condition in terms of its individualized psychodynamics and its cultural determinants, arguing that eating disorders are negotiated responses to "the general rule governing the construction of femininity [in patriarchal culture]: that female hunger—for public power, for independence, for sexual gratification—be contained, and the public space that women be allowed to take up be circumscribed, limited" (171). Women must fulfill an emotional economy that is other-directed, yet they must also exhibit the mastery and emotional discipline required to be accepted into spaces of public visibility. Disciplinary self-starvation is one kind of negotiation of this double bind.

If the contradictions surrounding these expectations for femininity in contemporary culture are constructed around power through possibility of visibility, certainly the female star—as a figure constituted through mediated instances of visibility to a mass public—would seem to particularly emblematize the vicissitudes of femininity in patriarchy. *Superstar* is interested in Karen Carpenter's biography in these terms, and in the irony of using a "shrinking" star to take on the burden of "embodying" feminine visibility. The use of Barbie dolls to portray the characters is the most obvious strategy of the film to contextualize Carpenter's dilemma within an immediately recognizable and widely accessible representation of femininity in postwar American culture. In other words, Barbie brings her own intertextual baggage to the film—a prehistory that includes one of the great success stories of any product of postwar corporate America, the most significant achievement of which was to wed a notion of an ideal, sexualized female body centered on commodity purchases—clothing, accessories, and dream houses—to little girls' fantasy narratives of successful maturation.

Barbie, modeled after a very sexualized German doll named Lili, has qualities of the star. Her "resilience, appeal, and profitability stems from the fact that her identity is constructed primarily through fantasy and is consequently open to change and re-interpretation" (Urla and Swedlund 1995, 285). In the years of the women's movement, sexual revolution, and counterculture after the 1960s, Barbie—like Karen Carpenter, who was derided for representing reactionary values—became a "bad object" for those who reject aspects of patriarchal and corporate ideology. Lynn Spigel argues that Barbie "has been a primary vehicle through which strained relations between different points of views of feminism surface in our culture" (2001, 315). Spigel reveals that adult female collectors of Barbie dolls, some of whom are self-identified feminists, find her image—that resilience, that openness to change and to multiple fantasies of female possibility—empowering. In contrast, other groups of self-identified feminists define the ideals, especially body image ideals, that Barbie seems to represent as highly problematic. In interviews, Haynes never articulates a wholesale condemnation of Barbie, but it is clear that his film speaks to the ways in which Barbie is a bad commodity fetish, or part of the culture's false consciousness (see Farber 1989 and Wyatt 1993).

To underscore the point that stardom and Karen's self-starvation are to be associated with the false consciousness of contemporary mass culture via their connection to Barbie, televisual images from other examples of sixties and seventies pop culture are juxtaposed with the Barbie dolls,

12.4 The Carpenters sing of "good things, not bad" at Nixon's White House, chosen as a singing group whose wholesomeness could counter the subversiveness of contemporary youth rebellion.

whose stiff limbs and movements render them zombielike. In a rapid montage sequence near the end of *Superstar*, images from *The Brady Bunch* and *The Partridge Family*—television shows contemporaneous with the rise of the Carpenters in the seventies that, like the musical group, were presumed to represent a return to more wholesome family values after the sixties—function as a visual backdrop to Karen's purging routine. As the film lets us glimpse what is "real" about Karen behind the constructed image of a happy, sweet femininity, video clips remind us of how popular culture products of this time formed a web of constructed images of ideal youth—a web in which Karen was hopelessly caught.

Also in this montage sequence, television images of Nixon, the Vietnam War, and student protests, accompanied by voiceovers describing the Carpenters' music, embed the history of popular culture into a larger history that sees the sixties and seventies as periods of massive resistance to capitalism and military imperialism. In this context, the Carpenters are depicted as a singing group whose function was to cover up the subversiveness of contemporary youth rebellion. The group's invitation to sing at Nixon's White House is a highlight of the film, and Karen's song there implores the audience to also sing, but of "good things, not bad." As the images of spankings inserted throughout the film suggest the personal psychodynamics of Karen's acts of punishment and repression, the Carpenters' music is depicted in the film as a sociocultural fantasy mechanism of repression that keeps more troubling realities from surfacing to consciousness. Similarly, the film's use of documentary found footage depicting the abundant availability of mass-marketed food products in American chain grocery stores during the postwar period puts Karen's relation to food and self-starvation into a larger history of consumption in a nation of abundance, and within the cultural prescriptions for women to consume, but not too much.

The most problematic use of documentary conventions in the film is its use of found-footage images of dead, emaciated bodies from Nazi concentration camps. Early in the film, intertitles explain the psychodynamics of anorexia as one in which victim and punisher are one—anorexic as fascist is the comparison explicitly made. Although the metaphorical construction of anorexic as fascist may have some explanatory power vis-à-vis an individualized psychodynamic, comparing self-imposed starvation with the forced starvation of victims of genocide raises more questions than it answers. But the use of the images of emaciated concentration camp victims for their shock or comparative value exposes again the difficulties in representing the anorexic body within traditional narrative, or even untraditional biographical narrative conventions. Another body must substitute for Karen's anorexic body, whether it is that of the concentration camp victim or the Barbie body in its shiny plastic carapace.

Superstar does not really need to show us concentration camp victims to suggest how Karen's anorexia was leading to death, because the very use of dolls and miniature props already does part of that work. Susan Stewart, in her 1993 study of the gigantic and the miniature as cultural forms, argues that the miniature evokes a removal from lived experience, a perfected self "protected from contamination" because absolute boundaries are maintained (69). It mimes perfection known only in death. In other words, the anorexic's self-imposed ideal of the perfect body—uncontaminated by food or unacceptable feminine desires—is uncontaminated by the material processes of living. Stewart also describes the function of the miniature, such as the dollhouse, in terms of the way the spectators experience it as a tableau representing the tension between inside and outside. *Superstar* evokes such a tension in its juxtaposition of scenes using dolls with the repeated live-action tracking shots taken on the streets of the Carpenters' Downey neighborhood. The "frozen-in-life" quality of ideal femininity epitomized in the rigid, unchanging miniature doll is contrasted with the movement of the camera as an endless searching in suburban America. This contrast suggests, as Stewart does about the miniature, that the house is simultaneously prison and haven and represents an interior self that always remains unrecoverable (44).

Like *The Karen Carpenter Story*, *Superstar* uses recordings of Karen's voice as a way to recall her presence in the melancholy void that characterizes these representations of her life and body. At times, both films actually use the same songs as soundtrack in representing particular moments in Karen's life. For example, both depict Karen's short courtship and marriage through a couple of brief scenes in which her rendering of "Masquerade," a song about the masquerades of identity we assume in relationships, serves as vocal backdrop. Despite the television movie's inscription of a sincere melodrama, like *Superstar* it lets Karen's voice take on the burden of authorial irony. In Haynes's film, he and other actors portray music critics in a mock documentary sequence in which three of the four talking heads claim that Karen's genius, the basis of her stardom, was the way she could control or create ironic inflections in otherwise uninteresting kinds of mass-produced music.

In the need to produce a star body and an acting agent for filmic biography, each film recovers Karen through her voice. In working out these representational challenges and determining what agency might mean in a political context that also sees women as afflicted by the images and constraints produced by patriarchal ideology, Haynes's film also affirms some of the norms that its ironic citations seek to undermine. But *Superstar* and, to a lesser degree, *The Karen Carpenter Story* thematize issues of control and agency that also inform their own production contexts and the legal fights between Haynes's status as author and the ownership claims of Richard Carpenter, A&M Records, and Mattel Toys. This discussion has been able to make claims about agency only in relation to these particular production and textual contexts. A study that would go further in terms of possible reception contexts would still be involved in those same dilemmas. Fans and readers surely claim to possess the star in their own ways, while patriarchal culture continually raises its stakes on the female body. These two film biographies of Karen Carpenter ask—and only sometimes answer—a few of the questions of stardom and the female body: Who owns the star's voice and image? Who owns the female body?

Coda (2021)

At the time I originally wrote this essay in 2003—and when I wrote an earlier version of it as a conference paper in the mid-1990s—I was thinking through theories of the female body, stardom, and biography. Now, I am preoccupied with the relation of biography to history—not only with their storytelling practices, but with how they elevate representative subjects, that is, make certain subjects visible as agents. Perhaps influenced by film theory's assent to the death of the author, feminist film scholarship has not been that interested in biography as an object of theoretical inquiry, but recent feminist scholarship about women's historical role in filmmaking asks questions that overlap with, or are at least relevant to, theorizing biography from a feminist perspective: How does the historical female subject become an agent? How does her agency relate to that of other women whose material conditions under patriarchy intersect with hers and form a historical constellation? How does the historian/biographer share (and not share) that history with her subject?[7]

Superstar, if it is a history, is a history of a recent past—the era of Haynes and Schneider's childhood and adolescence, the era of baby boomers whose shared cultural references included movie stars, pop singers, and Barbie dolls as "representative subjects." The use of a Barbie doll as a replacement for Karen's body is a reference to feminine body norms in patriarchal culture, a metaphor for the split subjectivity of Lacanian psychoanalysis and critical theory that was the intellectual historical context for Haynes and Schneider's coming-of-age as filmmakers, and a symbol of the disappearance of "real women" in traditional biographies and histories, but it is not merely any of these. Barbie dolls, like stars, are all too visible in patriarchal culture. *Superstar* uses the hypervisibility of Barbie to distance the viewer from the belief that she is seeing Karen, that a "true Karen" can be seen. Mary Ann Doane argues that Haynes's work demonstrates how "the generic invades the image, reducing its singularity, making it available for *recognition*" (2004b, 13; emphasis in the original). We recognize Karen, without having access to her.

In *Superstar*, we recognize Karen's life story through both the film's citation of the star biopic and in what it includes of her particular tragic trajectory (i.e., her death by anorexia). In the best tradition of experimental film and in anticipation of the interventions of feminist historiography, *Superstar* offers recognition of the conditions for and contradictions in Karen's interpellation as a subject in the past. Because these intersect with the conditions and contradictions in which we also live in the present, we share a history with Karen (and this is doubly true for those of us who were alive during all or part of Karen's actual earthly existence).

Superstar's use of Karen's voice enacts how Karen remains present to us. The voice is what makes the history of Karen's life worth telling, what makes us seek the film out—despite the legal and technological challenges in doing so. I still stand by my claim that *Superstar*, like the television movie *The Karen Carpenter Story*, attempts to "recover" Karen through her voice, but I believe that the productive effects of its employment are not exhausted by this fetishism. Karen's voice, still present in recording (if not legally available for reproduction), is also a call. It is not so different from the call of home that is conjured by the film's shots of the Carpenter's house from a moving car—a call for us to pay attention to our uncanny historical coexistence with Karen, as we live within the same ideological contradictions as she did, even as we long for and imagine a different history.

NOTES

This chapter originally appeared, in slightly different form, in "Todd Haynes: A Magnificent Obsession," special issue, *Camera Obscura: Feminism, Culture, and Media Studies* 19, no. 3 (2004): 23–55. The author expresses gratitude to the *Camera Obscura* collective, especially Amelie Hastie, for comments on the original version of the essay.

1 For discussions of how feminist criticism has participated in these debates around traditional biography's naturalization of representative figures, see hooks (1989), Wagner-Martin (1994).

2 I discuss *Rock Hudson's Home Movies* and *Joan Sees Stars* in conjunction with the films under examination in this essay in my book *Recycled Stars: Female Stardom in the Age of Television and Video* (Desjardins 2015).

3 *Superstar* had already been shown extensively on the film festival circuit and had even been transferred to video for rental and purchase at the time A&M and the Carpenters stopped it from legally circulating any further. See Hilderbrand (2004) for more on the viewing and distribution history of *Superstar*.

4 None of the dolls used were actually the "Barbie" doll. The doll used to portray Karen was a "Tracy" doll manufactured by Mattel to be Barbie's friend. A Mattel "Ken" doll portrays Richard, but wigs were used on it for the film (Farber 1989, 19–20).

5 For a small sampling of the work done on this issue in feminist film studies, see Gledhill (1987).

6 See, for instance, Farber (1989, 18), and Wyatt (1993, 4–5). See also the original press kit for *Superstar*.

7 Bingham (2010) references feminist *literary* scholars of biography in his discussion of the biopic. Recent historiographic work being done by participants in the biannual Women and the Silent Screen conference and for the Women Film Pioneers Project, for instance, that by Dall'Asta (2010) and Gaines (2018), has been concerned with the material conditions under which women produce and become subjects for historical inquiry.

13 Having a Ball with Dottie
Queering Female Stardom from MGM to Todd Haynes

Noah A. Tsika

The study of sexuality is not coextensive with the study of gender; correspondingly, antihomophobic inquiry is not coextensive with feminist inquiry. But we can't know in advance how they will be different.

—EVE KOSOFSKY SEDGWICK, *Epistemology of the Closet* (1990)

What is the use of being a boy if you are going to grow up to be a man.

—GERTRUDE STEIN, "What Are Master-Pieces and Why Are There So Few of Them?" ([1936] 2008)

In the early sixties dreamscape of Todd Haynes's *Dottie Gets Spanked* (1993), Stevie (J. Evan Bonifant) might as well be a Martian—much like the otherworldly spirit of Oscar Wilde, which so gracefully weaves its way through Haynes's 1998 film *Velvet Goldmine*. Perhaps Stevie, in about ten years' time, will become one of the teen rock fans of that later film, finally finding, amid the glamor of 1970s London, the fellowship that American suburbia cruelly withholds (at least for little boys who love female television stars). The giggling girls who torment Stevie, brushing him off on the bus to school, or seeking to censure his respect for a television icon—the irrepressible Dottie Frank—whom they themselves openly worship, represent some

13.1 Stevie feels anxious on the bus ride home.

of the queer contradictions at the center of Haynes's film. These mean little girls—miniature versions of their starched mothers—aspire to resemble an actress whose childlike femininity is as much of a masquerade as their own, while they also police both Stevie's fandom and identity by outing him as a "feminino." Throughout *Dottie Gets Spanked*, the star persona of Dottie Frank repeatedly, if unpredictably, incites these suburban contests (and psychic fantasies) in relation to postwar norms of gender and sexuality. Moreover, Dottie's awesome, allusive power—her "obvious" resemblance to Lucille Ball and to that star's always hybridized iconicity—is at the heart of the film, and of this chapter.

Alert to the queer inversions that mark the private underside of publicly (and "properly") gendered performances, Haynes's film also troubles this dichotomy, presenting seemingly hermetic moments as expansive displays, as when Stevie, blissfully consuming *The Dottie Show* in that stereotypical locus of "private" spectatorship—the suburban living room—is revealed to be under increasingly anxious surveillance by adults, including visiting strangers. This violation of the boundaries between public and private, illusion and reality, evinces a queer inquiry that finds its most memorable expression in breaches between Stevie and Dottie, the object of his obsessive, amorphously eroticized fandom. At the age of six (or, as he so proudly puts it, "six and three-quarters"), Stevie may well be "presexual"—unidentifiable as "gay," "straight," or "queer"—but the plainly homophobic surveillance to which he is subjected would seem to suggest otherwise, even as it evokes Foucault's argument ([1989] 1996) that "homosexuality threatens people as a 'way of life,' rather than a way of having sex" (310). That Stevie's "way of life" consists of compulsively watching and ruminating over *The Dottie Show* is a matter of much concern for his parents, particularly his football-loving father, who tries to "remediate" Stevie through force, aiming to plant the boy in front of a televised game that he presents as a masculinizing alternative to a "silly" domestic sitcom.

Dottie is scarcely the soothing savior figure that Stevie seems to need, however, as he discovers during a trip to the set of her series, where he finds himself faced with a "backstage" persona that, in its sheer "bossiness," seems to echo his father's own brand of authoritarianism. Yet it is precisely Dottie's queer recasting of conventional gender roles, coupled with her capacity to swing skillfully between dominance and submission, that Stevie finds compelling—so much so, in fact, that his dreams begin to reflect (or perhaps produce) a growing attachment to eroticized role play. Ominously, however, the film ends with Stevie's incipient sadism directed inward, at his own transgressive fandom: shamed by dreams of disciplinary rituals, he buries a self-produced *Dottie* tie-in—a crayon portrait of the character getting spanked. Punishment for his own material production, this burial is also, perhaps, a strategy—however naive—for precluding continued fantasy, even as it suggests a sort of time capsule to be consulted at a later, more liberated date. But Stevie has already discovered that Dottie cannot be confined to a single medium; tuning into a football game is no more effective a means of effacing her than burying a piece of paper that bears her likeness. Dottie has long since infiltrated Stevie's confused dreams, and she is hardly depicted as an unambiguous feminist icon; her appeal for Stevie seems to reside not in her being a "fabulous" model for an effeminate boy, but rather in her Ball-like capacity to contest what counts as "feminine" and "masculine" in the first place—much as Stevie forces us to question what could possibly constitute proto-gay male subjecthood.

Dependent, in part, on the careful, often contentious disarticulation of sex and sexuality from the category of gender, queer theory has certainly had its share of negative encounters with a feminism premised on the inviolability of "woman." "The binary between 'men' and 'women' seemed not only to be a constant presupposition within feminist work," writes Judith Butler of the period just before the emergence of queer theory, "but was elevated to the theological status of the 'irrefutable'" in some circles (1997, 2). Butler's *Gender Trouble: Feminism and the Subversion of Identity*, first published in 1990, was the author's polemical response to this state of affairs—what she calls "the acerbic culmination of [a] history of unease and anger within feminism" (2). Completed in 1993, *Dottie Gets Spanked* seems to reflect some of the earliest and most generative intersections between feminist theory and queer theory, contesting stable notions of stardom, fandom, womanhood, and boyhood—not to mention various categories of sexuality—through Stevie's encounter with a Lucille Ball clone. It is instructive that Ball, who died in 1989, was by 1993 at the center of so many attempts to self-consciously recuperate her career for feminism. Haynes's take on the star thus acquires a disruptive force akin to that of contemporaneous clashes between feminist theory and queer theory.

Dottie Gets Spanked combines a familiar, Ball-like brand of shape-shifting stardom with a queer critique of identity, consistently foreclosing epistemic certainty, especially regarding little Stevie. If, as Butler (1991) puts it in her gloss on Foucault, "identity categories tend to be instruments of regulatory regimes" (13), *Dottie Gets Spanked* presents at least two registers through which they may be evaded: female stardom in the age of television—a time of "massive recycling" that, according to Mary R. Desjardins (2015), required aging stars to become "transmutable"—and queer fandom, here defined as an affective relation irreducible to legible markers of gender and sexuality. Freud is well represented in the film, and, as Tim Dean (2000) reminds us, his theory of the unconscious "introduces a constitutive subjective division that undermines the possibility of any seamless identity" (24). Stevie, whose identity is inchoate at best, forms what Dean would call an "identificatory alliance" with Dottie—both the character and the star who plays her. This alliance, characterized as it is by various fantasy scenarios, is hardly a unidirectional or unambiguous process, however, particularly as Stevie's "polymorphously perverse nightmares," as Michael DeAngelis calls them, "compel the boy to move among a number of positions in relationships of identification" (2004, 44). Stevie's dreams, with their irrational transfigurations, recall, in fact, Ball's fantastical Hollywood musicals, with their shared requirement that the star "become" someone else at any moment—a requirement whose capitalist essence ("in a flexible economy that rewards global subjects for their quick changes") should hardly diminish its queer potential (Love 2011, 186). Much as Dottie, in Stevie's final nightmare, suddenly becomes the mustachioed stand-in for "the strongest man in the kingdom," Ball in *Meet the People* (Charles Reisner, 1944) transforms herself from an ultrafeminine stage star (complete with extravagantly feathered costume) into "one of the boys"—a butch welder in a wartime shipyard. Throughout Ball's work in classical Hollywood, dreamlike mutations characterize her star persona, even reaching cross-racial extremes in *You Can't Fool Your Wife* (Ray McCarey, 1940), in which her character "becomes" Latina, the better to understand (and ultimately contain) her husband's racially coded sexual desires.

Centered on six-year-old Stevie, *Dottie Gets Spanked* is less explicitly attuned to questions of sexuality, and, as DeAngelis reminds us in his gloss on Freud's "A Child Is Being Beaten" (the essay to which Haynes dutifully refers in the film), "the child's movement among various positions of identification is less an act of liberation than a result of repressive processes" that ultimately prevent the formation of a lastingly queer subject-position (2004, 44). Haynes's invitations to viewers to read the film as a form of autobiography have often produced confident accounts of Stevie's incipient "gayness"—of his status as a "proto-gay boy" whose love for Dottie inheres in his "sissydom" (Hilderbrand 2007, 45).[1] Haynes has spoken extensively of his childhood visit to the set of Lucille Ball's sitcom *Here's Lucy* (1968–74)—the very stage on which the star, in a manner that would structure the director's depiction of Dottie, performed both backstage dominance and on-screen submission. "That duality was fascinating to me," Haynes told Scott MacDonald (2015), "partly because it mirrored a different duality in my life and my fantasy world" (364). On the basis of the film itself, however, there is little reason to limit this duality to familiar gay/straight and male/female binaries. It is, at least potentially, far more complicated than that, as Ball's own iconicity attests, and as queer theory has, of course, long endeavored to demonstrate. Despite (or perhaps because of) the frequency with which he is tendentiously positioned as an avatar of "pre-pubescent gay sexuality," Stevie is an ideal conduit for the film's fusion of queer theory and star studies (Davies 2007, 63). What better figure than a prepubescent child to demonstrate that queerness "exceeds sexuality, sexual practices, sexual identities" (T. Dean 2000, 24)? There is little textual justification for believing that Stevie will "grow up gay," nor is there any reason to assume that Stevie is necessarily a boy or will necessarily "become" a man. The Ball-like transformations that Dottie undergoes—from "flapper to infant to Chaplin to housewife" (Davies 2007, 61–62)—suggest the elusiveness of identity for a star whose continued success depends, in Desjardins's terms, on dynamic change. But they also reflect a specifically queer-theoretical critique of identity, even gay (or proto-gay) identity, as an object of regulation.

Consider, for instance, the liberatory potential of Dottie's persona that Stevie's schoolgirl bullies seem both to recognize and to resist. The sadomasochistic charge of Stevie's interactions with these preteen tormentors certainly invites a queer reading, particularly as the girls appear to invert their own, practiced femininity during moments of abuse, thus exposing its sheer performativity. Even as their sadistic proclivities seem to depend upon Stevie as an object of easy denigration, however, the girls function as an almost euphoric homosocial unit. With its historicizing attention to suburban women (like Stevie's mother) who dutifully capitulate to their husbands' gender-essentialist demands, *Dottie Gets Spanked* would seem to critique Stevie's bullies for their potential to reproduce normative gender dynamics. But other interpretive possibilities are certainly available, provided one is willing to consider the pre- or proto-sexual charge of the girls' cruelty, evident in their giddy regroupings after shaming poor Stevie. That Stevie may well derive incipient sexual pleasure from such cruelty is clear from his fantasy life, which pivots around a spanking that—instructively—he is as likely to receive as to administer. Although it would be as naive to position the film's schoolgirls as proto-lesbians as it would be to situate Stevie as an embryonic gay man, it is worth stressing the extent to which their behavior seems to justify, however provisionally, the efforts of lesbian feminists to contest the cultural-feminist production of a "unitary female sexual nature," in which the woman and the girl are "essentially nurturing, tender"—and certainly far removed from sadomasochistic praxis (Seidman 1993, 123). Haynes's suburban girls seem very much to enjoy—to derive more than just social pleasure from—disciplining the submissive Stevie, but they are nevertheless, in the basic terms of the filmmaker's queer critique, housewives in the making. As they grow older and grow into their normative roles, overtly sadistic treatment of Stevie will plainly be forbidden—a taboo of which one girl seems well aware as she struggles to prevent her irrepressible little sister from skipping over to Stevie to cruelly share her opinion of him as a "feminino."

A similar process of repression and displacement seems to structure Dottie's star persona: comfortable with her own backstage power and influence, she must feign submissive "girlishness" for the camera (and thus for public consumption). And yet it is precisely her mastery of cultural production that links her not only to Lucille Ball (the legendary "business

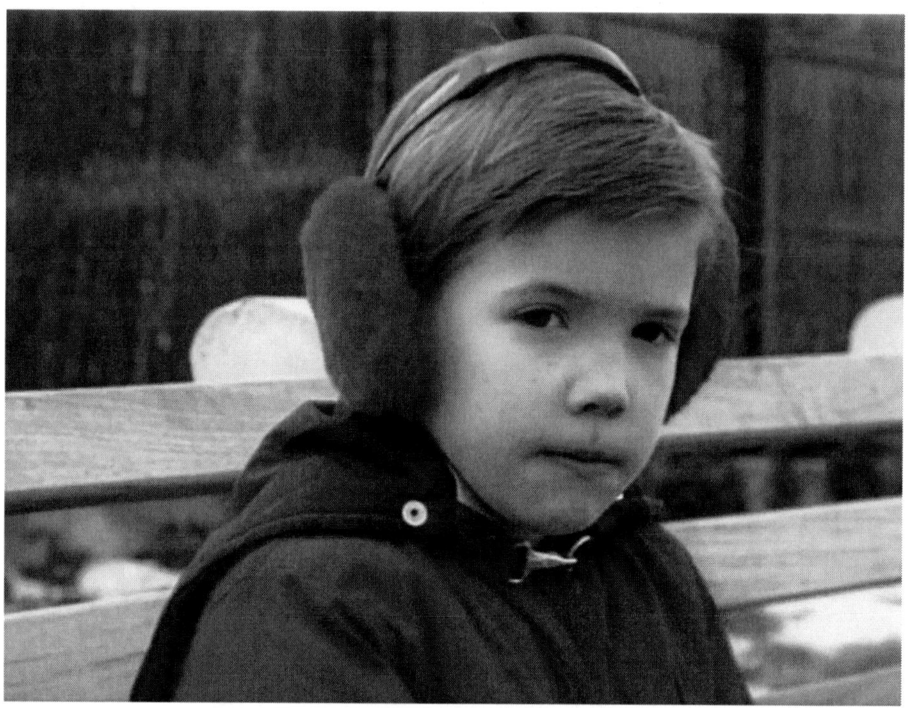

13.2 Stevie listens as schoolmates mischaracterize his idol in *Dottie Gets Spanked.*

genius") but also to Gayle Rubin's influential elaboration of the "sex/gender system"—"a systematic social apparatus which takes up females as raw materials and fashions domesticated women as products" ([1975] 2017, 902). Dottie is thus complicit in the very sociocultural dynamics that will ultimately demand that Stevie's bullies cultivate a nurturing femininity, but her close resemblance to Ball offers additional avenues of interpretation. For Ball's work in the classical Hollywood system tended, with remarkable consistency (if with scant commentary and box-office returns), to foreground the queer transformations required of such a production of womanhood, suggesting that the end result—the domesticated female—is achievable only through a role-playing process that, coded as masculine (and even sadomasochistic), would become anathema to cultural feminists before being reclaimed for queer theory.

Dottie's "Ball-ness"—an allusive quality that no piece on the film fails to mention—is queerly compelling in itself, irrespective of Ball's mutable star image, and its queerness qua allusion demands closer scrutiny, for

Dottie is both "obviously" Ball and "obviously" not—a sign whose referent is at once abundantly evident and oddly elusive (or perhaps intimidatingly multiple). Even beyond its apparently autobiographical trappings, *Dottie Gets Spanked* invites us to consider the interplay between "the worlds inside and outside the text" in a manner that calls to mind the roman à clef, a literary genre whose filmic inheritors include works as otherwise dissimilar as *The Goddess* (John Cromwell, 1958), Paddy Chayefsky's scandalously pseudonymous take on Marilyn Monroe, and Haynes's own *Velvet Goldmine*, a fantasia on themes from David Bowie's life and career (and a film whose script Bowie reportedly disliked, forcing Haynes to scrap plans to use the artist's music). As Sean Latham (2009) argues, the roman à clef has often functioned as an instrument with which to "queer the binary opposition between fact and fiction" (64), and that is precisely how it seems to function in Haynes's hands, especially in *Dottie Gets Spanked*. The "tantalizing ambiguity" of the roman à clef—the genre's conduciveness to questions of passing and closeting, gossipy confidence and epistemic uncertainty—is very much in evidence in Haynes's film, in which Dottie Frank remains powerfully, inescapably evocative of Lucille Ball, even as Haynes seems to incorporate amusing references to Carol Burnett (as when Stevie, anxiously correcting a classmate's take on Dottie's "natural" hair, charmingly mispronounces the word "brunette") (14). Specifically, Dottie calls to mind the Ball whom Patricia Mellencamp (1985) and Alexander Doty (1990), in separate essays, both describe as at once castrated *and* castrating. Mellencamp and Doty argue that this dual symbolic function has its roots as much in the semiotics of Ball's particular performance style as in her much-mediated biography, which has been recounted with remarkable consistency since the early 1940s, gaining facts and allegations with each telling, and a carefully curated (if hardly uncontroversial) relationship to feminism. Indeed, Ball's biography, whether rendered in the rote prose of fan magazines (such as *Silver Screen* and *Hollywood Life Stories*, which Haynes parodies here) or in the form of a quasi-biographical feature film, has never ceased to suggest a barometer both of feminist criticism and of an ongoing antifeminist backlash.

Frankly Ball

In presenting Ball as a woman whose "significance" is socially constructed, and who seems to queer the binary oppositions between public and private, male and female, acting and "authenticity," "real" work and "simulated" labor, Haynes draws on a remarkable and rarely acknowledged array of similar depictions of Ball that began circulating during the era of the Hollywood studio system and gained greater prominence through later transmedia platforms. However, he also fashions a Ball whose evocation of anti-essentialism benefits from the very fictionalization that turns Ball into Dottie, and that productively distorts a fair number of Ball's biographical details, such as her "mixed-race" marriage, which for Haynes becomes something far less controversial (at least according to mid-twentieth-century social proscriptions), or her iconic red hair, which here competes with a blonde wig for public adulation.

It is precisely by showing that Ball/Dottie is *not*, in fact, extraordinary in her lack of an "essence"—that she is actually close in spirit and experience to the film's prepubescent male protagonist—that Haynes complicates her claims to feminism. As the subject of a wide variety of film and television biographies—and in a range of dramatic and comedic incarnations—Ball has, to borrow a phrase from Luce Irigaray, consistently functioned to "undo by overdoing" both puerile dependence and "pants-wearing" strength (quoted in Aston 1999, 63). Ball shows herself to exist in a potentially feminist yet ultimately indeterminate middle ground that is explicitly explored in works as diverse as the wartime musicals *Best Foot Forward* (Edward Buzzell, 1943) and *Meet the People*; the nonfiction films *Hedda Hopper's Hollywood* (William Corrigan, 1960) and *Hollywood without Make-Up* (Ken Murray et al., 1963); and Haynes's *Dottie*. Ball is a star whose business acumen has long been at the center of biographical accounts, which, in the words of Desjardins (2012), tend to position her simultaneously as both a performance "genius" and "an independent woman television executive" (159).

What has made Ball so ripe for feminist recuperation is, arguably, her long-standing association with creative control and ownership of media production. Lucille the business-savvy star could easily be painted according to misogynist cultural presumption—as a "bitch" or worse. It is by directly addressing her industrial function(s), rather than her motherhood or her "failed" marriage to Desi Arnaz, that most media portrayals of Ball have endeavored to disable misogynist conclusions about her dominant, even "bossy" personality, demonstrating that self-reflexive fictions—in which Ball "plays herself" or in which someone else plays a "version" of her (as in *Dottie*)—operate to destabilize the biopic genre (through recourse to the queer techniques of the roman à clef) while strengthening certain understandings of feminism.

It is precisely this "backstage" aesthetic that Haynes has consistently adopted throughout his career as a filmmaker. In 1987's *Superstar: The Karen Carpenter Story*, 1998's *Velvet Goldmine*, and 2007's *I'm Not There*, this aesthetic finds its most direct expression, as a variety of public figures are depicted in moments of disturbing anguish but also of repose—the latter position perhaps the more shocking for its transgression of one of the central tenets of stardom, which is that the star herself is superhuman, or at least regal, and certainly never subject to the embodied boredom of the everyday, never reduced to the purely physical sensation of lounging listlessly on a couch (as Cate Blanchett's Bob Dylan does so memorably in *I'm Not There*, impassively viewing a television program about his life). But if the couch is a marker of the star's persistent humanity—and ripeness for psychoanalysis—in *Velvet Goldmine* and *I'm Not There*, two films in which public figures are rendered "mere" flesh and blood by being, at times, too comfortably ensconced in the most quotidian of sofas, then this particular piece of furniture serves a far more star-making, even feminist function for Dottie Frank: her character is spanked while flanking it, but her "off-stage" self is securely (if curtly) competent when altering its position, the better to be captured by television cameras.

In contrast to Cate Blanchett's Bob Dylan discovering the public breach in his own star-making mythology while strapped to a sofa, *Dottie*'s Ball uses the sitcom couch as a signifier of her character's culturally sanctioned subservience, whereas the behind-the-scenes woman herself—the "real" person inside the familiar TV figure—demonstrates her strength of character as well as her sheer gender- and genre-defying willingness to transcend a sitcom's shameful domestic setup, its whole "his-and-hers" aesthetic. The irony is extreme: the infantile and incompetent character who's spanked on a sofa is played by a woman who is powerful and professional enough to deliver her own figurative blows, and who not only owns the media property itself but also masters its mode of production, checking a camera lens in order to secure a close-up of her stand-in's spanked bottom. The psychosexual significance of this spanking—what it means for the possibly sadomasochistic Stevie, who witnesses it in both its backstage and on-screen iterations—has received the most attention in the scant scholarship on *Dottie* (Hilderbrand 2007). Equally worthy of critical attention, however, is what the spanking fantasies suggest about Ball's legend. As early as 1943, that legend was already combining a conscious exploitation of "girlish" qualities with a certain estrangement from the bodily mechanics of "feminine" manipulation: in *Best Foot Forward*,

13.3 Dottie performs infantile femininity in *Dottie Gets Spanked*.

in which Ball "plays herself," she proudly proclaims that, because she is so deeply "delicate," she in fact does *not* do all of her own stunts (an assertion that *Hollywood without Make-Up* later sought to undo, showing Ball's strenuous, "masculine" efforts to perfect a particularly demanding, even dangerous pratfall). As the Ball of *Best Foot Forward* so haughtily announces, there is "always some girl" to perform stunts for her—some double, some stand-in whose identity can easily be effaced through the magic of the movies, helping through her own physical labor to ensure the legibility of the "delicate" Lucille Ball, even as her efforts contribute to the construction of a "death-defying" star image. In *Dottie Gets Spanked*, such a stand-in must take orders from the bossy Dottie Frank, who, in a telling inversion of Stevie's suburban experience (in which his rather meek mother routinely defers to her husband's normative authority), rules the roost over her own, ultimately powerless spouse.

Through her "backstage" deliberations and on-screen shape-shifting, Dottie Frank further complicates Irigaray's famous conception of feminist mimicry, whose purpose, in Toril Moi's words, is "miming the miming imposed on woman"—a sort of metaperformance based on knowledge of patriarchy and its demands (1993, 140). Lucille Ball's "hidden" feminism is typically positioned in terms of her business control, but it can also be read in her willingness to consciously imitate—and thereby parody—a subservient yet harmlessly mischievous femininity, a performance technique that is of course so crucial to her beloved Lucy. Moi, in her discussion of Irigaray's feminist theory, lingers on the role of acting—on the capacity of conscious mimicry to subvert "the straitjacket of phallocentrism" (140). Dottie Frank makes this process even more legible through the use of an intermediary: forcing her stand-in to "mim[e] the miming imposed on woman," Dottie proceeds to mime it herself, after her double (played, in fact, by a man in drag) has fulfilled her limited yet indispensable function. *Dottie Gets Spanked* is, however, far from alone in seeking to expose the complexly feminist and even queer construction of Ball's star image. It is thus useful to situate the film in relation both to individual Ball biographies and to the broader Ball industry that has developed over the past eight decades.

The Business of Biography

In her account of the contradictory cultural currents surrounding *I Love Lucy*, Susan M. Carini (2003) argues that the historical Lucille Ball, in what seems a marked contrast to Haynes's Dottie, was eager to seem strictly feminine at all times: "In her publicity forays, Ball would express a gender conservatism—an 'anything for my man' ethos—that might well have strained the sympathies of 1950s female fans hungering for a plucky Lucy both on and off camera" (47). But Carini also concedes that the "reality" of Ball's divorce from Desi Arnaz conspired to complicate her public persona even beyond the all-too-familiar moralizing dimensions. Indeed, Ball's ever-changing relationship to gender norms has made her a popular subject of biographical analysis. As Desjardins writes in her account of Ball's most recent biographers, "Perhaps no other media star has been the subject of such a huge number and variety of biographies, and the . . . publicly celebrated one hundredth birthday of Ball . . . reminds us how important biographical 'facts' about Ball's marriage and career, and their alleged relationship to her comic performance 'genius,' are to the media circulation and public discussions that proclaim her value to American history" (2012, 159). The questioning quotation marks that Desjardins places around the word *facts*, however, were actually central to the earliest critical efforts to interrogate Ball's image—as Desjardins herself contends. As in *Dottie*, these efforts explicitly examined the extent to which Ball's on-screen life conformed to the parameters of her offscreen circumstances and vice versa. In the process, they often deliberately blurred the lines between public and private, acting and "authenticity," even in view of the sort of pronounced gender performance that Carini suggests was essential to all of Ball's public appearances, and that may well call to mind Irigaray's conception of the gender-conscious mime, "undoing by overdoing." Ball the wifely good girl was as exaggeratedly "feminine" as Ball the business executive was stereotypically "masculine"; the "truth," according to a 1953 issue of *TV Fan* magazine, was queerly situated "somewhere in between" ("Does Lucy Love 'Lucy'?," 2).

A vast number of magazine, television, and film biographies of Ball have similarly presented the liminal as the site of the star's "true self," to take a phrase used in a 1952 *People* magazine cover story that openly eschews concern for any "singular" or "essential" personality type ("Lucille Ball: 'Funny Face,'" 17). Authenticity is, in other words, very much a matter of plurality and mutability, rather than of particularity and fixity. For fan culture as much as for feminist and queer theory, multiple and multidirectional performance modes make interpretation both tempting and tremendously challenging. *Dottie Gets Spanked* helpfully provides an intervention, recalling precisely this reliance on an anti-essentialist approach to star studies; it is instructive that Stevie, in defending Dottie's "genius" against accusations that she is simply "playing herself," uses the phrase "in true life," thereby introducing the public/private binary as one not of reality and fantasy but of truth and fiction—a crucial distinction given the film's focus on the fabrications that inhere in ostensibly "authentic" situations and the verities that make even "play-acting" a source of personal and social certainties.

Billed as a brand of feminist biography and as a "warts-and-all" look at the Ball-Arnaz union, the television movie *Lucy & Desi: Before the Laughter* (Charles Jarrott, 1991), which preceded *Dottie Gets Spanked* by two years, tells a similar "backstage" story. Like Haynes's film, *Lucy & Desi* relies on the ironic contrasts between a performer's on-screen and offscreen personas and their combined effects on private fandom. Partly in response to what she felt were the film's egregious deviations from fact, Lucie Arnaz produced and appeared as a "talking head" in *Lucy and Desi: A Home Movie*, a 1993 TV special whose title not only removed the ampersand that had signified a strictly business relationship in the 1991 biopic, replacing it with a more connubial conjunction, but also added a marker of authenticity that had, with the astonishing success of ABC's *America's Funniest Home Videos* (1989–), gained considerable cultural traction by the early 1990s. In making the film, Arnaz essentially curated her family's home movies; the end result itself suggests another uncomfortable intersection between public and private, one that had long characterized accounts of Ball.

Consider, for instance, the compilation film *Hollywood without Make-Up*. Produced, directed, and narrated by Ken Murray—"the man who makes movies of people who make movies"—the film is invested in revealing the "masculine" labors required of female film stars (particularly mothers). Footage of Debbie Reynolds on the set of *The Mating Game* (George Marshall, 1959) shows the star cradling "her new baby" (son Todd Fisher). In his capacity as "interactive" voiceover commentator, Murray exhorts the infant to make way for his mother's professional duties: "Go to sleep, my little honey—mommy has to make some money!" Murray's footage next shows Reynolds effortlessly shedding the trappings of motherhood, executing a seemingly death-defying stunt (sans stand-in) with a powerful, "tomboyish" athleticism. Murray's "day-by-day personal film diary" purports to show how female film stars juggle the contradictory demands of their lives and careers. Introducing his own "home movies" of Lucille Ball, Murray remarks that many were made "long before television" (by which he means before *I Love Lucy*). Footage of Ball on the set of the film *Fancy Pants* (George Marshall, 1950) shows the star in a state of "scandalous" undress. Clad only in her undergarments, Ball boldly addresses the camera before director George Marshall attempts to cover her near-nakedness, shielding her breasts with his baseball cap. Next, Lucy's stand-in enters the frame, wearing the same pair of undergarments, and Lucy puts her arms around her as the two women smile conspiratorially. Footage from the set of another film—*Critic's Choice* (Don Weis, 1963)—pointedly demonstrates that a stand-in is hardly necessary for the "brave" Ball, who here (like Debbie Reynolds) does her own stunts. "This particular day, Lucy had to do a scene where she took some falls—and, boy, did she work hard!" exclaims Murray on the soundtrack. "Now, mind, that was just a rehearsal!" Footage of Ball repeatedly performing a painful stunt is accompanied by Murray's comments about her tenacity. Again and again, she must fall backward onto a table, breaking the table in the process, and end up on her back, battered and bruised. This persistence makes Ball "the greatest comedienne of our time"—comic genius being as much the product of repetitive labor as

Lucy's "glamour" (which, Murray suggests, comes only after hours spent with costume designers, hairstylists, and makeup artists). Like Haynes's version of her, Ball in *Hollywood without Make-Up* exhibits an obsessiveness that separates her from her television persona—a grim determination to perform a difficult task "until she gets it right."

Produced in 1944, Ball's musical *Meet the People* suggests that the queer potential of "total war"—its capacity to disturb the home front's gender norms—affects major stars as much as the "ordinary folks" referenced in the film's title. Ball plays a "famous Broadway star" named Julie Hampton who, at the start of the film, is "auctioned off" for the war effort. Having "generously donated herself as first prize" in a bond-selling competition, Julie becomes an object of lust for the rowdy male workers in a vast shipyard, but, in a telling gesture, she later "transitions" (as she puts it) into "one of the boys," becoming a "tough riveter" who renounces her erstwhile "softness." *Meet the People* repeatedly examines the wartime reversibility of gender norms, at one point depicting a man who does "women's work"—a so-called male homemaker who, wearing an apron, must cook, clean, and care for children while his wife, a mechanic, is away at work. Faced with his unruly brood, the man warns, "Now, if you children don't stay in your room, when your mother comes home, I'll have her give you a good spanking!" Affirming his mother's disciplinary "toughness," one child says, "She can do it too!" In the following scene, more than a dozen female mechanics return home to meals prepared by their apron-wearing husbands, while Julie stakes her claim to an even less conventional setup, one that sees her posing for provocative publicity photos while wearing little more than her welding helmet—an image of queer hybridity that, as in other Ball vehicles, serves the purpose of "denying the possibility of a single grounding for identity" (Desjardins 2015, 160).

The Ball film that bears perhaps the most striking resemblance to *Dottie Gets Spanked*, the MGM musical *Best Foot Forward*, employs a similar "backstage" aesthetic. Like Haynes's film, it features a fictionalized Ball (who is here permitted to retain her name, and who is played by Ball herself) and several of the biographical avenues that I have been exploring. In *Best Foot Forward*, a teenage boy and bona fide Ball fan writes a letter to the star, asking her to accompany him to his military academy's senior prom. He doesn't think that she'll reply; she does, and she arrives on the school's campus for what she openly describes as a "publicity stunt"—one designed, at a time of war, to render her more "warmly patriotic" than her cold-yet-sexy screen persona would suggest. The film expends considerable narrative energy, for roughly its first third, establishing recognizable biographical details: Ball's struggles with the studio system, her fears of aging and of competition that comes, in this case, in the form of a sweater-wearing Lana Turner. The familiar "facts" thus established, the film proceeds to show Ball's lack of a stable identity, eventually locating a degree of heroism in her refusal (or inability) to maintain an unwavering persona. This Ball—anticipating Dottie as well as queer theory—can help a boy by rejecting the constraints of identity.

The Irreducible Ball

Lucille Ball, in the first major phase of her career, complicated then-familiar conceptions of female film stardom. Throughout the 1940s, before her ascension to television celebrity, Ball was perhaps best known for her especially adaptable beauty. She played dual roles in no fewer than four films between 1940 and 1946, perfecting precisely the kind of shape-shifting that would come to characterize her star persona—and, perhaps, motivate the contrarian efforts of some biographers (and of Lucie Arnaz) to present Ball as an unusually unified personality. In *You Can't Fool Your Wife*, for instance, Ball plays Clara Fields, a meek woman who loves being married and who, as a response to suspicions that her husband is cheating, becomes the "dark" South American temptress Mercedes Vasquez in order to "win him back." The film thus demonstrates—as do a striking number of Ball's vehicles—that Joan Riviere's 1929 conception of womanliness as masquerade was, whether consciously or not, rendered distinctly relevant to Ball's screen persona, as were certain ethnic and erotic transformations. Three years later, in *Du Barry Was a Lady* (Roy Del Ruth, 1943), Ball played both the "modern" nightclub star May Daly and—in dream sequences that anticipate the fantasmatic aspects of the Freudian *Dottie Gets Spanked*—the eighteenth-century Madame Du Barry, whom the film fashions as a more "obvious" (yet no less carefully constructed) seductress.

Throughout the 1930s and 1940s, Ball was routinely called upon to impersonate a range of major Hollywood stars—a demand that seemed to reflect her ultimately indeterminate status at MGM, her liminal position as neither the lowliest of bit players nor a bona fide, "bankable" star. In her pre-*Lucy* publicity appearances, Ball was often asked to ape the iconicity of more familiar figures, from Judy Garland to Veronica Lake to Marlene Dietrich. For instance, in a color photograph on the cover of the November 1943 issue of *Movie Show*, Ball is wearing Garland's costume from

The Wizard of Oz. However, the iconicity of the 1943 image is hybrid: Ball's hair is her own henna-enhanced red, and in Dorothy's basket she carries four kittens, while the photo's Toto stand-in watches "suspiciously" from behind. Such suggestions of hybridity would become downright monstrous in the context of popular renderings of the Ball-Arnaz marriage, such as the July 30, 1952, cover of *People* that presented the two as a pair of disembodied heads next to the caption "Lucille Ball and Desi Arnaz: Two-Headed Family." Significantly, it is Arnaz who is made to assume a feminized position, smiling widely and gazing wistfully into the distance, while Ball, staring sternly in direct address, her lips pressed sourly together, looks strikingly unhappy. This connubial iconography is precisely what Haynes adopts and adapts for *Dottie*, in which Adam Arkin's Dick Gordon is the resplendently handsome (and ultimately powerless) male ingénue to Dottie Frank's surly star. The latter, in fact, seems far more "masculine" than little Stevie could have imagined, hailing as he does from a chillingly gender-normative family.

In *Best Foot Forward*, Lucille Ball presents an equally shocking persona to a baffled, anxious boy. The film introduces her via an autographed "pinup" in which she is wearing a bikini. Signed "To Bud," the publicity photograph signals both Ball's sexualized stardom and its significance for public and private fandom—the stridently patriotic dimensions of the pinup here competing with Bud's "illicit" desires. The film then cuts to the interior of a speeding train, in which Ball, appearing "as herself," gazes angrily at her manager, remaining every bit as flinty as her future reconfiguration as Dottie Frank. "We need something to get you on the front page!" shouts the manager, recalling Ball's real-life struggles to solidify her stardom. He talks about the "standard publicity ploys," which he and Ball have tried and which have clearly failed. (Significantly, they all involve "private" yet "cutesy" occurrences: Ball's dog having puppies or her date taking her "someplace special.") On the train, Ball is wearing a suit with broad, padded shoulders—hardly the image of beachside, bikini-clad femininity presented in the autographed publicity photo. Further emphasizing her relatively lowly status in Hollywood, Ball's manager tells her that she has been "left hanging" and that she must now "crawl back from the end of the limb." Further masculinizing her, and suggesting her frightening impact on young boys, he reads the headline that he imagines will be occasioned by her visit to the military academy: "Schoolboy Invites Screen Star to Senior Prom—The Lion and the Mouse!" (The mouse, he makes clear, will be the boy, not Ball.) Her arms folded in indignation, Ball threatens to fire him if he fails to make such a headline appear.

Upon her arrival at the military academy, Ball (anticipating Dottie) chain-smokes and paces nervously, often barking orders at her manager, a man she conspires to infantilize through her complaints about his many inadequacies. After a local reporter agrees to photograph her, the manager tells her, "I'll talk; you just raise his blood pressure." When the reporter appears, Ball drops the butch bossiness, emerging from the bathroom as a "fully feminine and flirtatious woman"—a guise that she abandons as soon as the social-climbing reporter tries to sell her his script. This facility for feminine disguise, which even the manager refers to as "a masquerade," has another opportunity to dazzle when, later in the film, Ball poses for publicity pictures with Bud, who has asked her to pretend to be his "real" girlfriend, Helen Schlesinger, so that no one at the school will suspect him of cheating. To his surprise and delight, Ball agrees. Bud has banked on her shape-shifting abilities, and she successfully "becomes" Helen even as all hell breaks loose at the school, in show-stopping MGM fashion.

Through its explicit focus on Ball's "many masquerades," and through the further blurring of fact and fantasy, *Best Foot Forward* demonstrates that efforts to present Ball as irreducible are not limited to *Dottie Gets Spanked*. But Haynes's film, in extending Ball's iconicity through the use of a proxy, offers its own rendering of Irigaray's feminist theory of mimicry. Putting this theory into practice, Haynes has Julie Halston imitate Dottie imitating "Dottie"—all within a broader, multidirectional evocation of the many lives of Lucille Ball. What Haynes would do to Dylan in *I'm Not There* or to Bowie in *Velvet Goldmine* he'd already done to Ball in *Dottie*—and with feminist reverberations worthy of continued analysis.

NOTE

1 To his credit, Hilderbrand resists "subscribing to a reading that fixes on the anal-sadistic pleasure of spanking as indicative of precocious gay male identity" (2007, 45).

14 Bringing It All Back Home, or Feminist Suppositions on a Film concerning Dylan

Nick Davis

Raise your hand if you have ever referred to *I'm Not There* as "the movie where Cate Blanchett plays Bob Dylan." Blanchett's image, defamiliarized by thick shades and a black tumbleweed of hair, has been the film's dominant emblem since its debut in 2007. She earned the Venice Film Festival's Best Actress prize and a Golden Globe for her work as Jude Quinn, the mid-1960s Dylan surrogate who electrifies his sound, alienates folk music congregants, and absconds on a pill-popping, conflict-ridden sojourn to the UK. Despite *I'm Not There*'s bravura reviews, Blanchett reaped its sole Oscar nomination, serving as the film's ambassador on red carpets and media junkets throughout awards season.

When I shared with fellow cinephiles or gender scholars my plan to write a feminist essay about *I'm Not There*, they all assumed Blanchett's Jude would again take center stage, as something like "a vision of feminist, polysexual queering" (Darby 2013, 334). After all, when Judith Butler theorized gender as a citational practice—a premise of much queer theory that followed, which Blanchett's performance readily recalls—she did so as a feminist intervention. From its opening pages, *Gender Trouble* (1990) denies that labels related to sex, gender, or sexuality denote biological facts. These include the category of women, often posited as a clear-cut constituency for feminist activism: "Precisely because 'female' no longer appears to be a stable notion, its meaning is as troubled and unfixed as 'woman,'" and so "we ought to ask, what political possibilities are the consequence of a radical critique of the categories of identity" (Butler 1990, ix). Women, then, just like gays, lesbians, trans folks, or self-identified queers, are a highly multifarious group, blurry around every edge. Anatomically, rhetorically, or politically, it is neither possible nor desirable to stipulate who is included within or excluded from their purview.

Butler's rebuttals to any naturalized ground for sex or gender, insisting they arise from reiterated cultural codes, remain her most famous assertions in three decades of work. Not everyone who cited these claims, however, preserved Butler's caveats that gender performativity holds no innate political character, progressive or otherwise: "Parody by itself is not subversive," she counsels, "and there must be a way to understand what makes certain kinds of parodic repetitions effectively disruptive, truly troubling, and which repetitions become domesticated and recirculated as instruments of cultural hegemony" (1990, 139).[1] Nor did everyone heed alarums from Teresa de Lauretis, Biddy Martin, Steven Seidman, and others that the early 1990s surge of queer scholarship might ramify poorly for feminism, even though this movement was barely thinkable without feminist activism and knowledge projects preceding and coinciding with it.[2] Nor did all readers catch B. Ruby Rich's concern, echoed by fellow journalists and filmmakers, that the "Homo Pomo" trend in '90s-era New Queer Cinema yielded fewer profits for women, on or off the screen, than for gay male directors like Haynes (1992, 32). In short, not every cross-cast performance or debunked essentialism, in art or in life, constitutes a feminist parlay—especially when the character in question is, like Jude, a narcissistic, starlet-chasing, vagina-fearing misogynist. Building a case for Blanchett's performance as a feminist undertaking, rather than presuming those credentials, thus constitutes one goal for this chapter.

Meanwhile, a more obvious subject for feminist sympathy hides in plain sight within *I'm Not There*. Charlotte Gainsbourg plays Claire, a bohemian painter who in the mid-1960s meets and marries Robbie Clark (Heath Ledger), the actor cast as an ersatz Dylan in a kitschy film-within-a-film called *Grain of Sand*. Off the set, Robbie embodies other traits of the freewheelin' Bob Dylan: his unlikely teen idol status, his hunger for cosmopolitan culture, and his errant stab at idyllic domesticity amid his cresting fame. Initially Robbie's guide through New York's creative warrens, Claire later idles inside a cavernous kitchen, explaining away his absences and perusing reprints of works from her long-ago gallery shows—now just items to clear off the table, with her daughters' drawings and dirty dishes. Cradling a book in several shots, Claire suggests a case study in *The Feminine Mystique* (published in 1963, the same year as Bob Dylan's breakthrough album) but also a likely reader of it, cognizant of every choice and structural trap that has stoked her gathering melancholy.

Reasons abound why Claire's role in the film might feel marginal, especially compared with Jude's. From its first outline, bearing the title *I'm Not There: Suppositions on a Film concerning Dylan*, to its marketing and reception, the hallmark of Haynes's film was always how it splintered the singer-songwriter into seven alter egos, delegated to six different actors: Blanchett's trickster, Ledger's pinup, Marcus Carl Franklin's child prodigy, Richard Gere's aging recluse, Ben Whishaw's Rimbaudian poet, and Christian Bale's dual role as young folkie phenom and Reagan-era evangelical. Everyone else in the film seems indentured to the goal of showcasing Dylan's proliferating facets. That said, Claire receives as much screen time as several of the Dylan avatars do—more, certainly, than Whishaw's or Bale's. Haynes testified that Gainsbourg was the only actor whom he mentally cast while writing the script, which also suggests her centrality to his overall design.[3] Though Claire lacks the vocal and cosmetic embellishments of Dylan's surrogates, Butler reminds us that seemingly normative comportments of gender are just as citational as more transgressive or hyperbolic iterations. The willowy, soft-spoken Claire is thus no less *performed* than Blanchett's Jude, and no less semiotically rich.[4]

I underline this point because Gainsbourg's understated approach—as typical of her work as Blanchett's rigorous mannerisms are of hers—could imply a simplistic foil to "riskier" experiments undertaken by her costars and director.[5] Blanchett's style of working, honed during the very years when deconstructive theories of gender rose to prominence, confounds any search for naturalized essences. Ingenious at overhauling her look, sound, and bearing for each film, Blanchett specializes in bold, gestural performances that present each character as what *Gender Trouble* calls "a stylized repetition of acts" (Butler 1990, 140), not a realistic figure for audience identification. Gainsbourg, by contrast, via her more muted economy of gestures, repeatedly presents as herself on screen—implying, moreover, that a "real Charlotte" exists to play. To value reflexively Blanchett's ornate style of acting over Gainsbourg's could reinscribe unfair reputations that feminism accrued in the 1990s. At that time, in Biddy Martin's view, as scholars increasingly portrayed queer theory, queer gender, or queer sexuality as "figural, performative, playful, and fun" (1994, 104), feminism got pigeonholed as its antonym: literal, familiar, stabilizing gendered and sexual categories rather than complicating or multiplying them.

As if these contrasts were not loaded enough, the women's trajectories in *I'm Not There* may further polarize impressions. Blanchett, the lone woman playing Dylan, beats the boys at their own game, anchors a storyline that eschews tidy resolution, and wins plaudits for a stylized verisimilitude we know to be an act—compelling the gazes of camera and viewer while refusing objectification and preserving her auratic allure. Meanwhile, Gainsbourg's Claire navigates a beginning-middle-end arc redolent of 1970s feminist consciousness-raising and of more traditional biopics. Amid the dazzling promiscuity of Haynes's signifiers, her plot reminds us that times did not a-change for everyone in Dylan's generation, especially for mother-wives abandoned to noncreative and unpaid labors.

Despite these stark divergences, I decline to frame Jude and Claire strictly as opposites or to vaunt either character's value for feminism at the other's expense. Rather, in a film that presents contrary refractions of Dylan's identity without imposing false hierarchies, Claire and Jude offer a fruitful double occasion for rethinking femininity's links to notions of materiality and signification, authenticity and pastiche. Both characterizations evince performative virtuosities but also reflect stubborn legacies of how sex/gender is often lived: as a falsely naturalized male-female dyad, socially mobilized in ways that limit women's individual and collective power. They also indicate different strategies by which dissimilar actresses and characters destabilize those legacies. In the first case, Blanchett's Jude suggests not just a spectacular dismantling of gender binaries but a recognizably female-bodied agent staking her ground within the sexist milieu of mid-1960s rock. She exposes fissures in "masculine" self-presentation while claiming for herself the ecstatic, nonobjectifying joys of onstage exhibitionism. Gainsbourg's appearances also rely on meticulous inflections of body, voice, and image, and on pointed intertextual allusions, exposing Claire's womanhood as a more subtly stylized and multisourced collage. Her scenes, especially her climactic assertion of autonomy, thus avoid connoting some more "literal" version of feminism that precedes or denies the performative turn, even as it conjures different paradigms of gendered rebellion.

I'm Not There clears space, then, for two modes of feminism often seen as exclusive: one historically aligned with the 1970s and linked to bodily difference, domestic discontents, and structural inequalities; the other elaborated across the 1990s and tied to androgyny, transitivity, rewritable discourses, and performative contingencies. Furthermore, the movie refuses to align Claire exclusively with the first mode and Jude entirely with the second, demonstrating instead how each characterization reflects dimorphic *and* deconstructive legacies of womanhood, in and out of quotation marks. *I'm Not There*'s feminism thereby echoes Butler's, not just by foregrounding gender as a parodic act, but by acknowledging the durable power of sexual binarisms even while exposing them as false. The movie also sustains feminist insights developed during the years evoked on screen, with second-wave essayist and rock connoisseur Ellen Willis an especially resonant influence and interlocutor. Ultimately, the film rewrites various histories toward feminist ends—not just Dylan's but those of '60s-era music, nouvelle vague cinema, and leftist ideology. Haynes accomplishes this mission not as a solo auteur but in collaborative synchronicity with two actresses whose thespian styles and extratextual connotations make them ideal co-prosecutors of the movie's feminist case.

A Tale of Two Feminisms

The opening of *I'm Not There* foregrounds the figure of Jude, making gender trouble a privileged sign for broader ontological uncertainties and representational crises in the film. The first image is a black-and-white tracking shot, filmed with a handheld camera, from Dylan's implied point of view as he enters a concert hall. Similar point-of-view tracking shots open Haynes's *Superstar: The Karen Carpenter Story* (1987) and *Poison* (1991), culminating in the deaths of main characters. In that signature tradition, *I'm Not There* quickly kills off its subject, or seems to. The ensuing wide shot observes a motorcyclist hurtling down a road before an audible collision, recalling Dylan's 1966 crash that prompted rumors of his passing. The film briefly prints that legend, cutting to a cropped, off-center close-up of Jude's head on an embalmer's table as a nondiegetic narrator gravely intones, "There he lies. God rest his soul." The eyes and brow are recognizably Blanchett's. After a montage of five mugshots introduces the other faces of Dylan, named by the voiceover as Poet (Whishaw), Prophet (Bale), Outlaw (Gere), Fake (Franklin), and Star of Electricity (Ledger), the "dead" Jude, seeming to speak from inside his coffin (figure 14.1), offers a brief homily that begins, "A poem is like a naked person . . . ," purloined from Dylan's sometime collaborator Leon Russell. Beyond her uncanny visual transformation, Blanchett's mimesis of Dylan's Minnesota vowels and slurry, stuttering cadence is remarkable. Having dangled this prospect of dazzling impersonation, however, the film again shatters its subject,

14.1 Cate Blanchett's Jude is *I'm Not There*'s most seductive entry point and most deliciously deferred spectacle.

cutting harshly to all six stars in rapid, reordered succession (Blanchett, Gere, Franklin, Ledger, Bale, Whishaw), each edit amplified by the sound of a bullet discharging. We do not reencounter Jude for another forty-five minutes, making him the movie's seductive entry point (the first Dylan we see and hear, the closest copy of the real thing, the starting point for two quick-cut montages) but also its most deliciously deferred spectacle.

Meanwhile, as *I'm Not There* unspools, each narrative thread deploys different aesthetics, correlating to epochs in Dylan's career and in cinematic style. Thus, Jude's profligate parties and creative paralysis recall Fellini's *8½* (1963). The bright but ill-fated Robbie-Claire romance blends the color and dolor of Godardian New Wave. Billy the Kid's backwoods hamlet recalls the eccentric milieus of Watergate-era Westerns like *McCabe & Mrs. Miller* (Robert Altman, 1971). Along the way, creative incongruities denaturalize these templates: piebald props and costumes in Billy's sequences make their era difficult to pinpoint; Franklin's young black hobo pulls stylistic homages to Douglas Sirk and Hal Ashby, themselves an odd pair, in unexpected directions. *I'm Not There* handles genre the way Butler approaches gender, as a regime of performative codes, recalibrated even as they are reiterated. This analogy is not idle: the prologue juxtaposes young men and old, black actors and white, females and males serving Dylan Realness to the camera, denying authenticity to any one rendition. Even the title, emerging in peekaboo permutations, links basic vagaries of being to those of gender: *I, I he, I'm he, I'm her, not her, not here, I'm not there*. The copresence of so many film styles and Dylan facsimiles exposes both singer and cinema as performative repertoires, each "a personal/cultural history of received meanings subject to a set of imitative practices which refer laterally to other imitations" (Butler 1990, 138).

I'm Not There is not, however, a pure foray into poststructuralist thinking and praxis. Haynes's prologue hints at prior feminist genealogies, presaging Butler in some ways while balancing her model against more quotidian, embodied experiences of gender and selfhood. In 1967, before emerging as a leading second-wave activist and essayist, Ellen Willis published a 7,500-word article titled "Dylan" that secured her post as *The New Yorker*'s first popular music critic. Opening with the crash, drawing links to Rimbaud, depicting Dylan's "baroque press conference inventions" as "extensions of his work, full of imaginative truth and virtually devoid of information" (E. Willis 2012, 4), she furnishes Haynes's script with many early and recurrent tropes. In turn, his reprising of her take on Dylan entails a feminist gesture in itself, after decades of rock criticism by men such as Greil Marcus interpolated her insights without bothering to cite her.

Most prescient of all was Willis's antifoundational, prismatic notion of Dylan, now a critical axiom and the structuring precept of *I'm Not There*. She effectively coins her own language for what Butler later calls performative reiteration: "Bob Dylan as identifiable persona has been disappearing into his songs, which is what he wants ... his masks hidden by other masks" (E. Willis 2012, 4–5). In later profiles, reflecting ever greater preoccupations with sexual politics, Willis praised Dylan's refusal of rock's dominant models of masculinity, whether white and Puritanical or black-coded and blues-derived, as essential to his "radicalism" (2011, 207). His exposure of these scripts *as* scripts subtends Willis's lasting enthusiasm for Dylan, despite her broad critiques of patriarchy and her well-earned irritation at sexist clichés in his lyrics, which fawn over "child-women, bitchy, unreliable" or "goddesses like Johanna and the mercury-mouthed, silken-fleshed Sad-Eyed Lady of the Lowlands" (E. Willis 2012, 21).

Crucially, Willis balanced the chimerical with the material in her vantage on Dylan—unlike her male colleagues, who elevated his not-thereness to levels of mystical abstraction—distinguishing her perceptions from Butler's more rigorously anti-identitarian stance. After tendering the masks-upon-masks conceit, Willis insists that "there is a continuing self" who is Dylan, one whose "eye for detail, sense of humor, and skill at evoking the archetypal sexual skirmishes show that some part of him is of as well as in the world" (2012, 5). Moreover, for all her attention to Dylan's uniqueness, Willis focused repeatedly on the complex bonds linking mostly male rock musicians of the 1960s and 1970s to their fans, including women like herself, who felt liberated but also coerced into identifying with celebrated chauvinists, relationships that "all too often found us digging them while they put us down" (2011, 136). Indeed, for all Dylan's rebukes to hegemonic masculinity, his songs regularly indulge sexist rhetoric that could require female fans to conduct intrapsychic triage: distancing themselves from the parasite sister in "Ballad in Plain D," pondering whether Dylan would have noticed Hattie Carroll if she had lived, or asking whether the heroine of "Lay, Lady, Lay" really needs the singer's "big brass bed" to see the "colors of her own mind."[6] These aspects of Willis's critique frame *I'm Not There* in ways that complement but exceed Haynes's presentation of Dylan as a paragon of performative (anti-)identity and, as we shall see, complicate Jude's apparent status as his queerest incarnation.

Cate Blanchett: Not Him, Not Her

Cate Blanchett shares Dylan's penchant for self-revision and self-concealment. Willis's emphasis on how such figures are nonetheless "of as well as in the world" cues us, though, to note the agentic labor of an actress who so skillfully renders not-thereness on screen. Combining the Butlerian idea of Dylan as unruly signifier with Willis's stress on artistic agency and on sociocultural histories of rock, we can observe how Blanchett folds into her Dylan homage a corollary tribute to his female fans, invigorated by his music but denied his expressive outlets.

Early in Blanchett's career, her pace and range of work, averaging four films per year between her Golden Globe for *Elizabeth* (Shekhar Kapur, 1998) and her Academy Award for *The Aviator* (Martin Scorsese, 2004), inspired a "reputation as a chameleon—a term that she despised, as it implied facile mimicry rather than a skilled process of becoming" (Keil 2012, 195). Often the actress stresses those artisanal processes of becoming over any seamless inhabitation of character. In *Elizabeth*, the monarch's attempts to cultivate physical and vocal authority before her mirror, filmed straight-to-camera, also suggest the actress's own process of building her performance. In the 1940s-inspired pastiche *The Good German* (Steven Soderbergh, 2006), one of many films to capitalize on Blanchett's knack for heightened mannerism, her Dietrich-esque siren is an undisguised "type," unburdened by personalized details or psychological thickness. The one time Blanchett played herself, in Jim Jarmusch's *Coffee and Cigarettes* (2003), she served as her own costar, rendering a coarse, jealous, and entirely fabricated look-alike cousin named Shelly in a bitterly comic pas de deux. This doubling undoes the ostensible simplicity of her turn as Cate Blanchett, disclosing yet another case of "masks hidden by other masks."

Whereas critics laud Dylan for abjuring any "real" self, reactions to Blanchett's similar gift have varied. Favoring discourses of imitation rather than genius, these disparate valuations carry sexist connotations in a culture that mandates women's self-exposure in so many senses, especially from female artists. Charlie Keil (2012), intending to praise Blanchett in the first scholarly study of her work, takes as a given that "'Bob Dylan' exists as a composite of different representations at different moments" and thus calls Blanchett "a particularly apt choice to play [him] because, ultimately, 'she' is not there either" (199). He frets, though, in assessing other Blanchett performances that an actress worth her salt should be able to "fill up the empty shell onscreen with her own persona … but that is precisely what a skilled shapeshifter such as Blanchett cannot supply" (197). Blanchett's triumph as Jude finally registers as Dylan's more than hers, despite having "all the famous Dylanisms down pat" (199). The singular troubadour saves the day, his fascinating enigmas accommodating the actress's worrisome impersonality.

Rather than conflate her with Dylan, though, or frame her labor as simple mimesis, *I'm Not There* showcases Blanchett as an authorial agent. Within the context of the film's overall "production of the figures of fantasy through the play of presence and absence on the body's surface" (Butler 1990, 135), extending also to the *screen's* surface, the role of Jude finds Blanchett presenting Dylan at some times, herself at others, and often a semi-legible blur of the two. Such nimble bricolage (*I'm he, I'm her, not her, not here*) marks an astonishing Butlerian feat. Moreover, Jude's ambiguous gendering is only one aspect of how Blanchett and Haynes simultaneously assemble, dismantle, flaunt, conceal, preserve, and remake Dylan. At the same time, aided by marketing and by Blanchett's recognizable celebrity, viewers of *I'm Not There* know they are seeing an actress "doing" Dylan, even as she downplays and complicates that fact. To that end, Blanchett's Jude entails one woman's retort to a mid-'60s rock economy that sidelined female patrons and participants. She seizes for herself not just the spotlight but the male artist's swaggering pleasures beneath it, in a performance distinguished by its vibrant physicality. This level of wild, loose-limbed expressivity was unusual for Blanchett by that point in her career—as if she, like Dylan, had gone electric—and unusual, too, for women in that moment and milieu of popular music.

Jude's final shot encapsulates the slippery qualities of Blanchett's performance, only *seeming* to cap a bravura act of impersonation. "Everybody knows I'm not a folk singer," Jude swears, before aiming a long, sphinx-like smirk at the lens. To the extent Blanchett, not Dylan, pronounces these words, they ring literally true. Moreover, her performance choice departs markedly from its ostensible model. In documentaries such as *Don't Look Back* (D. A. Pennebaker, 1967) and *Eat the Document* (Bob Dylan, 1972), recording Dylan during the very years that Haynes allots to Jude, the singer-songwriter's preferred mode of cultivating mystery is a disingenuous deadpan; he rattles interlocutors during increasingly tortuous dialogues while acting as if he makes perfect, offhanded sense. Dylan, then, rarely baited viewers with the overt coyness we witness in this final, Cate-ate-the-canary smile. *Ceci n'est pas Bob Dylan*, her expression insinuates—or, in English, *It ain't me, babe*. Here, Blanchett is not "being" Dylan but acknowledging a conspiratorial rapport with the viewer that has structured all her scenes. We have recognized throughout that we are watching not just Dylan but Blanchett, and she knows we know it. A key decision in preparing any performance, Blanchett attests, involves determining when "to find internal connections [so] the camera will find your performance," or when the idioms of, say, *The Good German* require that "you have to find your audience and reach out for that ... [such] that the energy production is outward rather than inward" (Porton 2007, 16, 19). Jude often requires both at once, as in that final image: taciturn yet winking, calling attention to his aloofness but also to his intense performativity. Especially at such instances, Blanchett's energies converge at a dynamic threshold where actress and character meet, as do "inwardness" and "outwardness"—a play of presence and absence upon a liminal surface, to reprise Butler's performative schema.

Still, it is remarkable how often *I'm Not There* finds Blanchett conveying this famously guarded, often clenched performer through kinetic, outward-facing physicality: stalking Coco Rivington through the woods, cavorting with the Beatles, convulsing with glee upon spotting Allen Ginsberg through a limousine window, then dancing a jig with him at the foot of a cross. While spitting out the vituperative "Ballad of a Thin Man" at Royal Albert Hall, a song rendered more caustic through cross-cuts to Bruce Greenwood's journalist prying into Jude's past, Blanchett is a whirlwind: her head and neck wheel, chin outstretched, fingers wild as anemones, torso spasmodically lurching toward the microphone while she hammers the piano like a hard rain (figure 14.2).[7] Jude's corporeal agitation exceeds anything we behold from the only other Dylans who perform

14.2 Blanchett's ecstatic body mirrors Dylan's but also showcases her own performative exuberance as both interpreter and fan.

in the film: Woody, seated for his porch-front jam session with Richie Havens; Jack, solemnly reciting "The Lonesome Death of Hattie Carroll" amid protesters and farmhands; and Pastor John, giving a stiff-backed, choir-boosted rendition of "Pressing On."

Comparing scenes like Jude's performance at Royal Albert Hall with footage that inspired them, especially that in *Eat the Document*, reveals Blanchett's consummate grasp of that "skinny and strange and feline and amorphous" Dylan who undertook that UK tour in 1966 (Haynes 2008). Such comparisons warrant more praise for Blanchett's imitative gift, yet the physical vocabularies are not exact matches; her rhapsodies do not color strictly within lines that Dylan sets. What, then, if Blanchett steps into Dylan's skinny shoes and polka-dot shirt not to disappear into him, nor just to queer regimes of masculinity, but to gratify her own pleasures, staking claims for specifically female presence and exaltation inside the rock arena?[8] Willis describes how rock's rhythmic, body-centered insolence got tangled up in misogynist mind-sets and yet, "insofar as it pitted teenage girls' inchoate energies against all their conscious and unconscious frustrations, it spoke implicitly for female liberation" (2011, 135). In that sense, "for all its limitations, rock was the best thing going, and if we had to filter out certain indignities—well, we had been doing that all our lives, and there was no feminist movement to suggest that things might be different" (136). In that spirit, Willis famously danced to rock albums as part of her protocol for reviewing them, using her body, not just her mind, to gauge how the music inhibited her but also to discover what it released.

Blanchett engages in an analogous process in *I'm Not There*, reviving Dylan at arguably the queerest *and* most sexist period of his public life (as *Eat the Document* also reveals) while indicating capacities for physical exuberance and cross-gendered identification that coexisted with vectors of chauvinistic exclusion. Taking for granted our simultaneous awareness of actress and character, her performance offers a rare chronicle of a woman delectating in rock without having to die for it like Bette Midler in *The Rose* (Mark Rydell, 1979). This aspect of Jude Quinn represents an astutely feminist intervention aimed not just at bygone music scenes but also at lingering tensions between skilled exhibitionism and sexist objectification on the movie screen. On one hand, Blanchett has admitted to feeling "constantly amazed watching female actresses on film and on stage play up to the male gaze because that's what they are being looked at for" (Schafer and Smith 2003, 215). On the other, Blanchett wonders, after seeking greater opportunities outside Australia, where "acting is much more bold, more adventurous, more vivid in the space" (165), why "the British don't engage their bodies as much" (213). Previously discouraged, then, for gendered *and* transcultural reasons from "engaging her body," and frequently cast in period dramas that corseted her movements and emphasized her close-ups, Blanchett devises in *I'm Not There* a way to utilize her physical instrument to avoid "freezing the flow of action" or feeding fetishistic appetites for feminine "to-be-looked-at-ness" (Mulvey 1986, 203).

Blanchett's Jude merges uncanny impersonation with strategic departures, inviting the spectator's gaze upon herself while also staring back with wry opacity. She works adroitly within the grain of *I'm Not There*'s poststructuralist mythobiography but sets out on other adventures, carrying Dylan's physicality and her own to newfound, flamboyant extremes. In so doing, she evokes a guarded, mercurial, imperious performer but also a legacy of women who relished his music while refusing parts of its ideological packaging. No mere mimic, Blanchett turns Dylan's artistry into a platform, not a container, for her own.

Charlotte Gainsbourg Stands Up for Herself (But Not Just for Herself)

The associations Charlotte Gainsbourg carries into *I'm Not There* differ markedly from Blanchett's. In four of her first six films, she played women named Charlotte Marker, Charlotte Castang, Charlotte, and "Daughter of J.," in Agnès Varda's playful meditation on her mother, Jane Birkin. She again impersonated "Charlotte Gainsbourg" in *Dead Tired* (Michel Blanc, 1994) and in *My Wife Is an Actress* (2001), one of three films in which her real-life partner Yvan Attal directed her. Gainsbourg's merging of personal and professional identities famously began when her father, Serge, that titan of twentieth-century French popular culture, wrote all the songs on her first album, *Charlotte for Ever* (1986), linked to an eponymous film he wrote and directed. "It was like being an instrument," Gainsbourg reminisces, "but the pleasure of seeing his pleasure was very intense" (Wagner 2006, 103). To this day, Gainsbourg frames her singing career as other people's accomplishment: "I don't have a singer's voice. I just have my personality, and in my mind it is not much. It is terrifying because I'm not a performer" (Knowles 2009/2010, 46). No chameleon, she invokes a different, more deferential not-thereness.

No huge leap, then, for Haynes to cast Gainsbourg as a painter subsuming her creativity to her husband's, inside a film whose story and score privilege his persona, not hers. Her reedy frame and river of hair patently recall Suze Rotolo, Dylan's first girlfriend in New York and his docent through its artistic scene. A shot of Claire and Robbie strolling through the Village is a dead ringer for the photo of Dylan and Rotolo gamboling down an avenue on his second album cover; portentously, we hear nothing Claire says, her voice supplanted on the soundtrack by Dylan's. Robbie and Claire's divorce-themed plotline, bracketing the same years as Dylan's marriage to Sara Lowndes and replete with songs from his breakup album *Blood on the Tracks* (1975), makes Gainsbourg an evident stand-in for her, too. The sexual rhetoric of Claire's scenes feels as plainspoken as Gainsbourg's acting, especially because Haynes draws legible links to his past work. Like Carol White in *Safe* (1995), Claire is engulfed by her home's colossal interiors; both women's most loyal domestic companions are their televisions.[9] Even more direct is a café scene in which, while Claire nurses their child, Robbie tells a female friend that she believes the world might improve only "because you're a chick." He belittles female poets, essentializes gender difference (women and men cannot communicate, he says, because they feel "different kinds of pain"), and mocks women's liberation ("I worship women! Everybody should have one!").

Such explicit appeals for feminist sympathy, as Claire wearies of both her husband's company and his absences, may obscure subtler layers of Gainsbourg's acting and Haynes's writing, reprising elements of earlier films while strengthening their feminist implications. For example, by dialing up her Gallic accent, stronger here than in prior US films like *21 Grams*

(Alejandro González Iñárritu, 2003), Gainsbourg establishes distance from erstwhile alter egos such as Rotolo and Lowndes, while linking Claire's scenes to Jean-Luc Godard's French New Wave dramas, suffused with what Haynes calls "a great romanticism towards women but with it, at times, a quiet condescension" (*I'm Not There* 2015, 8). That tension peaks in *Masculin féminin* (Jean-Luc Godard, 1966), a portrait of strained affection between Chantal Goya's Pepsi-drinking, apolitical songbird and Jean-Pierre Léaud's baleful syndicalist. The title suggests more antagonism than fluidity between genders. The diner scene where Claire and Robbie meet lifts frames and lines from *Masculin féminin*, a film that also namechecks Dylan in its script and inspired that sonic effect of edits joined to gunshots in *I'm Not There*'s prologue. These appropriations suggest a dialogue with Godard that is concentrated within Claire's subplot but at stake throughout the film.

Indeed, that engagement extends to other Godardian intertexts, to a mode of midcentury leftism they typify, and to a mixture of progressive and regressive orientations toward women in both. *I'm Not There*'s superwidescreen lensing, Haynes's first use of that format, and its proscenium-style vantages on bright, sprawling sets evoke Godard's quasi-feminist opus *2 or 3 Things I Know about Her* (1967), released just as Dylan emerged from self-imposed exile in Woodstock. Chronicling rapid changes in Paris, where ostensibly middle-class women undertake sex work to avoid insolvency (including one whose anonymous letter inspired the script), *2 or 3 Things* approaches women as modern citizens in tight socioeconomic binds but also as metaphysical conundrums. A famous scene juxtaposing two close-ups of Marina Vlady—first as herself and then "in character" as Juliette Janson, but occupying the same balcony and wearing the same outfit—problematizes the relation of performer to role, just as those Charlotte-playing-Charlotte movies would do two or three decades later. Stymied throughout the film by inchoate musings ("I've changed and yet I've gone back to being myself, so what does it mean?"), unable to interest her husband in her questions, Juliette ends her film drifting into sleep as a male voiceover catalogs global realities she ignores, from Hiroshima to the Parisian housing crisis.

Claire, however, refuses the self-commodification or the acquiescent somnolence of Godard's mid-'60s heroines. Furthermore, because aspects of Claire and her images explicitly recall Godard's chic but doomed women—and also recall, albeit differently, female characters from Haynes's own back pages—her climactic self-assertion resonates as a literal and vicarious stand on their behalf. The scene of Claire's withdrawal from her marriage starts with her making a direct-to-camera speech that Robbie

14.3 Gainsbourg takes a stand on behalf of Claire and earlier female film characters who had been forced to remain seated.

imagines while reading her farewell letter. Haynes's framing, grammar, and color palette at this moment are prototypically Godardian, and the narrated lines in fact derive from a speech in *2 or 3 Things*: "For all of these reasons, and many more still unknown, I must listen, I must look around more than ever, I must leave." After silently flashing back to their first date, the sequence lands on a wide shot of Claire on an enormous couch before Venetian-blinded windows, duplicating a shot from *Safe* where Carol faces an unseen therapist from a similar couch, before an identical window. Refusing, however, Carol's stuttering panic in that parallel scene, Claire's confident voice and firm gaze connote reclamations of personal will. Her sudden rise from the couch, following a man's mental projection of her plea for freedom and an interior shot awash in film references, forces a new shot from a different angle, unencumbered by intertextual footnotes (figure 14.3). By asserting herself as Juliette Janson could not in 1967 and as Carol White will not in 1987, echoing both but taking risks they avoided, Claire's mid-'70s epiphany realizes in feminist terms Billy the Kid's dream of "yesterday, today, and tomorrow, all in the same room," from the end of *I'm Not There*. No less a palimpsest of personas and epochs than Dylan or Jude, Claire is also an *actor* in two senses, theatrical and volitional, breaking from precedents, fond of neither pedestal nor cage.

Claire's reclamation of herself is as decisive as the Gere character's exit from pastoral seclusion, with which Haynes intercuts it. Just as suggestively, its initial sonic accompaniment comes from "Pressing On," the gospel mantra of Bale's Pastor John. Sound and editing indicate, then, that

Claire isn't just breaking from a Dylan figure but acting as one. The scene also, like Jude's performance at Royal Albert Hall, finds a performer speaking through her body in potent, newfound ways. It finishes with the couple embracing on the floor, Claire's legs wrapped around Robbie in a sculptural pose, awkward but carnal, that visualizes their enduring bond even as they separate. The scene's conclusion is scored to the song "Idiot Wind," a big-band tantrum from *Blood on the Tracks* whose raucous production sharpened its lyrical ferocity: "Idiot wind / blowing every time you move your mouth." *I'm Not There*, however, uses an acoustic version, recorded earlier but not released until 1991: again, yesterday, today, and tomorrow at once. In a film obsessed with the day Dylan went electric, this orchestration works oppositely, alchemizing a loud chauvinist kiss-off into a quiet storm of an apology, in a hushed and streamlined register mirroring Gainsbourg's performance aesthetic. She brings the end of *I'm Not There* back home by enlisting her trademark directness in service of a character at last roused to action, and as reconnected to her body as Jude is to his, notwithstanding the contrast of her austerity to his ornamentation. Her arc is a triumph for Haynes, too, because women in his films rarely know what they want or, when they do, often fall short of coherent, full-bodied expression.

Perhaps Claire's victory seems demure, rejecting one domestic arrangement for some barely intimated alternative. It is vital, though, that in leaving Robbie, Claire denounces marital expectations of subservience and sequester and that the film treats this action as directly political. *I'm Not There* thus breaks further from its Godardian influences while sustaining ideas in Ellen Willis's 1970 essay "Women and the Myth of Consumerism." That piece contests a mid-'60s leftist mantra that consumerism, not sexism, is the real engine of female misery within Western capitalism. *2 or 3 Things I Know about Her* reflects that kind of thinking; its closing image is a scale model of a tenement made of grocery items, as if conflating structural oppression with supermarket purchases. Willis, with a feminist politic that Haynes echoes, instead frames capitalist and patriarchal power formations as the dual root of women's despair, and consumerism as a convenient symptom favored by male demagogues. Conceding that "consumerism as applied to women is blatantly sexist" (E. Willis 2014, 42), Willis maintains that, "under present conditions, people are preoccupied with consumer goods not because they are brainwashed but because buying is the one pleasurable activity not only permitted but actively encouraged by our rulers" (40–41). Haynes likewise blames sexism and power, not Saran Wrap, for Claire's despondency. Her kitchen sports the same cereals and detergents as Juliette's, captured in similar frames, but it is Robbie and his politics, not the groceries and housewares, against which Claire rebels. Notably, too, Juliette ends her movie recumbent on her pillow, as if initiative or material change is impossible, whereas Gainsbourg's Claire stands and acts.

Importantly, Willis's jab at leftist doxa dovetails with her claims about rock, itself an enterprise in vexed consumerism—especially for women. "Consumerism at its most expansive," Willis wrote in 1982, savoring capitalism's unintended consequences, "encouraged a demand for fulfillment that could not so easily be contained by products" (E. Willis 2012, xvi). Moreover, "the history of the sixties strongly suggests that the impulse to buy a new car with the radio blasting rock-and-roll"—or, as it were, a motorcycle, which Claire drives much better than Robbie does—"is not unconnected to the impulse to fuck outside of marriage, get high, stand up to men or white people or bosses, join dissident movements" (xvi). Godard, the kind of leftist artist who believed Marxist critique outstripped or encompassed gender-based analyses, might as well be Willis's reference point here, as he so often serves as Haynes's, particularly in Gainsbourg's scenes. He emblematizes a mid-'60s cinema that, for all its professed progressivism, mirrors an "ideological sexism" in popular music that Willis dates to 1967, the year *2 or 3 Things* premiered, and right around the time Claire and Robbie's marriage enters its long downturn: "When rock was taken over by upper-middle-class bohemians, it inherited a whole new set of contradictions between protest and privilege. . . . Their sexism is smugger and cooler, less a product of misdirected frustration, more a simple assumption of power consistent with the rest of their self-image. It is less overtly hostile to women but more condescending" (E. Willis 2011, 135–36). As Willis achieved this realization, which captures Robbie's attitudes to a tee, she staged her own exit, largely abandoning rock criticism in favor of feminist writing, teaching, and activism.

Having reached a comparable epiphany, what will Claire do? Might she revive her dormant artistry? The script refuses to say, but Gainsbourg, that semireluctant performer, implies some hope by raising her own voice, not just in the film but on *I'm Not There*'s soundtrack, where she gives the world's breathiest reading of "Just like a Woman." That tune remains embroiled in arguments about Dylan's sexism, its lyrics adoring but paternalistic toward a subject who "breaks like a little girl." Gainsbourg's version, in which she never achieves full voice, is quintessentially self-effacing. Still, to claim this song of all songs—which, even when sung in a fragile whisper, suggests a first step toward vocal authority—is to appropriate

Dylan in an especially chauvinist moment, just as Blanchett does by dancing and shuffling in his shoes in the druggy, womanizing *Eat the Document* years. Both actresses, in league with their writer-director, marshal Dylan as a performative prompt for women's expression, a staging ground for female-bodied pleasure, and an unexpected promontory from which feminists, male and female alike, offer new perspectives on the world.

NOTES

1 See, too, Butler's comments in *Bodies That Matter* (1993) about such Hollywood films as *Some Like It Hot* (1959), *Tootsie* (1982), and *Victor/Victoria* (1982) that expose false groundings of gender normativity as a form of "high het entertainment," accruing no subversive force (126).

2 De Lauretis (1991) worries about feminism and gender parity within the very article hailing queer theory's arrival. Jagose (2009) offers a more recent assessment of tensions between these disciplines. See also Martin (1994) and Seidman (1993, esp. 117–27).

3 Haynes states this in his commentary track and the "Conversation with Todd Haynes" included on the *I'm Not There* DVD. Gainsbourg recalls for Freydkin (2007) how Haynes engaged her in conversation before finishing the script.

4 Joshua Clover, swimming against the tide, opens a review of *I'm Not There* by critiquing Blanchett ("she veers closer to impersonation than invention") in explicit contrast to Gainsbourg ("riveting and absolute, even as she stays within herself"), and by speculating that critics' ardor for the former may be helping them "displace the hots for the historical Bobby" (2008, 6).

5 Even Gainsbourg felt intimidated watching Blanchett film her scenes (Freydkin 2007).

6 Proving you can never generalize, in Barbara O'Dair's stimulating study of gender politics in Dylan's work, she names "Lay, Lady, Lay" as catalyzing her teenage investments in Dylan (2009, 80). Gainsbourg also specifies it as her favorite Dylan song, while characteristically testifying that "it was my father's pick" (Freydkin 2007).

7 O'Dair likens Blanchett's performance to those of female singer-songwriters of her era, including Cat Power, Lucinda Williams, and PJ Harvey, who complicate gender categories as Dylan did and occasionally use his songs to do it (2009, 85).

8 Blanchett's efforts thus counter what Susan Knobloch (1999) notes as a formal sidelining of women, fans and intimates alike, in the classic Dylan-centered documentary *Don't Look Back* (1967).

9 This motif realizes Ellen Willis's fears that in buying a TV set her husband craved, she "would wake up and find myself transformed into a suburban housewife" (2012, 143).

FILMOGRAPHY

All about Eve. 1950. Directed by Joseph L. Mankiewicz. USA.
"All I Ever Wanted." 2013. *Enlightened*, series 2, episode 6. Directed by Todd Haynes. USA.
All That Heaven Allows. 1955. Directed by Douglas Sirk. USA.
Angels in America [miniseries on HBO]. 2003. Directed by Mike Nichols. USA.
Assassins: A Film concerning Rimbaud [short film]. 1985. Directed by Todd Haynes. USA.
Best Foot Forward. 1943. Directed by Edward Buzzell. USA.
The Birth of a Nation. 1915. Directed by D. W. Griffith. USA.
Blue Is the Warmest Colour. 2013. Directed by Abdellatif Kechiche. France.
The Bold and the Brave. 1956. Directed by Lewis R. Foster. USA.
Boys Don't Cry. 1999. Directed by Kimberly Peirce. USA.
Brief Encounter. 1945. Directed by David Lean. UK.
Carol. 2015. Directed by Todd Haynes. USA.
Carol Support Group. 2017. Directed by Allison Tate. USA.
Charlotte for Ever. 1986. Directed by Serge Gainsbourg. France.
Chinatown. 1977. Directed by Roman Polanski. USA.
Chinese Roulette. 1976. Directed by Rainer Werner Fassbinder. West Germany.
Coffee and Cigarettes. 2003. Directed by Jim Jarmusch. USA.
Committed. 1984. Directed by Sheila McLaughlin and Lynne Tillman. USA.
Critic's Choice. 1963. Directed by Don Weis. USA.
Dance, Girl, Dance. 1940. Directed by Dorothy Arzner. USA.
Dark Waters. 2019. Directed by Todd Haynes. USA.
Daughter Rite. 1980. Directed by Michelle Citron. USA.
Daughters of Darkness. 1971. Directed by Harry Kümel. France.
Dead Tired. 1994. Directed by Michel Blanc. France.
"Domestic Violence" [installation piece]. 1996. Directed by Todd Haynes and Christine Vachon. USA.
Don't Look Back. 1967. Directed by D. A. Pennebaker. USA.
Dottie Gets Spanked [short film]. 1993. Directed by Todd Haynes. USA.
Dry Kisses Only. 1990. Directed by Jane Cottis and Kaucyila Brooke. USA.
Du Barry Was a Lady. 1943. Directed by Roy Del Ruth. USA.
Eat the Document. 1972. Directed by Bob Dylan. USA.
8½. 1963. Directed by Federico Fellini. Italy.

Elizabeth. 1998. Directed by Shekhar Kapur. UK.

Erin Brockovich. 2000. Directed by Steven Soderbergh. USA.

Fancy Pants. 1950. Directed by George Marshall. USA.

Far from Heaven. 2002. Directed by Todd Haynes. USA.

Fassbinder's Women [originally titled *Fassbinder Was the Only One for Me: The Willing Victims of Rainer Werner F.*]. 2000. Directed by Rosa von Praunheim. Germany.

The Forsyte Saga [miniseries on BBC, PBS]. 1967/1969–70. Produced by Donald Wilson. UK.

Frances. 1982. Directed by Graeme Clifford. USA.

Freeheld. 2015. Directed by Peter Sollet. USA.

Frida. 2011. Directed by Julie Taymor. USA

From the Journals of Jean Seberg. 1995. Directed by Mark Rappaport. USA.

Go Fish. 1994. Directed by Rose Troche. USA.

The Goddess. 1958. Directed by John Cromwell. USA.

The Good German. 2006. Directed by Steven Soderbergh. USA.

Grey Gardens [miniseries on HBO]. 2009. Directed by Michael Sucsy. USA.

Gypsy. 1962. Directed by Mervyn LeRoy. USA.

Happiness. 1998. Directed by Todd Solondz. USA.

Hedda Hopper's Hollywood. 1960. Directed by William Corrigan. USA.

Hilda Crane. 1956. Directed by Philip Dunne. USA.

Hitchcock, Selznick and the End of Hollywood [American Masters]. 1999. Directed by Michael Epstein. USA.

Hollywood without Make-Up. 1963. Directed by Ken Murray et al. USA.

Imitation of Life. 1959. Directed by Douglas Sirk. USA.

I'm Not There. 2007. Directed by Todd Haynes. USA.

"I'm Still Here" [segment of anthology film *Six by Sondheim*, directed by James Lapine]. 2013. Directed by Todd Haynes. USA.

"In the Mirror" [installation piece]. 1971. Directed by Chantal Akerman. Belgium.

I Shot Andy Warhol. 1996. Directed by Mary Harron. USA.

Jeanne Dielman, 23 quai du Commerce, 1080 Bruxelles. 1975. Directed by Chantal Akerman. Belgium.

Joan Sees Stars. 1993. Directed by Joan Braderman. USA.

John Adams [miniseries on HBO]. 2008. Directed by Tom Hooper. USA.

The Karen Carpenter Story. 1989. Directed by Richard Carpenter and Joseph Sargent. USA.

Kids. 1995. Directed by Larry Clark. USA.

Klute. 1971. Directed by Alan J. Pakula. USA.

La Chambre. 1972. Directed by Chantal Akerman. Belgium.

L'enfant aimé ou je joue à être une femme mariée. 1971. Directed by Chantal Akerman. Belgium.

Letter from an Unknown Woman. 1948. Directed by Max Ophüls. USA.

Lili Marleen. 1981. Directed by Rainer Werner Fassbinder. West Germany.

Lucy and Desi: A Home Movie. 1993. Produced by Lucie Arnaz. USA.

Lucy & Desi: Before the Laughter. 1991. Directed by Charles Jarrott. USA.

Mala Noche. 1986. Directed by Gus Van Sant. USA.

Masculin féminin. 1966. Directed by Jean-Luc Godard. France.

The Mating Game. 1959. Directed by George Marshall. USA.

McCabe & Mrs. Miller. 1971. Directed by Robert Altman. USA.

Meet the People. 1944. Directed by Charles Reisner. USA.

Mildred Pierce. 1945. Directed by Michael Curtiz. USA.

Mildred Pierce [miniseries on HBO]. 2011. Directed by Todd Haynes. USA.

Miracle in the Rain. 1956. Directed by Rudolph Maté. USA.

Mommie Dearest. 1981. Directed by Frank Perry. USA.

My Wife Is an Actress. 2001. Directed by Yvan Attal. France.

The Notorious Bettie Page. 2005. Directed by Mary Harron. USA.

Now, Voyager. 1942. Directed by Irving Rapper. USA.

Office Killer. 1997. Directed by Cindy Sherman. USA.

One Flew over the Cuckoo's Nest. 1985. Directed by Milos Forman. USA.

Orphans of the Storm. 1921. Directed by D. W. Griffith. USA.

Party Monster. 2003. Directed by Randy Barbato. USA.

Poison. 1991. Directed by Todd Haynes. USA.

Postcards from America. 1994. Directed by Steve McLean. UK.

Psycho. 1960. Directed by Alfred Hitchcock. USA.

Raging Bull. 1980. Directed by Martin Scorsese. USA.

Rear Window. 1954. Directed by Alfred Hitchcock. USA.

The Reckless Moment. 1949. Directed by Max Ophüls. USA.

Red Desert. 1964. Directed by Michelangelo Antonioni. Italy.

Rich Man, Poor Man [miniseries on ABC]. 1976. Produced by Jon Epstein. USA.

Riddles of the Sphinx. 1977. Directed by Laura Mulvey and Peter Wollen. UK.

Rock Hudson's Home Movies. 1992. Directed by Mark Rappaport. USA.

Rome, Open City. 1945. Directed by Roberto Rossellini. Italy.

Roots [miniseries on ABC]. 1977. Produced by Stan Marguiles. USA.

Rosetta. 1999. Directed by Jean-Pierre and Luc Dardenne. France.

Safe. 1995. Directed by Todd Haynes. USA.

Savage Grace. 2007. Directed by Tom Kalin. USA.

Star Wars: Episode VII—The Force Awakens. 2015. Directed by J. J. Abrams. USA.

Stella Dallas. 1937. Directed by King Vidor. USA.

Still Alice. 2014. Directed by Richard Glatzer and Wash Westmoreland. USA.

Stonewall. 1995. Directed by Nigel Finch. USA.

The Suicide [short film]. 1978. Directed by Todd Haynes. USA.

Superstar: The Karen Carpenter Story. 1987. Directed by Todd Haynes. USA.

Swoon. 1992. Directed by Tom Kalin. USA.

Sybil. 1976. Directed by Daniel Petrie. USA.

Temple Grandin [miniseries on HBO]. 2010. Directed by Mick Jackson. USA.

Therese and Isabelle. 1968. Directed by Radley Metzger. France.

This Close [series on Sundance TV]. 2018–. Created by Joshua Feldman and Shoshannah Stern. USA.

The Three Faces of Eve. 1957. Directed by Nunnally Johnson. USA.

Thriller. 1979. Directed by Sally Potter. UK.

21 Grams. 2003. Directed by Alejandro Gonzalez Inarritu. USA.

Twin Peaks [ABC]. 1990–91. Created by David Lynch and Mark Frost. USA.

Twin Peaks: Fire Walk with Me. 1992. Directed by David Lynch. USA.

2 or 3 Things I Know about Her. 1967. Directed by Jean-Luc Godard. France.

Velvet Goldmine. 1998. Directed by Todd Haynes. USA.

Velvet Underground. 2021. Directed by Todd Haynes. USA.

Vertigo. 1958. Directed by Alfred Hitchcock. USA.

Wanda. 1970. Directed by Barbara Loden. USA.

The Wizard of Babylon. 1982. Directed by Dieter Schidor. West Germany.

Wonderstruck. 2017. Directed by Todd Haynes. USA.

Working Girl. 1988. Directed by Mike Nichols. USA.

Written on the Wind. 1956. Directed by Douglas Sirk. USA.

You Can't Fool Your Wife. 1940. Directed by Ray McCarey. USA.

You Don't Know Jack [miniseries on HBO]. 2010. Directed by Barry Levinson. USA.

Z: The Beginning of Everything [series on Amazon Prime]. 2015–17. Created by Dawn Prestwich and Nicole Yorkin. USA.

Zola. 2021. Directed by Janicza Bravo. USA.

REFERENCES

Aaron, Michele, ed. 2004. *New Queer Cinema: A Critical Reader*. New Brunswick, NJ: Rutgers University Press.

Aftab, Kaleem. 2017. "Todd Haynes: 'You Have to Be Alone to Be Inspired.'" *The Talks*, August 23. https://the-talks.com/interview/todd-haynes/.

Ahmed, Sara. 2003. "Feminist Futures." In *A Concise Companion to Feminist Theory*, edited by Mary Eagleton, 236–54. London: Blackwell.

Ahmed, Sara. 2017. *Living a Feminist Life*. Durham, NC: Duke University Press.

Anderson, Christopher. 2008. "Producing an Aristocracy of Culture in American Television." In *The Essential HBO Reader*, edited by Gary R. Edgerton and Jeffrey P. Jones, 23–41. Lexington: University Press of Kentucky.

Anderson, Melissa. 2015. "Todd Haynes's *Carol*." *Artforum* 54 (1): 113–14.

Ang, Ien. 1996. *Living Room Wars: Rethinking Media Audiences for a Postmodern World*. London: Routledge.

Aston, Elaine. 1999. *Feminist Theatre Practice: A Handbook*. New York: Routledge.

Baker, Torah. 2019. "Cindy Sherman's Groundbreaking Images That Capture the Look of the 1950s and '60s Hollywood." *Creative Boom*, June 27. https://www.creativeboom.com/inspiration/cindy-sherman/.

Balsamo, Anne. 1996. *Technologies of the Gendered Body: Reading Cyborg Women*. Durham, NC: Duke University Press.

Baron, Cynthia, and Sharon Marie Carnicke. 2008. *Reframing Screen Performance*. Ann Arbor: University of Michigan Press.

Barrett, Michèle, and Mary McIntosh. 1982. *The Anti-social Family*. London: Verso.

Barthes, Roland. 1977. *Image-Music-Text*. Translated by Stephen Heath. New York: Farrar, Straus and Giroux.

Barthes, Roland. 1978. *A Lover's Discourse: Fragments*. Translated by Richard Howard. New York: Hill and Wang.

Bennett, Chad. 2010. "Flaming the Fans: Shame and the Aesthetics of Queer Fandom in Todd Haynes's *Velvet Goldmine*." *Cinema Journal* 49 (2): 17–39.

Benshoff, Harry M., and Sean Griffin. 2006. *Queer Images: A History of Gay and Lesbian Film in America*. New York: Rowman and Littlefield.

Berger, Richard. 2010. "Out and About: Slash Fic, Re-imagined Texts, and Queer Commentaries." In *LGBT Identity and Online New Media*, edited by Christopher Pullen and Margaret Cooper, 173–84. New York: Routledge.

Bergstrom, Janet. 1999. "The Innovators 1970–1980: Keeping a Distance." *Sight and Sound* (November): 26–28.
Berlant, Lauren. 2008. *The Female Complaint: The Unfinished Business of Sentimentality in American Culture*. Durham, NC: Duke University Press.
Berlant, Lauren. 2011. *Cruel Optimism*. Durham, NC: Duke University Press.
Berman, Judy. 2015. "*Carol*: A Rare Movie That Escapes the Male Gaze." *The Cut*, November 18. https://www.thecut.com/2015/11/carol-a-rare-movie-that-escapes-the-male-gaze.html.
Bernstein, Matthew. 2008. "The Producer as Auteur." In *Auteurs and Authorship: A Film Reader*, edited by Barry Keith Grant, 180–89. Malden, MA: Blackwell.
Bersani, Leo. 1987. "Is the Rectum a Grave?" *October* 43: 197–22.
Bersani, Leo. 1995. *Homos*. Cambridge, MA: Harvard University Press.
Bingham, Dennis 2010. *Whose Lives Are They Anyway? The Biopic as Contemporary Film Genre*. New Brunswick, NJ: Rutgers University Press.
Biskind, Peter. 2016. *Down and Dirty Pictures: Miramax, Sundance and the Rise of Independent Film*. London: Bloomsbury.
Bolton, Lucy. 2015. *Film and Female Consciousness: Irigaray, Cinema and Thinking Women*. London: Palgrave Macmillan.
Boorman, John, and Walter Donohue, eds. 1996. *Projections 5: Filmmakers on Filmmaking*. London: Faber and Faber.
Bordo, Susan. 1993. *Unbearable Weight: Feminism, Western Culture, and the Body*. Berkeley: University of California Press.
Bouchard, Danielle, and Jigna Desai. 2005. "'There's Nothing More Debilitating than Travel': Locating US Empire in Todd Haynes' *Safe*." *Quarterly Review of Film and Video* 22 (4): 359–70.
Bowie, Angela, with Paul Carr. 1993. *Backstage Passes: Life on the Wild Side with David Bowie*. New York: Putnam.
Bratton, Jacky, Jim Cook, and Christine Gledhill, eds. 1994. *Melodrama: Stage, Picture, Screen*. London: British Film Institute.
Brecht, Bertolt. 1992. *Brecht on Theatre: The Development of an Aesthetic*. 13th ed. Translated by John Willett. London: Hill and Wang.
Brown, Mark. 2016. "*Carol* Named Best LGBT Film of All Time." *Guardian*, March 15. https://www.theguardian.com/film/2016/mar/15/carol-named-best-lgbt-film-of-all-time.
Brumberg, Joan Jacobs. 2000. *Fasting Girls: The History of Anorexia Nervosa*. New York: Vintage.
Bryson, Norman. 1999. "Todd Haynes's *Poison* and Queer Cinema." *InVisible Culture: An Electronic Journal for Visual Studies*. https://www.rochester.edu/in_visible_culture/issue1/bryson/bryson.html.
Burgoon, Judee K., Laura K. Guerrero, and Kory Floyd. 2010. *Nonverbal Communication*. New York: Routledge.
Butler, Judith. 1990. *Gender Trouble: Feminism and the Subversion of Identity*. New York: Routledge.
Butler, Judith. 1991. "Imitation and Gender Insubordination." In *Inside/Out: Lesbian Theories, Gay Theories*, edited by Diana Fuss, 13–31. New York: Routledge.
Butler, Judith. 1993. *Bodies That Matter: On the Discursive Limits of "Sex."* New York: Routledge.
Butler, Judith. 1997. "Against Proper Objects." In *Feminism Meets Queer Theory*, edited by Elizabeth Weed and Naomi Schor, 1–30. Bloomington: Indiana University Press.

Butler, Judith, and Biddy Martin. 1994. "Cross-Identifications." *Diacritics* 24 (2–3): 3.

Byars, Jackie. 1991. *All That Hollywood Allows: Re-reading Gender in 1950s Melodrama*. Chapel Hill: University of North Carolina Press.

Cain, James M. 2002. *Mildred Pierce*. London: Phoenix. Originally published in 1941.

Çakırlar, Cüneyt. 2011. "Cinephilic Bodies: Todd Haynes's Cinema of Queer Pastiche." *KÜLT: Istanbul Bilgi University Cultural Studies Journal* 1 (1): 162–200.

Carini, Susan M. 2003. "Love's Labors Almost Lost: Managing Crisis during the Reign of *I Love Lucy*." *Cinema Journal* 43 (1): 44–62.

Carnicke, Sharon Marie. 2004. "Screen Performances and Directors' Visions." In *More than a Method: Trends and Traditions in Contemporary Film Performance*, edited by Cynthia Baron, Diane Carson, and Frank P. Tomasulo, 42–67. Detroit: Wayne State University Press.

Caserio, Robert L. 2006. "The Antisocial Thesis in Queer Theory." Forum: Conference Debates. *PMLA* 121 (3): 819–21.

Churchwell, Sarah. 2011. "Rereading: *Mildred Pierce* by James Cain." *Guardian*, June 24. https://www.theguardian.com/books/2011/jun/24/mildred-pierce-sarah-churchwell-rereading.

Cills, Hazel. 2020. "Tonight, You Should Watch *Safe*, Which Predicted the Horror of Wellness." *Jezebel*, March 12. https://themuse.jezebel.com/tonight-you-should-watch-safe-which-predicted-the-hor-1842298374.

Ciment, Michel, and Hubert Niogret. 2014. "Entretien avec Ed Lachman." *Positif: Revue mensuelle de cinéma* 635 (January): 32–38.

Ciment, Michel, and Yann Tobin. 2016. "Entretien avec Todd Haynes: Je voulais exprimer le désir et les obstacles qu'il rencontre." *Positif: Revue mensuelle de cinema* 659 (January): 17–21.

Citron, Michelle, Julia Lesage, Judith Mayne, B. Ruby Rich, and Anna Marie Taylor. 1978. "Women and Film: A Discussion of Feminist Aesthetics." *New German Critique* 13: 83–107.

Clover, Joshua. 2008. "Marx and Coca-Cola." *Film Quarterly* 61 (3): 6–7.

Cole, Susan G. 2015. *Carol* (review). *Now Toronto*, December 9. https://nowtoronto.com/movies/reviews/carol.

Collins, K. Austin. 2020. "Watching *Safe* at the End of the World." *Vanity Fair*, April 14. https://www.vanityfair.com/hollywood/2020/04/shut-in-movie-club-safe-coronavirus.

Comolli, Jean-Louis. 1978. "Historical Fiction: A Body Too Much." *Screen* 19 (2): 41–54.

"A Conversation with Todd Haynes." 2008. *I'm Not There*. 2007. Directed by Todd Haynes. Santa Monica, CA: Genius Products. DVD.

Cook, Pam. 1980. "Duplicity in *Mildred Pierce*." In *Women in Film Noir*, edited by E. Ann Kaplan, 68–82. London: British Film Institute.

Cook, Pam. 2013. "Beyond Adaptation: Mirrors, Memory and Melodrama in Todd Haynes's *Mildred Pierce*." *Screen* 54 (3): 378–87.

Cook, Pam. 2015. "Text, Paratext and Subtext: Reading *Mildred Pierce* as Maternal Melodrama." *SEQUENCE: Serial Studies in Media, Film and Music* 2: 2.

Cooke, Rachel. 2015. "Todd Haynes: 'She Said, There's a Frock Film Coming Up, with Cate Attached … It Sounded Right Up My Alley.'" *Guardian*, November 15. https://www.theguardian.com/film/2015/nov/15/todd-haynes-interview-carol-frock-film-cate-blanchett-rooney-mara.

Corber, Robert J. 2011. *Cold War Femme: Lesbianism, National Identity, and Hollywood Cinema*. Durham, NC: Duke University Press.

Crane, David. 2002. "Projections and Intersections: Paranoid Textuality in *Sorry, Wrong Number*." *Camera Obscura: Feminism, Culture, and Media Studies* 17 (3): 70–97.

Cunha, Darlena. 2016. "The Divorce Gap." *Atlantic*, April 28. https://www.theatlantic.com/business/archive/2016/04/the-divorce-gap/480333/.

Custen, George F. 1992. *Bio/Pics: How Hollywood Constructed Public History*. New Brunswick, NJ: Rutgers University Press.

D'Acci, Julie. 1994. *Defining Women: Television and the Case of Cagney and Lacey*. Chapel Hill: University of North Carolina.

D'Alessandro, Anthony. 2017. "Kevin Smith to Donate Dividends from Weinstein-Made Movies to Women in Film." *Deadline*, October 18. https://deadline.com/2017/10/harvey-weintein-kevin-smith-wif-donation-1202190654/.

Dall'Asta, Monica. 2010. "What It Means to Be a Woman: Theorizing Feminist Film History beyond the Essentialism/Constructionism Divide." In *Not So Silent: Women in Cinema before Sound*, edited by Sofia Bull and Astrid Soderbergh Widding, 39–57. Stockholm, Sweden: Stockholm University Press.

Darby, Helen. 2013. "I'm Glad I'm Not Me: Subjective Dissolution, Schizoanalysis, and Post-structuralist Ethics in the Films of Todd Haynes." *Film-Philosophy* 17 (1): 330–47.

Davies, Jon. 2007. "Nurtured in Darkness: Queer Childhood in the Films of Todd Haynes." In Morrison 2007, 57–67.

Davis, Glyn. 2010. *Far from Heaven*. Edinburgh: Edinburgh University Press.

Davis, Nick. 2007. "'The Invention of a People': *Velvet Goldmine* and the Unburying of Queer Desire." In Morrison 2007, 88–100.

Davis, Nick. 2013. *The Desiring-Image: Gilles Deleuze and Contemporary Queer Cinema*. London: Oxford University Press.

Davis, Nick. 2015a. "Interview: Todd Haynes." *Film Comment*, November 11, 30–35. https://www.filmcomment.com/blog/interview-todd-haynes/.

Davis, Nick. 2015b. "The Object of Desire." *Film Comment*, November 4. https://www.filmcomment.com/article/todd-haynes-carol-interview/.

Dean, James Joseph. 2007. "Gays and Queers: From the Centering to the Decentering of Homosexuality in American Films." *Sexualities* 103: 363–86.

Dean, Tim. 2000. *Beyond Sexuality*. Chicago: University of Chicago Press.

DeAngelis, Michael. 2004. "The Characteristics of New Queer Filmmaking: Case Study—Todd Haynes." In *New Queer Cinema: A Critical Reader*, edited by Michele Aaron, 41–52. New Brunswick, NJ: Rutgers University Press.

DeCordova, Richard. 1990. *Picture Personalities: The Emergence of the Star System in America*. Urbana: University of Illinois Press.

de Kuyper, Eric, and Annie van den Oever. 2015. "Temps mort: Speaking about Chantal Akerman (1950–2015)." NECSUS: *European Journal of Media Studies* (November 27). https://necsus-ejms.org/temps-mort-speaking-about-chantal-akerman-1950-2015/.

de Lauretis, Teresa. 1984. *Alice Doesn't: Feminism, Semiotics, Cinema*. Bloomington: Indiana University Press.

de Lauretis, Teresa. 1987. *Technologies of Gender: Essays on Theory, Film, and Fiction*. Bloomington: Indiana University Press.

de Lauretis, Teresa. 1991. "Queer Theory: Lesbian and Gay Sexualities: An Introduction." *differences: A Journal of Feminist Cultural Studies* 5 (2): iii–xviii.

de Lauretis, Teresa. 1994. *The Practice of Love: Lesbian Sexuality and Perverse Desire*. Bloomington: Indiana University Press.

Derschowitz, Jessica. 2019. "Two to Tango." *Entertainment Weekly*, April 12: 60–61.

Desjardins, Mary R. 2012. "Loving Lucy, Performing Biography." *Cinema Journal* 51 (Spring): 157–62.

Desjardins, Mary R. 2015. *Recycled Stars: Female Film Stardom in the Age of Television and Video*. Durham, NC: Duke University Press.

DeVito, John, and Frank Tropea. 2010. *The Epic Miniseries*. Jefferson, NC: McFarland.

Diprose, Rosalind. 1994. *The Bodies of Women: Ethics, Embodiment, and Sexual Difference*. New York: Routledge.

Doane, Mary Ann. 1987. *The Desire to Desire: The Woman's Film of the 1940s*. Bloomington: Indiana University Press.

Doane, Mary Ann. 1991. *Femmes Fatales: Feminism, Film Theory, Psychoanalysis*. New York: Routledge.

Doane, Mary Ann. 2004a. "Aesthetics and Politics." *Signs: Journal of Women in Culture and Society* 30 (1): 1229–35.

Doane, Mary Ann. 2004b. "Pathos and Pathology: The Cinema of Todd Haynes." *Camera Obscura: Feminism, Culture, and Media Studies* 19 (3): 1–20.

Doane, Mary Ann, Patricia Mellencamp, and Linda Williams, eds. 1984. *Re-vision: Essays in Feminist Film Criticism*. Los Angeles: American Film Institute.

doCarmo, Stephen N. 2002. "Beyond Good and Evil: Mass Culture Theorized in Todd Haynes's *Velvet Goldmine*." *Journal of American and Comparative Cultures* 25 (3): 395–98.

"Does Lucy Love 'Lucy'?" 1953. *TV Fan* (August): 2.

Donaldson, Laura. 1999. "On Medicine Women and White Shame-ans: New Age Native Americanism and Commodity Fetishism as Pop Culture Feminism." *Signs: Journal of Women in Culture and Society* 24 (3): 677–96.

Doty, Alexander. 1990. "The Cabinet of Lucy Ricardo: Lucille Ball's Star Image." *Cinema Journal* 29 (Summer): 3–34.

Doty, Alexander. 1993. *Making Things Perfectly Queer: Interpreting Mass Culture*. Minneapolis: University of Minnesota Press.

duCille, Ann. 1994. "The Occult of True Black Womanhood: Critical Demeanor and Black Feminist Studies." *Signs: Journal of Women in Culture and Society* 19 (3): 591–629.

Dyer, Richard. 1993. "Seen to Be Believed: Some Problems in the Representation of Gay People as Typical." In *The Matter of Images: Essays on Representations*, 19–51. London: Routledge.

Dyer, Richard. 1997. *White*. London: Routledge.

Dyer, Richard. 1998. *Stars*. London: British Film Institute.

Dyer, Richard. 2002. "Rock: The Last Guy You'd Have Figured?" In *The Culture of Queers*, 159–74. London: Routledge.

Dyer, Richard. 2007. *Pastiche*. London: Routledge.

Ebrahimian, Babak A. 2004. *The Cinematic Theater*. Toronto: Scarecrow.

Edelman, Lee. 2004. *No Future: Queer Theory and the Death Drive*. Durham, NC: Duke University Press.

Edgerton, Gary R. 2008. "Angels in America." In *The Essential HBO Reader*, edited by Gary R. Edgerton and Jeffrey P. Jones, 135–50. Lexington: University Press of Kentucky.
Elliott, Jane. 2006. "The Currency of Feminist Theory." PMLA 121 (5): 1697–703.
Ellis, John. 1982. *Visible Fictions: Cinema, Television, Video*. London: Routledge.
Elsaesser, Thomas. 1972. "Tales of Sound and Fury: Observations on Family Melodrama." *Monogram* 4: 2–15.
Elsaesser, Thomas. 1987. "Tales of Sound and Fury: Observations on Family Melodrama." In *Home Is Where the Heart Is: Studies in Melodrama and the Woman's Film*, edited by Christine Gledhill, 43–69. London: British Film Institute.
Elsaesser, Thomas. 2016. "Media Archaeology as Symptom." *New Review of Film and Television Studies* 14 (2): 181–215.
Emily. 2015. "Carol's Ghost: Chantal Akerman, Todd Haynes, and the Problem of Representation." *Femina Ridens*, December 3. https://feminaridens.club/2015/12/03/carols-ghost-chantal-akerman-todd-haynes-and-the-problem-of-representation/.
Eng, David. 2010. *The Feeling of Kinship: Queer Liberalism and the Racialization of Intimacy*. Durham, NC: Duke University Press.
Epstein, William H. 1987. *Recognizing Biography*. Philadelphia: University of Pennsylvania Press.
Farber, Sheryl. 1989. "Karen Carpenter: Getting to the Bare Bones of Todd Haynes's *Superstar: The Karen Carpenter Story*." *Film Threat* 1 (20): 16–22.
Farmer, Brett. 2000. *Spectacular Passions: Cinema, Fantasy, Gay Male Spectatorships*. Durham, NC: Duke University Press.
Feuer, Jane. 1983. "The Concept of Live Television: Ontology as Ideology." In *Regarding Television: Critical Approaches—An Anthology*, edited by E. Ann Kaplan, 12–22. Frederick, MD: American Film Institute/University Publications of America.
Feuer, Jane. 1995. *Seeing through the Eighties: Television and Reaganism*. Durham, NC: Duke University Press.
Fischer, Lucy, ed. 1991. *Imitation of Life: Douglas Sirk, Director.* New Brunswick, NJ: Rutgers University Press.
Fischer, Paul. 2002. "Julianne Moore's *Far from Heaven*." *Film Monthly*, November 2. http://www.filmmonthly.com/Profiles/Articles/JMoore/JMoore.html.
Fishbein, Leslie. 1983. "*Roots*: Docudrama and the Interpretation of History." In *American History/American Television*, edited by John E. O'Connor, 279–305. New York: Frederick Ungar.
Fiske, John. 1987. *Television Culture*. London: Methuen.
Fontenot, Andrea. 2008. "The Dandy Diva." *Camera Obscura: Feminism, Culture, and Media Studies* 23 (1): 165–71.
Foucault, Michel. (1989) 1996. "Friendship as a Way of Life." In *Foucault Live: Collected Interviews, 1961–1984*, edited by Sylvère Lotringer, 308–12. New York: Semiotext(e).
Freeman, Elizabeth. 2010. *Time Binds: Queer Temporalities, Queer Feelings*. Durham, NC: Duke University Press.
Freud, Sigmund. (1907) 1953. "Creative Writers and Day-Dreaming." In *The Standard Edition of the Complete Psychological Works of Sigmund Freud*, vol. 9, edited and translated by James Strachey, 141–53. London: Hogarth.
Freud, Sigmund. (1919) 1953. "'A Child Is Being Beaten': A Contribution to the Study of the Origin of Sexual Perversion." In *The Standard Edition of the Complete Psychological Works*

of Sigmund Freud, vol. 17, edited and translated by James Strachey, 175–204. London: Hogarth.

Freydkin, Donna. 2007. "Charlotte Gainsbourg Was Totally There for Dylan Film." *USA Today*, November 19. http://usatoday30.usatoday.com/life/people/2007-11-19-gainsbourg_N.htm.

Fricke, David. 1998. "Weird Scenes from the *Velvet Goldmine*." *Rolling Stone*, November 26, 64.

Friedberg, Anne. 1993. *Window Shopping: Cinema and the Postmodern*. Berkeley: University of California Press.

Frueh, Joanna. 1999. "Tarts, Stars, Jewels, and Fairies." *Art Journal* 58 (4): 88–89.

Gaines, Jane. 1986. "White Privilege and Looking Relations: Race and Gender in Feminist Film Theory." *Cultural Critique* 4 (Autumn): 59–79.

Gaines, Jane. 2018. *Pink-Slipped: What Happened to Women in the Silent Film Industries*. Urbana: University of Illinois Press.

Geller, Theresa L. 1992. "Deconstructing Postmodern Television in *Twin Peaks*." *Spectator* 12 (2): 64–71.

Geller, Theresa L. 2003. "Arzner, Dorothy." *Senses of Cinema*, May. http://sensesofcinema.com/2003/great-directors/arzner/.

Geller, Theresa L. 2006. "The Personal Cinema of Maya Deren: *Meshes of the Afternoon* and Its Critical Reception in the History of the Avant-Garde." In "Self-Projection and Autobiography in Film," edited by Linda Rugg. Special issue, *Biography* 28 (1): 140–58.

Geller, Theresa L. 2013. "Is Film Theory Queer Theory? Or, Everything I Know about Queerness I Learned at the Movies." *Camera Obscura: Feminism, Culture, and Media Studies* 28 (3): 159–67.

Geller, Theresa L. 2018. "Thinking Sex, Doing Gender, Watching Film." In *The Anthem Handbook of Screen Theory*, edited by Tom Conley and Hunter Vaughan, 49–69. New York: Anthem.

Gilbey, Ryan. 2015. "The Interview: Todd Haynes." *Sight and Sound* 25 (December): 18–23.

Gilbey, Ryan. 2017. "The Muse and the Monster: Fassbinder's Favorite Star on Surviving His Abuse." *Guardian*, March 27. https://www.theguardian.com/film/2017/mar/27/rainer-werner-fassbinder-bfi-season-hanna-schygulla-interview.

Gilbey, Ryan. 2018. "Strange Vibrations." *New Statesman* 147 (April 6–12): 55.

Gilchrist, Tracy E. 2018. "*Carol* Producer Elizabeth Karlsen Confirms Weinstein 'Stole' Credit." *The Advocate*, May 24. https://www.advocate.com/film/2018/5/24/carol-producer-elizabeth-karlsen-confirms-weinstein-stole-credit.

Gilman, Charlotte Perkins. 1997. *The Yellow Wallpaper*. New York: Dover. Originally published in 1892.

Gledhill, Christine, ed. 1987. *Home Is Where the Heart Is: Studies in Melodrama and the Woman's Film*. London: British Film Institute.

Goldberg, Jonathan. 2016. *Melodrama: An Aesthetics of Impossibility*. Durham, NC: Duke University Press.

Gorfinkel, Elena. 2005. "The Future of Anachronism: Todd Haynes and *The Magnificent Ambersons*." In *Cinephilia: Movies, Love and Memory*, edited by Marijke de Valck and Malte Hagener, 153–68. Amsterdam: Amsterdam University Press.

Gray, Tim. 2017. "Sounds of Silence Ring Out in *Wonderstruck*: Millicent Simmonds Leads Ground-Breaking Young Cast." *Variety* 338 (1): 14–15.

Gross, Larry. 2014. "Antibodies: Larry Gross Talks with *Safe*'s Todd Haynes." 1995. In Leyda 2014, 60–72.

Grossberg, Lawrence. 1992. "Is There a Fan in the House? The Affective Sensibility of Fandom." In *The Adoring Audience: Fan Culture and Popular Media*, edited by Lisa A. Lewis, 50–66. New York: Routledge.

Grossman, Julie. 2015. *Literature, Film, and Their Hideous Progeny: Adaptation and ElasTEXTity*. London: Palgrave Macmillan.

Grundmann, Roy. 1995. "How Clean Was My Valley: Todd Haynes's *Safe*." *Cineaste* 21 (4): 22–25.

Hahn, Rachel. 2020. "What the Style of Todd Haynes's *Safe* Can Tell Us about Fashion in Isolation." *Vogue*, April 15. https://www.vogue.com/article/todd-haynes-safe-film-quarantine-self-isolation-style.

Halberstam, Jack. 2011. *The Queer Art of Failure*. Durham, NC: Duke University Press.

Halley, Janet. 2006. *Split Decisions: How and Why to Take a Break from Feminism*. Princeton, NJ: Princeton University Press.

Halliday, Jon. 1972. *Sirk on Sirk*. London: Secker and Warburg.

Halliday, Jon, and Laura Mulvey, eds. 1972. *Douglas Sirk*. Edinburgh: Edinburgh Film Festival.

Haraway, Donna. 1984. "Teddy Bear Patriarchy: Taxidermy in the Garden of Eden, New York City, 1908–1936." *Social Text* (11): 20–64.

Harvey, Steve. 1987. "Then: Hooverville—Refuge for L.A.'s Homeless in Depression Years." *Los Angeles Times*, June 15. https://www.latimes.com/archives/la-xpm-1987-06-15-me-4229-story.html.

Hastie, Amelie. 2011. "Sundays with Mildred." *Film Quarterly* 65 (1): 25–33.

Hayek, Selma. 2017. "Harvey Weinstein Is My Monster Too." *New York Times*, December 13. https://www.nytimes.com/interactive/2017/12/13/opinion/contributors/salma-hayek-harvey-weinstein.html.

Haynes, Todd. 1995. "Liner Notes for *Safe* [Album]." London: Fine Line.

Haynes, Todd. 1998. *Velvet Goldmine: A Screenplay*. New York: Miramax-Hyperion.

Haynes, Todd. 2003. *Far from Heaven, Safe, and Superstar: The Karen Carpenter Story: Three Screenplays*. New York: Grove.

Haynes, Todd. 2008. Audio Commentary. *I'm Not There* (2007). Directed by Todd Haynes. Santa Monica, CA: Genius Products. DVD.

Haynes, Todd. 2015. "Todd Haynes on Chantal Akerman." Vimeo, November 6. https://vimeo.com/144887444.

Hebron, Sandra. 2003. "Haynes's Manual." *Guardian*, February 20. https://www.theguardian.com/film/2003/feb/21/features.

Hedren, Tippi. 2016. *Tippi: A Memoir*. New York: HarperCollins.

Hemmings, Clare. 2011. *Why Stories Matter: The Political Grammar of Feminist Theory*. Durham, NC: Duke University Press.

Hendrickson, Paul. 2004. *Bound for Glory: America in Color, 1939–43*. New York: Harry N. Abrams and Library of Congress.

Highsmith, Patricia. 2010. Afterword to *Carol*, 308–11. London: Bloomsbury.

Hilderbrand, Lucas. 2004. "Grainy Days and Mondays: Superstar and Bootleg Aesthetics." *Camera Obscura: Feminism, Culture, and Media Studies* 19 (3): 57–91.

Hilderbrand, Lucas. 2007. "Mediating Queer Boyhood: *Dottie Gets Spanked*." In Morrison 2007, 42–56.

Hoberman, J. 2002. "Film; Back to the Sunny Suburban 50's and Its Dark Secrets." *New York Times*, November 10. https://www.nytimes.com/2002/11/10/movies/film-back-to-the-sunny-suburban-50-s-and-its-dark-secrets.html.

Hole, Kristin Lené, and Dijana Jelača. 2019. *Film Feminisms: A Global Introduction*. London: Routledge.

Hollinger, Karen. 2006. *The Actress: Hollywood Acting and the Female Star*. New York: Routledge.

hooks, bell. 1989. *Talking Back: Thinking Feminist, Thinking Black*. Boston: South End.

Hopewell, John. 2017. "Todd Haynes to Direct Velvet Underground Documentary." *Variety*, August 7. https://variety.com/2017/film/festivals/locarno-todd-haynes-velvet-underground-documentary-1202517233/.

Huffer, Lynne. 2013. *Are the Lips a Grave? A Queer Feminist on the Ethics of Sex*. New York: Columbia University Press.

Huyssen, Andreas. 1986. *After the Great Divide: Modernism, Mass Culture, Postmodernism*. Bloomington: Indiana University Press.

I'm Not There. 2015. Production notes. The Weinstein Company. www.twcpublicity.com.

Jacobs, Amber. 2014. "On Maternal Listening: Experiments in Sound and the Mother-Daughter Relation in Todd Haynes' *Mildred Pierce*." In *The SAGE Handbook of Feminist Theory*, edited by Mary Evans, Clare Hemmings, Marsha Henry, Hazel Johnstone, Sumi Madhok, Ania Plomien, and Sadie Wearing, 163–77. London: SAGE.

Jacobs, Lea. 1991. *The Wages of Sin: Censorship and the Fallen Woman Film, 1928–1942*. Berkeley: University of California Press.

Jagernauth, Kevin. 2016. "Cate Blanchett Finds Lack of Oscar Recognition for Todd Haynes & *Carol* 'Bewildering,' Talks Industry Diversity." *IndieWire*, February 26. https://www.indiewire.com/2016/02/cate-blanchett-finds-lack-of-oscar-recognition-for-todd-haynes-carol-bewildering-talks-industry-diversity-265994/.

Jagose, Annamarie. 2009. "Feminism's Queer Theory." *Feminism and Psychology* 19 (2): 157–74.

Jenkins, David. 2015. "Todd Haynes: The Amorous Imagination." *Little White Lies*, November 25. https://lwlies.com/interviews/todd-haynes-carol-interview/.

Jenkins, Henry. 1992. *Textual Poachers: Television Fans and Participatory Culture*. London: Routledge.

Jennings, Ros. 2002. "Making Movies That Matter: Christine Vachon, Independent Film Producer." In *Fifty Contemporary Filmmakers*, edited by Yvonne Tasker, 353–60. New York: Routledge.

Johnston, Claire. 1973. "Women's Cinema as Counter-Cinema." In *Notes on Women's Cinema*, edited by Claire Johnston, 24–31. London: Society for Education in Film and Television.

Johnston, Claire. 2000. "Women's Cinema as Counter-Cinema." In *Feminism and Film*, edited by E. Ann Kaplan, 22–33. Oxford: Oxford University Press.

Joyrich, Lynne. 1988. "All That Television Allows: TV Melodrama, Postmodernism, and Consumer Culture." *Camera Obscura: Feminism, Culture, and Media Studies* 6 (1): 128–53.

Joyrich, Lynne. 1996. *Re-viewing Reception: Television, Gender, and Postmodern Culture*. Bloomington: Indiana University Press.

Joyrich, Lynne. 2001. "Epistemology of the Console." *Critical Inquiry* 27 (3): 439–67.

Jurca, Catherine. 2002. "*Mildred Pierce*, Warner Bros., and the Corporate Family." *Representations* 77 (1): 30–51.

Kantor, Jodi, and Megan Twohey. 2017. "Harvey Weinstein Paid Off Sexual Harassment Accusers for Decades." *New York Times*, October 5. https://www.nytimes.com/2017/10/05/us/harvey-weinstein-harassment-allegations.html.

Kaplan, E. Ann. 2000. "The Case of the Missing Mother: Maternal Issues in Vidor's *Stella Dallas*." In *Feminism and Film*, edited by E. Ann Kaplan, 466–78. Oxford: Oxford University Press.

Kaplan, E. Ann. 2012. "Troubling Genre/Reconstructing Gender." In *Gender Meets Genre in Postwar Cinemas*, edited by Christine Gledhill, 71–83. Champaign: University of Illinois Press.

Keil, Charlie. 2012. "Kate Winslet and Cate Blanchett: The Performance Is the Star." In *Shining in Shadows: Movie Stars of the 2000s*, edited by Murray Pomerance, 182–99. New Brunswick, NJ: Rutgers University Press.

Killer Content. 2018. "Statement from Killer Content on Reported Interest in the Assets of the Weinstein Company." PR *Newswire*, January 15. https://www.prnewswire.com/news-releases/statement-from-killer-content-on-reported-interest-in-the-assets-of-the-weinstein-company-300582569.html.

Klinger, Barbara. 1994. *Melodrama and Meaning: History, Culture, and the Films of Douglas Sirk*. Bloomington: Indiana University Press.

Knegt, Peter. 2009. "10 Things You Want to Know about Julianne Moore." *IndieWire*, October 27. https://www.indiewire.com/2009/10/10-things-you-want-to-know-about-julianne-moore-246325/.

Knobloch, Susan. 1999. "(Pass through) the Mirror Moment and Don't Look Back: Music and Gender in a Rockumentary." In *Feminism and Documentary*, edited by Diane Waldman and Janet Walker, 121–36. Minneapolis: University of Minnesota Press.

Knowles, Patrick. 2009/2010. "Charlotte Gainsbourg: A Portrait of an Ethereal Icon." *Soma* 23 (8): 42–47.

Kohn, Eric. 2011. "Todd Haynes on 'Mildred Pierce': Too Racy for Indies, but Perfect for TV." *IndieWire*, April 8. https://www.indiewire.com/2011/04/interview-todd-haynes-on-mildred-pierce-too-racy-for-indies-but-perfect-for-tv-243045/.

Koresky, Michael. 2017. "Review: *Wonderstruck*." *Film Comment* 53 (5): 68–69.

Kouvaros, George. 2006. "Improvisation and the Operatic." In *Falling for You: Essays on Cinema and Performance*, edited by Lesley Stern and George Kouvaros, 49–71. Sydney: Power.

Kronke, David. 2010. "Winslet, Haynes Team for 'Mildred Pierce.'" *Variety*, November 8. https://variety.com/2010/tv/news/winslet-haynes-team-for-mildred-pierce-1118026829/.

Kugler, Ryan. 2002. "Life Affirmed: An Interview with *Far from Heaven* Director Todd Haynes." *Cinemaspeak*, November 4. www.cinemaspeak.com/Interviews/lifeaffirmed.

Kuhn, Annette. (1982) 1994. *Women's Pictures: Feminism and Cinema*. London: Verso.

Laffly, Tomris. 2015. "8 Things We Learned from Carol Director Todd Haynes at NYFF." *Film School Rejects*, October 15. https://filmschoolrejects.com/8-things-we-learned-from-carol-director-todd-haynes-at-nyff-af1538885668/.

Lagerwey, Jorie, Julia Leyda, and Diane Negra. 2016. "Female-Centered TV in an Age of Precarity." *Genders* 1 (1). https://www.colorado.edu/genders/2016/05/19/female-centered-tv-age-precarity.

Lahr, John. 2019. "Todd Haynes Rewrites the Hollywood Playbook." *New Yorker*, November 4. https://www.newyorker.com/magazine/2019/11/11/todd-haynes-rewrites-the-hollywood-playbook.

Landy, Marcia. 1991. *Imitations of Life: A Reader on Film and Television Melodrama*. Detroit, MI: Wayne State University Press.

Landy, Marcia. 1993. "'The Dream of the Gesture': The Body of/in Todd Haynes's Films." *boundary* 2 30 (3): 123–40.

Lane, Christina. 2020. *Phantom Lady: Hollywood Producer Joan Harrison, the Forgotten Woman behind Hitchcock*. Chicago: Chicago Review Press.

Lantos, Jeffrey. 2014. "Todd Haynes: The Intellectual from Encino." In Leyda 2014, 13–18.

Laplanche, Jean, and Jean-Bertrand Pontalis. (1967) 2006. "Phantasy." In *The Language of Psychoanalysis*, translated by Donald Nicholson-Smith, 318–19. London: Karnac.

Laskawy, Michael. 2014. "*Poison* at the Box Office." 1991. In Leyda 2014, 19–32.

Latham, Sean. 2009. *The Art of Scandal: Modernism, Libel Law, and the Roman à Clef*. Oxford: Oxford University Press.

Lawrence, Amy. 1991. *Echo and Narcissus: Women's Voices in Classical Hollywood Cinema*. Berkeley: University of California Press.

Leclere, Margaret. 2018. "The Death of Auteur Director in the #MeToo Age." *The Conversation*, May 18. http://theconversation.com/the-death-of-the-auteur-director-in-the-metoo-age-95254.

Lesage, Julia. 1974. "Feminist Film Criticism: Theory and Practice." *Women and Film* 1 (6): 12–20.

Lessing, Gotthold Ephraim. 2005. *Laocoön: An Essay upon the Limits of Painting and Poetry*. Translated by Ellen Frothingham. Reissue edition. Mineola, NY: Dover. Originally published in 1766.

Leyda, Julia. 2012. "'Something That Is Dangerous and Arousing and Transgressive': An Interview with Todd Haynes." *Bright Lights Film Journal* 78 (October 31). Reprinted in Leyda 2014, 201–26.

Leyda, Julia, ed. 2014. *Todd Haynes: Interviews*. Jackson: University Press of Mississippi.

Lim, Dennis. 2010. "When 'Poison' Was a Cinematic Antidote." *New York Times*, November 5. https://www.nytimes.com/2010/11/07/movies/07poison.html.

Lim, Dennis. 2011. "'Mildred Pierce': A Mother's House of Love and Hurt." *New York Times*, March 18. https://www.nytimes.com/2011/03/20/arts/television/kate-winslet-in-todd-hayness-mildred-pierce-on-hbo.html.

Lim, Dennis. 2014. "Heaven Sent." In Leyda 2014, 105–9.

Lippe, Richard. 1987. "Rock Hudson: His Story." *CineAction* 10: 46–54.

Littwin, Susan. 1988. "The Family's Memories vs. Hollywood's Version." *TV Guide*, December 31, 26–29.

Love, Heather. 2007. *Feeling Backward: Loss and the Politics of Queer History*. Cambridge, MA: Harvard University Press.

Love, Heather. 2011. "Queers ____ This." In *After Sex? On Writing since Queer Theory*, edited by Janet Halley and Andrew Parker, 180–91. Durham, NC: Duke University Press.

Lovell, Glenn. 1999. "Hitchcock, Selznick and the End of Hollywood." *Variety*, January 24. https://variety.com/1999/film/reviews/hitchcock-selznick-and-the-end-of-hollywood-1200456404/.

Luciano, Dana. 2007. "Coming around Again: The Queer Momentum of *Far from Heaven*." *GLQ* 13 (2): 249–72.

"Lucille Ball: 'Funny Face.'" 1952. *People*, January 30, 17.

Lyons, James. 2016. "'A Woman with an Endgame': Megan Ellison, Annapurna Pictures and American Independent Film Production." In *Indie Reframed: Women's Filmmaking and Contemporary American Independent Cinema*, edited by Linda Badley, Claire Perkins, and Michele Schreiber, 54–69. Edinburgh: Edinburgh University Press, 2016.

MacDonald, Scott. 2014. "From Underground to Multiplex: An Interview with Todd Haynes." 2009. In Leyda 2014, 152–69.

MacDonald, Scott. 2015. *Avant-Doc: Intersections of Documentary and Avant-Garde Cinema*. Oxford: Oxford University Press.

Macfarlane, Steve. 2015. "Review: *Carol*." *Slant Magazine*, October 2. http://www.slant magazine.com/film/carol.

MacKenzie, Steven. 2016. "Todd Haynes: 'Cinema Still Has a Problem with Women.'" *Big Issue*, April 6. https://www.bigissue.com/interviews/todd-haynes-interview-cinema-still -problem-women/.

MacLean, Alison. 2014. "Todd Haynes." In Leyda 2014, 49–59.

Maddison, Stephen. 2000. *Fags, Hags, and Queer Sisters: Gender Dissent and Heterosocial Bonds in Gay Culture*. London: Palgrave Macmillan.

Malcolm, Janet. 1994. *The Silent Woman: Sylvia Plath and Ted Hughes*. New York: Vintage.

Marghitu, Stefania. 2018. "'It's Just Art': *Auteur* Apologism in the Post-Weinstein Era." *Feminist Media Studies* 18 (3): 491–94.

Margulies, Ivone. 1996. *Nothing Happens: Chantal Akerman's Hyperrealist Everyday*. Durham, NC: Duke University Press.

Margulies, Ivone, and Jeremi Szaniawski. 2019. *On Women's Films: Across Worlds and Generations*. London: Bloomsbury Academic.

Marks, Elaine. 1979. "Lesbian Intertextuality." In *Homosexualities and French Literature*, edited by George Stambolian and Elaine Marks, 353–77. Ithaca, NY: Cornell University Press.

Martin, Biddy. 1994. "Sexualities without Genders and Other Queer Utopias." *Diacritics* 24 (2–3): 104–21.

Mayer, So. 2016a. *Political Animals: The New Feminist Cinema*. London: I. B. Tauris.

Mayer, So. 2016b. "Where We Are Is Here: On the Influence of Female Filmmakers." *Another Gaze*, March 14. https://www.anothergaze.com/where-we-are-is-here-on-the-influence -of-female-filmmakers/.

Mayne, Judith. 1990. *The Woman at the Keyhole: Feminism and Women's Cinema*. Bloomington: Indiana University Press.

McCabe, Janet, and Kim Akass. 2007. "Sex, Swearing and Respectability: Courting Controversy, HBO's Original Programming and Producing Quality TV." In *Quality TV: Contemporary American Television and Beyond*, edited by Janet McCabe and Kim Akass, 62–76. New York: I. B. Tauris.

McCallum, E. L. 1999. "Mother Talk: Maternal Masquerade and the Problem of the Single Girl." *Camera Obscura: Feminism, Culture, and Media Studies* 14 (3): 70–95.

McDougall, Danny. 2017. "*Wonderstruck* Splits the Deaf Baby." *Terp Theater*, May 24. http:// www.terptheatre.com/wonderstruck-deafface/.

McGovern, Joe. 2015. "*Carol* Stars Cate Blanchett, Rooney Mara, Director Todd Haynes on the Film's Forbidden Love Story." *Entertainment Weekly*, November 21. http://ew.com /article/2015/11/21/carol-cate-blanchett-rooney-mara-todd-haynes/.

Meagher, Michelle. 2009. "Final Girls: Appropriation, Identification, and Fluidity in Cindy Sherman's *Office Killer*." In *There She Goes: Feminist Filmmaking and Beyond*, edited by Corinn Columpar and Sophie Mayer, 135–45. Detroit, MI: Wayne State University Press.

Mellencamp, Patricia. 1985. "Situation and Simulation: An Introduction to *I Love Lucy*." *Screen* 26 (March–April): 30–40.

Mercer, John, and Martin Shingler. 2004. *Melodrama: Genre, Style, Sensibility*. London: Wallflower.

Meyer, Richard. 1991. "Rock Hudson's Body." In *Inside/Out: Lesbian Theories, Gay Theories*, edited by Diana Fuss, 258–88. New York: Routledge.

Michael, David. 2003. "Interview: Todd Haynes, *Far from Heaven*." BBC, February 13. http://www.bbc.co.uk/films/2003/02/13/todd_haynes_far_from_heaven_interview.shtml.

Millett, Kate. 1970. *Sexual Politics*. New York: Doubleday.

Millman, Noah. 2016. "'Carol' Is Beautiful but a Bit of a Drag." *American Conservative*, January 6. https://www.theamericanconservative.com/millman/carol-is-beautiful-but-a-bit-of-a-drag/.

Mitchell, John Cameron. 2014. "Flaming Creatures." 1986. In Leyda, 2014, 86–92.

Mitchell, Wendy. 2020. "The Centrepiece Interview: Killer Films Chief Christine Vachon on the Fluctuating State of Indie Film." *Screen Daily*, February 28. https://www.screendaily.com/features/the-centrepiece-interview-killer-films-chief-christine-vachon-on-the-fluctuating-state-of-indie-film/5147212.article.

Mittell, Jason. 2015. *Complex TV: The Poetics of Contemporary American Television Storytelling*. New York: New York University Press.

Modleski, Tania. 1984. "Time and Desire in the Woman's Film." *Cinema Journal* 23 (3): 19–30.

Moi, Toril. 1993. *Sexual/Textual Politics*. London: Routledge.

Montagne, Renee. 2017. "Todd Haynes on 'Wonderstruck' and Evolution of Deaf Culture in the U.S." NPR, October 15. https://www.npr.org/2017/10/15/557863719/todd-haynes-on-wonderstruck-and-evolution-of-deaf-culture-in-the-u-s.

Moore, Suzanne. 2018. "From Tippi Hedren to Uma Thurman, Being a Muse Means Being Abused." *Guardian*, February 5. https://www.theguardian.com/film/commentisfree/2018/feb/05/from-tippi-hedren-to-uma-thurman-being-a-muse-means-being-abused.

Mora, Gilles, and Beverly W. Brannan, eds. 2006. *FSA: The American Vision*. New York: Abrams.

Morgan, Claire [Patricia Highsmith]. 1983. Afterword to *The Price of Salt*, by Patricia Highsmith, n.p. Tallahassee, FL: Naiad Press.

Morley, David. 1992. *Television, Audiences, and Cultural Studies*. London: Routledge.

Morrison, James, ed. 2007. *The Cinema of Todd Haynes: All That Heaven Allows*. London: Wallflower.

Morse, Margaret. 1986. "The Television News Personality and Credibility: Reflections on the News in Transition." In *Studies in Entertainment: Critical Approaches to Mass Culture*, edited by Tania Modleski, 55–79. Bloomington: Indiana University Press.

Moverman, Oren. 1998. "Superstardust: Talking Glam with Todd Haynes." In *Velvet Goldmine: A Screenplay*, by Todd Haynes, ix–xxxi. New York: Miramax-Hyperion.

Mulvey, Laura. 1975. "Visual Pleasure and Narrative Cinema." *Screen* 16 (3): 6–18.

Mulvey, Laura. 1977–78. "Notes on Sirk and Melodrama." *Movie* 25: 53–56.

Mulvey, Laura. 1986. "Visual Pleasure and Narrative Cinema." In *Narrative, Apparatus, Ideology*, edited by Philip Rosen, 198–209. New York: Columbia University Press.
Mulvey, Laura. 2015. "Introduction: 1970s Feminist Film Theory and the Obsolescent Object." In *Feminisms: Diversity, Difference and Multiplicity in Contemporary Film Cultures*, edited by Laura Mulvey and Anna Backman Rogers, 17–26. Amsterdam: Amsterdam University Press.
Mulvey, Laura, and Anna Backman Rogers, eds. 2015. *Feminisms: Diversity, Difference and Multiplicity in Contemporary Film Cultures*. Amsterdam: Amsterdam University Press.
Munzenrieder, Kyle. 2020. "Why Julianne Moore in *Safe* Is Everyone's Social Distancing Panic Mood Right Now." *w Magazine*, March 17. https://www.wmagazine.com/story/safe-julianne-moore-coronavirus-social-distancing.
Murray, Noel. 2014. "Todd Haynes." 2007. In Leyda 2014, 143–48.
Nash, Jennifer. 2014. *The Black Body in Ecstasy: Reading Race, Reading Pornography*. Durham, NC: Duke University Press.
Nash, Jennifer. 2019. *Black Feminism Reimagined: After Intersectionality*. Durham, NC: Duke University Press.
Neale, Stephen. 1976–77. "Douglas Sirk." *Framework* 5: 16–18.
Neale, Stephen. 1986. "Melodrama and Tears." *Screen* 27 (6): 6–23.
Newman, Michael Z., and Elana Levine. 2012. *Legitimating Television: Media Convergence and Cultural Status*. New York: Routledge.
Nienaber, Georgianne. 2012. "Minnesota Wolf Hunt Desecrates Ojibwe Creation Symbol." *Huffington Post*, November 14. Updated December 6, 2017. https://www.huffingtonpost.com/georgianne-nienaber/minnesota-wolf-hunting_b_2112944.html.
O'Dair, Barbara. 2009. "Bob Dylan and Gender Politics." In *The Cambridge Companion to Bob Dylan*, edited by Kevin J. H. Dettmar, 80–86. Cambridge: Cambridge University Press.
O'Hehir, Andrew. 2002. "Far from Heaven." Salon.com, November 9. https://www.salon.com/2002/11/08/far_from_heaven/.
O'Hehir, Andrew. 2015. "'Carol' Isn't Just a 'Lesbian Movie': Cate Blanchett and Rooney Mara's '50s Love Story Is a Classic American Screen Romance." Salon.com, November 25. http://www.salon.com/2015/11/25/carol_isnt_just_a_lesbian_movie_cate_blanchett_and_rooney_maras_50s_love_story_is_a_classic_american_screen_romance/.
O'Neill, Edward R. 2004. "Traumatic Postmodern Histories: *Velvet Goldmine*'s Phantasmatic Testimonies." *Camera Obscura: Feminism, Culture, and Media Studies* 19 (3): 156–85.
Onion, Rebecca. 2017. "We've Got the '70s-Style Rage. Now We Need the '70s-Style Feminist Social Analysis." *Slate*, November 20. http://www.slate.com/articles/double_x/doublex/2017/11/amid_the_flood_of_stories_about_harassment_and_abuse_there_s_been_a_scarcity.html.
Osenlund, R. Kurt. 2017. "The Gay Agenda." *Out* 26 (3): 20–23.
Pardo, Alejandro. 2010. "The Film Producer as a Creative Force." *Wide Angle* 2 (2): 1–23.
Pendleton, David. 1993. "My Mother, the Cinema." *Wide Angle* 15 (2): 39–49.
Penley, Constance, ed. 1988. *Feminism and Film Theory*. New York: Routledge.
Penley, Constance. 1992. "Feminism, Psychoanalysis, and the Study of Popular Culture." In *Cultural Studies*, edited by Lawrence Grossberg, 479–500. New York: Routledge.
Phipps, Keith. 2014. "Interview with Todd Haynes." 1998. In Leyda 2014, 93–100.

Pick, Anat. 2004. "New Queer Cinema and Lesbian Films." In *New Queer Cinema: A Critical Reader*, edited by Michele Aaron, 103–18. Edinburgh: Edinburgh University Press.

Pick, Anat. 2007. "Todd Haynes's Melodramas of Abstraction." In Morrison 2007, 145–55.

Pinkerton, Nick. 2018. "Wonderstruck." *Sight and Sound* 28 (5): 58–59.

Polito, Robert. 2008. "An Interview with Todd Haynes." *Believer Magazine*, March 1. https://believermag.com/an-interview-with-todd-hanes.

Pollock, Griselda, Geoffrey Nowell-Smith, and Stephen Heath. 1977. "Dossier on Melodrama." *Screen* 18 (2): 105–19.

Pomerance, Murray. 2007. "*Safe* in Lotosland." In Morrison 2007, 79–87.

Pogrebin, Robin. 2013. "Send in the Cameras: Sondheim on TV." *New York Times*, December 6. https://www.nytimes.com/2013/12/07/arts/television/send-in-the-cameras-sondheim-on-tv.html.

Porton, Richard. 2007. "Trusting the Text: An Interview with Cate Blanchett." *Cineaste* 32 (2): 16–19.

Potter, Susan. 2004. "Dangerous Spaces: *Safe*." *Camera Obscura: Feminism, Culture, and Media Studies* 19 (3): 125–54.

Pratt, Mary Louise. 1995. *Imperial Eyes: Travel Writing and Transculturation.* New York: Routledge.

Queens Museum. 2018. "Building History: The Queens Museum—New York City Building." https://queensmuseum.org/building-history.

Ramanathan, Geetha. 2006. *Feminist Auteurs: Reading Women's Films*. London: Wallflower.

Rappaport, Mark. 1996. "Mark Rappaport's Notes on *Rock Hudson's Home Movies*." *Film Quarterly* 49 (4): 16–22.

Rapping, Elayne. 1992. *The Movie of the Week: Private Stories/Public Events*. Minneapolis: University of Minnesota Press.

Rhiel, Mary, and David Suchoff. 1996. "Introduction." In *The Seductions of Biography*, ed. Mary Rhiel and David Suchoff, 1–5. New York: Routledge.

Rhodes, John David. 2007. "Allegory, Mise-en-scène, AIDS: Interpreting *Safe*." In Morrison 2007, 68–78.

Rich, Adrienne. 1980. "Compulsory Heterosexuality and Lesbian Existence." *Signs: Journal of Women in Culture and Society* 5 (4): 631–60.

Rich, B. Ruby. 1992. "New Queer Cinema." *Sight and Sound* (September): 30–34.

Rich, B. Ruby. 2001. "Queer and Present Danger." In *American Independent Cinema: A Sight and Sound Reader*, edited by Jim Hillier, 114–18. London: British Film Institute.

Rich, B. Ruby. 2013. *New Queer Cinema: The Director's Cut.* Durham, NC: Duke Univeristy Press.

Riviere, Joan. 1929. "Womanliness as Masquerade." *International Journal of Psychoanalysis* 10: 303–13.

Romney, Jonathan. 1991. "Poison." *Sight and Sound* 1 (6): 56–57.

Rony, Fatimah Tobing. 1996. *The Third Eye: Race, Cinema, and Ethnographic Spectacle*. Durham, NC: Duke University Press.

Rosenberg, Rebecca. 2019. "Harvey Weinstein: I Deserve Pat on Back When It Comes to Women." *Page Six*, December 15. https://pagesix.com/2019/12/15/harvey-weinstein-i-deserve-pat-on-back-when-it-comes-to-women/.

Roth, David. 2020. "Todd Haynes's Masterpiece 'Safe' Is Now a Tale of Two Plagues." *New Yorker*, March 28. https://www.newyorker.com/culture/culture-desk/todd-hayness-masterpiece-safe-is-now-a-tale-of-two-plagues.

Rowin, Michael Joshua. 2019. "Interview: Todd Haynes on *Dark Waters* and Being in the Crosshairs of Everything." *Slant*, November 18. https://www.slantmagazine.com/features/interview-todd-haynes-on-dark-waters-and-being-in-the-crosshairs-of-everything/.

Rubin, Gayle. 2017. "The Traffic in Women." In *Literary Theory: An Anthology*, 3rd ed., edited by Julie Rivkin and Michael Ryan, 901–24. Oxford: Wiley Blackwell. Previously published in *Toward an Anthropology of Women*, edited by Rayna R. Reiter. New York: Monthly Review Press, 1975.

Ryan, Mike. 2017. "Todd Haynes Discusses the Beauty of 'Wonderstruck' and the Bigger Problem behind Harvey Weinstein." UPROXX, October 19. http://uproxx.com/movies/todd-haynes-wonderstruck/.

Satellite of Love: A Velvet Goldmine *Fan Fiction Archive*. 2005. Last updated February 5. http://satellite.shriftweb.org.

Saunders, Michael William. 2014. "Appendix: An Interview with Todd Haynes." In Leyda 2014, 33–41.

Savage, Jon. 1991. "Tasteful Tales." *Sight and Sound* 1 (6): 15–17.

Schafer, Elizabeth, and Susan Bradley Smith, eds. 2003. *Playing Australia: Australian Theatre and the International Stage*. Amsterdam: Rodopi.

Schatz, Thomas. 1981. "Family Melodrama." In *Hollywood Genres: Formulas, Filmmaking, and the Studio System*, edited by Thomas Schatz, 221–60. New York: Random House.

Scherr, Rebecca. 2008. "(Not) Queering 'White Vision' in *Far from Heaven* and *Transamerica*." *Jump Cut: A Review of Contemporary Media*, no. 50 (Spring). https://www.ejumpcut.org/archive/jc50.2008/Scherr/index.html.

Schorr, Collier. 2014. "Diary of a Sad Housewife: Collier Schorr Talks with Todd Haynes." 1995. In Leyda 2014, 42–48.

Schulze, Laurie. 1990. "The Made-for-TV Movie: Industrial Practice, Cultural Form, Popular Reception." In *Hollywood in the Age of Television*, edited by Tino Balio, 351–75. Boston: Unwin Hyman.

Schweitzer, Dahlia. 2010. "Another Kind of Monster: Cindy Sherman's 'Office Killer.'" *Jump Cut: A Review of Contemporary Media*. https://www.ejumpcut.org/archive/jc52.2010/schwitzerOfficeKiller/.

Sedgwick, Eve Kosofsky. 1990. *Epistemology of the Closet*. Berkeley: University of California Press.

Seidman, Steven. 1993. "Identity and Politics in a 'Postmodern' Gay Culture: Some Historical and Conceptual Notes." In *Fear of a Queer Planet: Queer Politics and Social Theory*, edited by Michael Warner, 105–42. Minneapolis: University of Minnesota Press.

Seiter, Ellen, Hans Borchers, Gabrielle Kreutzner, and Eva-Maria Warth, eds. 1989. *Remote Control: Television, Audiences, and Cultural Power*. London: Routledge.

Seltzer, Sarah. 2017. "Can the Weinstein Co. Be Saved? The Women Putting Their Money on It." *Refinery29*, December 21. https://www.refinery29.com/en-us/2017/12/185919/weinstein-company-bids-female-investors.

Seymour, Nicole. 2011. "'It's Just Not Turning Up': Cinematic Vision and Environmental Justice in Todd Haynes's *Safe*." *Cinema Journal* 50 (4): 26–47.

Shah, Nayan. 2005. "Policing Privacy, Migrants, and the Limits of Freedom." *Social Text* 23 (3–4): 275–84.

Shambu, Girish. 2018. "Time's Up for the Male Canon." *Film Quarterly*, September 21. https://filmquarterly.org/2018/09/21/times-up-for-the-male-canon/.

Silverman, Kaja. 1988. *The Acoustic Mirror: The Female Voice in Psychoanalysis and Cinema*. Bloomington: Indiana University Press.

Simon, Rachel. 2015. "'Carol' Is a Feminist Dream." *Bustle*, November 23. https://www.bustle.com/articles/125103-the-women-behind-carol-on-why-director-todd-haynes-was-the-perfect-choice-for-the-feminist.

Smith, Victoria L. 2018. "The Heterotopias of Todd Haynes: Creating Space for Same Sex Desire in *Carol*." *Film Criticism* 42 (1). http://dx.doi.org/10.3998/fc.13761232.0042.102.

Sondheim, Stephen. 1971. "I'm Still Here." *Follies*.

Spigel, Lynn. 1992. *Make Room for TV: Television and the Family Ideal in Postwar America*. Chicago: University of Chicago Press.

Spigel, Lynn. 2001. *Welcome to the Dreamhouse: Popular Media and Postwar Suburbs*. Durham, NC: Duke University Press.

Staat, Wim. 2019. "Todd Haynes' Melodramas of the Unknown Woman: *Far from Heaven*, *Mildred Pierce*, and *Carol*, and Stanley Cavell's Film Ethics." *Quarterly Review of Film and Video* 36 (6): 520–38.

Stein, Arlene. 1995. "Crossover Dreams: Lesbianism and Popular Music since the 1970s." In *Out in Culture: Gay, Lesbian, and Queer Essays on Popular Culture*, edited by Corey K. Creekmur and Alexander Doty, 416–26. Durham, NC: Duke University Press.

Stein, Gertrude. 2008. "What Are Master-Pieces and Why Are There So Few of Them?" (1936). In *Gertrude Stein: Selections*, edited by Joan Retallack, 308–20. Berkeley: University of California Press.

Stern, Lesley, and George Kouvaros. *Falling for You: Essays on Cinema and Performance*. Sydney: Power Publications.

Stern, Michael. 1979. *Douglas Sirk*. Boston: Twayne.

Stewart, Susan. 1993. *On Longing: Narratives of the Miniature, the Gigantic, the Souvenir, the Collection*. Durham, NC: Duke University Press.

Stockton, Kathryn Bond. 2009. *The Queer Child, or Growing Sideways in the Twentieth Century*. Durham, NC: Duke University Press.

Taubin, Amy. 1998. "Fanning the Flames." *Village Voice*, November 3.

Taubin, Amy. 2014. "All That Glitters: Todd Haynes Mines the Glam Rock Epoch." In Leyda 2014, 77–80.

Thompson, Anne. 2016. "Todd Haynes and Oscar-Nominated Writer Phyllis Nagy Talk 'Carol,' Glamorous Stars, Highsmith and More." *IndieWire*, January 15. https://www.indiewire.com/2016/01/todd-haynes-and-oscar-nominated-writer-phyllis-nagy-talk-carol-glamorous-stars-highsmith-and-more-175265/.

Thomson, David. 1982. "The Missing Auteur." *Film Comment* 18 (4): 34–39.

Tinkcom, Matthew. 2002. *Working like a Homosexual: Camp, Capital, Cinema*. Durham, NC: Duke University Press.

Tobias, Scott. 2014. "Todd Haynes on the Unsafe World of *Safe*." *Dissolve*, December 18. https://thedissolve.com/features/interview/856-todd-haynes-on-the-unsafe-world-of-safe/.

"Todd Haynes: A Magnificent Obsession." 2004. Special issue, *Camera Obscura: Feminism, Culture, and Media Studies* 19 (3).

Urla, Jacqueline, and Alan C. Swedlund. 1995. "The Anthropometry of Barbie: Unsettling Ideals of the Feminine Body in Popular Culture." In *Deviant Bodies: Critical Perspectives on Difference in Science and Popular Culture*, edited by Jennifer Terry and Jacqueline Urla, 277–313. Bloomington: Indiana University Press.

Vachon, Christine. 2017. "Film-Makers Can Defy Trump. Depicting the Lives of Others Is an Act of Resistance." *Guardian*, February 24. https://www.theguardian.com/commentisfree/2017/feb/24/oscars-arent-just-so-white-theyre-also-so-straight.

Vachon, Christine, and Austin Bunn. 2006. *A Killer Life: How an Independent Film Producer Survives Deals and Disasters in Hollywood and Beyond*. New York: Simon and Schuster.

Vachon, Christine, and David Edelstein. 1998. *Shooting to Kill*. New York: Harper Perennial.

Van Sant, Gus. 2015. "Interview: Todd Haynes." *Issue Magazine*, no. 6 (October). https://issuemagazine.com/todd-haynes/#/.

Wagmeister, Elizabeth. 2020. "Kate Beckinsale Alleges Harvey Weinstein Berated Her after 'Serendipity' Premiere." *Variety*, March 12. https://variety.com/2020/film/news/kate-beckinsale-harvey-weinstein-serendipity-screaming-cunt-1203531809/.

Wagner, Alex. 2006. "French Revolutions: The Quiet Industry of Charlotte Gainsbourg." *Fader* 41: 98–107.

Wagner-Martin, Linda. 1994. *Telling Women's Lives: The New Biography*. New Brunswick, NJ: Rutgers University Press.

Warner, Michael. 1993. *Fear of a Queer Planet*. Minneapolis: University of Minnesota Press.

Waters, John. 2015. "John Waters' Top 10 Films of 2015, from 'Cinderella' to 'Tangerine.'" *IndieWire*, December 1. http://www.indiewire.com/2015/12/john-waters-top-10-films-of-2015-from-cinderella-to-tangerine-213506/.

White, Patricia. 1999. *UnInvited: Classical Hollywood Cinema and Lesbian Representability*. Bloomington: Indiana University Press.

White, Patricia. 2015a. "A Lesbian *Carol* for Christmas." *Public Books*, December 24. http://www.publicbooks.org/blog/a-lesbian-carol-for-christmas.

White, Patricia. 2015b. "Sketchy Lesbians: *Carol* as History and Fantasy." *Film Quarterly* 69 (2): 8–18.

White, Patricia. 2015c. *Women's Cinema, World Cinema: Projecting Contemporary Feminisms*. Durham, NC: Duke University Press.

White, Patricia. 2016. "Killer Feminism." In *Indie Reframed: Women and the Contemporary American Independent Cinema*, edited by Linda Badley, Claire Perkins, and Michele Schreiber, 36–53. Edinburgh: Edinburgh University Press.

White, Rob. 2013. *Todd Haynes*. Urbana: University of Illinois Press.

Wiegman, Robyn. 2014. "The Times We're In: Queer Feminist Criticism and the Reparative 'Turn.'" *Feminist Theory* 15 (1): 4–25.

Wiegman, Robyn. 2017. "Sex and Negativity; or, What Queer Theory Has for You." *Cultural Critique* 95 (Winter): 219–43.

Wilkinson, Alissa. 2017. "Wonder Wheel Is Impossible to View Apart from Woody Allen's Family Controversies." *Vox*, November 30. https://www.vox.com/2017/11/28/16692006/wonder-wheel-review-woody-allen-oedipus-rex.

Willemen, Paul. 1971. "Distanciation and Douglas Sirk." *Screen* 12 (2): 63–67.

Willemen, Paul. 1973. "Towards an Analysis of the Sirkian System." *Screen* 13 (4): 128–34.

Williams, Linda. 1984. "'Something Else besides a Mother': *Stella Dallas* and the Maternal Melodrama." *Cinema Journal* 24 (1): 2–27.

Williams, Linda. 1991. "Film Bodies: Gender, Genre, and Excess." *Film Quarterly* 44 (4): 2–13.

Williams, Linda. 2000. "Something Else besides a Mother: *Stella Dallas* and the Maternal Melodrama." 1984. In *Feminism and Film*, edited by E. Ann Kaplan, 479–504. Oxford: Oxford University Press.

Willis, Ellen. 2011. *Out of the Vinyl Deeps: Ellen Willis on Rock Music*. Edited by Nona Willis Aronowitz. Minneapolis: University of Minnesota Press.

Willis, Ellen. 2012. *Beginning to See the Light: Sex, Hope, and Rock-and-Roll*. Minneapolis: University of Minnesota Press.

Willis, Ellen. 2014. *The Essential Ellen Willis*. Edited by Nona Willis Aronowitz. Minneapolis: University of Minnesota Press.

Willis, Sharon. 2003. "The Politics of Disappointment: Todd Haynes Rewrites Douglas Sirk." *Camera Obscura: Feminism, Culture, and Media Studies* 18 (3): 131–75.

Willis, Sharon. 2015. "The Lure of Retrospectatorship: Hitting the False Notes in *Far from Heaven*." In *The Poitier Effect: Racial Melodrama and Fantasies of Reconciliation*, 119–60. Minneapolis: University of Minnesota Press.

Winslet, Kate. 2011. "Interview with Todd Haynes." *Interview Magazine*, February 22. http://www.interviewmagazine.com/film/todd-haynes/#.

Wyatt, Justin. 1993. "Cinematic/Sexual: An Interview with Todd Haynes." *Film Quarterly* 46 (3): 2–8.

Wyatt, Justin. 2014. "Cinematic/Sexual: An Interview with Todd Haynes." In Leyda 2014, 26–32.

Zacharek, Stephanie. 2015. "Cold and Dreamy, *Carol* Examines Women in Love." *Village Voice*, November 15.

Zemler, Emily. 2015. "11 Male Directors Who Actually *Get* Women." *Elle*, June 5. https://www.elle.com/culture/movies-tv/a28713/male-directors-pro-woman/.

CONTRIBUTORS

DANIELLE BOUCHARD is an associate professor of women's, gender, and sexuality studies at the University of North Carolina at Greensboro. She is the author of *A Community of Disagreement: Feminism in the University* (2012).

NICK DAVIS is an associate professor of English and gender and sexuality studies at Northwestern University. He is the author of *The Desiring-Image* (2013), a contributing editor at *Film Comment*, and the author of Nick-Davis.com (http://nick-davis.com).

JIGNA DESAI is a professor in the Department of Gender, Women, and Sexuality Studies and the Asian American Studies Program at the University of Minnesota. She is the author of *Beyond Bollywood* (2004) and several coedited collections, including *Bollywood: A Reader* (2009), *Transnational Feminism and Global Advocacy in South Asia* (2012), and *Asian Americans in Dixie* (2013).

MARY R. DESJARDINS is a professor of film and media studies at Dartmouth College, where she also teaches women's, gender, and sexuality studies. She is the coeditor of *Dietrich Icon* (2007) and author of numerous essays published in various journals and collections and of the books *Recycled Stars: Female Film Stardom in the Age of Television and Video* (2015) and *Father Knows Best* (2015).

PATRICK FLANERY is the author of the novels *Absolution* (2012), *Fallen Land* (2013), *I Am No One* (2016), and *Night for Day* (2019) and the creative-critical memoir *The Ginger Child: On Family, Loss, and Adoption* (2019). He is chair of Creative Writing in the Department of English and Creative Writing at the University of Adelaide and Professor Extraordinary at the University of Stellenbosch.

THERESA L. GELLER is a scholar-in-residence with the Beatrice Bain Research Group at the University of California, Berkeley. She is the author of *The X-Files*

(2016) and several scholarly essays and articles on feminist theory, film, and television.

REBECCA M. GORDON is a film studies scholar and archivist-in-training at Ryerson University. She has taught cinema studies and literature at Northern Arizona University, Reed College, and Oberlin College. Her work has appeared in the *Journal of Cinema and Media Studies*, *Film Quarterly*, *Reception*, and other venues.

JESS ISSACHAROFF is a postdoctoral fellow in law and society at the Newcomb College Institute at Tulane University. She holds a PhD in literature from Duke University's Program in Literature and a certificate in feminist studies. Her dissertation is titled "Big House: Women, Prison, and the Domestic."

LYNNE JOYRICH is a professor of modern culture and media at Brown University and a member of the editorial collective of the journal *Camera Obscura*. She is the author of *Re-viewing Reception* (1996) and of articles on film, television, and gender and sexuality studies that have appeared in such journals as *Critical Inquiry*, *Cinema Journal*, *differences*, and the *Journal of Visual Culture*.

BRIDGET KIES is an assistant professor of cinema studies at Oakland University, where she researches gender and sexuality in film and television. She has coedited issues of *Queer Studies in Media and Popular Culture* and *Participations*.

JULIA LEYDA is a professor of film studies at the Norwegian University of Science and Technology. Her books include *American Mobilities* (2016) and *Anthroposcreens: Mediating the Climate Unconscious* (2022) and the edited volumes *Todd Haynes: Interviews* (2014) and *Post-cinema: Theorizing 21st-Century Film* (with Shane Denson, 2016).

DAVID E. MAYNARD is an independent scholar and freelance editor with interests in cultural production, Marxian economic theory, contemporary work and workers, and representations of labor and capital. He has published on cultural studies and financialization.

NOAH A. TSIKA is an associate professor of media studies at Queens College, City University of New York. His books include *Gods and Monsters* (2009), *Nollywood Stars* (2015), *Pink 2.0* (2016), *Traumatic Imprints* (2018), *Screening the Police* (2021), and *Cinematic Independence* (2022).

PATRICIA WHITE is a professor of film and media studies at Swarthmore College. She is the author of *Rebecca* (2021), *Women's Cinema, World Cinema* (2015), and *UnInvited* (1999) and is coauthor, with Timothy Corrigan, of *The*

Film Experience (6th ed., 2021). White is a coeditor of *Camera Obscura* and its book series.

SHARON WILLIS is a professor of art history and visual and cultural studies at the University of Rochester. A coeditor of *Camera Obscura,* she is the author of *Marguerite Duras: Writing on the Body* (1987), *High Contrast* (1997), and *The Poitier Effect* (2015), as well as numerous articles on race and gender in popular cinema.

INDEX